PRAISE FOR 99 NEW MEXICANS...AND A FEW OTHER FOLKS

This compilation of old-time stories illustrates how the Wild West really was during New Mexico's frontier era. In a showdown between folklore and fact, Don Bullis is triumphant. *99 New Mexicans...and a few other folks* is a must read for Western history buffs.

Bob Alexander, Author/Historian
Dangerous Dan Tucker
Lawmen, Outlaws and S. O. Bs.
And others

Read Don Bullis' essays in *99 New Mexicans...and a few other folks* and journey back to a time long since forgotten. Don possesses a deep, intrinsic knowledge of New Mexico's history and his prose flows flawlessly to capture the essence and true flavor of the state's vivid past.

Betta Ferrendelli, Editor
Rio Rancho (New Mexico) *Observer*

Tales of courage and cowardice, sinners and saints—all fascinating and exceptionally well referenced. *99 New Mexicans...and a few other folks* is a must-have, must read compendium of New Mexico's most enchanting historical figures.

Karl Lassiter, Author
Sword and Drum, White River Massacre,
Warriors of the Plains, and others

Author Don Bullis has mined old newspapers and scholarly publications to present interesting short stories about famous, infamous and controversial figures in *99 New Mexicans...and a few other folks.* It is an entertaining primer for anyone seeking facts, legends and trivia about New Mexico's past.

Deborah C. Slaney
Curator of History
The Albuquerque Museum

Ellos Pasaron Por Aqui

ELLOS PASARON POR AQUI

(THEY PASSED BY HERE)

99

NEW MEXICANS...

AND A FEW OTHER FOLKS

DON BULLIS

Science & Humanities Press
Chesterfield Missouri

Graphics Credits:

The cover design is by Dana McCausland. Credits and acknowledgements for the various historical photos are in their respective legends.

ISBN 1-888725-92-3 Science & Humanities Press Edition
ISBN 1-8887293-1 MacroPrintBooks Edition (large print)
Publication date January, 2005
First Printing, January, 2005

Library of Congress Cataloging-in-Publication Data
Is on file with the Library of Congress

𝕾cience & 𝕳umanities 𝕻ress
PO Box 7151
Chesterfield, MO 63006-7151
(636) 394-4950
sciencehumanitiespress.com

DEDICATION

To Gloria Bullis, to whom I owe just about everything.

Ellos Pasaron Por Aqui

TABLE OF CONTENTS

INTRODUCTION

Ask us New Mexicans why we love our high, dry state and we'll first tell you it is because of our mountain-desert landscape and our big blue skies. Talk a bit longer and you'll learn that we also delight in the interesting citizens our state has been collecting from the Ice Age down to modern times. Give them a little time and New Mexicans will begin telling you about some of them. You'll hear of Popé, who led the only successful Indian revolution against new comers in North American history, and captured Santa Fe in 1680. You'll hear about U. S. Senator Albert Bacon Fall of New Mexico, later Secretary of the Interior, who gave America its famous "Teapot Dome Scandal" in the 1920s. You'll even hear about the "determined citizens" of Silver City who wiped out Kit Joy's gang of bandits in 1884.

Every New Mexican should have a head full of accounts of our colorful heroes and villains to educate visitors from the less interesting states, and Don Bullis has provided us with the fullest and most useful collection of them ever created.

Since this is New Mexico, many of these accounts tend to involve violence of one sort or another. Bullis spent a lot of his life involved in New Mexico law enforcement making the endless effort to maintain some sort of order in a landscape that contributed more than its share to America's wonderful legends of the Wild West and wild westerners. Thus he is just the man to take a backward look and explain what happened, and why, and to whom. As a lawman, he made a career of "being there and doing that." He's given us a book that deserves a place in every Westerner's library.

Many of the names you'll encounter in *99 New Mexicans...and a few other folks* belong to people familiar to those of us who know something of Western history. There's Clay Allison, the first "shootist," and Elfego Baca, New Mexico hero as the Socorro County deputy sheriff who fought off eighty Texans and now has a beer (Elfego Bock) named for him, and Lieutenant Ed Beale, whose assignment was to make a U. S. Army Camel Corps practical in New Mexico's desert, and, on the darker side, Col. John Chivington of the Sand Creek Massacre.

On the brighter side Bullis re-introduces us to Edmund Ross whose vote in the U. S. Senate stopped the impeachment of President Andrew Johnson, and who as our territorial Governor created the University of New Mexico. And he reminds us of Sally Rooke, who gave her life as operator of the Folsom telephone exchange, staying at her post and warning folks of the flood roaring down on the northeastern New Mexico village until the waters swept her away.

But we're wasting time here. The rest of the cast of characters in *99 New Mexicans...and a few others*, await us in the pages to come—starting with Clay

Allison who was "dangerous and deadly when he was sober, and a downright terror when he was drunk, which was often."

Tony Hillerman
Albuquerque, New Mexico

PREFACE

About forty years ago, I undertook the task of writing a short item on William H. Bonney, better known as Billy the Kid. I didn't know much about the man (or boy), but I figured I would find plenty of resources that would provide me with the information I needed. What I almost immediately discovered was that while there was indeed a lot of information available, almost none of the writers agreed about the facts surrounding the outlaw's life. Some wrote that the Kid's *real* name was not Bonney, but McCarty; others claimed his name was Antrim. No one seemed to know how the outlaw came to call himself William Bonney, and some couldn't even agree on the spelling of the name (Bonny, Bonnie, etc.).

The debate about Billy continues to this day, and many of the questions about him, and his life and death (particularly his death), will never be answered to the satisfaction of everyone.

I wondered about other characters in the history of New Mexico and the Old West. Was there as much disagreement about them as there was about Billy? It didn't take long to learn that the answer to the question was an emphatic *yes*. And the problem, I noted, was compounded by the fact that many writers of Western history (perhaps writers of *all* history) tell their versions of events as if each is absolute fact. Very few make any effort to reconcile the several different accounts of the same event, and the people involved in each.

Could, for instance, New Mexico Governor Manuel Armijo have been as bad as he has often been portrayed? Probably not. Armijo's primary antagonists had personal reasons for attacking him. At the same time, was Sheriff Pat Garrett really as heroic as some portrayed him? Also probably not. Perhaps he did one brave deed, but the rest of his life tended to fade in heroic luster, and even arduous self-promotion couldn't completely restore it.

So when I started writing regular newspaper columns about twenty-five years ago, I thought it would a valuable service to my readers to present the divergent points of view offered by the several writers on any given historical subject. General readers, I thought, would be able to make up their own minds about people and events of a time in the distant past, and those so motivated could dig deeper into items of particular interest to them. Those not stirred to further study, would at least know that many *facts* about the history of New Mexico and the Old West were not facts at all, but merely legends that have been around for so long that no one questions them.

99 New Mexicans...and a few other folks includes essays, published and unpublished, over the past thirty or so years; newspaper columns published in a half-dozen papers—but primarily the Rio Rancho (New Mexico) *Observer*—over the past eighteen years; and items excerpted from my earlier book, *New Mexico's Finest: Peace Officers Killed in the Line of Duty, 1847-1999*. Each item has been reviewed, revised and updated for inclusion in this book.

This effort is interactive inasmuch as I would like to hear from readers who have knowledge of the people and events described on these pages, or readers who know of historic characters who *should* be included here. I won't promise to answer each missive, but I will consider each as I continue to research and write about the people who populated New Mexico from the days before recorded history to modern times. I can be reached at don.bullis@att.net.

Maybe your name will find its way onto the pages of the next *99 New Mexicans*...

Don Bullis
Rio Rancho, New Mexico

NEW MEXICO KILLER CLAY ALLISON: THE ORIGINAL SHOOTIST

He was dangerous and deadly when he was sober, and a downright terror when he was drunk, which was often. Robert A. "Clay" Allison was not a man to be trifled with. He called himself a shootist, and he was. Writers on the Old West generally agree on these points, but little else about the man or his life. A look at a few sources will provide readers with several different Clay Allisons.

Try these five books: *The Gunfighters* by the editors of Time-Life Books with text by Paul Trachtman; *The Gunfighters* with paintings and text by Lea Franklin McCarty; *The Album of Gunfighters* by J. Marvin Hunter and Noah H. Rose; the *Encyclopedia of Western Gunfighters*, by Bill O'Neal and *The Encyclopedia of Lawmen, Outlaws, and Gunfighters* by Leon Metz. A word on these sources. Trachtman is comprehensive and readable. McCarty is exactly the opposite; he claims to have known a man who knew Wyatt Earp. No other sources are cited and he is wrong much more than he is right. Hunter and Rose are reliable and so is O'Neal. Metz is among the best.

All five sources agree that Allison was born in Tennessee, probably at or near Waynesboro in 1840. From this point on the departures are many. Take his military career for instance.

The Album of Gunfighters says this: "... [He] became a [Confederate] spy. He was captured and sentenced to be shot, but killed his two guards and escaped the night before he was to be executed." That's pretty exciting stuff.

The McCarty book reports, "... [He] had been a soldier in the Confederate Army where he learned about easy-go killing. As a guerrilla he became adept at the art of gunslinging." None of that seems to make sense.

The Time-Life book says, "When the Civil War began, [Allison] enlisted in the Tennessee Light Artillery. Three months later he was given a medical discharge by ... army doctors; they described him as "incapable of performing the duties of a soldier because of a blow received many years ago. Emotional or physical excitement produces paroxysmals of mixed character, partly epileptic and partly maniacal."

O'Neal says this: "At the outbreak of the Civil War, Allison ignored his clubfoot and defended his native state, serving throughout the conflict in various Confederate units." O'Neal and Metz are the only sources to report that Allison had a clubfoot.

So much for Allison's military career.

Sources generally agree that he left Tennessee after the Civil War and migrated first to Texas and then on to Colfax County, New Mexico, with stops in Colorado and Kansas along the way. In 1870, a Missouri newspaper alleged that Allison had already killed 15 men. Allison replied, "I have at all times tried to use my influence toward protecting the property holders and substantial men of the country from thieves, outlaws, and murderers, among whom I do not care to be classed." Note that he did not deny killing 15, or any other number, of men.

Despite his protestations of respectability, people living in Colfax County knew him for what he was: not only a killer, but also a man who took perverse pleasure in killing.

Trachtman, O'Neal and Metz tell variations on the following story. A man named Kennedy was accused of killing several strangers and his own infant daughter. He was arrested and taken to jail at Elizabethtown, New Mexico. Some bones were found at Kennedy's cabin several days later, but they were not determined to be human in origin. No matter. Allison and some of his drunken friends judged Kennedy guilty and sentenced him to death. They broke into the jail and removed the condemned man to a nearby slaughterhouse where they lynched him. That wasn't enough for Allison. He decapitated the corpse, mounted the head on a long stick, and then rode to Cimarron where he carried the grisly trophy into Lambert's saloon (Metz does not include the beheading incident).

Another event in Allison's life shows something of the nature of "gunfighting" in the old west. The McCarthy book says that a man by the name of William Chunk arrived in town one day with the expressed purpose of killing Allison. But instead of going into the street and shooting at one another, the two men went into a restaurant for dinner. During the course of the meal, Allison is said to have become annoyed at Chunk's table manners and killed the man for eating salad with his mouth open.

Time-Life agrees that the man probably intended to kill Allison, but his name was not William Chunk, but Chunk Colbert (all other sources agree about the name except Metz who reports the man's name as Chuck and his last name as possibly Tolbert), and he was the nephew of a man Allison had fought years earlier. The two did go to dinner. When coffee was being served, Colbert attempted to kill Allison by pulling his gun from under the table. His gun barrel struck the edge of the table, however, and his shot went wide, deflected by the wood. Allison then calmly pulled his own gun and shot Colbert in the forehead, killing him instantly. Asked later why he would take a meal with a man who meant to kill him, Allison said, "Because I didn't want to send a man to hell on an empty stomach."

O'Neal says the fight between Allison and Colbert resulted from a contested horse race.

Only the Hunter/Rose book says that Allison killed 18 men in his lifetime, and even they point out that the figure is based on Allison's reputation, and not documented fact. Other sources do not offer a total. Research indicates that he killed at least three or four men, and participated in the killings of several others. Eighteen is an unlikely number.

One would imagine that a man such as Allison would die by the gun, as he had lived. Not so. He was killed when run over by a freight wagon. Sources, again, do not agree as to the details. *The Album of Gunfighters* reports that his team ran away and in the process, Allison was thrown under the wagon wheels and his neck broken. McCarthy says the wagon struck a chuckhole, which caused Allison to drop the reins and fall off and be run over, breaking his back. Time-Life says Allison was hauling supplies to his ranch when a bag of grain slipped. He reached for it, lost his balance and fell off the wagon, was run over and killed. Metz generally agrees with this version. O'Neal says he fractured his skull on a wheel when he fell off the wagon, and died an hour later. (A sixth source agrees that he fractured his skull, but claims the wagon hit a clump of salt grass, throwing Allison from the seat.)

And when? McCarthy says it happened in 1877. Other sources agree that the year was 1887. Three of them say July 1, and one of them asserts Allison died on July 3.

Here is what one newspaper editor had to say on the occasion of Allison's death:

"Certain it is that many of his stern deeds were for the right as he understood it to be."

Damned by faint praise, all would likely agree.

MANUEL ARMIJO: TRAITOR OR SAINT?

Except for some heinous criminals and few others who were utterly loathsome to society, it is hard to find anyone as badly treated by history as Manuel Armijo who served three times as governor of New Mexico under Mexican rule (1821-1846). He was probably deserving of some of the derision and by his own statements he gave proof to some of the allegations made about him. He was also libeled by several writers of the day.

Armijo was born in Albuquerque in 1790, the youngest of 12 children. A fourth generation New Mexican, his great-grandfather, José de Armijo, came north with Don Diego de Vargas in the 1690s.

Manuel Armijo served his first term as governor from 1827 to 1829. There was nothing notable about his administration except that he is said to have resigned rather than face an investigation into his behavior in office. He returned to Albuquerque where he was promptly elected *alcalde*, an office akin to the modern-day mayor. He bided his time for about eight years, but he saw opportunity in the late 1830s.

Albino Pérez, appointed governor in 1835, was ordered to raise taxes, which he attempted to do. The result was open rebellion by many small farmers and Pueblo Indians. In the summer of 1837, with a small force of soldiers, Pérez set out to quell the disturbance. He confronted the rebels, was quickly defeated and forced to retreat back to Santa Fe. The insurgents soon captured and decapitated him, and killed most of his officers. In a grand gesture, Manuel Armijo raised an armed force in Albuquerque, marched north, and put down the rebellion and restored order in the capital.

What is interesting about this chain of events is that it was widely believed that Armijo organized the rebellion in the first place. When the uprising succeeded, he abandoned it, and then organized the militia to put it down. Once that was successful, he described himself to Mexico City officials as the savior of New Mexico. They must have believed him. He was once again named governor, with the added title of general. The following year, he marched north to Santa Cruz where he captured the other leaders of the rebellion and executed them. None of them could betray him.

Armijo greatly expanded his business activities during his second term in office. He had many dealings with the Missouri traders who arrived in significant numbers in New Mexico over the Santa Fe Trail after 1821. Among them were Adolph Speyer, with whom he formed a partnership, and James Magoffin.

It was also during his second term, in 1841, that 300, or so, Texans "invaded" New Mexico with the expressed purpose of capturing Santa Fe for the new Republic to the east and south. General Armijo took credit for capturing them, but in reality, by the time he and his troops found the Texans, the invaders were nearly dead from hunger and lack of water because they had become lost on the vast Llano Estacado of eastern New Mexico. The Texans were marched to Albuquerque then south to Mexico. Among them was a newspaperman named George W. Kendall who reported on the mistreatment they received. He later wrote some of the most scurrilous reports about Armijo.

Armijo was out of office for a time in 1844-45, but was into his third term when General Stephen Watts Kearny and his Army of the West set out for New Mexico from Fort Leavenworth, Kansas in the summer of 1846. Armijo knew they were coming; 1,700 of them. A couple of his spies were captured at Bent's Fort and freed, sent to Santa Fe to tell Armijo that the Americans were coming, in peace, Kearny said.

With great bluster and braggadocio, Armijo sounded the alarm to resist the invasion. He propagandized that if the Americans captured New Mexico, women would be captured and branded, the Catholic religion would no longer be allowed and looting would be the order of the day. Armijo had 200 to 300 regular troops to which he was able to add 1,500 to 2,000 volunteers, many of them Pueblo Indians. Most of his army did not have firearms and were expected to fight with lances, bows and arrows.

The point of defense was to be at Apache Canyon, about 15 miles east of Santa Fe. The Americans would be obliged to march through a narrow defile which could be defended by few against many. But some defenders soon realized that there would be no fighting at Apache Canyon. Armijo allowed the troops to go home if only they paid him a bounty of $20 to $200. Some of his higher-ranking officers wanted to fight, but the Governor General ignored them and left the field himself, headed south, for Mexico. The Americans met no resistance when they passed through Apache Canyon and entered Santa Fe on August 18.

Why did Armijo flee? Was it because he knew he had no chance against the Americans? Was he simply a coward? Did he accept a bribe? It may have been a little of all three.

History records that James Magoffin and Phillip St. George Cooke visited Armijo in Santa Fe in the days before the Americans arrived at Apache Canyon (August 12). Armijo wined and dined them. Magoffin is said to have simply told the Governor that it would be futile to resist the American advance. What history does not specifically record is whether or not Magoffin bribed Armijo to the tune of $50,000 in gold. Many people at the time, American and Mexican, believed that he did. In fact, some time later, Magoffin applied to the U. S. Government for reimbursement in the amount of $50,000, money owed him, he said, for his dealings with Armijo. He was awarded $30,000, but even so, it is not known if he actually gave Armijo any money. Documentation that would have proven the point, one way or the other, was somehow lost or destroyed.

Armijo left his wife in Albuquerque as he fled all the way to Chihuahua. An Englishman named George Ruxton met him there and reported that the Governor had seven wagons loaded with trade goods. He said Armijo was more interested in prices being paid in Durango than he was in affairs at Santa Fe. Ruxton described Armijo as "a mountain of fat."

What hurts Armijo most, historically, is that he admitted to his own avarice and lack of fortitude. He acknowledged that he stole from Missouri traders by the way in which he taxed them and their goods. And then there's this: he had a personal motto that he often recited. *Vale más estar tomado por valiente que serlo.* "It is better to be thought brave than to really be so."

The Governor General was tried for treason by the Mexican government, and acquitted. He returned to New Mexico in 1848 and ran for public office under the American Occupation. He was defeated and said this: "I am here as a Saint whose day has passed."

When he died in December of 1853, the Territorial legislature, at the behest of his friend, Dr. Henry Connelly (who would become territorial governor in 1861), passed a resolution that described Armijo as one of the territory's "greatest benefactors."

Former New Mexico State Historian Robert Tórrez correctly points out that many of the uncomplimentary things written about Governor Armijo are unsubstantiated. George Kendall (1809-1867), cited above, for whom Kendall County, Texas, is named, notoriously disliked "Mexicans" after his experiences as a member of the Texan Santa Fe Expedition of 1841. (Kendall spent a couple of years in a Mexican prison.) He was also wounded during the Mexican War.

Young George Ruxton (1821-1847), also cited above, was an English writer of the time. He also distained "Mexicans," except, as one writer noted, "the kindness of their women." He scorned Roman Catholics, the "upper families" of New Mexico and he wrote that Santa Fe reminded him of a prairie dog town.

Neither of these writers, and others, could scarcely be considered objective in their stated opinions of Governor Armijo, or his contemporaries.

SHERIFF ARMIJO SOLVES POTTER CASE: PERPETRATORS LYNCHED

Santiago Baca, Sheriff of Bernalillo County, 1885-86.
(Photo Symes Collection, Courtesy of the Albuquerque Museum Photoarchives, PA 1980.21.9)

As sheriff of Bernalillo County in the late 1870s and early 1880s, Perfecto Armijo participated in some of the most noted events of his time, and the way in which he attained office is unique in the history of the New Mexico Territory.

Armijo, a Democrat, was first elected sheriff in 1877 when he succeeded Manuel Sanchez y Valencia. In subsequent elections he faced Santiago Baca, an ardent, and influential, Republican. Historian Marc Simmons tells how their campaign efforts came together:

"Preceding the balloting, both candidates rode into the surrounding county to enlist the aid of their brawniest and toughest supporters. On the appointed day, partisans of each man gathered in a vacant lot ... between Third and Fifth Streets [in Albuquerque]. On signal, the two sides flew at one another with sticks, stones, gun butts, fists and profane language. A throng of Albuquerqueans regularly assembled on the steps of the Armijo House to watch the fray. To the winner, whether Armijo or Baca, they gave their votes."

No one was killed in these melees, according to Judge William C. Heacock, who often served as referee. But, he said, "the fights were real." Armijo prevailed in a couple of elections, but the Baca forces won in 1884. It was in the intervening six years that Armijo made his name as a lawman. (Armijo remained out of the sheriff's office until 1905 when he was appointed to the job by Governor Miguel Otero.)

In May of 1880, William H. Bonney (Billy the Kid) and another man stole a couple of horses in Albuquerque and started for Santa Fe with them. Sheriff Armijo gathered a posse and took up pursuit, soon overtaking the thieves. A "sharp fight" ensued and the sheriff took Bonney into custody. The Kid plead guilty on May 11 and was sentenced to five years in prison.[1]

On the same evening, a mob appeared before the jail and demanded that Bonney be turned over to them for the purpose of summary punishment by hanging. Sheriff Armijo confronted the crowd and prevented the lynching. The Albuquerque *Advance* for May 8, 1880 reported: "For a while Wednesday night it was thought Kid would be taken out of the jail and hung, but it was not done and Albuquerque has for the present escaped the notoriety which such affairs give."

They spoke too soon.

In October of the same year, Colonel Charles Potter, a surveyor for the U. S. Government, disappeared while en route from Albuquerque to Santa Fe by way of Tijeras Canyon and then north along the east slope of the Sandia Mountains and what was called the San Pedro Mining District. Potter had scoffed at warnings about the bandits who prowled the area. His disappearance was the big news of the day and sizable rewards were offered for information concerning the matter. No information was forthcoming.

In January of 1881, Sheriff Armijo located a pocket watch that contained a picture of Mrs. Potter in an Albuquerque pawnshop. He learned that one Pantaleon Miera of Bernalillo had hocked it. Unfortunately, the sheriff was aware that Miera had been hanged by vigilantes for stealing a horse a month or so earlier. Armijo was also aware, however, that Miera had been a member of the Marino Leyba gang of bandits that roamed the Sandia Mountains. The sheriff soon secured arrest warrants for Leyba and other gang members.

One of them, Escolastico Perea, was soon arrested at Isleta and returned to Albuquerque. He confessed and told the sheriff the details of the crime, and the location of the body. Armed with that information, Armijo rode into the Mountains and recovered the body. He also arrested two additional members of the gang, Miguel Barrera and California Joe.[2]

On the very day that the sheriff returned to Albuquerque with his prisoners, talk of lynching them began to circulate in the town's saloons and cantinas. By late that evening, three of the Leyba gang members were "Dancing on air," as the newspaper headline read. Several weeks later, a fifth member of the gang, Faustino Gutierres, was captured and he too was promptly lynched. Only Leyba himself avoided the rope. (He was shot to death near Golden by Santa Fe County sheriff's deputies Joaquin Montoya and Carlos Jacomo in the spring 1886.)

While Sheriff Armijo was not able to prevent the hangings of the Leyba gang—and some said he didn't try very hard—he was successful in preventing the lynching of one Milt Yarberry. Yarberry was Albuquerque's first city marshal, appointed in 1881. While he was a man with a shady reputation—some said he was a cattle rustler from Arkansas—he was a handy man with a gun and that was the major requisite for the job.

The marshal got into trouble soon after taking the job when he shot and killed one Harry Brown. Yarberry and Brown both sought the attentions of a young grass widow named Sadie Preston. Yarberry surrendered himself to Sheriff Armijo and claimed self-defense in the shooting, in spite of the fact that Brown was not armed at the time of the shooting. The marshal was acquitted of murder charges and returned to patrolling the streets of Albuquerque.

In June of 1881, Yarberry was in trouble again, and that time he was not so lucky. He shot and killed a man named Charles Campbell for no good reason except that he was on the street at the wrong time. Again the marshal surrendered himself to the sheriff and again he claimed self-defense. The jury didn't buy it. Yarberry was convicted and sentenced to hang. But some of the good folks of Albuquerque, about 100 of them, seemed to think the process of justice took too long. They gathered at a local livery stable to organize a lynching. Sheriff Armijo heard about the meeting and marched himself into the gathering and single-handedly brought it to a halt. Armijo properly executed Yarberry on February 9, 1883.[3]

One source described Perfecto Armijo as "...one of New Mexico's most effective lawmen." He must have been.

---

[1] One source says Bonney was sentenced to New Mexico Territorial prison, but that could not be so since the Territorial prison didn't open until August of 1885.
[2] History does not record additional information about this particular California Joe.
[3] There were hard feelings about one lawman hanging another, and some observers believed that this event contributed to Armijo's defeat at the polls to Santiago Baca the following year.

ELFEGO BACA FIGHTS 80 TEXANS AT FRISCO PLAZA

The saga of Elfego Baca began in November of 1884. He was 19 years old at the time and a resident of Socorro, New Mexico. He decided that he wanted to be a lawman, and Sheriff Pedro Simpson commissioned him as a deputy.[1] When he learned that Texas cowboys were in the habit of hoorawing a small town in western Socorro County, near the Arizona line, he pinned on his badge, armed himself, and rode off to put a stop to it.

Upper San Francisco Plaza [2] was located about 130 miles west of Socorro. It was a quiet town of little note until several Texas cattle outfits began grazing large herds in the area. The original inhabitants of the village were almost entirely Hispanic and the Texas drovers were almost entirely Anglo. The latter group found entertainment in getting drunk and shooting up the town and generally terrorizing the native population. On one occasion the cowboys tied a young boy named Martinez to a tree and used him for target practice. He was wounded four times, but survived.

Little, it seemed, could be done to stop the disorder because the Texans were better armed than the natives and they clearly demonstrated their willingness to disregard the law by force of arms. A local justice of the peace had once bothered to jail one of the cowboys for disturbing the peace only to be set upon by a band of rowdies and sent scurrying with gunshots at his heels. The cowboys then broke down the jail door and released their friend.

On the same day that young Elfego arrived in town, so did a cowboy named McCarty [3]. McCarty went to work at getting drunk in Milligan's saloon, and then shooting up the village. He rode up and down the street taking potshots at anything or anyone he chose. Baca went to the justice of the peace and demanded an arrest warrant for the miscreant, but the judge refused saying he feared more harm would befall the town in trying to stop the cowboy than if they just let the matter pass. Elfego would have none of that. He was a peace officer, he announced, and he would do his duty.

He did. He found McCarty standing in the street visiting with some of his friends. The self-appointed deputy grabbed the cowboy by the collar, shoved the barrel of his pistol into the drover's ear and ordered him to hotfoot it for the jail. McCarty complied and no one interfered.

Late the same afternoon a bunch of cowboys made an effort to free their friend. Baca appeared at the door, gun in hand. He gave the drovers until the count of three to get out of town. He quickly made the count and opened fire. One shot hit a cowboy in the knee and the noise of the gunshots spooked a horse ridden by the ranch foreman, a man named Perham, who was killed when the animal fell on top of him. The Texans retreated.

Word of the shooting, and the death of Perham, spread quickly and soon a large number of cowboys assembled in Upper Frisco Plaza. Fearing the worst, a group of citizens, led by a man named J. H. Cook, arranged a truce. Baca agreed to deliver McCarty to the justice of the peace who by then had agreed to hear the case. The cowboy was fined five dollars and released.

Baca prepared to leave town, but it was the Texans turn to take aggressive action. A shot was fired and Elfego retreated down an alley. After evicting a woman and two small children, took cover in a small one-room house of a type called a *jacal*, little more than a shack made of vertical sticks and daubed with mud. Under the leadership of a Texas man named Jim Herne, an attack was soon made. Herne held the Hispanic residents of Frisco Plaza in utter contempt, and often said so in certain and blasphemous terms. He demanded that Baca leave his shelter and Elfego's response was two well-placed shots into the cowboy's body. He fell dead on the spot. It was nine o'clock in the morning.

The Texans took cover nearby and put a steady barrage of gunfire into the hut. They kept it up all day, firing hundreds of rounds of ammunition. Baca returned fire from time to time, but no one was hit. None of the Texans attempted to approach and Elfego was unscathed.

The floor in the *jacal* was about 18 inches lower than the ground around it, so the deputy had protection from the bullets. By late afternoon the cowboys had fired enough lead into the house that one wall collapsed. Around midnight, they used dynamite to try and dislodge Baca, and part of the roof and another wall collapsed.

The Texans hoped they had killed Baca with the dynamite, but they learned better on the morning of the second day when they smelled food cooking. Elfego had managed to make a fire in the stove and prepare his breakfast. At midmorning, a cowboy attempted to approach by hiding behind the front part of a cast iron stove. Baca watched and waited for an opportunity, which the cowboy provided when he peeked above his armor. Elfego split his scalp with a single shot. The cowboy did not die.[4]

Late in the afternoon of the second day, a deputy sheriff named Ross and J. H. Cook, with the help of Francisquito Naranjo, convinced Baca to surrender. They agreed to protect him from the Texans as he was taken to Socorro to face charges for killing Herne. Elfego agreed provided that he did not have to give up his guns until he reached Socorro, and that he be allowed to ride backwards on the buckboard so that he could not be taken by surprise. Ross and Baca left town that same evening.

Thus ended the gunfight at Upper Frisco Plaza, and thus began the legend of Elfego Baca. About 80 Texans had fired an estimated 4,000 rounds of ammunition into the *jacal* during a period of 36 hours[5]. Eight bullets had hit a broom handle inside. Every spoon, fork and knife was struck by at least one bullet. About 370 bullets penetrated the door. The only thing in the shack not hit, besides Elfego, was a plaster statue of *Mi Senora Santa Ana*.

Elfego was jailed for four months and tried twice for the killings at Upper Frisco Plaza. He was acquitted both times.

This was only the beginning.

---

[1] Legend holds that Simpson refused to commission Baca, and that the young man took it upon himself to act as a deputy. Records show that the sheriff commissioned Baca on October 26, 1884. Baca himself perpetuated this myth.

[2] Also known as Milligan's Plaza, after a local saloonkeeper, now called Reserve, it is the seat of Catron County.

[3] Not to be confused with William Henry McCarty, AKA Billy the Kid.

[4] Some legends hold that three or four Texans were killed at Upper Frisco Plaza, but it is more likely that Herne was the only one shot to death while several were wounded.

[5] Eighty is the generally accepted number. One writer puts the number at "several dozen."

ELFEGO BACA CAPTURES THE KILLER, JOSÉ GARCIA WITHOUT FIRING A SHOT: OR DID HE?

This is one of those great stories that may or may not be fact.

Elfego Baca's personally approved biographer, Kyle Crichton, recounted the tale in Law and Order, LTD., The Rousing Life of Elfego Baca. *Other historians and biographers do not repeat the story. The date of these events is not known, but Baca served as sheriff of Socorro County in 1919 and 1920, and Undersheriff at an earlier time. Baca is of course famed for his gunfight with 80 Texans at Frisco Plaza in western Socorro County in 1884.*

José Garcia killed a man in Belen, Valencia County, and ran off with the dead man's wife. She seemed to have been a willing accomplice in the crime. They disappeared into the rugged mountains of western Socorro County. No great effort was made to locate them and the entire matter was all but completely forgotten.

Then one day, mountain shepherds found the remains of a human body. It had been cut up into four pieces and strung up on the limb of a tree in much the way a butchered animal carcass would be treated. Authorities soon learned that the body was that of the woman with whom Garcia had fled.

Elfego Baca was not about to let this woman's murder go unpunished, as the Valencia County officials had done with the previous killing. The trail was cold, but after three months of investigative effort Baca learned that Garcia was likely hiding at a sheep camp somewhere in northern Sandoval County. He also learned that the men with whom Garcia was hiding were themselves at least marginal outlaws. Finding Garcia in the mountains would be difficult, and capturing him even harder.

Baca took the train to the town of Bernalillo where he enlisted the help of one Alfredo Montoya. Montoya was only 16 years old at the time, but he knew Sandoval County well (in fact later in life he was elected sheriff). The two set out on their quest. For six days they looked for the elusive sheep camp. Elfego became concerned that Garcia's friends might have the time to ride out from Bernalillo and warn the killer that lawmen were in the district. Baca also knew that Garcia could recognize him. So each day that Baca and Montoya were on the trail, Baca covered his face with burnt cork to make it appear as if he were a Negro. The plan was that if they encountered anyone, Baca was to be introduced as Montoya's groom.

On the evening of the sixth day they came upon the camp they sought. Garcia was there along with three other men. Horses were tied nearby and all four were armed. The lawmen entered the camp as previously planned: Montoya in the lead and

Baca, as groom, following behind. The ruse worked. The sheepherders were acquainted with Montoya and took little notice of his Black companion. Garcia did not recognize Baca, either, until it was too late and the killer was looking down the wrong end of the lawman's pistol.

Montoya covered the other three men, and then disarmed them. Once the arrest was complete, Baca made the following speech:

"This man Garcia is a murderer. He killed his wife and cut her in four pieces. In four pieces. A very bad man. We are taking him back to Socorro. Alfredo will ride on ahead to show the way. Garcia will come next and then me. You will stay here. You know Alfredo's father. He knows you, and he knows that Alfredo is up here to visit you. If Alfredo doesn't come back, or if anything happens to Alfredo, Alfredo's father will come up here and kill you. Remember that, and don't try to move from this camp after we leave."

The three sheep men did not interfere, nor did they follow the lawmen and the prisoner. While it had taken six days to get from Bernalillo to the sheep camp, it only took eight hours to arrive at the railroad station at the town of Thornton.[1]

But Baca, Montoya, and Garcia too, had another problem. Word had somehow reached Thornton as to exactly who Garcia was, and why he was in custody. A crowd formed at the railroad station and it was made clear that its purpose was to take Garcia away from Baca and to hang him from a nearby tree. It would be four hours until the next train to Albuquerque arrived. It would, however, only be 15 minutes until a north-bound train arrived.

It is interesting to note that the mob outside the railroad station knew who Garcia was, but did not recognize Baca who had gained a measure of fame by then. Baca pulled two revolvers from holsters, pointed them at the crowd and said that if anyone made a move toward him, or Garcia, he would start shooting. He said that with 12 shots he would certainly kill at least four of them. At that point, someone in the mob finally asked Baca who he was. Baca told them. The story goes that with that announcement, the crowd fell back and when the northbound train arrived a few minutes later, Baca, Montoya and Garcia were allowed to board it unmolested.

Such was the reputation of Elfego Baca.

History doesn't record what became of José Garcia.

---

[1] The name of the town was later changed to Domingo. It was located about six miles south of Peña Blanca in Sandoval County.

THE LONGHORN WILL-O-WISP KILLS EDDY CO. SHERIFF GEO. BATTON: HIMSELF KILLED IN GUNFIGHT

In early June, 1922, word reached Eddy County Sheriff George Batton that a Texas outlaw called the "Longhorn Will-O-Wisp" (Pedro Galindo) and two women were hiding at a house—some said a shack—in the town of Hope, about 20 miles west of Artesia in the far northwest corner of the county. Galindo had escaped from the Huntsville, Texas, prison while serving a life sentence for murder.

Batton, along with his deputies and a posse of local cowboys and citizens surrounded the place and ordered those inside to surrender. The women emerged and said no one remained inside.

The sheriff approached the front door and one of his deputies, Stone Wilburn, approach the back door. The "Will-O-Wisp," from concealment behind a dresser, opened fire immediately as the officers entered the house. A soft-nosed bullet bounced off Wilburn's rib and the sheriff took a bullet in the bowel near hip level. Both officers opened fire in a rapid succession of shots. The lights inside were blown out and the firing stopped. As Wilburn staggered outside, the women tried to escape, only to be caught by a couple of cowboys. The younger woman was then forced to go back into the house. She crawled in on her hands and knees and soon returned with Galindo's gun, a .44 caliber automatic. She said both men inside were dead.

She was right. The posse found Sheriff Batton on the floor, dead. The outlaw was in a corner, shot through the neck and heart. Deputy Wilburn recovered from his wound.

George Batton, 58, previously served four years as deputy sheriff of Brown County in central Texas where he killed an outlaw who shot the sheriff. Batton also served eight years as Brown County sheriff.

After he arrived in New Mexico, Batton served as Artesia town marshal and Eddy County deputy sheriff before he was elected sheriff in 1920. His wife, Lillie Bell, and four children— Sam, Grace, Cecil, and Dot—survived Sheriff Batton. Sam succeeded his father as sheriff. Reports at the time showed that Sam was present at the gunfight that claimed his father's life, but his involvement is not known.

LT. ED. BEALE & THE U. S. ARMY CAMEL CORPS: EXERCISE IN STRANGENESS

The camel train arrived in Albuquerque from Camp Verde, Texas, in the autumn of 1857. It had caused quite a stir in each town it passed through as the camels plodded along, attended by handlers from far-away lands: Arabs and Turks dressed in the attire of their native lands. The train stayed in the Duke City for three days before moving on to the west, to Fort Defiance.

There is some debate about who first came up with the idea of using camels for military purposes in the American southwest. One source credits Lt. Edward F. Beale with promoting the notion that the beasts could be put to good use as mounts and pack animals. Beale was a native of Washington, D. C. and a graduate of the Naval Academy at Annapolis. During the Mexican American War he was detached to serve with land forces in California. He was designated as a dispatch bearer and made six coast to coast trips carrying official documents and news of the far west to Washington. It was Beale, in 1848, who carried the news that gold had been discovered in California, setting off the Gold Rush of 1849. He knew what he was talking about when he suggested using camels.

Another source reports that the original idea belonged to Henry C. Wayne, an army artillery officer who also served in the southwest during the Mexican War. It was Wayne who took the idea to a U. S. Senator from Mississippi named Jefferson Davis in 1851.[1] Davis left office soon afterwards but became Secretary of War under President Franklin Pierce in 1853. Through Davis' good offices, $30,000 as appropriated in late 1854 for the purpose of importing camels for military purposes. Davis placed Henry Wayne, then a major, in charge of buying the animals. A navy ship, the USS Supply, commanded by Lt. D. D. Porter was assigned the duty of transporting the camels.

Major Wayne traveled first to England to study the animals at the London Zoo. He then met up with Porter and the *Supply* in Italy and they sailed further east on the Mediterranean Sea. They purchased three camels in Tunis, nine in Egypt, and 21 in Smyrna; nine were dromedaries (one humped) and the rest were Bactrian (two humped). They arrived at Indianola, Texas in May 1856, and the animals were moved on to Camp Verde, about 60 miles north of San Antonio.

Lt. Porter was ordered back to the Middle East for more animals and returned in February 1857 with 41 more.

Local folks poked a great deal of fun at the odd looking animals and expressed doubt that they could each do the work of four horses.[2] To prove the point Major Wayne offered a demonstration. He put a single camel on display and made the animal kneel. He affixed two bales with a total weight of more than 600 pounds to the beast, and then affixed two more of equal weight, a total of 1,256 pounds. The animal stood without effort and walked away. As a rule, each camel carried about twice the load of a pack mule.

In basic logistics, a camel ate and drank about the same amount as a horse, but it could travel 300 miles, loaded, in three to four days without drinking. The troops working with them, however, did not like their charges. Camels required more care than horses, the soldiers complained; they were not as maneuverable as horses in combat; they were more stubborn than mules; and they defecated at random and smelled bad. Camels also tended to spook horses and mules.

Secretary of War (under president James Buchanan) John B. Floyd officially created the U. S. Army Camel Corps in March 1857 and Edward Beale was placed in command. Beale was assigned the task of using the beasts to forge a road west from New Mexico to California; hence the Camel Corps visit to Albuquerque. Beale completed his task and opened the new road in 48 days, a remarkable feat.

Beale reported thus to congress, "I have tested the value of the camels, marked a new road to the Pacific, and traveled 4,000 miles without an accident."

Secretary Floyd agreed and ordered an additional 1,000 of the animals, but before an appropriation could be approved by congress, war between the states became a very real possibility and the entire program was abandoned. In 1859 Beale was ordered to dispose of the camels. He managed to avoid doing so until about 1863, keeping some of them on his own property in California.

Some were later given to the city of Los Angeles where they were used to transport mail and baggage. In 1864 many others were sold to highest bidders and used by private interests to haul freight. Some were used in circuses. Texas Confederates captured the camels remaining at Camp Verde, but couldn't figure out what to do with them, so they set them free to fend for themselves.

Apparently, no one kept tabs on the beasts after that and reports continued for years of camel sightings in the remote corners of the deserts of the far west. In 1907 a Nevada prospector encountered a couple of them, and as recently as the early 1970s, there was a rumor that one had been seen in a remote area of west Texas.

One source concluded with this: "The U. S. Army Camel Corps, which had successfully...carried military loads throughout the new West, finally died of mistreatment and neglect—because it was [just] too strange."

---

[1] One source reports that Wayne was only the messenger who conveyed the camel idea that had originated with Professor George Glidden. Another writer says the idea was suggested as early as 1837 by an army major named George Crossman.

[2] The Duke of Tuscany told Major Wayne that his 250 camels did the work of 1,000 horses.

JUDGE KIRBY BENEDICT: JUSTICE NEW MEXICO STYLE

Judge Kirby Benedict (1809-1874) was one of the most colorful characters in Territorial New Mexico.

Benedict was born in Connecticut. He practiced law in Illinois in the 1840s during which time he became acquainted with Abraham Lincoln. He also became acquainted with President Franklin Pierce who appointed him to the New Mexico bench in 1853. He kept his seat through the administration of James Buchanan (1857-1861) and continued after Lincoln was elected. Benedict and the president carried on a regular correspondence and the Judge was fond of showing off his letters.

"Physically, Kirby Benedict looked the part of a judge, with his habitual taciturn expression, his backbone ramrod stiff, and a wavy beard that spilled onto his chest." He also had a crippled right hand, the result of a wound from a Bowie knife.[1] Even though he had difficulty in writing, he distinguished himself by his lyrical pronouncements from the bench.

In one 1854 case which involved some questionable documents, allegedly stolen, in a land grant adjudication case, the justice asked: "How, and when did, it [the grant document] desert its secure abode, among the archives of El Paso, and separated from its companions upon the shelf, wander like a bird, from the arik [ark] of her safety, to be found lost & floating, upon the revolutionary ocean, which the imagination of the defendant, has pictured in his answer?"

Then there was the occasion when Benedict was holding court in Las Vegas (New Mexico) at a time when the territory's ordinance against gambling was being strictly enforced. The Grand Jury returned a long list of indictments for gambling infractions against many of the territory's most upstanding citizens, including several members of the bar. Most appeared and promptly paid the statutory $50.00 fine. One of them, Tom Catron, intended to embarrass the judge by pointing out that he, the judge, was known to engage in poker playing on a regular basis. As the court processed those accused, the sheriff read out the names, and at last he called, "Kirby Benedict, for gambling."

The judge promptly stood and listened as the sheriff read the indictment. "Kirby Benedict enters a plea of guilty," he said loudly, and then added, "and the court assesses his fine at $50.00 and cost; and, what is more, Kirby Benedict will pay it." Tom Catron subsequently plead guilty, too.

But Benedict's most famous pronouncement came at the conclusion of 1864 murder trial in Taos. The defendant was accused of brutally killing blacksmith Julian Trujillo. The judge said this upon conviction of the accused:

"José Maria Martin, stand up! José Maria Martin, you have been indicted, tried and convicted by a jury of your countrymen of the crime of murder, and the court is now about to pass upon you the dread sentence of law. As a usual thing, José Maria Martin, it is a painful duty for the judge of a court of justice to pronounce upon a human being the sentence of death. There is something horrible about it, and the mind of the court naturally revolts from the performance of such a duty; happily, however, your case is relieved of all such unpleasantness, and the court takes positive delight in sentencing you to death.

"You are a young man, José Maria Martin, apparently of good physical constitution and robust health. Ordinarily you might have looked forward to many years of life, and the court has no doubt you have, and have expected to die at a green old age, but you are about to be cut off as the consequence of your own act. José Maria Martin, it is now the spring time; in a little while the grass will be springing up in this beautiful valley, and on these broad mesas and mountains sides, flowers will be blooming; birds will be singing the sweet carols, and nature will be putting on her most gorgeous and most attractive robes, and life will be pleasant and men will want to stay; but none of this is for you, José Maria Martin; the flowers will not bloom for you, José Maria Martin, the birds will not carol for you, José Maria Martin; when these things come to gladden the senses of men, you will be occupying a space about six by two beneath the sod, and the green grass and those beautiful flowers will be growing above your lowly head.

"The sentence of the court is that you be taken from this place to the county jail; that you there be kept safely and securely confined in the custody of the Sheriff until the day appointed for your execution. Be very careful, Mr. Sheriff, that he have no opportunity to escape, and that you have him at the appointed place at the appointed time; that you be so kept, José Maria Martin, until—Mr. Clerk, on what day of the month does Friday about two weeks from this come?"

"March 22nd, Your Honor."

"Very well, until Friday the 22nd day of March, when you will be taken by the sheriff from your place of confinement, to some safe and convenient spot within the county... and that you be there hanged by the neck until you are dead and—the Court was about to add, José Maria Martin, 'May God have mercy upon your soul,' but the court will not assume the responsibility of asking an All Wise Providence to do that which a jury of your peers has refused to do.

"The Lord couldn't have mercy upon your soul. However, if you affect any religious belief, or are connected with any religious organization, it might be well enough for you to send for your priest or your minister and get from him—well, such consolation as you can, but the Court advises you to place no reliance upon anything of that kind.

"Mr. Sheriff, remove the prisoner."[2]

For all his earnest integrity, Judge Benedict had two character flaws: he was known to drink too much from time to time, and he cheated at poker, and apparently he was a poor cheat. This latter item is not mere speculation. He was caught at it more than once, and on one occasion in Albuquerque in the late 1850s, he had to be sprinted away by friends before an irate loser could shoot him.

In the early 1870s, Benedict became embroiled in some controversy with the Territorial Supreme Court, in part having to do with "his habits, including the excessive use of intoxicating drinks." He was suspended from the practice of law.[3] In January 1874 he petitioned the Court thus: "I present this petition to your honors in the spirit of confession, respect, obedience and supplication. I confess to have committed against this court, its dignity and judges, disorder, improprieties and contempts for which I should be punished.... I now come as a supplicant and sincerely crave the pardon and forgiveness of your honors.... Accumulating age, want and desolation press upon me, and I desire to be at peace and maintain just and honorable relations with the courts, the judges and others, in such remaining days as may be allotted to me...."

The Court declined to restore Benedict to practice. He died on February 27, 1874.

---

[1] The nature of the incident which caused the injury is not discussed by any source consulted.

[2] Former New Mexico State Historian Robert Tórrez points out that no documentary evidence, official or otherwise, exists to prove that Judge Benedict actually recited this speech. It has, though, been passed along as fact for nearly a century and a half. Tórrez writes, "I hope our history books continue to tell the story because it is a great story that deserves to be told—as long as it is not presented as historical fact."

Governor Miguel Otero in his memoirs says that Martin (he is sometimes called Martinez) escaped from custody and was never executed. Other sources, however, report that Martin was executed on Friday, the 13th of May in 1864.

[3] Even Will Keleher, himself an attorney and meticulous historian, does not provide details of this controversy. That Benedict was a so-called Radical Republican in the years after the Civil War might well have had something to do with it.

ON THE DEATH OF WILLIAM H. BONNEY: BILLY THE KID

If New Mexico had a state outlaw, as it has a state cookie (the *bizcochito*) or a state question (red or green?) or a state bird (the roadrunner), it would certainly be William H. Bonney, better known as Billy the Kid. Mention of his name never fails to incite interest and in many cases, controversy. In 2003, 122 years after the fact, a dispute, again, arose concerning whether or not Sheriff Pat Garrett actually killed Billy in 1881 in Pete Maxwell's bedroom at Fort Sumner, New Mexico. The question has arisen periodically since 1948 when a man who called himself Ollie "Brushy Bill" Roberts came on the scene. He claimed that Garrett killed someone other than Bonney, and that he, Roberts, was in fact 89-year-old Billy the Kid.

A brief retrospective of Billy. Born in New York City in the late 1850s, he arrived in Silver City, New Mexico, along with his mother, brother and stepfather in the early 1870s. His claim to fame there was for sneak-thievery, and he fled rather than face jail for a petty crime. He shot and killed an unarmed bully named Frank Cahill near Fort Grant, Arizona Territory in the summer of 1877. Billy fled back to New Mexico. By fall of that year, he was loitering around Lincoln County where he worked briefly for John H. Tunstall as a cowboy, likely the only honest job he ever held. The Lincoln County War swung into full swing when Tunstall was murdered in February 1878. Billy took that as justification for a spate of murder, rustling and horse thievery; practices he pursued until his death three and one half years later.

By 1880, folks around Lincoln County had put up with about all of young Billy's activities they cared to, and they elected Pat Garrett to the office of sheriff of Lincoln County, based on his promise to get rid of the outlaw. Garrett set upon his task even before he officially took office and captured Bonney at Stinking Springs, near Fort Sumner, in December 1880. Billy was tried at Mesilla and on April 13, 1881 he was convicted of murdering Lincoln County Sheriff William Brady. The penalty was death by hanging, the sentence to be executed on May 13, of the same year. On April 28, Billy murdered two lawmen, J. W. Bell and Bob Olinger, and escaped custody at the town of Lincoln.

The other thing Billy seems to have been busy with in 1879-80 was fathering children. One researcher reports at least four children as his offspring, all obviously illegitimate.

Billy returned to Fort Sumner after his escape. Sheriff Garrett's early efforts to recapture the outlaw were unsuccessful but at last he received word that Billy was in his old haunts. Garrett, with two deputies—Tip McKinney and John Poe—rode to

Fort Sumner and on July 14, in a darkened room, Garrett killed the Kid with a shot to the heart.

A coroner's jury convened the next morning and its members examined the body of the deceased and declared thus: "We of the jury unanimously find that William Bonney has been killed by a bullet entering the left side of his chest... and shot from a gun in the hands of Pat F. Garrett, and our dictum is that the act of said Garrett was justifiable homicide and we are of the opinion that the gratitude of the whole community is owed to said Garrett for his deed, and that he deserves to be rewarded."

The verdict was signed by M. [Milnor] Rudulph, Antonio Saavedra, Pedro Antonio Lucero, Jose Silba, Sabal Gutierrez and Lorenzo Jaramillo.[1]

Others in Fort Sumner that day who viewed the body included, of course, Garrett and his two deputies, Pete Maxwell, and Nasaria, Abrana, Paulita and Luz Maxwell. The local *Alcalde*, Alejandro Segura, presided at the inquest. Two local men constructed the Kid's coffin. That makes a total of 17 people with first-hand knowledge as to who was killed.

It is impossible to believe that these (at least) 17 people could have entered into a conspiracy to cover-up the death of the Kid, and then kept it a secret for all of the years that followed, until their own deaths. What would their motives have been? Bonney had no money with which to pay them off, and there is little evidence that he was so beloved in the community that such a large number of people would carry out such an elaborate plan. In fact there is evidence to the contrary.

The fathers of the young women Billy impregnated could not have been happy with the outlaw, particularly in those conservative times. There is also evidence that Pete Maxwell's sister, Paulita, planned to run off with Billy, a prospect that was completely unacceptable to her brother. Pete is the one, the story goes, who got word to Garrett that Billy was hiding in Fort Sumner. He actually hoped the Sheriff *would* kill the outlaw. It seems unlikely that Maxwell would then enter into the conspiracy of silence that allowed the Kid to escape.

Sheriff Garrett's son, Oscar, carried the point one step further in later years by suggesting that an entire generation of southern New Mexicans had to have been accessories to the lie of Billy's death by keeping silent about it until Brushy Bill made his claim nearly 70 years later.

And the conspiracy would have involved more than silence. If, as Roberts claimed, another man was killed that night in Fort Sumner, who was he?[2] And did that make Garrett guilty of murder, or at least manslaughter? It would be asking the impossible to think that so many people could hide such a secret.

What became of Ollie Roberts and his claim? Probably the most complete debunking of Roberts' book, *Alias Billy the Kid*, was done by Albuquerque history writer Don Cline who subsequently published his own biography of young Bonney. Step by step, he contradicts virtually everything Roberts said in claiming to be Billy the Kid. Cline concluded that Roberts lied in nearly every particular, and that he was too young to have even taken part in the Lincoln County War.[3] Roberts died of an apparent heart attack on a street in Hico, Texas on December 27, 1950.

---

[1] This document, apparently, was never officially filed. Conspiracy theorists count that as evidence that Bonney was not killed as the document attests.

[2] Roberts claimed the man killed that night was his "partner," Billy Barlow. Researchers have found no evidence that such a person existed in Lincoln County at the time.

[3] Even William V. Morrrison, one of Roberts' most ardent supporters, said that upon first meeting Brushy Bill, he thought him too young to be Billy the Kid.

FOUL MURDER OF SHERIFF WILLIAM BRADY:
COWARDS ALL!

One of the most cowardly acts of murder in frontier New Mexico took place on April 1, 1878 in the town of Lincoln.

At mid morning on that day, Sheriff William Brady and deputies George Hindman, Billy Mathews, George Peppin and John Long walked down Lincoln-town's only street.[1] Suddenly from behind cover—either an adobe wall or a heavy gate, depending on who is telling the tale—there erupted a fusillade of small arms fire. Sheriff Brady was killed instantly, penetrated by numerous bullets. Deputy Hindman also went down, mortally wounded. The remaining deputies scattered and took cover. Billy Mathews was able to return fire. He shot and wounded one of the assailants as the killer picked over Brady's body.[2] The shooters all escaped from the scene.

The question is, who were the assassins?

Historians Will Keleher and Bill O'Neal identify them as William H. Bonney (Billy the Kid), Henry—or Hendry—Brown, John Middleton, Fred Wait—or Waite— and Jim French. To those five, historians John P. Wilson and Robert Utley add Frank McNabb. Don Cline says there were at least 12 men behind the wall, but he does not identify them except for Bonney and French.

A man named Abneth McCabe, who lived near Lincoln at the time, wrote the following in a letter to Lily Klasner not long after the events described.

"Now for the War news.... Brady and George Hindman were killed in the streets of Lincoln by men hid in the corral behind the new store of McSween and Tunstall, shot in the back as they were passing. John Middleton, [Robert] Weiderman, a Negro, George Washington, and another Negro, Little Henry, 'the kid' [sic] and a man called French were seen to come out the corral after the firing. All must have shot.

Keleher, and Utley are most likely correct, as their scholarship rises to the top in a cauldron full of historians on the subject of the Lincoln County War. It is hard to imagine a dozen gunmen behind that wall, but there were certainly that many, and more, partisans involved in other aspects of the war.

As for Ab McCabe's letter, it is unlikely that Weiderman participated although one writer claims he was there, but did not shoot. Until that date he was a deputy U. S. Marshal. George Washington and George Robinson, both former members of the Negro 10th Cavalry, were arrested after the killings, but probably had nothing to do with it. So, he seems to correctly list Middleton, Brown, Bonney and French.

Bonney, Brown and Middleton were indicted for the crime. It seems odd that Jim French would avoid indictment since witnesses claimed that he helped Bonney molest the bodies after the killings. Of course, there are those who claimed it was

Middleton, not French. In the final analysis, only one man was ever convicted, for killing Sheriff Brady, and that was Bonney. He claimed that he did not fire a fatal shot since he spent his time shooting at Billy Mathews, a man with whom he had a personal grudge.

What became of the other known shooters?

Frank McNabb lasted only one month after the killings. On April 30, he and two others, while watering their horses, were jumped by about two-dozen members of Brady's faction. Frank was shot numerous times and his body left where it fell.

Henry Brown returned to Texas by 1880 and became a deputy sheriff. He then moved on to Caldwell, Kansas, where he became the city marshal in 1882. He seems to have been well regarded and married in March 1884. The following month, his true character emerged. He and his deputy, Ben Wheeler, and two local cowboys attempted to rob the bank at Medicine Lodge, Kansas. Things did not go well. A bank employee went for a gun and was shot dead for his faithfulness to duty. The bank president managed to close the door to the safe, and he too was killed. The robbers got no money.

But that wasn't all. A posse quickly took up pursuit, and the robbers could not find their extra horses. They were soon captured. Back in Medicine Lodge, it wasn't long before a lynch party was formed and when the dust settled, Brown was dead, shot while trying to escape, and the other three were also dead and hanging from a tree.

John Middleton was severely wounded in the gunfight at Blazer's Mill four days after Brady's assassination. He recovered at Fort Sumner and then migrated to Kansas where he entered the grocery business. In 1885 he'd moved on to Oklahoma where he became a consort of famed lady outlaw Belle Starr. Her husband, Sam, seems to have been away at the time, but maybe not. Someone shot and killed Middleton from ambush in May 1885. It is noteworthy that Belle was shot from ambush and killed less than four years later.

Fred Waite lasted a little longer. Fred was a quarter blood Cherokee Indian. After the killings, he remained with Bonney for a few months, but ultimately returned to the Cherokee Nation in Oklahoma. He became the tax collector. He died in 1895, at age 42, of unknown causes.

And no one knows what became of Jim French. He too remained with Bonney for a time and probably participated in some cattle rustling. But at some point he and the Kid parted ways and French drifted off into obscurity. In one of those odd historical coincidences, at this exact same time, one Lt. James H. French was stationed at nearby Fort Stanton, and he sided with Brady. Apaches killed him in 1880.

And William H. Bonney? Every one knows that he was shot and killed by Sheriff Pat Garrett at Fort Sumner, New Mexico, late on the evening of July 14, 1881.

---

[1] One historian claims they were all on horseback.

[2] Some writers claim that Bonney only intended to take the sheriff's rifle; others claim he was after a warrant that Brady carried in his coat pocket.

TEXAS CONFEDERATES INVADE NEW MEXICO: COL. CANBY UNABLE TO HALT THEM AT VALVERDE FIGHT

Historians often overlook the importance of events in New Mexico during the early days of the American Civil War. Many reference books make no mention of the battles at Valverde and Glorieta Pass, or the skirmishes at Apache Canyon or Peralta.

But on the very same day that Confederate forces under the command of General Simon Bruckner surrendered to Union troops under General U. S. Grant at Fort Donelson along the Cumberland River in Tennessee, February 16, 1862, another Confederate force under General Henry H. Sibley[1] advanced on Fort Craig, near the Rio Grande, in southern New Mexico, a post commanded by Union Colonel Edward R. S. Canby.

General Sibley chose not to attack Fort Craig. He by-passed it and thus forced the Union troops out into the open. Canby attempted to stop the Rebels further north along the Rio Grande four days later, at Valverde, south of Socorro. Unlike Fort Donelson, Confederate forces won at Valverde and continued their march north toward Albuquerque.

What led up to the invasion is also consistent with New Mexico's place in history. In the years prior to the Civil War, both northern and southern politicians worried about places like Kansas, California and Texas, and their respective positions on the issue of slavery, and hence their predispositions toward potential Union or Confederate allegiances. No one seemed to care much about New Mexico.

And ante-bellum New Mexico wasn't much concerned, either. A large segment of the population had been Mexican citizens until only 15 years before. Negro slavery as an institution, while legal, was not something New Mexicans cared much about. There were no more than two-dozen slaves in the territory (which at the time included Arizona), and U. S. Army officers from southern states owned most of them. Slavery was not an economic factor or social issue, and state's rights didn't matter much since New Mexico was not a state.

Many of the Anglo settlers in southern New Mexico had roots in Texas, and they leaned toward the Confederacy. Many of the Anglo traders in northern New Mexico held sympathies for the Union. Dr. Henry Connelly was one of them. He'd been a New Mexico merchant since 1824 and was well regarded. President Abraham Lincoln named him territorial governor in September 1861. He rallied the Hispanic population to the Union cause. One of the ways he encouraged support was to consistently refer to the invaders as "Texans" and not "Confederates" or "Southerners." Hispanic New Mexicans had ample reason to dislike Texans.

By 1861 there were U. S. Army forts scattered all over New Mexico. The question for the officers commanding them became whether to remain loyal to the Union or to join forces with the Confederates. Becoming a Confederate officer often meant a substantial promotion in rank. On the other hand, if the Confederacy lost the war, it could mean a treason charge and a firing squad. The risk must have been worth it. Many officers defected.

Henry Sibley was one of them. In early 1861, he was the commander at Fort Union in northeastern New Mexico, with the rank of major. He joined the Texas Confederates soon after the war began with the rank of colonel (he was promoted to brigadier general a month later). He traveled east to visit with CSA President Jefferson Davis. He had no trouble convincing Davis that the capture of New Mexico could be important to the Southern cause. From New Mexico, attacks could be launched on Colorado and California and the gold and silver deposits in both places would bolster southern coffers.

Davis could offer no troops in support of the effort, but he authorized Sibley to raise his own army of volunteers. Sibley recruited about 3,000 men and trained them near San Antonio. They had no uniforms and many provided their own equipment. He marched them north to El Paso in December 1861.

After the battle of Valverde, February 21, 1862, Sibley continued north. While Colonel Canby and most of the Union troops returned to Fort Craig, some of his officers, including Colonel Kit Carson, skirted around the Texas troops and sped north to prepare Albuquerque for the invasion. Along the way they warned farmers and ranchers to hide their livestock and bury their valuables. As a result, Sibley found the pickings slim as he lengthened his supply line from El Paso.

Confederate troops marched into Albuquerque on March 2, 1862 but they found few usable supplies. Union Captain Henry Enos, an army quartermaster, had loaded wagons with what supplies he could and burned the rest in several warehouses located of west of what is now old town.

Along the march from Albuquerque to Santa Fe, the Confederates stopped off in Bernalillo long enough to search for the fortune that was rumored to be in the possession of Don José Leandro Perea, known as the Sheep King of New Mexico. It would not have been difficult for General Sibley to hear about the treasure since Don José was quite ostentatious about his wealth. Soldiers reduced several building to rubble, but they found nothing. One story goes that the trove was buried and covered with rawhides and dirt, over which a herd of sheep were driven thus concealing the location. Another historian reports that the money was not in Bernalillo at the time; that Don José had previously secured it elsewhere.

In Santa Fe, Sibley found the same situation he'd encountered in Albuquerque. Retreating Union troops had taken their supplies with them as they abandoned Fort Marcy and marched east toward Fort Union. The rebels were able to re-supply to some extent by looting local merchants.

The Confederate path of little or no resistance was about to end. Governor Connelly had requested assistance from Colorado Governor William Gilpin, and about 3,000 mixed regular soldiers and volunteers marched from Denver to Fort Union.

Colonel John Slough was in command and he believed the place to stop the southern advance was in the mountains between Las Vegas and Santa Fe. He left Fort Union on March 22 with about 1300 men. His troops met Sibley's volunteers first at Apache Canyon on March 26.

It is generally agreed that the fight at Apache Canyon was a draw. When it was over, five Union soldiers had been killed, and 14 wounded. Four rebels were dead and 20 wounded. The two armies met again on the 28th at Glorieta Pass.

Many historians call the Battle at Glorieta a draw, too. Each side had about 50 killed and 60 wounded in a day of fighting. Militarily, though, the really important action took place when Union troops under the command of Lieutenant Colonel Manuel Chavez and Major John Chivington [2] flanked the confederate troops and attacked the Rebel headquarters at Johnson Ranch. They quickly over-powered the defenders and then destroyed about 80 wagons which contained military supplies, rations, personal effects, and the like. One southerner said, "Here we are ... 1,000 miles from home, not a wagon, not a dust of flour, not a pound of meat."

With its supplies destroyed, Sibley's "Army of New Mexico" went no further. The troops fled with great hast and in considerable disarray to Santa Fe and Albuquerque. At the same time, Colonel Canby and his troops were heading north from Fort Craig. The two forces met once again, this time at Peralta, near present-day Los Lunas, and engaged in a skirmish. Canby noted the deplorable condition the Texans were in and he could see no value in capturing them. After all, if he made them prisoners or war, he'd have to feed and care for them. There were precious few resources in New Mexico with which to do so. He allowed them to continue traveling south, back to Texas, from whence they would never return. New Mexico remained in the Union.

General Sibley declared his adventure in New Mexico a success in a report to Jefferson Davis. But, he said, there was no point in returning to the territory to the north. He said his troops had learned to dislike the place and people greatly.

The feeling among New Mexicans must have been mutual.

---

[1] General Henry Hopkins Sibley, who commanded the Confederate invaders of New Mexico, should not be confused with General Henry Hastings Sibley, who led U. S. troops against the Sioux in Minnesota during the 1860s.

[2] This is the same John Chivington who as a colonel led 400 troopers of the 3rd Colorado Volunteers at the Sand Creek Massacre on November 29, 1864.

SILVER CITY MARSHAL CHARLES CANTLEY SLOW ON THE DRAW: KILLED IN BARROOM GUNFIGHT

Gunfights are part and parcel of the literature—including television and movies—of the Old West. Such events were usually portrayed as matters of honor, or villainy, in which two men faced each other in the middle of a dusty street, drew holstered six-guns and fired at one another. Readers will recall that Marshal Matt Dillon of TV's *Gunsmoke* fame only required a single shot to bring down his adversary. So did Roy Rogers, Gene Autry, John Wayne and many others.

The problem is that history does not record a single instance of such a fight ever taking place.[1]

Western historian Leon Metz has observed thus: "In reality, few people were stupid enough to stand in the middle of the street and risk being shot down, and those who did were usually intoxicated. Sensible and sober individuals took cover behind a barrel...."

What follows is an abridged account of a real-life gunfight, which appeared in the Silver City (New Mexico) *Enterprise* for October 11, 1895 under the headline, "A DUEL TO DEATH."

"At twenty-five minutes past ten o'clock on Tuesday evening (Oct. 8), the citizens of Silver City were startled by the loud reports of six pistol shots fired in regular and precise order of about a half second apart, followed by an interval of a few seconds by two more shots...."

"The affray occurred at the White House Saloon, into which place Mr. [James] Fielder had stepped for a few moments before going home [after] simply taking a stroll through the town before retiring for the night. Walking through the club room to go out he was accosted by Marshall [*sic*] [Charles] Cantley, who had been drinking and was considerably under the influence of liquor. Their conversation at first was of a pleasant and jovial character, but soon Cantley became angry and aggressive, as he often did while drinking. Mr. Fielder strove to placate and pacify him but without avail."

Witness John Gillett described what happened then.

"Cantley was drinking during the evening and Mr. Harvey, myself, and others had been trying to get him home for an hour and a half but could not. I had been in the back room a short time when I heard the words uttered by Mr. Fielder, 'liar or damned liar.' I stepped out of the back room and walked up and stood by Mr. Cantley. Mr. Cantley said to Mr. Fielder, 'I've been told that you said you were going to beat the stuffing out of me.' Mr. Fielder said he had never said so, and that whoever told him so was a liar. After some farther parley about some lawsuit, Cantley said he had personal reasons for knowing he had it in for him. Fielder told Cantley, 'Cantley I have nothing on earth against you; I've always been your friend.' Cantley asked Mr. Fielder if he was armed. Mr. Fielder replied, 'I do not think you have any right to ask me that question.'

"Mr. Cantley then pulled his pistol and fired; Mr. Fielder pulled his pistol and fired; his pistol apparently going off before he had it up and I think the first shot went into the floor. Then they both continued to fire. After the third or fourth shot Cantley staggered and started to fall. After Cantley fell or was falling Mr. Fielder stepped forward and fired another shot with his pistol in both hands, he then snapped his pistol once or twice more at Cantley but it was empty."

Under the heading, **INCIDENTS OF THE SHOOTING**, the *Enterprise* reporter provided the following details.

"When Cantley pulled his gun Mr. Fielder coolly reached for his cigar and placed it in the other side of his mouth, at the same time freeing his elbows from the place they occupied between the pickets of the railing against which he was standing, and stepped to one side of the railing so that his arms were unobstructed.

"From the relative positions of the combatants and the bullet marks in the wall behind where Mr. Fielder stood, it is evident that each of the bullets fired from Mr. Cantley's pistol only missed his opponent by a few inches. One bullet went too high and to the left of Mr. Fielder's head, one just to the right of his breast. Mr. Fielder's first shot evidently went into the floor between them, his second evidently struck the deceased above and outward of the nipple of the left breast, another struck him in the neck above the left clavicle, when he commenced to stagger and fall, and another after he had fallen grazed his chin on the left side, going downward through the neck into the body. One of the bullets fired by Mr. Fielder went over his antagonist's head and bedded itself in the wall. Mr. Fielder testified that after the first shot was fired by Cantley he could not see him on account of the [gun] smoke, and he just fired at the point where the flashes were coming from, until Cantley fell."

Charley Cantley, a native of Anderson County, Texas, had resided in Silver City for about ten years at the time of his death, and had served as a lawman for the entire period, first as a deputy sheriff and then as city marshal. He was well regarded and generally considered fearless in the face of the outlaw element. The *Enterprise*, though, said this: "His long continued authority as an officer ... had caused him to assume an arbitrary demeanor, which at times tended toward aggressiveness. Liquor, to which he was slightly addicted, would aggravate this tendency...

"The business houses in the city all closed during the funeral which was largely attended by all of our best citizens."

Justice of the Peace Isaac Givens ruled the case a matter of self-defense, and the *Enterprise* concluded thus:

"The whole affair is to be deplored."

---

[1] The closest to a "classic" western duel was probably the fight between James Butler "Wild Bill" Hickok and Dave Tutt in Springfield, Missouri on June 21, 1865. At a range of about 100 yards, they both drew their guns at about the same time and began firing. Hickok made what had to be a lucky shot at that range and killed Tutt with a bullet to the heart.

GUNFIGHT AT THE GREATHOUSE RANCH: DEPUTY CARLYLE KILLED, OUTLAWS ESCAPE

James Bermuda Carlyle is not a name that springs to mind when one recalls the famous gunfights and gunfighters of the old west. He didn't live long enough to acquire much of a reputation, but those who bother themselves with the esoterica of the late 19th century American Frontier know his name.

Carlyle is believed to have been born in Trumbull County, Ohio, around 1861. He left home at a young age and by the time he reached his middle teens he was working on the buffalo hunting ranges of West Texas. In the summer of 1874 he participated in the second battle at the Adobe Walls in which thirty men—famed lawman Bat Masterson among them—and one woman, held off a thousand Comanche, Kiowa and Cheyenne Indians. Carlyle's name appears on the monument there as Bermuda Carlile.

The route he took is not known, but by November of 1880 Jim Carlyle was living in the thriving mining town of White Oaks, New Mexico, and working as a blacksmith. That was in the waning days of the famed Lincoln County War. William Bonney (Billy the Kid) remained free, making a general nuisance of himself, and Patrick F. Garrett had just been elected sheriff of Lincoln County, on the campaign promise that he would bring a halt to Bonney's criminal career.

Bonney along with Billy Wilson and Dave Rudabaugh, and perhaps others, stole a herd of horses and drove them into White Oaks on November 28. The nuances of ownership of the animals could be overlooked as a result of great demand for mounts. But a local deputy sheriff named Will Hudgin became suspicious and took up the trail of the outlaws. In the gunfight that followed, Bonney and Wilson both had their horses shot from under them and they were obliged to run for their lives. The outlaws rode back into White Oaks on November 30 and for no very good reason, Bonney, or one of his toadies, took a shot at another deputy sheriff named James Redman on White Oak's main street.

Jim Carlyle, who also served as a Lincoln County deputy sheriff,[1] took a leadership position in the 12-man posse that pursued the miscreants. The chase ended about 40 miles to the north at the Greathouse and Kuch ranch on the White Oaks-Las Vegas Road, near the present-day town of Corona. The ranch house, sometimes called Greathouse Tavern, was actually a saloon and way station for travelers. The outlaws had the better of the situation. As a standoff developed, the outlaws were inside where it was warm and the posse was out in the cold. Snow covered the ground and the temperature stood at below freezing.

A Greathouse and Kuch employee named Joe Steck became an intermediary between the two groups. It was agreed that Jim "Whiskey Jim" Greathouse—who acquired his nickname name by illegally selling liquor to Indians—would join the posse as a hostage if a representative of the law would enter the saloon and discuss the situation with William Bonney.[2] Carlyle agreed and traded places with Greathouse. By late evening the deputy had not returned and the other possemen became concerned. They sent a note into the house saying that if Carlyle was not promptly released, they would shoot Greathouse. Shortly afterward, a shot was heard from outside and what happened next has been the source of debate from that day to this.

One theory is that Carlyle heard the shot and thinking his posse had killed Greathouse, he dived out a window to save his own life, only to be shot to death by Bonney and the outlaws. Bonney's version of events agreed that Carlyle jumped out the window after the first shot was fired, but Bonney claimed the deputy was actually shot and killed by members of his own posse who, not recognizing him, thought he was attacking them.

The posse withdrew after Carlyle was shot, leaving his body where it fell in the snow. Less than an hour later, the outlaws also fled the scene. Carlyle's body was frozen stiff when Joe Steck found it at daybreak. Another White Oaks posse, this one led by Will Hudgin, burned the road ranch to the ground the following day.

It is not known who fired the shot that created the circumstances leading to Deputy Carlyle's death. Jim Greathouse was arrested in March 1881, and charged as an accessory to the murder of Jim Carlyle. He was released on bond two days later. In December 1881, after rustling some 40 head of cattle from Joel Fowler of Socorro, Fowler shot Jim "Whiskey Jim" Greathouse to death in the San Mateo Mountains, west of Socorro.

Lincoln County Sheriff Pat Garrett killed William H. Bonney at Fort Sumner on July 14, 1881. Dave Rudabaugh was killed in Mexico in 1886.

Billy Wilson was later convicted of counterfeiting and sentenced to Leavenworth Prison in Kansas, from which he escaped. President Grover Cleveland pardoned him in 1896 at the behest of Pat Garrett. One source says he later became sheriff of Terrell County, Texas. A drunken cowboy killed him there in 1911. Most important is that Wilson was born in 1861 in Trumbull County, Ohio. One source says that Carlyle and Wilson attended school together. That may explain why Carlyle was willing to go into the ranch house/tavern in the first place. But whatever the reason, the result was that Jim Carlyle's career on the western frontier ended before he reached his 21st birthday.

---

[1] Historian Don Cline, who spent many years researching Billy the Kid and the Lincoln County War, says that these law officers may not have been deputy sheriff's, but deputies of the White Oaks town marshal.

[2] Cline believes that Kuch was the hostage, and not Greathouse.

"SHERIFF CARMICHAEL AND 1 KILLED, 7 WOUNDED AS UNEMPLOYED RIOT"

(Headline, Gallup *Independent*, April 4, 1935)

Things were tough in the United States in 1935. The Great Depression was firmly in place, unemployment was high and money was scarce. Banks foundered or failed. The drought, and resulting Dust Bowl, worsened monthly. Farms and ranches failed. Manufacturing declined and mines of all kinds closed. Distrust, agitation and violence were the unfortunate results.

Gallup, New Mexico, found itself in the maelstrom of the times.

Coal mining was a significant factor in the Gallup economy. So important was it that the community of Gamerco, located a couple of miles north of town, was named for the Gallup American Coal Company. By the middle 1930s, with the demand for coal down, many miners found themselves out of work.

Many of them lived in company housing at a place called Chihuahuita. In 1934 a local state senator named C. F. Vogel bought the settlement from Gamerco. At the time it consisted of about 100 houses, many of them occupied by unemployed miners. Vogel offered those living there an opportunity to either begin paying rent, or in the alternative to purchase their respective homes on the installment plan. Most refused and they were supported by the National Miners Union[1], the International Labor Defense organization, and the Community Party's Unemployed Union.

Vogel took legal action in early 1935 to enforce his ownership prerogatives and Justice of the Peace William J. Bickel soon issued eviction orders against the squatters. One of those evicted was Victor Campos whose house was boarded up by officers after the eviction was carried out.

The house didn't stay boarded up for very long. Campos, along with Ezquio Navarro, Jennie Lovato and a "mob" of about 50 other miners tore the boards off and moved Campos' belongings back into the house. All three were promptly arrested on a complaint signed by Vogel. Mrs. Lovato was released on her own recognizance, but the men were jailed pending a court appearance scheduled for the morning of April 4.

Sheriff Mack Carmichael did not take the matter lightly. Along with Undersheriff Dee Roberts and deputies Bobcat Wilson and Hoy Boggess he had no problem in getting the prisoners to Bickel's courtroom. A crowd began to gather outside as the proceedings got underway inside. Bickel took no action but continued the case until the following day to allow the Navarro time to secure the services of legal counsel. Carmichael decided that rather than risk taking his prisoners through the crowd, he'd take them out the back way; through the judge's chambers, down an alley from Third St. to Second St. and to the jail. The mob—75 to 300 strong, depending on who told the story—learned of the maneuver and thought the suspects had been railroaded and were being returned to jail.[2] The crowd confronted the sheriff on Third Street and demanded the release of Campos and Navarro.

No one knows for sure who fired first. Some believe it was either Ignacio Valarde or Solomon Esquibel. It is known that Sheriff Carmichael was the first to fall, shot in the left arm and just below the right eye; dead on the ground before he drew his own gun. Dee Roberts pulled his gun but could not make the trigger work. He fanned the hammer with the heel of his hand and managed to kill Valarde and seriously wound Esquibel, who died eight days later.

Gunfire continued on both sides. Bobcat Wilson was hit in the chest and rioters Doroteo Andrade, Juan Castro and Pete Moreno were also wounded, along with innocent bystander Mrs. Solidad Sanchez.

Deputy Boggess was beaten about the head with clubs and stabbed in the chest with an ice pick.

Gallup Police Chief Kelsey Presley and his officers moved into the area and helped break up the mob. Campos and Navarro managed to escape as the crowd scattered. Wounded rioters were taken to St. Mary's hospital in Gallup and wounded officers were taken to Rehoboth Mission hospital. They all survived. In fact, Hoy Boggess, with five stitches and his head swathed in a bandage, rejoined the posse that same evening.

Dee Roberts had previously served as McKinley County sheriff and within minutes of Carmichael's death, he was again elevated to that position. He immediately mobilized a posse of about 100 special deputies that included all the able-bodied members of the American Legion and the Veterans of Foreign Wars, and other citizens. By noon, Gallup was an armed camp. By 2:30 that afternoon, 30 suspects were in custody. By nightfall, the number had reached about 100. The Sheriff's goal was to arrest everyone in McKinley County connected with the "radical movement," and in those days that meant Communists and Communist sympathizers.

Later the same day, New Mexico Governor Clyde Tingley ordered E. A. House, chief of the New Mexico State Police[3], and twelve officers to Gallup. The governor also made the state penitentiary available to confine those arrested and a special railroad car was assigned to take them to Santa Fe. Tingley declined to mobilize the National Guard.

When the dust settled 10 days later, about 150 people had been arrested; 47 of them, including 11 women, charged with murder. The murder charges were possible because of a state statute which provided that all participants in illegal mob activity could be so charged in the event that a peace officer was killed as a result of that activity. Ten of the suspects were bound over for trial after a preliminary hearing.

Trial of the 10 took place in Aztec on a change of venue in October 1935. On the 17th, three of the defendants, Juan Ochoa, Manuel Avitia and Leandro Valarde (the brother of Ignacio Velarde) were convicted of second-degree murder for the death of Mack Carmichael. Judge James McGhee sentenced them to not less than 45, nor more than 60, years in prison. The remaining seven were convicted of rioting. Two of them, Joe Bartol and Willie Gonzales, both American citizens, were ordered to leave New Mexico. The other five, Mexican citizens, were deported to their native country.

The convictions were, of course, appealed. The state Supreme Court reversed Velarde's conviction. Ochoa and Avitia served short prison terms before they were pardoned and set free.

Thus it ended, one of the darker chapters in New Mexico history.

---

[1] The National Miners Union should not be confused with the United Mine Workers of America. The United Mine Workers cooperated with Gallup authorities after the riot and cancelled local meetings until order was restored.

[2] Bickel was sometimes referred to as "Bail-less" Bickel.

[3] The New Mexico State Police was created by the legislature on February 25, 1935.

MARSHAL J. CARSON KILLED IN LAS VEGAS SALOON FIGHT: FOUR KILLERS DIE FOR THE CRIME

In mid January 1880, four young toughs rode into Las Vegas, New Mexico and set about making drunken fools of themselves. A rumor circulated around town that they were horse and cattle rustlers looking for stock to steal; other gossip held that they were nothing more than young hot-bloods out for a good time. Whichever it was, they soon wore out their welcome.

If the gang had a leader, it was Thomas Jefferson House. He called Colorado home and used the alias Tom Henry. The other three were Anthony Lowe, alias Jim West, John Dorsey, and William "Big" Randall. All of them were drunk—and armed—in the Close and Patterson Saloon and Variety Hall on the evening of January 22. Marshal Joe Carson, alone, approached the four men and asked them to comply with a local ordinance that required them to check their guns with the bartender. History does not record what words were exchanged—one writer says Carson received "a barrage of profane insults"—but what happened next is pretty well documented. Tom Henry likely fired first, two of his bullets hitting Carson in the arms. The other three scofflaws commenced firing as the marshal went down. Carson may have got off two shots—he carried two guns, one in a holster and one in his hip pocket—before he died with eight bullets in his upper body and one in his leg.

Present in the saloon at the time was deputy city marshal Dave Mather who joined the fracas and his aim was true. He quickly killed Big Randall with two bullets to the chest. He put two bullets into Jim West's body and another into Tom Henry's leg. When the smoke cleared, only Mather remained in the saloon, uninjured. Dorsey wasn't wounded, either, but he and Henry had managed to escape leaving the wounded Jim West behind. Reports at the time indicated that about 40 shots were exchanged in the period of a few seconds. (Some newspaper accounts failed to mention that Mather participated in the gunfight, but *someone* assisted the Marshal. Carson's wounds would have prevented him firing five or six shots.)

Henry and Dorsey didn't go far. Two weeks later they were seen at Mora, 30 miles north of Las Vegas. A seven-man posse set out after the killers. Joined along the way by Sheriff A. P. Branch of Mora County, they soon surrounded a farmhouse where the outlaws were holed up. Henry wanted to fight it out but Dorsey talked him out of it based on a promise from the posse that the outlaws would be protected from mob violence back in Las Vegas.

Henry and Dorsey were in jail on the afternoon of February 6 when Henry told a local newspaper reporter that the "fatal fuss" in which Joe Carson died was the result of drunkenness and he had no recollection of it. He seemed nonchalant and unconcerned about the seriousness of the crime he and his friends had committed.

In the early morning hours of February 8, 1880, a large group of vigilantes, probably led by Dave Mather, took the three killers out of the jail—without any serious resistance—and led them to the windmill in the town plaza. What followed was as gruesome as any deed done by vigilantes in the annuls of New Mexico history.

It started out civilized enough, as lynchings go. The condemned were asked if they had any final words.

West told the crowd his real name.

Dorsey said he had nothing to say and not a friend or relative in the world.

Tom Henry said this: "Boys, it's pretty rough to be hung, but I wish someone would write to my father and mother. I will stand the consequences and die like a man."

The wounded Jim West had been kept in jail rather than in the hospital since the night of Carson's murder. His condition had not improved. The mob decided to hang him first. Sick, bleeding and shivering in the winter cold, the young killer whimpered.

"Jim, be still and die like a man," Tom Henry said.

Strong hands pulled the rope and hung West, but the amateur executioners had neglected to tie his hands and he grasped the noose around his neck as his pants dropped around his thighs.

"Please button my pants," West gasped as he swung about.

Joe Carson's widow was in the crowd. She picked up a rifle and fired, probably at West first since he made the best target. Instantly, it seemed, everyone in the crowd with a gun began firing at the killers. West was riddled and hung dead from the noose. Dorsey was shot down and dying. So was Tom Henry. He crawled to the edge of the tower's platform, from which he would have been hung.

"Boys, for God's sake," he begged, "shoot me again. Shoot me in the head."

Someone obliged. All four of Marshal Joe Carson's killers were dead.

Joe Carson was 40 years old (one source says 43), happily married and the father of a 14-year-old daughter. He was born near Knoxville, Tennessee, and previously resided in Sherman, Texas.

The so-called "Hanging Windmill" was dismantled later the same year.

KIT CARSON: HERO OR VILLAIN?

Famed 19th century hunter, trapper, mountain-man and soldier Christopher Houston "Kit" Carson was in the news in the early 21st century when an effort was made to designate his home in Taos as a state monument. A couple of state legislators, both Navajo Indians, strongly objected. They claimed that Carson practiced genocide against the Navajo people 140 years earlier.

But did he really?

Carson was born on Christmas Eve, 1809, on a farm in Madison County, Kentucky. During the summer of 1811, he and his family moved west to Howard County, Missouri. Young Kit learned early about mortal combat. At not yet nine years of age, gun in hand, Kit helped repel an Indian attack upon the family farm in Missouri.

At about age 14, Kit was apprenticed to a saddle maker at Franklin, Missouri, a line of work he found "irksome." He stayed at it for two years before he joined a wagon train and ran away to the west. His talent in leatherwork was such that the man to whom he was apprenticed offered a *one-cent* reward for his return. Kit arrived in Santa Fe in the fall of 1826 and moved on to Taos where he spent the winter. While his adventures in life took him from Montana on the north to Chihuahua on the south, and from California to Washington, D. C., he always returned to Taos.

Historians and biographers do not agree as to the extent of Carson's education. One claims he was illiterate throughout his life; another that he attended school through the third grade and was able to read and write quite well. Literate or not, there is no argument that he was more comfortable with a rifle in his hands than a quill pen. He earned his way in life for many years as a hunter, trapper, scout and soldier.

It is noteworthy that Kit Carson was married three times in his life. His first wife was an Arapahoe woman named Waa-Nibe. Together they had one daughter, Adaline, in 1837. Waa-Nibe died in 1839. In 1840 or 41, he married a Cheyenne woman, Making out Road, but the union didn't last long. In 1843 he married Maria Josefa Jaramillo of Taos. They remained married until her death in 1868. They were the parents of eight children; the youngest, Josefita, born only a weeks before Josefa's death.

During his own lifetime he was lionized as a great Indian fighter. In his autobiography, Carson told of the time in 1849, after a fight with Jicarilla Apache Indians, who had killed a woman named White and her child, when he found a novel about himself among the litter in the Indian camp. He was surprised, and dismayed, to find that he was "...represented as a great hero, slaying Indians by the hundred."

The notion of removing the Indians from the white man's path was not simply a matter of immediate need among mountain men and trappers. It was an extension of the national policy of the time, the Monroe Doctrine. President James Monroe, in his seventh annual message to congress delivered on December 2, 1823, said the United States would strongly oppose any attempt by Russia, Great Britain or Spain to extend their colonies into North America and New York newspaperman John Louis O'Sullivan wrote in 1845: "Our manifest destiny is to over spread the continent allotted by Providence for the free development of our yearly multiplying millions."

Nowhere in any of that was mention made of the western Indian tribes. And while Carson and his friends were invading remote Indian lands in the Rocky Mountain west, the Indians of Illinois and Wisconsin were being driven west across the Mississippi and the Carolina and Florida tribes were being relocated in Oklahoma.

In his younger years, Carson seems to have been a believer in Manifest Destiny. At one point he said that he and his fellow mountain men attacked Indians "...to discover who had the best right to the country." And during the 1840s he served as scout into the remote corners of the American West with noted explorer John C. Frémont.

But during the 1850s, he served as Indian Agent for the Ute tribe, and was well regarded by his charges. An incident during this period bears repeating. A band of Ute warriors appeared at the Carson home one day when Kit was away. With them was a three-year-old Navajo boy. Josefa told the Indians that Kit was not at home, and she wondered why they had the child with them. The leader said the boy had been taken in an earlier raid, but that he had become a bother to them, and they intended to kill him once they left the town. Josefa understood the futility of pleading for the child's life, but she well knew the barter system. She offered to buy the young Navajo. The price agreed upon was one horse, which Mrs. Carson paid. The boy, Juan, adopted the name Carson and was raised to adulthood in the Carson household.

By 1863, Carson was a Colonel in the army and in command of the volunteer infantry regiment he had led during the Battle of Valverde. General James Carleton saw Carson as the man to lead an attack against the Navajo of eastern Arizona and western New Mexico who had committed serious depredations. In his middle 50s and not in the least convinced that extermination was the solution to the Indian "problem," Carson tried to beg off. General Carleton insisted and Carson obeyed orders.

Carson's regiment was about 700 men strong, more than 300 of which were Rio Grande Pueblo Indians, along with Utes, Hopis and Zunis—all traditional enemies of the Navajo. The Navajo population was estimated at 8,000 and they were well armed and often well fortified. Carson thought conventional tactics would not succeed but he believed he could out-gun them with cannon and starve them into submission by relentless pursuit. Through the summer and fall of 1863 Carson's troops ranged up and down the Navajo country. They fought no major battles, but in their wake they left destruction. Grain storage facilities were put to the torch. Fields were uprooted. Fruit trees were cut down. Livestock was slaughtered. Nothing of any use was left behind.

Here is what Carson wrote to his wife about the Navajo campaign: "I can take no pride in this fearful destruction. My sleep is haunted by dreams of starving Navajo squaws and children. If the elders of the tribe would listen to reason, we could make peace. But they're stubborn men, so I must finish what I have started."

In April 1964, the Navajo surrendered. Only about 50 Navajos had been killed during the course of the entire operation. Direct military action under any other commander would have claimed many times that number of Navajo lives.

There is further evidence, too, that Carson mellowed as he grew older. On November 29, 1864, Colonel John Chivington and a troop of Colorado volunteers, without provocation, attacked a camp of Cheyenne and Arapaho Indians at Sand Creek in eastern Colorado, killing more than 300 men, women and children. Carson's reaction to the slaughter was to call Chivington a "dog" and his troops "cowards."

Carson retired from the army in November of 1867 with the rank of brigadier general. In April 1868, his wife of 25 years, Maria Josefa Jaramillo Carson, died, and the following month, Carson himself died, too, in his own bed, the victim of a ruptured aneurysm in his trachea at 59 years of age.

Carson was a man who did what was expected of him. It seems unlikely that he questioned the national policies of the time, but it is equally certain that he became convinced that compromise was preferable to annihilation; that there was room for everyone in the vastness of the American West. One writer observed thus:

"Carson, a legendary American hero, was authentic and worthy of the adulation in most important respects."

COL. JOHN CHIVINGTON AND THE SAND CREEK MASACRE

Major John Chivington and Captain Edward "Ned" Wynkoop of the Colorado Volunteer Militia became heroes to many New Mexicans because they were key participants in the military effort to halt the invasion of New Mexico by Texas Confederate forces under the command of General Henry H. Sibley in March of 1862.

Chivington led a flanking movement by the Coloradoans during the battle of Glorietta that resulted in the destruction of 80 wagonloads of Confederate ammunition and supplies at Johnson's Ranch. Wynkoop was one of Chivington's company commanders.

Less than three years later, both men would have a role to play in one of the most infamous atrocities in the history of the old west: the Sand Creek Massacre.

John Milton Chivington was born at Lebanon in southwestern Ohio in 1821. By the late 1840s, he was ordained as a Methodist Episcopal preacher and until 1860 he did church work in Illinois, Nebraska and Missouri. Chivington stood six feet six inches tall and weighed 250 pounds. He had a booming voice and commanded the attention of those around him.

He arrived in Denver in 1860 where he served as leader of the Rocky Mountain conference of his church. When the 1st Colorado Volunteer Regiment was created in 1860, he was offered a commission as chaplain. He turned it down in favor of a regular commission: a "fighting" commission rather than a "praying" commission, he said. Because of his military success in New Mexico, he became something of a hero back in Denver. He was promoted to Colonel and placed in command of the Military District of Colorado.

The political bug soon bit him. He became allied with Governor John Evans who favored statehood for Colorado. Chivington aspired to become the new state's first congressman. He offered the services of the Colorado Volunteers, with himself in command, to the Army of the Potomac during the Civil War, but the offer was declined. He also made little secret of the fact that he believed that he should be at least a Brigadier General. As it was, he spent his time chasing small groups miscreant Indians in an effort to punish them for assorted minor depredations.

Edward Wanshear Wynkoop was born in Philadelphia, Pennsylvania in 1836. He too had an unlikely background for a military officer. He migrated west and arrived in Kansas the late 1850s. By 1859 he was serving as sheriff of Arapahoe County, Colorado, but failed to win election as Denver city marshal in 1861. One source described him as "a bad man from Kansas." He is said to have worn buckskin breeches and carried a knife and pistol in his belt. He was reportedly involved in a couple of shooting scrapes. He may have supplemented his income by working in a brothel and a saloon.

When the Colorado volunteer organizations were created in 1860, Wynkoop joined two of them; as a first lieutenant in the Denver Cavalry and a second lieutenant in the Jefferson Rangers. He went from there to second lieutenant in the 1st Colorado Volunteers and was soon promoted to captain in command of Company A, the position he held at the battle of Glorieta Pass in New Mexico.

Ned Wynkoop was promoted too, to major. In 1863 he and five companies of volunteers participated in the so-called Ute Campaign. Nothing much happened, really. By May of 1864, Chivington placed Wynkoop in command of Fort Lyon in southeastern Colorado.

In September of the same year, a Cheyenne Indian called Lone Bear by the tribe, and One Eye by white men, arrived at Fort Lyon. One Eye was able to move about freely because he had a pass signed by Col. Chivington.[1] He offered the trade of white hostages held by Indians for Indians held by the whites. Without orders to do so, Wynkoop took 125 men of the 1st Colorado out to secure the release of the captives. Near the Smokey Hill River, about 600 Indians under the leadership of Black Kettle, White Antelope, Bull Bear and others confronted him. The situation got a little tense, but it was finally agreed that the Indians would release four hostages and in return Wynkoop would arrange a peace confab with Colorado Governor Evans.

The problem was that Governor Evans, and his top military man, Col. Chivington, did not want peace with the Indians. Evans told the chiefs that he could not conclude a peace treaty with them, but that they should put themselves under the protection and jurisdiction of the army. Both Evans and Chivington believed that extermination was the solution to the Indian problem, and that there was political hay to be made in the process. On November 4, Wynkoop was relieved of command at Fort Lyon and reassigned to Fort Riley, Kansas.

Overt action against the Indians began late in November 1864. Chivington and about 600 men of the 3rd Colorado arrived at Fort Lyon late on the 28th. He surrounded the fort so that no one could leave and warn the Indians at Sand Creek. Some of the officers at Fort Lyon, those who had supported Wynkoop's peace efforts, objected to what Chivington intended to do. Chivington is said to have shaken his fist and roared, "Damn any man who sympathizes with Indians. I have come to kill all Indians and I believe it is right to use any means under God's heaven!"

That same evening he force-marched his troops to Sand Creek, arriving before dawn. There have been many accounts of the slaughter that followed. About 150 Indians were killed, most of them women and children. One source indicates that only 25 of the fatalities were men. Nine soldiers were killed, and some of them may have fallen victim to friendly fire.

Aside from humanitarian considerations, Chivington could not have made a worse career mistake. He was obliged to resign his commission to avoid court martial, and the remainder of his life was insignificant. Other than that, however, he was not punished for his barbarity. He said many times, "I stand by Sand Creek." He died of cancer in 1894.

Wynkoop was restored as commander of Fort Lyon in January 1865 and led an investigation into Chivington's actions. His findings were not favorable to his former commander. He resigned his commission in 1866 and served as an Indian agent for a time. He held a number of positions in his remaining years, including Adjutant General of the New Mexico Territorial Militia and warden of the territorial penitentiary. He died of Bright's Disease in 1891.

---

[1] One Eye was a paid agent of the white establishment. He received $125 per month, plus rations. Regular army troopers and volunteers were paid $12 to $15 per month at the time.

BLACK JACK CHRISTIAN AND THE HIGH FIVES GANG

By the last decade of the 19th century, the days of the roving outlaw bands were about over in the American West. But a few of them remained active in New Mexico and Arizona. As late as 1899, members of Butch Cassidy's Wild Bunch held up a train near Twin Mountains in Colfax County, New Mexico. Rustlers, robbers and killers Tom "Black Jack" Ketchum and his brother Sam remained active throughout the last years of the decade. Tom was hanged at Clayton, New Mexico in April 1901. Sam died in prison a couple of years earlier.

A somewhat lesser known gang roamed around the southwest about this same time. Its leader was also called "Black Jack." His real name was Will Christian. He was also called "202" because of his portly stature. There is nothing to indicate that the two Black Jacks ever worked together, but they were aware of each other and may have been acquainted. For a period of time officials blamed crimes committed by Black Jack Christian on Black Jack Ketchum, and vice versa. Christian's gang was called the High Fives after a card game popular at the time.

Will Christian and his brother, Bob, were born near Ft. Griffin, Texas; Will, the younger of the two, in 1871. They spent their early years in Oklahoma Territory where they busied themselves with petty theft and armed robbery. On one occasion, when confronted by the law, Bob shot and killed a deputy sheriff. Arrested for murder, the Christians were jailed in Oklahoma City. They managed to escape, killing a city policeman as they did so. They pulled a couple of robberies in Oklahoma and departed for New Mexico.

In New Mexico they ranged across the Territory, from Seven Rivers on the east to Lordsburg on the west, and as far north as Albuquerque and Grants. They occasionally wandered into Arizona. Along the way they picked up a group of thieves and killers who made up the original High Fives: George Musgrave, Cole Young, and Bob Hayes. Outlaws "Three Fingered Jack" Dunlap, Jess Williams and later, Theodore James joined them in several of their crimes.

The High Fives were not a particularly successful bunch. They robbed a lot of stores, post offices, stagecoaches and trains and stole very little. They robbed the store at Separ in southern New Mexico and got $250. They robbed the same store sometime later and only got $100. In August 1896, they attempted to rob the International Bank in Nogales, Arizona but the effort was interrupted when newspaperman Frank King opened fire on the robbers with his pistol. Jess Miller dropped the loot as he fled, and the gang came up empty handed.

A posse caught up with them a few days later and in the gunfight that ensued, a deputy sheriff was killed, while the gang escaped. Even later the same month, another posse caught up with them, and in that gunfight outlaw Bob Hayes was killed while the remainder of the gang got away again.

Arizona was just too hot for the High Fives, so they returned to New Mexico.

In October 1896 they attempted to rob an Atlantic & Pacific train about 35 miles southwest of Albuquerque near the Rio Puerco crossing. Little did they know that a deputy U. S. Marshal by the name of H. W. Loomis was aboard the train that night. Cole Young fired a couple of shots in taking control of the train, and that attracted Loomis who was armed with a large bore shotgun. He observed a group of men near the engine, with one man standing apart from the rest. The deputy picked him as target, and fired. The man went down, but regained his feet and staggered off into the dark and disappeared. The other gang members returned fire but Loomis was not hit. The Christian brothers and friends acted as if they would go ahead with the robbery, but they couldn't get the express car uncoupled and after a while they gave up. They did manage to rob the train's fireman of his personal belongings, but that was all they got. They left wounded and dying Cole Young behind when they rode away. Loomis later found the outlaw's body not far from the railroad tracks. He'd been hit with five buckshot pellets: four in the chest and one in the face. The gun in his hand contained three spent cartridges. Young was 25 years old when he died.

The gang pulled off a few more small-time robberies in Lincoln County—they actually robbed the same stagecoach three or four times—before they fled back to Arizona. The one thing that all this activity did accomplish was to attract the attention of every law enforcement officer in the two territories and a number of bounty hunters as well. The reward offered was $6,000 for Will "Black Jack " Christian, dead or alive, an enormous sum at the time.

Even the famed scout, Pinkerton detective and assassin Tom Horn offered his services to Arizona's U. S. Marshal William Meade in bringing down the High Fives, "if there is anything in it for me." There is no indication that Marshal Meade took him up on the offer.

In April 1897, a group of bounty hunters learned that the High Fives, or what remained of the gang, were holed-up in a cave not far from Clifton in southeastern Arizona. Four of them surrounded the place, and waited. Three men emerged from the cave just after dawn, presumably the Christian brothers and George Musgrave. The posse opened fire and the outlaws fled. The bounty hunters returned to town with nothing to show for their effort. It was discovered later that Black Jack had been wounded in the fight, and later died. His body was hauled into town on top of a load of lumber.

The oddity of Will Christian's death was that no one around Clifton had ever seen him alive, so he could not be positively identified after he was killed. Since he was never seen alive again, it is a safe bet that they got the right guy.

Only two of the original High Fives gang members remained alive: Bob Christian and George Musgrave. The two of them, along with Theodore James, set out once again to rob an Atlantic & Pacific train, and in the same general area where they'd made an unsuccessful attempt a year earlier that cost the life of Cole Young. They did better the second time.

On the evening of November 6, 1897 they boarded the train's engine at a place called Saint's Siding, east of Grants, New Mexico and captured the fireman, Henry Able. The engineer hid under a loading dock and the express messenger locked the express car and escaped into the darkness. At gunpoint, the outlaws ordered Able to uncouple the express car from the passenger cars and pull it on down the line for a half-mile or so. Then they used dynamite to blast open the express car and to blow the door off the safe they found inside. Able said they were quite leisurely about what they were doing and even took the time to eat the express messenger's lunch, washing it down with whiskey. They gave Able $15 in cash as a gift and they left behind a bottle of whiskey for the engineer.

Railroad officials originally believed that after they robbed the train, the outlaws stoked up the engine, put it into reverse, and drove it backward into a collision with the passenger cars. They later learned that Able actually caused the accident. He said in backing up the engine, he misjudged the distance and "bumped the empty cars." His "bump" caused the stove in one of the cars to overturn and set the unit on fire, destroying it.

No one knows for sure how much money was taken that night. It was common practice for railroad officials to report that nothing was taken after a train robbery, and that's what they reported in this case. They did that for two reasons. The first was to reassure shippers that their consignments were safe. The second was to make robbers believe that there was no profit in robbing trains. Henry Able, however, publicly declared that the loot, removed in a sugar sack, was so heavy that one man could hardly carry it. Other, later, sources declared that the amount taken was at least $100,000.

There is one other curiosity about this robbery. As the bandits were riding away, one of them called out to Henry Able, "Tell him (the engineer) that Black Jack has come back to life!"

In that connection, it should also be noted that as he was about to be hanged in April 1901, Tom "Black Jack" Ketchum said this: "That man they killed in Arizona [in 1897] was not Black Jack Christian. He is not dead to my certain knowledge. Oh, yes; I have an idea where he is, but I won't tell." He didn't, either.

Whether Black Jack Christian was alive or not, the holdup at Saint's Siding was the last robbery committed by the High Fives. Bob Christian, George Musgrave and Theodore James are known to have fled to Mexico. They were all arrested after shooting up the town of Fronteras, Sonora on November 25, 1897. They were released from jail on December 9. Christian and James are believed to have fled further south into Mexico where they disappeared from history. There are those who believe that Tom Horn assassinated Christian and James since neither was ever seen after December 9, 1897.

George Musgrave apparently headed north. He was recognized in Colorado in 1909, and subsequently arrested at North Platte, Nebraska, on Christmas Day of that year. He was never charged with any of the crimes he'd committed as a member of the High Fives, but only for a murder he'd allegedly committed on a ranch near Roswell, New Mexico in 1896. He was acquitted of that charge in 1910 and left the United States for South America. He died there in 1947.

NEWSPAPERMAN A. M. CONKLIN MURDERED AT SOCORRO: ONE KILLER SHOT—ONE LYNCHED

Railroad construction moved rapidly south from Albuquerque and reached Socorro in July of 1880. An economic boom resulted and the town became one of New Mexico's largest territorial communities with an increase in population from about 600 to 4,000 in less than two years. Silver mining was a primary attraction at the time, but farming and ranching were also significant economic factors.

Times were good but life in Socorro was wild and wooly. Very shortly after the railroad arrived, the town was home to 44 saloons. That amounted to one drinking establishment for each 100 of resident cowboys and miners. Law enforcement was not up to handling the violence that tends to accompany rapid growth and the free-flow of whiskey. Local folks took a hand in solving the problem.

In the summer of 1880, as the railroad was being completed, A. M. Conklin decided to move his Albuquerque newspaper, the *Advance*, to Socorro. He made the move south by floating his press and staff on a raft down the Rio Grande. In Socorro, he established a new paper called the Socorro *Sun*.

On Christmas Eve of the same year, Conklin, after attending church services, became involved in an altercation with several thugs who had created a disturbance. When it was over, the newspaperman was dead, shot through the heart as his wife watched. Two of the shooters were promptly captured and lodged in jail. One of them attempted to "escape" and was shot dead in the effort. The other one was shortly taken out of the jail by vigilantes and hanged near the courthouse.

An Albuquerque newspaper said this about the untimely demise of Conklin and his killers: "Moral: 'Tis a bad thing to assassinate editors in New Mexico."

Vigilance committees, or vigilantes, were common in New Mexico at the time. Beside Socorro they were active in Albuquerque, Bernalillo and Las Vegas.[1] Most, however, were not as well organized as the Socorro group. They called themselves *Los Colgandores*, which literally translated means "The hangers." They dealt out a lot of extra-legal justice and became greatly feared by the lawless element.

By the early 1890s, silver prices began to drop and the panic of 1893 drove them down even further. Mining became unprofitable and people began moving away from Socorro. The boom was over. The New Mexico School of Mines—which became the New Mexico Institute of Mining and Technology—was established in 1889, and it, along with tourism and agriculture, remain today as the community's economic base.

The recorded history of Socorro actually predates the 1880-1893 boom by nearly 300 years. It is likely that a member of Coronado's expedition (1540-41) got a glimpse of an Indian village on the site of present-day Socorro, but it was not until 1598 that the Spanish spent any time there. In that year, members of Juan de Oñate's expedition arrived at the Piro Indian village. They were nearly exhausted from the trek across what has come to be known as the "*Jornada de Muerto,*" or journey of death.

The Indians took in the Spanish soldiers and provided them with food and shelter. It was from these charitable acts that the town got its name. The Spanish word *socorro* means help or aid, the English cognate being "succor." When a mission church was built there sometime before 1627, it was called *Nuestra Señora del Socorro*, or Our Lady of Help, because of Oñate's experience with the Indians.

In 1680 when Popé led the Pueblo Revolt against the Spanish and effectively drove them out of New Mexico, Socorro was not spared. The mission was abandoned and ultimately destroyed. Interestingly enough, the Indian people living near the mission followed the Spanish south to El Paso del Norte, and they never returned. Instead they established a community there called *Socorro del Sur* (Soccoro of the South). When DeVargas marched north in 1692 to re-conquer New Mexico, he reported stopping at Nuestra Señora de Socorro. He noted that it was in ruins. It would stay that way for more than 100 years.

The ruins were situated on the main route—*El Camino Real* or Royal Road— between Santa Fe and Chihuahua and by 1815 trade along the way was often interrupted by Apache Indian attacks. In that year the Spanish Governor, Don Alberto Maynez, ordered the site resettled. He established the Socorro Land Grant made up of four square leagues of land.[2] It was a good spot for a village. There was plenty of water and the land was rich and productive. By 1850, the population of the town was about 600.

In spite of the town's success, its reoccupation did little to alleviate the problem of Indian attacks. In 1852, Colonel Edwin V. Sumner dispatched troops to Socorro to protect the town from attack. He also led a column of troops east from Albuquerque to engage the Navajo. His efforts were no more successful than had been those of the Spanish and Mexicans in the preceding 100 years. The U. S. troops of the time were insufficient in numbers, poorly equipped and ill experienced to locate and do damage to either the Navajo or Apache. Indian depredations decreased after Kit Carson defeated the Navajo in the 1860s and the last of the Apaches finally surrendered in the 1880s.

The town changed little until the railroad arrived and since the boom ended in the late 19th century, Socorro has grown steadily to about 9,000 residents. It is a quiet and friendly community easily reached by traveling about 70 miles south from Albuquerque.

---

[1] The Marino Leyba outlaw gang was wiped out—except for Leyba—by Albuquerque and Bernalillo vigilantes in 1881.

[2] One source says the grant boundaries were measured from the altar of the old church; another says from the corner of the building. Given that the league was an inexact measurement at best, it could not have made much difference at the time.

HORSE THIEF NICHOLAS ARAGON KILLS LINCOLN COUNTY DEPUTIES J. CORN & J. HURLEY

In early 1884 Nicholas Aragon and another man, both from San Miguel County, New Mexico, stole several horses along the Rio Hondo in Lincoln County and removed them to a canyon near Anton Chico on the Rio Pecos, south of Las Vegas. Lincoln County authorities learned where the horses were hidden and Deputy Sheriff Jim Brent and a posse soon recovered the animals, captured Aragon and his friend, and jailed them in Lincoln. Aragon escaped from jail on May 28 by climbing through a hole in the roof. In October of the same year, Sheriff John Poe[1] learned that Aragon had been seen in his old haunts around Gallinas Springs and Anton Chico in San Miguel County. Sheriff Poe told Deputy Sheriff Jasper Corn of Roswell[2] to take as many men as he needed to arrest the horse thief.

Corn took only one man: his brother-in-law, Bill Holloman[3]. He soon learned that Aragon regularly visited a particular woman near Anton Chico and they approached her house. The outlaw saw Deputy Corn coming and dashed out the back door, running for his horse that stood saddled and waiting some distance away, beyond a stone fence. Corn, from horseback, opened fire with his pistol as his mount galloped toward Aragon. Aragon, using the fence for cover, returned fire with a Winchester rifle. His first shot struck Corn's horse in the neck, knocking the animal down, and the deputy with it. Even though Corn was pinned to the ground, his leg caught under the horse and badly broken, he continued the fight until his gun was empty. Aragon took his time, then, aimed carefully, and shot Corn in the stomach. Aragon mounted his horse and escaped before Holloman could stop him. Corn suffered greatly and died thirty-six hours later without ever receiving medical treatment.

Aragon hid out for a few months and then, once again, returned to Anton Chico. In late January 1885, Sheriff Poe led a posse made up of Jim Brent, Johnny Hurley, Barney Mason, Billy Bufer and Jim Abercrombie in search of the killer. A little investigation led the posse to a house where Aragon was believed to be hiding. Two women living there said they were alone in the house; that Aragon was not there. Sheriff Poe assigned Deputy Hurley—who spoke fluent Spanish—to take the women into the kitchen and interrogate them carefully while the remainder of the posse surrounded the house. After a while, one of the women admitted that Aragon was in the house. She said the fugitive was heavily armed and ready to fight. In his haste to tell the sheriff that Aragon was there, Hurley allowed himself to be silhouetted in the kitchen doorway.

"We've got him! He's in there!" Hurley called out to Sheriff Poe.

"Johnny, get out from in front of the door or he'll kill you," Poe yelled just as Aragon fired.

"Are you hit, Johnny?" Poe asked.

"Yes," the deputy replied. "Gut shot."

Hurley staggered back into the kitchen and lay down before the fire. The women made him as comfortable as possible. He died 36 hours later just as Corn survived for 36 hours after Aragon shot him in the stomach. He, too, received no medical attention.

In the meantime, gunfire became general between Aragon inside the house, and the posse outside. Though badly wounded in three places—in the head and leg—the outlaw managed to hold off his pursuers for more than sixty hours. Aragon didn't surrender until the sheriff from Las Vegas, Hilario Romero, arrived and promised the outlaw he would not be harmed.

Sheriff Poe and Deputy Brent took Aragon to Santa Fe and lodged him in jail there.[4] Aragon was tried during the summer of 1885 and acquitted on charges of murdering Jasper Corn. Aragon's argument was that he didn't know Corn was a deputy, and that Corn fired first. In the fall of 1885, a Colfax County jury found Aragon guilty of second-degree murder for killing Johnny Hurley and gave him a life sentence.[5] He actually served about ten years before he was released and returned to Anton Chico where he died of natural causes many years later.

Jasper Corn was the brother of Martin Corn who migrated from Kerr County Texas and settled in the Pecos Valley in the late 1870s. Martin Corn was the father of 20 children and the Corn family remains prominent in Chaves County yet today. One chronicler of the times described Jasper Corn "...as brave as the bravest."

Deputy John Hurley was about 37 years old at the time of his death. At various times he'd been a Lincoln County cowboy, small farmer, and saloonkeeper near Fort Stanton. He served as deputy under several Lincoln County Sheriffs, including Pat Garrett. Hurley participated in several gun battles during the Lincoln County War, which makes it surprising that he needlessly made himself a target for Nicolas Aragon's rifle.

---

[1] John W. Poe succeeded famed lawman Pat Garrett as sheriff of Lincoln County. Jim Brent succeeded him.

[2] Roswell was in Lincoln County at the time. Chaves County was not created until 1889.

[3] The name may have been spelled Holliman.

[4] One source says Aragon was held in the Territorial Penitentiary, but that is not likely since New Mexico's first prison didn't open until August 1885.

[5] A later report held that Aragon was acquitted of killing Hurley and convicted of killing Corn.

[6] One historian claims that Aragon killed both Corn and Hurley as he escaped from jail in Lincoln. There seems to be little support for that version of the story.

DON FRANCISCO VÁZQUEZ DE CORONADO: ADVENTURE IN *LA TIERRA INCOGNITA*

Don Francisco Vásquez de Coronado was the first European to do any kind of extensive exploration in what is now New Mexico and the American southwest. How did he come to do that, and what became of him?

Coronado was born at Salamanca, Spain in 1510. He arrived in the New World in 1535 with the Viceroy of Mexico, Antonio de Mendoza. In 1538 Mendoza named him Governor of Nueva Galicia in western Mexico. Coronado married the beautiful Dona Beatriz, the daughter of Alonso de Estrada, said to have been the illegitimate son of King Ferdinand. As Coronado was well off financially, he and Beatriz lived a life of privilege and splendor.

Viceroy Mendoza listened as Estevan the Moor first, and Padre Marcos de Niza later, told tales of vast riches in *la tierra incognita* (the unknown land) to the north; the so-called Seven Cities of Cibola. The Viceroy financed an expedition, using both his own and the king's money, and he named Coronado commander. Mendoza had visions of besting Hernán Cortés, the conqueror of Mexico, and Francisco Pizarro, the conqueror of Peru, in the acquisition of riches in the New World.

Coronado set about organizing his excursion in Compostela, Nueva Galicia. It included 225 soldiers on horseback and 60 more on foot and between 800 and 1,000 Mexican Indians. The Indians drove along about 1,500 head of cattle, sheep, goats and pigs. There were hundreds of pack animals loaded with personal goods.

Five Franciscan Friars accompanied the expedition, one of whom was Padre Niza. Niza's job was to lead Coronado to Hawikuh, the village near Zuñi said to have been built of gold, and the place where Indians had killed Estevan the Moor in 1539.

The departure from Compostela was a splendid event. It was organized as a parade for Viceroy Mendoza and the few residents who remained in the town (there were more people in the parade than there were spectators). Coronado was described as "...wearing a golden helmet and breastplate, which sparkled in the sunlight so that they almost blinded those who looked on. He rode a white charger which danced nervously and arched his neck proudly. The horse was covered with a rich blanket, red and yellow, with a fringe of gold, and Coronado rode in a great saddle with heavy silver trimmings."

The young Spanish noblemen who were a part of the army were no less splendid. The parade took place on February 22, 1540. Departure was the following day.

The way north was arduous. Coronado and his troops quickly learned that they were burdened with too much finery and soon the trail was littered with rich clothing and other excess baggage.

They first marched northwest to the town of Culican, the last Spanish outpost in northern Mexico. From there they headed straight north into what is now Arizona. The trek across the desert claimed even more finery and a number of animals were lost because of a lack of forage and water.

For five months they marched north. Eventually Coronado became weary of the slow pace set by driving large herds of animals and he and a troop of soldiers and Padre Niza went on ahead. About the first of August 1540, they reached Hawikuh. What they found was "a small rocky pueblo, all crumpled up," and no gold. About 200 warriors lived there. Coronado promptly sent Padre Niza back to Mexico City, for his own safety.

The Zuñi Indians of Hawikuh resisted the Spanish invasion, and in the skirmish that followed, a warrior rolled a large rock off the roof of one of the houses and it struck Coronado on the head. It made a dent in his golden helmet and knocked him off his horse. A couple of his senior officers rescued him from further harm. This would not be the only knock in the head Coronado would suffer before his return to Mexico.

The Zuñi Indians were quickly subdued and Coronado remained at Hawikuh to allow his main force to catch up. While he waited, he sent Don Pedro de Tovar on an expedition to the northwest. Don Pedro made the first contact with the Hopi Indians of northeastern Arizona. Garcia Lopez de Cardenas was sent west and he is believed to have been the first European to see the Grand Canyon. And Captain Hernando de Alvarado was sent east. He encountered the Acoma Indians and marched on to the Rio Grande at a point near the present day Isleta Pueblo.

Alvarado sent a message back to Coronado suggesting that the main party move east as soon as possible to avoid the winter storms he was sure would come to the high Zuñi country. He then marched north to the Pueblo of Pecos where he met a Plains Indian he named El Turco, because he looked like a Turk. Alvarado rested for a few days before returning south to Tiguex, near the present day town of Bernalillo. He took El Turco with him. Coronado's army arrived there in December 1540.

The stay at Tiguex was not pleasant. When Coronado's advance party arrived, the Indians seemed to think the Spaniard's visit would be a short one. But as Alvarado arrived, and then the main party, the Indians became concerned that the newcomers would never leave. Coronado's army literally took over the entire Indian village of Alcanfor and forced its residents to move into homes in other nearby communities. But more than that, the Spanish soldiers took from the Indians whatever they pleased, including some of their women. The Indians determined to fight back and launched what was called the Tiguex War.

By later standards, it wasn't much of a war. The Indians were not equal to the Spanish matchlock guns (called harquebuses), armor and horses. During the various skirmishes, battles and sieges, at least 200 Indians were killed. In March 1541, they surrendered.

Coronado by then had been in the field for more than a year. He had found no gold, or anything else he considered of value. Still he heard rumors of great riches to be had at a place called Quivira, further yet to the east. These tales were provided by

El Turco who said he was "...a native of country toward Florida." El Turco was probably a Pawnee Indian. He described Quivira as abundant with gold, governed by nobles and ruled by a king. The down side was that another Pawnee slave, named Ysopete, claimed that El Turco was a liar and only intended to mislead the Spaniards.

On April 23, 1541, Coronado set out again, in search of Quivira, with El Turco as his guide. Would he prove more reliable than Padre Niza?

He traveled east to a point somewhere near the present-day city of Amarillo, Texas, probably Palo Duro Canyon. There he turned to the north and trekked into what is now Kansas. He did not find Quivira. What he did find were a few Plains Indian encampments and none of them contained metallic riches of any kind. Coronado figured that El Turco had lured him and his troops to the plains to slaughter and rob them. In retaliation, the Spaniards killed the Indian. Some sources say they hanged him, others that he was garroted.

Autumn was approaching so Coronado returned to Tiguex. He took a more direct route on the return march, one that would approximate the southern route of the Santa Fe Trail nearly 300 year later. He arrived at Tiguex in early October. In spite of it all, Coronado remained optimistic about his prospects and planned yet another foray into Kansas the following year. New troops had arrived from Mexico to assist in the effort. It was not to be.

In the early spring of 1542, Coronado was out riding with Captain Rodrigo Maldonado and challenged him to a horse race. Maldonado agreed and the race began. Unfortunately, the cinch on Coronado's saddle broke and he fell to the ground where he was promptly kicked in the head by one of the horses. The injury was serious and for a time it was felt that the leader would die. He survived, but his incapacitation marked the end of the expedition. No one stepped in to take over leadership, and the troops were frustrated that they had found no gold, and they had been away from home for more than two years. A rebellion seemed to be in the offing. At that point, a group of officers petitioned Coronado for his agreement that they return to Mexico. There seemed to be no alternative, and Coronado gave the order. The march south began in April.

Three Spaniards remained behind: Franciscan missionaries Fray Juan de Padilla, Fray Luis de Escalona and Fray Juan de la Cruz. They were never heard from again and it is believed that the Indians killed them.

Coronado had traveled nearly 2,000 miles from his home and had found nothing. He could not know that he crossed some of the richest farm land in the world, nor could he known that he rode past mountains which contained enormous mineral wealth.

Needless to say, Viceroy Mendoza was not pleased that Coronado returned to Mexico empty handed. It is recorded, however, that he did not blame Coronado personally for the failure, and he appreciated the hardships the expedition members had suffered. It was not likely, though, that Mendoza would finance another such adventure.

Only two years after his return to Mexico, Coronado was charged with a variety of offenses having to do with his administration of Neuvo Galicia, including neglect of duty and the use of slave labor. He was tried, convicted, fined five hundred pesos and removed from office, although he later regained his position.

And Coronado faced another problem by 1544; a judge of the Royal Audiencia of Mexico, Lorenzo de Tejada, launched an investigation into his management of the expedition. Specifically he was charged with perpetrating "great cruelties" upon the Indians he'd encountered. He was also accused of waging war against the Zuñi Indians, setting dogs on the Indians at Tiguex, executing El Turco, and a failure to colonize Quivira. He was cleared of these charges and the matter was dropped.

Coronado remained active in public affairs in Mexico, but his health declined and he died at the age of 44 in 1554. He and Doña Beatriz are buried in the Church of Santo Domingo in Mexico City.

But was Coronado's journey a failure? Yes, but only in the context of his times. In the broader context of history, it was a great success because it opened the vast frontier known as *Tierra Incognito*. A little over fifty years later, other Spaniards would move north and colonize the land the Coronado visited.

The one group of people who would not agree with that point of view were the Indians who ultimately lost a way of life forever. But they would have been the victims of history under any circumstances. If it had not been the Spanish in the 16th and 17th centuries, it would have been the French in the 18th or the Americans in the 19th. The American West was far too valuable to be left alone.

Historian Dan L. Thrapp sums up the explorer this way: "Coronado was an able leader, strict though scarcely a martinet. He was bold, brave in action and a man not entirely without mercy toward his enemies, although he could be ruthless in the manner of his day."

———————

DAVY CROCKETT SHOT DEAD AT CIMMARON: SHERIFF CLEARED OF WRONGDOING

It doesn't matter much that some debunkers have attempted to show that David Crockett of Tennessee didn't die bravely at the Alamo in Texas on March 6, 1836, but rather surrendered and was ingloriously executed by Mexican soldiers under General Antonio Lopez de Santa Anna; he remains a national—and Texas—hero nonetheless. The same cannot be said of his namesake.[1]

After Texas independence was gained later in 1836 with Sam Houston's victory over General Santa Anna at San Jacinto (April 21), the new government awarded Crockett's widow, Elizabeth, some property along the Brazos River in what is now Hood County, southwest of Fort Worth. Robert Crockett, the elder Davy's son, and his wife Matilda, moved to Texas from Tennessee in the mid 1850s. With the couple was their son David "Davy", who had been born in February 1853. Robert Crockett operated a toll bridge over the Brazos.

No one is certain when young Davy arrived in Cimarron, Colfax County, New Mexico. Some sources place him in New Mexico as early as 1870 when he is said to have participated—along with famed "shootist" Clay Allison—in the lynching of Charles Kennedy[2] who, according to legend, was decapitated and his head taken to the Lambert Saloon in Cimarron. Other sources discount this tale. "...A mob led by Allison and Crockett could not have been...possible [in 1870]. The Lambert Saloon was not in existence until 1872. Crockett was not yet in New Mexico, but in Texas."[3] Crockett would have only been 17 years old at the time.

Historians generally agree that Davy Crockett operated a small ranch near Cimarron by the mid 1870s. One of his neighbors was Clay Allison; another was Pete Burleson, with whom Crocket had been acquainted in Texas. Crockett's ranch foreman was Gus Heffron.[4] It is also generally agreed that Crockett was a likeable young man, and well received at local social events. Gus Heffron was exactly the opposite, considered by townsmen as a quarrelsome braggart and coward. All the same, Crockett and Heffron struck up a strong friendship.

The first of Crockett's assaults upon society took place on March 24, 1876 in the barroom of the St. James Hotel. The story goes that Crockett, Heffron and a third man, Henry Goodman, had spent the day drinking in Cimarron's saloons and that evening they stopped at the St. James to get one more bottle of booze to take with them, back to the ranch. Crockett had trouble leaving the establishment, as the door wouldn't seem to open. He discovered that the cause was a soldier, a Black soldier, on the other side of the portal, trying to get in. Crockett pulled his gun and shot the man dead, then whirled and shot three other Black soldiers who were sitting at a table and playing cards. Two of them died.[5]

Crockett later surrendered himself to a friendly court where he pleaded his innocence predicated on the notion that it was simply a matter of drunken behavior with no malice involved. The court agreed and fined Crockett $50.00 for "carrying arms."[6]

At some point, Crockett decided that cattle ranching was not for him, so he sold off his livestock and spent his time in hoorawing the town of Cimarron. Along with Heffron, he was often observed riding up and down the town's main street firing his pistol into the air, or taking casual shots at random targets. The county's new sheriff, Isaiah Rinehart, who had taken office on March 8, seemed powerless to stop the depredations.

On one occasion, Crockett was said to have roped a pedestrian, dragged him to the general store and outfitted him with a new suit of clothes, the bill for which he sent to Sheriff Isaiah Rinehart. Another time, the story goes, he forced the sheriff, at the point of a gun, to drink whiskey until the lawman was completely intoxicated. This behavior went on for six months. But Sheriff Rinehart and the people of Cimarron had had enough.

Late in September 1876, Crockett and Heffron were again in Cimarron on a drunken spree and making nuisances of themselves. On Saturday the 30th, Sheriff Rinehart approached a rancher named Joseph Holbrook and postmaster John McCullough and asked them to arm themselves and assist him in arresting Crockett and Heffron. They agreed. Late that afternoon the lawmen approached the drunken revelers, who were mounted and on the road out of town. Holbrook ordered them to stop. A drunken Crockett apparently did not take the officers seriously and told them to go ahead and shoot. They did! When the shots were fired, Crockett's horse bolted. When it was found some time later, Crockett was still aboard, shot dead, his hand gripping the saddle horn so strongly that his fingers had to be pried loose.

Heffron, wounded in the head, escaped only to be captured later. He then broke out of jail and disappeared from history. Sheriff Rinehart and his deputies were tried and acquitted of any crime associated with the killing of Crockett.

Pete Burleson, Crockett's friend from Texas, took charge of the outlaw's body and had it laid out in a Cimarron rooming house. Burleson is said to have been outraged when Rinehart, Holbrook and McCullough entered the room without removing their hats. One source says he had to be physically restrained. He must have stayed angry. Just over a month later Burleson defeated Rinehart and was elected sheriff of Colfax County.

---

[1] One historian reports that the younger Davy Crockett was the nephew of the one who died at the Alamo. Other sources tend to agree that he was the grandson of the hero.

[2] Kenney was a multi-murderer who made a practice of killing travelers and burying their bodies near his home.

[3] *Clay Allison, Portrait of a Shootist*, by Chuck Parsons, Pioneer Book Publishers, Seagraves, Texas, 1983.

[4] The name has been variously spelled as Hefferson, Heffner, and Heifner.

[5] One source lists the three soldiers killed as Privates George Small, John Hanson and Anthony Harvey, members of Troop "L", 9th Cavalry, better known as the Buffalo Soldiers.

[6] This crime is often attributed to Clay Allison, but he was not present when the soldiers were killed.

SHERIFF, GOVERNOR & CONGRESSMAN: GEORGE CURRY WAS A WITNESS TO NEW MEXICO HISTORY

George Curry, Governor, Congressman, et al.
(Photo from a painting by Sam Smith, Courtesy Albuquerque Musuem Photoarchives PA 1978.50.330)

Curry County in eastern New Mexico (county seat is Clovis) is named for George Curry who served as Territorial Governor (1907-11) and as one of the state's first two congressmen.[1] That rather pedestrian fact tells little of the story. Curry participated in, and was a witness to, some of the most stirring events in New Mexico during the late 19th and early 20th centuries. Close examination of almost any significant event between 1878 and 1913 will reveal the presence of Curry, more often than not on the periphery of the action.

He was born in Louisiana during the first year of the Civil War (1861) and lived long enough to see the conclusion of World War II (1947).

Curry's adventures began early. In 1870, when he was but nine years old, he witnessed the ambush assassination of his father by carpetbaggers near Greenwood Plantation in West Feliciana Parish, Louisiana. His mother was obliged, a few years later, to move on to Dodge City, Kansas. They arrived there in 1873, only a year after the town (and Ford County) had been organized. Young George went to work for Rath & Company, a mercantile business. In June 1874 he was dispatched to a place called Adobe Walls in the Texas panhandle with a load of merchandise. He promptly returned to Dodge City with the empty wagons and completely missed the Second Battle of the Adobe Walls that began on June 26. He was acquainted with some of the participants, however, including Bat Masterson and Jim Carlisle.

And becoming acquainted with the famous, and near famous, was a characteristic of Curry's entire life. He arrived in Lincoln, New Mexico in October 1878, only three months after the Five-Day battle of the Lincoln County War. He was thus in the right place at the right time to become acquainted with the likes of Billy the Kid, Pat Garrett, Col. Nathan Dudley, Judge Warren Bristol, and others.[2]

Once again, young George was close to the action, but saw none of it. In December 1880, he joined a posse that went in search of Billy the Kid and some of his cohorts, but by the time his group arrived at Stinking Springs, east of Fort Sumner, Pat Garrett and his posse had already arrested the Kid.

In 1882, Curry became interested in politics. He also moved on to Las Vegas, New Mexico. He had no luck at all at the gaming tables and soon found himself broke. He went to work as a hotel manager in Trinidad, Colorado for a few months before he found work in Raton, New Mexico, again with a merchant. His interest in politics grew into participation. He was a delegate to the 1884 territorial Democratic convention in Albuquerque.

By 1885 he was in the Colfax County jail charged with manslaughter and 15 other charges. This was the result of Curry involving himself in the disorder of the "Maxwell Land-grant Troubles." George's brother, John, had taken sides with a vigilante group headed by gunman Dick Rogers, and they were stirring up trouble in the town of Springer. George Curry tried to broker a peace between factions, at least a temporary one. He was not successful and when the shooting was over, both Dick Rogers and John Curry were dead and George was in jail, where he stayed for six weeks. The following May he pleaded guilty to unlawfully carrying firearms and was fined five dollars. The other 15 charges were dropped. George was erroneously reported killed in the Springer shootout.

George returned to Lincoln County after his unhappy experience in Colfax County. In 1888 he ran for county clerk on the Democratic ticket, and won.

In 1892 he was elected sheriff. He later said this about his work: "I told them (cattlemen and cowboys) that the 'statute of limitations' on cattle rustling and brand changing had run out the day I took office.... A large majority agreed to go along with me. A few of them, including Slick Miller, Henry Brown and George Craig, did not take my warning seriously and continued cattle stealing. They were arrested and convicted and sent to prison. I was frankly proud to hold it (the office of sheriff), for I followed a long list of Lincoln County sheriffs who had distinguished themselves for law enforcement under far more difficult conditions... I made many friends, also a few enemies, as must any sheriff who enforces the law."[3]

And George's political star continued to rise. In March of 1893 he was a member of a delegation that traveled to Washington, D. C. to attend the inauguration of president Grover Cleveland. While there, in conversation with the president, he learned, to his surprise, that he was number two on the list to become U. S. Marshal for New Mexico. As it was, the appointment went to a Grant County rancher named Edward L. Hall, whose brother served as Democratic congressman from Missouri.[4]

By the following year, Curry claimed "We had succeeded in cleaning out the cattle rustlers, brand-blotters and outlaws in Lincoln County. I announced my intention of retiring from the sheriff's office at the end of my term." He did resign the office in spite of an offer from cattlemen to pay him a $2,000 per year bonus to stay in office. He next ran for the territorial senate.[5]

Curry was elected and traveled to Santa Fe for the legislative session in late December 1894. What he found there was turmoil. As a result of it, and by a cabal of Democrats with the support of Republican Colonel J. Francisco Chavez, he was elected president of the senate his first day in office. It should be noted that at the time, the senate only had 12 members, seven of whom were Democrats. He did well enough during the session that Senate employees gave him a gold-headed cane and after adjournment the New Mexico Cattle Growers Association gave him a gold watch. Colonel Albert Jennings Fountain, a staunch Republican, made the presentation.

Voters returned Curry to office in 1896 but the balance of power had shifted slightly and the new senate was made up of six each Republicans and Democrats. Curry lost his seat as president and had to settle for the chairmanship of the Appropriations Committee. After adjournment, he went to work for Charles B. Eddy as a right-of-way-agent for the El Paso and Northeastern Railroad in southern New Mexico.

It was also in January of 1896 that Albert Jennings Fountain and his young son, Henry, disappeared from the face of the earth in the White Sands of southern New Mexico. Curry would naturally become a part of that drama, too. Much as been written about the case, but basically the circumstantial evidence pointed to cattleman Oliver Lee, and two of his friends, Jim Gilliland and Billy McNew. Former Lincoln County Sheriff Pat Garrett was brought in as Doña Ana County Sheriff for the primary purpose of solving the case. He eventually secured warrants for the suspects.

In the spring of 1898, according to Curry, there was a seventy-four hour poker game in Tobe Tipton's saloon in Tularosa. Players were Curry, Tipton, Oliver Lee, Albert Bacon Fall, Jeff Sanders and Pat Garrett. At the conclusion of the game, according to Curry, Garrett and Lee had a conversation during which Lee said, "Pat, you'll have no trouble serving a warrant on me. I have no reason or desire to resist the law." That was a lie on Lee's part. When the time came, Lee resisted service of the warrant with all his might.

Albert Bacon Fall, Lee's attorney, devised a ploy that would take jurisdiction in the Fountain disappearance/murder case away from Garrett. He pulled some strings in Santa Fe and the result was the creation of a new county, named for Governor Miguel Otero. The sheriff of the new county, appointed in March 28, 1899, was none other than George Curry. Lee, who had come to believe that Garrett would kill, rather than arrest him, now surrendered himself to Judge Frank Parker, who turned him over to Curry who moved Lee and Gilliland to Hillsboro, then the seat of Sierra County, where they were jailed pending trial. Garrett was effectively removed from the loop. (Lee and Gilliland were acquitted at trial in May 1899.)

Curry didn't last long as sheriff. He resigned in August of the same year to accept a captaincy in the Rough Riders, destined for fame in the Spanish American War. Curry was not a part of the action, though, and his unit was mustarded out after only four months of service, none of it in Cuba.

The most significant thing to happen to Curry during this time was his switch from Democrat to Republican. He said this: "I was but one of many Rough Riders who followed Colonel Roosevelt into the Republican party [sic]." The change would serve him well in the years to come.[6]

From 1899 to 1907, Curry spent most of his time in the Philippines where he served variously as chief of police and governor. He did see some combat while there, and in 1904, for the second time, his death was erroneously reported.

President Theodore Roosevelt appointed Curry territorial governor of New Mexico in April 1907 (he was inaugurated on August 7). He served until 1910, during some of the critical years leading up to statehood in 1912. He was elected to the U. S. Congress in 1911 and served from 1912-13, after which, he said, "I decided to get out of politics and into private business." He moved to Texas to do so.

There was one more anomaly in Curry's life. On April 12, 1932, and for the third time, he was wrongly reported to be dead. The Albuquerque *Journal* carried the headline that he had died suddenly while visiting in Hillsboro. Curry never found out how this mistake was made.

In fact, he died on Thanksgiving Day (November 24) 1947 in Veterans Hospital, in Albuquerque at age 86. He was state historian at the time. That was entirely appropriate. He was witness to a lot of it.

------

[1] The Enabling Act of 1910, the precursor to statehood, provided for two congressmen. Curry and Harvey B. Fergusson were elected in November 1911 and both served from January 1912 to March 1913, when only one of the two could continue. Fergusson then served until 1915.

[2] One source says that Curry was acquainted with Sheriff William Brady, but that could not be so. Brady was killed from ambush in April 1878, more than six months before Curry got to town.

[3] It is generally agreed among historians that Eli "Slick" Miller and his gang were put out of business by a cattle inspector named Les Dow, who later became Eddy County Sheriff, and prosecutor Albert Jennings Fountain. It is not at all clear what role sheriff George Curry had in the matter. Henry (Hendry) Brown was one of Billy the Kid's bunch. He was later hanged after a Kansas bank robbery. George Craig's name does not appear elsewhere in the annals of the day.

[4] The only other contender for the U. S. Marshal's job was Felix Martinez of Las Vegas. Because Martinez was a member of the Populist wing of the Democratic Party, President Cleveland considered him too "radical" for the job. There was also some opposition to the appointment of an Hispanic even though the previous marshal was Trinidad Romero.

[5] The upper house of the legislature was actually called the Territorial Council until statehood in 1912.

[6] Changes in party affiliation during the territorial period were common. The party in power in Washington had enormous influence over New Mexico affairs; so many folks changed party depending on which way the political wind blew. Most famous of the switchers was A. B. Fall. He was a rabid Democrat who became an equally rabid Republican. He was sentenced to prison for accepting a bribe during the Harding administration in the early 1920s.

ALBUQUERQUE NORTH OF SANTA FE: J. DISTURNELL'S MAP OF 1847

New Mexico lies between 103° and 109° west longitude and 32° and 37° north latitude. It measures 390 miles from north to south and 350 miles from east to west. Total land area is 121,666, or 121,594, square miles, depending on the source,[1] which makes New Mexico fifth in area among the fifty states (Alaska, Texas, California and Montana are larger). How these borders were established is a convoluted story.

In the 1600s, *Nuevo Mejico* had no specific boundaries. It was then under Spanish rule, and the Spaniards preferred it that way since they could then lay claim to all the lands north of Mexico, or New Spain, then called *la tierra incognita* or "the unknown land." This was a huge area. On the east it ran from the confluence of the Rio Grande and the Rio Pecos, northeast across what is now Texas, Oklahoma, Kansas and Nebraska. The northern boundary extended somewhere across Wyoming. The western limit was in central Utah, Arizona and into Mexico. Present day New Mexico and Colorado were completely within this vast domain.

By 1700, *Nuevo Mejico* began to lose territory. El Paso was established as an important trading point and river crossing. It and the territory extending from what is now Texas and Arizona, and south to Chihuahua became the Province of *Nueva Viscaya*, which would itself be later divided into the Mexican states of Chihuahua and Durango. The northern boundary of *Nueva Vizcaya* was somewhere north of the present day Las Cruces.

Boundary lines, both real and imagined, were established and withdrawn, and redrawn, for the next 100 years. Arguments raged between Spain and France about who owned what, and the young United States entered the fray with the Louisiana Purchase in 1803.[2]

Large numbers of American settlers poured into Mexican-ruled Texas in the 1820s, initially at the invitation of the Mexican government. By 1830 some 20,000 Americans were firmly established, and the Mexican government reconsidered its policy, but too late. In 1836, a substantial conflict arose between American Texans and the Mexican government. The result was the battle at the Alamo, and the subsequent defeat of the Mexican Army under General Antonio Lopez de Santa Anna at the Battle of San Jacinto. Texas became independent and it too began looking westward for expansion. In 1841, Texans claimed everything west to the Rio Grande (which included Santa Fe, then a major trading point on the Santa Fe and Chihuahua trails) and north to present day Wyoming.

Texas invaded New Mexico in the same year with the so-called Texan-Santa Fe Expedition. The effort failed when the Texans got lost on the plains of eastern New Mexico and were captured by Mexican troops under the command of Governor, and General, Manuel Armijo and marched off to Mexico City. After that, more moderate Texans suggested that a better western boundary might be the Rio Pecos, but that never happened, either.

The Mexican War broke out in 1846, and while it was fought almost entirely in California, Texas and Mexico, it had a profound effect on New Mexico's boundaries, and resulted in one of the great snafus in American geography.

The war ended with the signing of the Treaty of Guadalupe Hidalgo, which established the Rio Grande as the border between Texas and Mexico. It further described the border thus: "[North] to the point where it [the Rio Grande] strikes the southern boundary of New Mexico (which runs north of the town called *Paso* [El Paso] to its western termination, until it intersects the first branch of the River Gila." The treaty also provided that boundaries should be based on a map published by J. Disturnell in 1847. Therein rested the problem.

J. Disturnell did not know where El Paso was located. His map placed the city about 100 miles east, and a little north, of where is was, and is, located (Albuquerque was placed northeast of the correct location of Santa Fe, and Taos was in Colorado). This caused a considerable problem. First of all, President James K. Polk was not pleased with the treaty because he thought the United States should get more territory from Mexico as a result of the war and payment of $15,000,000; and second, the treaty gave Mexico the fertile farming area in the Mesilla Valley south of Las Cruces and the rich copper mines at Santa Rita.

A commission was established to resolve the problem. John R. Bartlett represented the United States and General Pedro Conde represented Mexico. They saw the problem with the Disturnell map and moved the line about 100 miles west, but they left the Mesilla Valley in Mexico while giving the copper mines to the United States. Congress failed to ratify the plan in 1852.

In the meantime, an armed conflict was shaping up in the Mesilla Valley. American settlers, mostly farmers, had been there for a number of years and as a result of the Treaty of Guadalupe Hidalgo they were being deprived of their land by the Mexican government. Open warfare was averted with the signing of the Gadsden Purchase in April of 1854. The United States acquired nearly 19,000,000 acres for payment to Mexico of another $10,000,000. U. S. troops entered the disputed area in November 1854 and it became firmly a part of the United States.

Thus was established the southern boundary of modern New Mexico. There were, of course, temporary changes during the Civil War when in 1861 Texas proclaimed the Confederate Territory of Arizona. That only lasted until 1862 when the Texas Confederates were driven out of New Mexico after the Battle of Glorieta.

New Mexico and Arizona were a single territory until the U. S. Congress created Arizona in February 1863. The Robbins Survey finally established the western New Mexico boundary in 1875.

The Clark Survey established the eastern New Mexico boundary in 1859. Because the survey started at both the north and the south, there is a small glitch where New Mexico borders on Oklahoma. The Darling Survey established the northern border in 1868, but the exact line was not firmly drawn until 1960.

Thankfully, future changes are unlikely although there are some who think New Mexico should make a trade with Texas in which everything east of the Pecos would go to the Lone Star state—Clovis, Portales, Lovington, Hobbs et al—and New Mexico would acquire everything west of the Pecos. That would include El Paso.
Not likely.

----

[1] *The Historical Atlas of New Mexico, The World Almanac* and *New Mexico Place Names* all agree on 121,666 square miles. *The Rand McNally Contemporary World Atlas* says the area of New Mexico is 121,594 square miles.
[2] The Louisiana Purchase amounted to 830,000 square miles of land extending from the Gulf of Mexico to Canada.

CHAVES COUNTY DEPUTY RUFE DUNNAHOO KILLED IN NEEDLESS GUNFIGHT

Chaves County Sheriff John Peck and his chief deputy, Rufe Dunnahoo drove out of Roswell on Sunday morning, August 2, 1931. They were en route to the Welch farm near Greenfield, north of Hagerman. They stopped in Dexter and picked up Deputy Sheriff Dwight Herbst who operated a gas station there. The purpose of their trip was to question Gilford Welch about some parts that had been taken from an auto which had burned and been left along a rural road.

The officers confronted Welch in his yard.

"I am looking for some parts off a car, a license plate and some parts...." Deputy Herbst said.

"The license plates are here. They should be in this truck bed," Welch replied.

But they were not there.

"My name is Peck. I am the sheriff. Do you object to me searching your place?"

"No," Welch said. "I will help you."

Herbst began searching in some of the farm's outbuildings while the sheriff looked around outside the house. Dunnahoo went into the house and soon emerged carrying some of the stolen items.

"We have found the [license] plate and you might as well come clean and tell us where the other articles are hidden." Dunnahoo said.

Dunnahoo, Peck and Welch returned to the house. Welch made no protest. As the lawmen searched, Welch was allowed to go outside, where he watched the search through a window. He saw Dunnahoo, down on his knees, searching under a bed. Welch said later that he thought the deputy was disturbing his baby who was asleep on the bed. He returned to the house and quickly retrieved a .380 automatic pistol he had hidden behind a dresser. He pointed it at the two officers.

"Don't come in here, ...damn you, I will kill you!"

"Why, man, you can't afford to do anything like that," the sheriff, said. "This case does not amount to anything."

Peck later recalled what happened then. "I saw that the man would not listen to reason and I nodded at Dunnahoo to come up from behind. I grabbed one arm and at the same time Rufe grappled him from the other side. We were attempting to take the gun away from him and in the mix-up the three of us fell on a bed in the corner of the room. In some manner Welch must of gotten his right arm loose and the [fatal] shot was fired."[1]

Investigation revealed that Dunnahoo was shot as he lay on the bed, the bullet ranging upward from his neck and into his brain. The deputy had not attempted to draw his own gun and Sheriff Peck was not armed. Neither was Deputy Herbst. None of the officers considered the situation dangerous, Peck said, even after Welch pulled the gun.

Peck fled from the house and ran to his car where he'd left his gun in the glove compartment. Welch fired at the sheriff repeatedly, until his gun was empty. Peck returned fire. Welch reloaded and resumed the fight. No one was wounded in the exchange of shots. Peck demanded that he be allowed inside the house to see what could be done for Dunnahoo.

"Don't you try to go into that house, or I will kill you," Welch yelled before he fled out the rear door. He ran across a cotton patch and into a cornfield. Welch reached the Hagerman-Dexter road only to be met by Sheriff Peck, who'd headed him off. Welch raced back to his house. His wife and stepdaughter begged him to surrender. A brief standoff followed until a number of armed men arrived from nearby communities. Welch finally agreed to surrender, but only to deputy sheriff Jim Williamson, who had arrived at the farm.

There was no further violence, but there might have been. One man at the scene, armed with a shotgun, offered to settle matters with Welch right then and there. The sheriff declined.

In custody, Welch remained angry. "I killed Dunnahoo because he made me mad when he started to search my home." He said he'd have killed Peck, too, if he had not run out of ammunition. But on the drive to Roswell, Welch seemed to realize the enormity of his crime. "Take me out to the side of the road and kill me," he said. "I'm a good man. Just kill me."

At his arraignment on the morning of August 3, 1931 Welch plead guilty to the murder of Rufe Dunnahoo. His plea, according to law, was not accepted and he was returned to custody. On a change of venue, he was tried at Carlsbad on October 16. He changed his plea to not guilty his main line of defense being that Dunnahoo's entry into his house was illegal because the officer did not have a warrant. Welch argued that he had a right to defend his home. It took a jury two hours and fifteen minutes to convict him of second-degree murder. Judge Miguel A. Otero sentenced him to 40 to 90 yeas in prison. But that was not the end of the matter.

The case, of course, was appealed and the New Mexico Supreme Court addressed the matter in 1933. The higher court ruled that the lower court had made mistakes in the instructions provided to the jury and it declared that it was lawful for Welch to have armed himself since the sheriff had no warrant. The shooting of Dunnahoo was, the court said, an act of involuntary manslaughter, not murder. The case was remanded to Eddy County for a new trial.

Welch's second trial took place in the fall of 1934, more than three years after the killing. Murder charges were not re-filed and Welch was accused only of voluntary manslaughter. He plead guilty to that charge and was sentenced to four to five years in prison. Since he had had already served more than three years, it is unlikely that he did any more prison time. He and his family disappeared from Chaves County, never to be heard from again.

Dunnahoo, a month shy of his 52nd birthday, had lived in Roswell for 51 years. A wife and two children survived him. He had been a peace officer for 20 years. "He was known as an efficient, courageous and faithful officer and yesterday his life was snuffed out while he was acting in the line of duty. [He] was well and favorably known," according to the Roswell *Daily Record*.

---

[1] Sheriff Peck was involved in another gunfight, in July 1933, and another of his deputies was killed. Barney Leonard was shot and killed, as was Oklahoma fugitive Frank Wallace.

"SMOOTH" STEVE ELKINS AND THE FIGHT FOR STATEHOOD

Stephen Benton Elkins had a long career in public life. He served as Secretary of War in the Benjamin Harrison administration (1889-1893) and then two terms as U. S. Senator from West Virginia, from 1895 until his death in 1911. He and his wife were prominent in Washington, D. C. social circles for many years.

His climb up the political and social ladder began in territorial New Mexico.

Elkins was born in Perry County in central Ohio in 1841. He was educated at the University of Missouri from which he graduated in 1861. One of his friends and classmates was Thomas B. Catron. Both became attorneys. They went their separate ways during the Civil War years, Elkins joining the Union forces and Catron the Confederate. Neither left much of a mark in the military service, and to the credit of each, they never used military titles—major or colonel—in their subsequent careers.

By 1864, Elkins resided in Mesilla, New Mexico where he entered the practice of law. He was elected to the Territorial House of Representatives the same year and within a few more years he'd been appointed District Attorney and Attorney General. By 1870, not yet 30 years of age, he was the U. S. District Attorney for New Mexico. Because of his facility in the world of politics, he came to be called "Smooth Steve."

He'd moved to Santa Fe by then, and in the meantime enticed his friend Tom Catron to relocate in New Mexico. Catron arrived in 1866 and became District Attorney for the Third District in 1867. They formed a law partnership in 1869. Any differences they might have had over Civil War issues seem to have been put aside. They both became integral parts of the famed Santa Fe Ring, a political bloc dedicated to taking advantage of New Mexico's wealth.[1]

Elkins was elected as territorial representative to the U. S. Congress in 1872 where he served two terms. It was during his tenure in Washington on behalf of New Mexico that he made one of the biggest mistakes of his career; a mistake that may well have cost New Mexico statehood status for a number of years.

By 1874, the prospects of statehood for New Mexico looked good. The territory had been waiting for nearly a quarter century, and the time seemed right. Elkins gave a speech in which he cited the nation's responsibility to admit New Mexico as a part of the Treaty of Guadalupe Hidalgo; the territory's strong support of the Union during the Civil War; the potential for resource development, not to mention the territory's "salubrious" climate.

A statehood bill passed the U. S. House of Representatives in May of 1875. It also passed the U. S. Senate, but the latter body made some amendments to the bill, which required that it go back to the House for concurrence. There seemed to be no trouble with that.

Elkins was not present on the floor of the House later that year when Representative Julius Burroughs of Michigan declaimed bitterly about events in the South following the Civil War, and the rise of the Ku Klux Klan. Smooth Steve returned to the chamber in time to see Burroughs receive considerable adulation from his northern colleagues in the House of Representatives so he joined in the chorus, shaking Burroughs' hand and offering congratulations. Southern representatives didn't appreciate the gesture and the New Mexico statehood bill was as good as dead. It never got out of the House Committee on Territories.[2]

But Elkins' days in New Mexico were numbered. In 1877 he married Hallie Davis, the daughter of U. S. Senator Henry G. Davis of West Virginia, and he shortly moved his law practice and political fortunes east. In addition to a successful political career, Elkins did well in the economic realm. He had amassed a considerable fortune before he left New Mexico, and he only added to it over the remainder of his life. The town of Elkins, West Virginia is named for him.

---

[1] The original Santa Fe Ring, according to historian Will Keleher, was made up of Tom Catron, Robert Longwill, H. L. Waldo, Frank Springer and Abe Staab, members of both political parties. It existed, in one form or another, from the years following the Civil War until about 1885. Some would argue that it lasted considerably longer than that. If Elkins was not, strictly speaking, a member, he was certainly associated with the group.

[2] Another source says the statehood bill failed by seven votes.

ESTEVAN AND SOME OTHER BLACK PEOPLE: THEIR IMPORTANCE IN THE HISTORY OF THE OLD WEST

The history of the American West is replete with tales of the good and bad deeds done by Anglo and Hispanic explorers, trappers, pioneers, settlers, soldiers and cowboys. Stories of Indians and Indian Wars are too numerous to mention. Asians, particularly the Chinese, are remembered for their contributions to railroad construction and various business enterprises in towns all over the West. Until recently, though, one group was frequently ignored in histories of the American Frontier. These were the Black explorers, soldiers, cowboys and mountain men.[1]

A Black man was involved in the earliest exploration of the Southwest. The Spanish explorer Alvar Nuñez Cabeza de Vaca set sail from Spain in 1528. When he reached Florida, his group was set upon by Indians and their numbers severely reduced. The Spaniards fled to what is now Texas where they were attacked again. When all was said and done, three men remained with Cabeza de Vaca, two Spaniards and a Black man, a Moor, named Estevan (or Estevánico).

For eight years they wandered the prairies, deserts and mountains of what is now Texas, New Mexico and Old Mexico.[2] They were the first to report the existence of the Seven Cities of Cibola, said to have been cities made of gold.

In 1539, Padre Marcos de Niza led an expedition into New Mexico seeking the Seven Cities. His guide was Estevan who was sent ahead with a small group of scouts. He sent back regular reports of great finds. Late in the year, Estevan and his group reached the Zuñi village of Hawikuh. He is said to have made unreasonable demands on the residents who retaliated by killing him and most of his scouts. At least one of the party escaped and reported the tragedy to Niza. The Padre insisted that he at least see the village, which later he did, from a distance. Apparently the adobe buildings under the bright New Mexico sun looked like gold. Niza reported to the Viceroy of New Spain that the town was made of the stuff.

In the intervening years, up to the American Civil War, hundreds of Black people settled in the West. They accompanied the Spanish as they settled old and New Mexico. There were Black slaves among the Americans who settled in Texas during the first half of the 19th century and there were Blacks among the Mountain Men who hunted and trapped in the Rocky Mountains during the same period, Jim Beckwith being probably the most famous.[3]

But it was after the Civil War that Black people and their activities made a marked difference in the West. A very large number of the soldiers who fought the various Indian tribes were Black. In 1866, the U. S. Congress created two Black infantry regiments, the 24th and 25th, and two Black cavalry regiments, the 9th and 10th.

They were called Buffalo Soldiers and they fought in every part of the West. About 3,500 Buffalo Soldiers served at 11 of New Mexico's forts between 1866 and 1900.

As a young officer, General John J. "Black Jack" Pershing commanded the 10th Cavalry for a decade. He said this: "It has been an honor which I am proud to claim to have been at one time a member of that intrepid organization of the Army which has always added glory to the military history of America—the 10th Cavalry."

The four Black regiments had a desertion rate far lower than comparable white regiments, and fewer Black soldiers were court-martialed. One military historian has noted that Black soldiers believed that wearing the uniform was a privilege and an honor. They took the business of soldiering very seriously and were quite good at it. Twelve members of the Black regiments that served in New Mexico won Congressional Medals of Honor.

In addition to the regular soldiers, there were some who were not quite so militarily oriented. They were called the Seminole Negro Indian Scouts. These men were descendants of slaves who had fled to Florida and settled with the Seminole Indians. They later moved west and settled in Old Mexico. Some of them fought with Santa Ana in the Mexican War.

The U. S. Army recruited about 50 of them in 1870. They were to serve as scouts in the war against the Plains Indians. Commander of the unit was Lt. John L. Bullis.[4] Bullis reported that the scouts were outstanding in military fitness in every area but appearance. They were not inclined to wear uniforms and preferred their normal dress that sometimes included feathered war bonnets.

Bullis commanded the scouts for nine years during which they were involved in 12 major engagements in New Mexico and Texas. None of them were killed, or even seriously wounded, and yet three of the Seminole Negro scouts were awarded Congressional Medals of Honor. Sergeant John Ward, bugler Isaac Payne and Private Pompey Factor were so honored for their part in an action against Comanche Indians along the Pecos River on April 25, 1875.

Another area in which Black men played a significant role was the development of the cattle industry. Hundreds of the cowboys who drove cattle north from Texas to railheads and the northern ranges were Black. One writer suggests that there were as many, or more, of them than there were Mexican vaqueros. They did every kind of work the trail drive required.

Bose Ikard was a Black cowboy who rode with Charles Goodnight, Oliver Loving, John Chisum and others. After Ikard died in 1929, Goodnight (shortly before his own death) placed the following marker on the grave:

"Bose Ikard. Served with me four years on the Goodnight-
Loving Trail, never shirked a duty or disobeyed an order, rode with me
in many stampedes, participated in three engagements with
Comanches, splendid behavior."

But of course, racial discrimination was a part of the picture, too. A Black cowboy named Jim Perry rode for the famed XIT Ranch for 20 years. He is reported to have said, "If it weren't for my damned old black face, I'd have been boss of one of these divisions (of the ranch) long ago." A white cowboy who rode with Perry agreed.

---

[1] Many history texts, especially those published 40 or so years ago, do not mention African-Americans as part of the history of the West after 1865.

[2] Some historians believe that Cabeza de Vaca did not range as far north as New Mexico.

[3] Jim Beckwith (or Beckwourth) was a contemporary of Kit Carson and Jim Bridger in the first half of the 19th century. Late in his life Bridger became a chief of the Crow Indian Tribe.

[4] Lt. John Lapham Bullis was a native of Macedon, New York. He first served with the 126th New York Volunteer Infantry during the Civil War and was commissioned in August 1864, as captain in the 118th U. S. Infantry, Colored. After the war, Bullis reverted to his permanent rank of second lieutenant and was posted to the West in 1865. He was assigned to the 24th Regiment in 1869. He remained in Texas for the rest of his life and retired as a Brigadier General. He died in May 1911. Camp Bullis, Texas, near San Antonio, is named for him.

THE SINS OF ALBERT BACON FALL, NEW MEXICO'S FIRST U. S. SENATOR

Albert Bacon Fall, Judge, U. S. Senator, Secretary of Interior, Disgrace to New Mexico.
(Photo Courtesy the Albuquerque Museum Photoarchives, PA 1978.050.565)

Albert Bacon Fall was one of New Mexico's great political chameleons, and he ultimately brought disgrace to the Land of Enchantment in the early years of statehood.

Fall was born at Frankfort, Kentucky in November 1861 to a strongly Confederate family. He received very little formal education, but studied law as a young man. Because of ill health, he moved west while in his early 20's. He worked on cattle and sheep ranches in Texas, and for a time served as a chuckwagon cook. Fall also spent some time in old Mexico, working as a miner. He married in Texas and arrived at Kingston, New Mexico in 1883. He did some prospecting in the Black Mountains and for a time worked as a miner there, too. Fall first met Edward Doheny in Kingston in the 1880's, and Doheny would play a significant role in Fall's life in the 1920's.

Fall is said to have grown weary of the miner's life and moved on to Las Cruces in 1887. He opened a book and stationery store and later took up the practice of law. He also became involved, as a Democrat, in the rough and tumble politics of the time. In 1888 he stood for election to the Territorial House of Representatives. The opposition press noted his recent arrival by writing that "Fall has not been here long enough to change his shirt." He lost the election by about 50 votes out of 2,000 cast.

Loss of the election didn't slow Fall's drive for political power. He, and the Democrats of the time, represented an Anglo population made up largely of Texans who had been Confederates, or were the descendants of southern sympathizers. The Republicans of the day were old-line Hispanic families and their supporters. The Republican leader was Albert Jennings Fountain, a former Union Officer, who was married to a Hispanic woman. Fall announced to anyone who would listen that Fountain had "gone native" by marrying her, and he meant it as a pejorative.

Fall was cynical enough, however, to run an advertisement in the local newspaper identifying himself as "Alberto B. Fall" when he again ran for the legislature in 1890. The slogan in the same ad read, "Faithful Friend of the Mexican Race." The Republicans countered by writing that Fall was a "Texas Democrat" whose campaign was "an appeal to passion, prejudice, ignorance and bigotry." Fall won the election anyway, defeating Fountain. His political star was on the rise.

The election two years later in 1892 was good for the Democrats. Grover Cleveland was elected President and Fall moved up to the Territorial Council, comparable to today's State Senate. An incident during this campaign illustrates how the politics of late 19th century in New Mexico worked.

Fall received word that a troop of New Mexico militia would ride into Las Cruces on Election Day to keep the peace at the polling place in the Masonic Temple. He believed that the real purpose was to intimidate Democrat voters, since the militia leadership was made up of Republicans. He sent word to his good friend, rancher Oliver Lee, that he needed help, and Lee, along with six or so of his cowboys responded. Early on the morning of Election Day, a company of militia led by Major H. H. Llewellyn rode into town, only to be confronted by Albert B. Fall. He raised his arms and halted the troop. "Llewellyn," he said in a commanding voice, "get the hell out of here with that damned militia inside of two minutes, or I will have you all killed!" He gestured toward the roof of the mercantile across the street where stood half of a dozen men, armed with rifles aimed at the volunteer soldiers. The troop did an about-face and retreated from the scene.

President Cleveland appointed Fall an associate justice for the Third Judicial District of New Mexico in March 1893, and he served until February 1895. One source says that he did not like the job; that he found judicial duties boring and irksome. Another reports that Fall was too much of an advocate to be happy in a role as jurist. Perhaps it had more to do with Fall's attitude toward law and order.

On the evening of September 15, 1895, as *Judge* Fall and his brother-in-law, Joe Morgan, walked along Las Cruces' main street, they encountered Ben Williams, a former deputy U. S. Marshal, current town constable, and strong supporter of Albert

Fountain. Fall and Morgan pulled their guns and began shooting. On of Morgan's shots was fired from such close range that Williams' face was powder burned. Williams was also wounded in the arm so severely that he had limited use of the limb for the remainder of his life. Fall and Morgan were arrested but a grand jury, made up of 16 Democrats and five Republicans, refused to indict them. Instead, they indicted Williams and Fountain (Fountain had not been at the scene of the shooting) on charges of assault with intent to kill. The latter indictment didn't bear close scrutiny and was dismissed. Williams removed himself to El Paso for a time afterwards.

The *Independent-Democrat* newspaper, owned by Fall's family, and edited by his father, reported thus: "There was no political significance to [Fall's] armed assault on Deputy Williams; he had simply succumbed to a personal dislike of the man and decided to take a shot at him; wasn't that any freeborn New Mexican's right and privilege?"

By the turn of the century in 1901, Albert Bacon Fall had established himself as an ardent leader in the New Mexico territorial Democratic Party and an effective attorney. After all, he'd taken on Tom Catron, leader of the Santa Fe Ring, in the defense of Oliver Lee charged with the murder of Henry Fountain, and won decisively.[1] One source said this: "In the eyes of New Mexico, the main issue had been decided; Fall was a better man than Catron.

But at about the same time, Fall took a hard look at his political future, and what he saw did not bode well for the Democrats. Fall drew two conclusions. First was that New Mexico would gain statehood status within a few years, and second, that the Republicans would hold sway in the foreseeable future. If he wanted to serve in the United States Senate, it was necessary that he change parties, and he did.

Many at the time thought he did so because the Democrats failed to nominate him for Delegate-in-Congress in 1900, and that may have contributed to his decision. He'd made it clear that he would accept such an opportunity. But it may have been as simple as what Fall himself said: "I know when to change horses."

The change was a shock to many. Fall had been "one of the most uncompromising Democratic partisans ever...in the history of New Mexico." One observer noted that he was "the most rabid and intense Democrat in the whole Southwest." And yet he not only changed parties, but at once sought to become a leader among the Republicans.

Fall's perception of New Mexico's political future was correct. Republican presidents William McKinley, Teddy Roosevelt and William Howard Taft controlled the territory from 1897 to 1913, and the territory gained statehood in 1912. Fall played his cards just right and, along with Tom Catron, was named one of New Mexico's first U. S. Senators in 1912.[2] He served until March 1921 when President Warren G. Harding named him Secretary of the Interior. Fall was the first New Mexican ever named to a presidential cabinet position.

His problems soon began.

Within a few months of taking over the Interior Department, Fall requested that President Harding transfer supervision of some of the nation's oil and gas reserves in California, Colorado, Utah, and Wyoming from the Secretary of the Navy to the

Secretary of the Interior. The locations that would become most troublesome for Fall were at Elk Hills, California and Teapot Dome, Wyoming. Leases at these two locations were negotiated and executed with the Pan American Petroleum and Transport Company and the Mammoth Oil Company. E. L. Doheny and H. F. Sinclair owned those companies, respectively, and both were close personal friends of Secretary Fall. Readers will recall that Fall's friendship with Doheny reached back to the 1880's in Kingston, New Mexico.

These deals caught the attention of conservationists who believed that Fall was attempting to circumvent congressional control of his office. It soon became common knowledge that Fall had received $100,000, in cash, from E. L. Doheny. The money became the focus of future events. Early on, before a congressional committee, but not under oath, Fall stated that the money had come from E. B. McLean, owner of the Washington *Post*. McLean was called before the committee and, under oath, he denied making the loan. It was obvious that the money had come from Doheny. The question was the purpose of it. Fall maintained that it was simply a loan he intended to use to make improvements at his Three Rivers ranch. Prosecutors didn't believe it. Fall was indicted for accepting a bribe. He resigned from the cabinet on March 4, 1923.

Fall defended himself against the charges for years, but in October 1929 he was convicted of accepting a bribe. He was sentenced to a year and a day in prison and fined $100,000. After all appeals failed, he reported to the State Penitentiary at Santa Fe on July 21, 1931 where he was enrolled as a federal prisoner. He spent most of his time in the prison hospital and was released on May 9, 1932. He died on December 1, 1944 in El Paso. He never paid his fine.

Many at the time did not believe that Fall was guilty. George Curry, territorial governor and congressman after statehood[3] said this: "It remains my belief that Fall was guilty of bad judgment rather than acceptance of a bribe." Historian Will Keleher wrote, "[I have] reached the conclusion that the testimony submitted in the various trials had not proved him guilty of wrongdoing 'beyond a reasonable doubt,' ...[but] his handling of the business relating to the Doheny loan was careless and inept."

No matter. Albert Bacon Fall's name will forever be associated with the corruption of the Harding administration and the Teapot Dome scandal.

If there is a lesson to be learned from Fall's professional life, it is that arrogance will only carry a man so far.

----

[1] The trial took place at Hillsboro in the late spring of 1899. Lee and Jim Gilliland were charged in connection with the disappearance of Albert Jennings Fountain and his eight-year-old son, Henry, in 1896.

[2] At the time, Senators were selected by state legislators and not by popular election.

[3] Curry was also a Democrat who bolted his party to become Republican as the times changed.

A NEW MEXICO MYSTERY: WHAT BECAME OF ALBERT & HENRY FOUNTAIN?

Albert Jennings Fountain [1] was born on October 23, 1838 at Staten Island, New York. He grew up there and attended public schools and Columbia University before he began a tour of the world. He landed in San Francisco after several adventures. [2] While in California, he engaged in the newspaper business—he covered the Walker filibuster expedition in Nicaragua for the Sacramento *Union*—and studied law. Shortly after the Civil War started in 1861, Fountain joined the volunteer infantry, the California Column, which brought him to New Mexico. Before the end of the century, Fountain would become the subject of one of New Mexico's greatest mysteries.

On January 31, 1896, or thereabouts, Fountain and his young son, [3] Henry, disappeared from the face of the earth, virtually without a trace.

For some years preceding his disappearance, the elder Fountain served as prosecutor for several livestock growers associations in southern New Mexico. In January 1896, he appeared before a grand jury at the town of Lincoln where on the 21st, true bills were returned against Oliver Lee and William McNew charging that they had rustled cattle belonging to W. A. Irwin of El Paso. They were also charged with defacing brands on Irwin's cattle. Neither man was in Lincoln at the time, but they soon learned of the grand jury's actions.

On January 30, the Fountains set out from Lincoln for home in Las Cruces. Some of Fountain's friends warned him not to make the trip alone and suggested that he wait until he could travel with the U. S. mail wagon. They were concerned that the prosecutor's life was in danger because of the many enemies he'd made among the cattle thieves of southern New Mexico and west Texas. Fountain patted his shotgun and said, "This will be my protection."

That Fountain believed he could take care of himself was no idle boast. He no doubt believed that he could handle just about any situation. At age 57, Fountain had a long record of military adventures. As in infantryman, he fought Indians in the deserts from California to New Mexico. Later, as a cavalry captain, he organized forays against Apache and Navajo Indians. He was wounded by Apaches in Arizona and sent to El Paso to recover.

In 1868 he was elected to the Texas State Senate representing more than 30 west Texas counties. He eventually became president of the Senate. He was also a custom's official. As a result of the so-called El Paso Salt Wars, he engaged in a shootout with one Frank Williams in 1870. He was wounded but managed to kill

Williams. In 1875, he returned to New Mexico and took up the practice of law in the town of Mesilla. He participated in the campaigns against the Apache—Victorio and Geronimo in particular—as a colonel in the New Mexico volunteer cavalry.

In 1888, Fountain was elected to the New Mexico Territorial Legislature. Even then he continued as a soldier in the field, only this time he was busy chasing cattle thieves and other outlaws. In 1894 alone, he was given credit for convicting 20 men on charges of cattle rustling.[4]

On the evening of January 30, 1896 the Fountains stopped for the night at the village of La Luz. While there, the Colonel gave Henry a quarter to buy some candy at the general store. The change for the purchase was one dime and one nickel which young Fountain tied into the corner of a handkerchief and put into his pocket.

On the morning of January 31, the Fountains set out for Las Cruces. They stopped at the midway point of the lower Tularosa Basin, at Luna's Well, to water the horses. There they met up with Santos Alvarado, driver of a mail stage who was also watering his horses. Alvarado told Fountain that he'd seen three riders who galloped away when he drew near. Soon, Fountain spotted them on the horizon, too far away to be recognized.

Fountain met up with Saturnino Barela just south of Luna's Well. As the two men visited, Barela pointed out three men silhouetted on the horizon. The Colonel told Barela that he'd been followed since he left Lincoln by two men at first, and then three. Barela suggested that the Fountains return to Luna's Well where they could spend the night with him and return to Las Cruces the following day in his company. Fountain declined saying that young Henry was ill and needed the attention of his mother.

The Colonel and Henry never arrived in Las Cruces.

On the evening of February 1, as soon as he returned to Las Cruces, Barela went to the Fountain home and inquired about the Colonel and Henry. When he was told that they had not arrived, Barela told the Colonel's adult sons, Albert and Jack, that he had seen a place along the road, near the Chalk Hills, where a buckboard had left the road. He also told the boys what their father had told him about the three riders. A posse made up of the Fountain boys, Antonio Garcia, Catarino Gallegos, Camimiro Chacón and Pedro Onapa set out for the Chalk Hills at once. A second posse followed a few hours later.

The searchers soon found the spot where the buckboard had left the road and it didn't take long to find the rig; the horses unhitched and gone. Nearby they found some lap blankets that were identified as belonging to Colonel Fountain. They also found the Colonel's cartridge belt and some other personal items. His necktie had been draped over a wheel spoke. And, nearby, in some bloody and crushed grass, they found two coins, a nickel and a dime, wrapped in a handkerchief. There was no trace of Albert Jennings Fountain or young Henry.

The only real clues at the scene were foot and hoof prints. Among the three sets of footprints, one set was made by cowboy boots with a pointed toe and high heels. Boots with box toes made up the other two sets, and one set of prints showed that the wearer had one foot smaller than the other.

The hoof prints led away from the scene in the general direction of Oliver Lee's ranch at Dog Canyon in the Sacramento Mountains. One source reports that the trail was lost about four miles from the spot where Fountain's buckboard was found. Another says that the three sets of horse tracks joined a huge number of cow tracks, and could not be followed. Thomas Branigan, chief scout from the Mescalero Reservation, using Apache trackers, was unable to follow the trail. He concluded that the Fountain's had been "foully dealt with and murdered." He could, of course, produce no bodies.

Another posseman, Carl Clausen, found a set of tracks, those of a large, shod horse, and he followed them to Oliver Lee's southern ranch headquarters at Wildey Well. Clauson visited with Lee there and said that he was searching for the two missing persons. When ask to help in the search, Lee declined saying that the Fountains meant nothing to him.

The search continued far and wide. The Masonic Lodge, of which Fountain was a member, offered a reward of $10,000 to anyone who could find the Fountains, alive or dead. A newspaperman from Las Cruces, Isidoro Armijo, set out on his own search in Old Mexico based on what he considered an important clue. In a year and a half, he found nothing and became convinced that neither of the Fountains were in Mexico.

The rumors started. It was said that Oliver Lee, if not personally involved, knew who did the deed and knew what had become of the Colonel and his son. The original indictments against Lee and McNew for rustling, those for which Fountain was responsible, were dismissed in April 1897. No action was ever taken on the charges.

For more than two years nothing much seemed to happen regarding the case. But in early April 1898, Doña Ana County Sheriff Pat Garrett[5] petitioned Judge Frank Parker for arrest warrants charging three men with the murders of Albert and Henry Fountain. The affidavit read in part, "[Garrett] knows persons and can have them before the court, who identified the tracks of Oliver M. Lee, William McNew and James Gililland[6] at the first camp where they stopped with Colonel Albert J. Fountain and his little son...." Parker issued the warrant on April 3.

Garrett promptly arrested Billy McNew and lodged him in the Doña Ana County Jail, held without bond. The sheriff's efforts to arrest Lee and Gililland over the following year were almost tragicomedy. At one point, the trial led to Lee's ranch at Wildey Well. In a gun battle there, one of Garrett's possemen, Kent Kearney, was killed, but Lee and Gililland avoided arrest. The wanted men came to believe that Garrett meant to kill them rather than take them to trial. After the Wildey Well fight, they both grew beards and hid out at remote ranches in the Sacramento Mountains.

Oliver Lee was not without powerful friends. They generally agreed that Garrett wanted to do to Lee and Gililland what he had done to William H. Bonney and his friends. A solution to the problem would be to remove the entire matter from the jurisdiction of Doña Ana County, and therefore Pat Garrett. Albert Bacon Fall[7] and W. A. Hawkins[8] devised a plan whereby they would simply create a new county. With some deft political maneuvering, they succeeded in gaining territorial legislative approval of the change: Otero County was created on January 30, 1899.

The point from which the Fountains disappeared was within the boundaries of the new county, and therefore beyond the jurisdiction of Pat Garrett. All matters pertaining to the case would now fall to the new Otero County Sheriff, George Curry, a close personal friend of Oliver Lee[9].

Through the good offices of Sheriff Curry, Lee and Gililland then agreed to surrender to Judge Parker provided they not be turned over to Pat Garrett and that they not be jailed in Doña Ana County. Parker, along with Governor Miguel A. Otero[10] agreed to the plan and in March 1899 the two men surrendered their guns to the judge. They were held at Socorro since Otero County had not had time to construct a jail.

As a trial strategy, Lee and Gililland were only tried for the murder of Henry Fountain and on a change of venue the trial was held in Hillsboro, Sierra County. The trial began on May 25, 1899 and lasted for 18 days. It took the jury just eight minutes to return a verdict of not guilty. No one was ever tried for the murder of Col. Fountain.

In later years, Jim Gililland was heard to boast on several occasions: "...if the bodies had to found before a murder could be proved, no one would ever be convicted [of killing the Fountains]."

----

[1] He was born Albert Jennings. He adopted the use of his mother's maiden name, Fountain, at a later date.

[2] On one occasion, Albert and his friends boarded a ship in Calcutta bound for Hong Kong only to learn that they were aboard an opium smuggler. They were arrested but apparently acquitted of all charges.

[3] Different sources give different ages for young Henry, ranging from 8 to 12.

[4] While Fountain was successful as a prosecutor, he was not always successful as defense attorney. In April 1881 he was appointed by Judge Warren Bristol at Mesilla to defend Billy the Kid. He lost. Billy was convicted of killing Lincoln County Sheriff William Brady and sentenced to hang.

[5] Garrett was appointed Doña Ana County Sheriff in April, 1986. Readers will recall that he was sheriff of Lincoln County when he killed Billy the Kid in July 1881.

[6] Some sources spell the name Gililand, others as spelled here.

[7] This is the same A. B. Fall who went to prison in 1931 for accepting bribes while serving as Secretary of the Interior in the administration of President Warren G. Harding.

[8] Hawkins, an attorney, had once been associated with Pat Garrett in the Pecos River irrigation project.

[9] Throughout his life, Curry maintained that Lee was innocent of any complicity in the disappearance or murder of the Fountains.

[10] It is more than coincidence that Otero County was named for Governor Miguel Otero.

SOCORRO KILLER JOEL FOWLER: DEAD AT THE END OF A ROPE

Joel A. "Joe" Fowler was a killer. No question about it although no one knows exactly how many men he killed. Estimates range as high as 26 in New Mexico alone, and probably a few more in Texas. Realistically, he may have killed eight or ten. He shot most of his victims, often using a shotgun, but he stabbed the last one, in November 1883. That murder would be his undoing, and would lead to what little fame he ever achieved.

Like many men of his time, there is a great deal of confusion as to where and when he was born. Newspaper accounts of the time couldn't agree. One claimed that he was born in Indiana in 1849 and another that he was born and raised in Mississippi. A modern source asserts that he was born in Massachusetts in 1854. One source even suggests that his real name may not have been Fowler, but it probably was. Sources do agree that he was a bantam of a man at five feet four inches tall and weighing 130 or so pounds.

Legend holds, and most sources agree, that Fowler arrived in Fort Worth, Texas, in the 1870s. He lived there with an uncle, a prominent politician. He may have studied law, but there is no proof of it. He got married, but ended up killing his wife's lover when he caught the two of them together. He seems to have taken up the outlaw trail about then, rustling cattle and robbing stagecoaches for sustenance. There is no complete record of his criminal activity in Texas. He arrived in Las Vegas, New Mexico, in 1879.

He brought enough money from Texas that he was able to open a saloon in Las Vegas, and he very shortly married again. His new wife was a dance hall girl named Josie.[1] They left Las Vegas after about six months and moved on to Santa Fe. Fowler opened the Texas Saloon on San Francisco Street near the plaza.

In Santa Fe in February 1880, Fowler came to the attention of the press. The *Daily New Mexican* reported that he got drunk one day, and remained drunk the next. With a shotgun in hand, he shot up the street near his saloon, and held off a sizable crowd of citizens for about half an hour. A passer-by finally pounced upon and restrained him until help arrived and carried the miscreant off to jail. It was an omen of things to come. Joe and Josie moved on again.

They arrived in White Oaks, in Lincoln County, in the late spring of 1880. They promptly opened yet another saloon. An incident occurred in late May that seems to record Fowler's first killing in New Mexico. Two prospectors got drunk in town one day, and proceeded to shoot up the community, narrowly missing some women and children. An incensed and armed male populace addressed the problem, firing 30 to 40 shots at the ruffians. One of them was knocked off his horse and the other fled. Joe Fowler and another man took up the chase. They soon encountered the man, and Fowler killed him with a rifle bullet to the chest. No charges were ever filed in the matter.

His business ventures, legal or illegal, must have been successful. By the following year, 1881, Fowler was engaged in the cattle business on a ranch he owned at Bear Spring, north of the present day Magdalena in Socorro County. He managed to enhance his reputation as a drunkard and a bully by occasionally riding into Socorro and terrorizing the citizenry. He is reported to have made people stand on their heads in a barroom corner, at gunpoint; or to have made them dance with gunshots around their feet. An unsubstantiated story goes that he once encountered a one-legged man on the street and proceeded to shoot holes in the poor fellow's wooden leg until it splintered and collapsed. Then Fowler shot him in the good leg.

Fowler was also reputed to have killed buyers to whom he'd just sold cattle so that he could sell the same livestock over and over again. He was never caught or prosecuted for any such crimes.

As a rancher, he often complained about his cattle being stolen, and it was sometimes true. In December, 1881, Jim Greathouse,[2] Jim Finley and a man named Forrest stole 40 head of Fowler's beef. They drove the stolen herd to Georgetown, a silver mining community in northern Grant County where they sold it. Fowler and one of his hired hands caught up with the rustlers. When the confrontation was over, all three rustlers were dead, two of them from shotgun blasts.

In the fall of 1883, Forrest's brother, Pony, attempted to settle up for the killing of his sibling. He and another man, "Butcher Knife Bill" Childes, set a trap for Fowler at his home ranch. As Fowler rode into sight, Pony and Butcher Knife Bill opened fire with their revolvers. Fowler returned fire with a shotgun and killed Butcher Knife Bill immediately. Pony retreated into a nearby stone house and continued to fire at Fowler. A man named McGee arrived on the scene, and Pony killed him with a pistol shot to the head. The story goes that Fowler set the house on fire and that Pony Forrest then shot himself to death rather than surrender to Fowler. Most newspapers of the time doubted that Pony's death was a suicide. All three men were buried on Fowler's ranch, and no charges were ever filed in the matter, although Fowler did appear before Judge Beall in Socorro to explain himself.

In November of 1883, Fowler sold his ranch for more than $52,000, an enormous sum at the time. He and Josie arrived in Socorro to celebrate. As it turned out, Josie stayed in their rooms at the Grand Central Hotel, and Joe went from saloon to saloon until he was roostered, as they called drunkenness at the time. The Socorro Sun reported thus: "About daylight, he [Fowler] reached the Grand Central Hotel.... With two pistols in his hands, he terrorized those who happened to be there. Mr. Dorman came in and was forced to dance, was slapped in the face several times and finally struck on the head with a revolver." The newspaper described Fowler as "in a state of crazy intoxication."

Things went downhill from there.

As Joe shot up the Grand Central Hotel, a group of men descended on the drunkard and attempted to take his guns away from him, and they succeeded.

Unfortunately, Fowler had a knife hidden on his person. He withdrew it and plunged it into the chest of James Cale, a clothing drummer from Vermont. Fowler was quickly taken into custody and jailed and Cale, badly injured but alive, was taken to a hotel room. Cale made the following declaration before he died.

"J. E. Cale, being duly sworn, disposes and says: That he ... was at the Grand Central Hotel on the night of the 6th of November; Joel A. Fowler was with me; I was holding him off from a stockman when he struck me with a Spanish dagger; I had no trouble with Fowler; I was taking a gun from Fowler; he was drunk and swinging around; was afraid Fowler would shoot somebody else."

Because of the money Joe had, he was able to hire some of the best-known attorneys in the territory: Thomas B. Catron of Santa Fe and Neill B. Field of Socorro. Rumor had it that Fowler paid Catron $5,000. No amount of money, though, could persuade a jury that Joe was anything but guilty. He was convicted of first-degree murder on December 8, just a month after he killed Cale. Judge Joseph Bell sentenced him to death by hanging, the sentence to be executed on January 4, 1884. Catron, of course, filed notice of appeal and that date was vacated. The appeal could take as much as a year.

Active in Socorro at the time was a group that called itself the Committee of Safety. They were, in the parlance of the time, vigilantes. The local Hispanic population referred to them as *los colgadores*, literally, "the hangers." As Joe Fowler languished in jail, he contemplated the fact that the committee had already hanged two robbers, two killers and a child rapist. He and his lawyers feared that he would be next.

Fowler contacted his uncle, the Fort Worth politician, who contacted Socorro officials and demanded that his nephew be protected. Also, a group of Texas outlaws arrived to help protect their former partner in crime.

Socorro County Sheriff Pedro Simpson feared for Fowler's safety, too. He was well aware that his jail was not secure and the county commission refused to pay for additional guards or to pay the added cost involved in housing the killer in another jail. New Mexico Territorial Governor Lionel Sheldon authorized the sheriff to use the local militia company as guards, but the governor could only pay for them through the third week in January.

Along about this time, Sheriff Simpson felt called upon to leave town, to go in pursuit of train robbers. He left jailer F. W. Gaddis in charge. Gaddis knew there was vigilante activity afoot; that Fowler's friends had threatened to liberate the killer; and that the militia had withdrawn. The jailer even found a pistol under Fowler's bunk. The visiting Texans offered to serve as jail guards to protect Fowler, and Gaddis accepted the offer on January 21.

Local citizens were alarmed. The newspaper pointed out that one of the volunteer guards was the father of one of the train robbers Sheriff Simpson was chasing.

In the early morning hours of January 23, 1884, the Committee of Safety, about 200 strong, entered the Socorro County Jail. They met little resistance as they removed Fowler. The killer did not go quietly. According to one eyewitness, he

"...was howling and begging for his life," as he lost control of his functions. A witness reported that the condemned man called for protection from heaven, and someone in the mob answered, "It's a cold night for angels, Joel. Better call on someone nearer town."

He was placed on a wagon and hauled to the edge of the city where there stood a cottonwood tree with a convenient limb. The vigilantes simply put the noose around his neck and drove the wagon out from underneath him. One witness reported that he thought Fowler was dead, of fright, before he was hanged. Another reported that after the hanging was complete, someone in the crowd shot the killer a couple of times for good measure.

It was learned later that Sheriff Simpson was actually back in town at the time of the lynching. He'd arrived just after midnight and stopped at the Grand Central Hotel when someone rushed in and announced that the committee had taken Joe out of the jail. The Sheriff commented that he thought the proper course of action would be for him to cut down the body at the "first streak of day."

A coroner's jury ruled that Fowler had died by strangulation "at the hands of persons unknown." Of course, the jury was made up of the very people who had done the deed.

The lynching of Joel Fowler was the last one done by *los colgadores.*

The Texans who'd arrived in Socorro to protect Fowler were escorted to the railroad station by the Committee of Safety. They were put aboard a southbound train and told never to return.

Josie Fowler, newly a widow, saw to it that her late husband had new clothing for the public display of his body in Socorro before it was shipped back to Texas for burial. She then withdrew his fortune from the bank and left with his body. She returned to Socorro the following year with a new husband, Jack Acres, described as a well-known sporting man.

---

[1] One source said she was really named Belle.

[2] "Whiskey Jim" Greathouse was a partner with Fred Kuch in a road-ranch located about 40 miles north of White Oaks, New Mexico. It was there that Billy the Kid's gang shot and killed a deputy sheriff named James Carlysle in November 1880. Greathouse was called "Whiskey Jim" because he was known for selling booze to Indians, quite illegal at the time.

STATE POLICE OFFICER NASH P. GARCIA SLAIN ON ACOMA RESERVATION: KILLERS IN CUSTODY

State Police Officer Nash Garcia sat in his parked police car along U. S. Route 66 about 20 miles east of Grants on Friday, April 11, 1952. He may have been doing paperwork. A pickup sped passed him. Then it turned around and passed him again, operating erratically. The officer took up pursuit.

Garcia followed as the truck turned off the highway a couple of miles to the west and drove south on dirt roads across Acoma Pueblo Indian Reservation land for about 19 miles at which point it stopped. As Officer Garcia approached the pickup, two subjects opened fire from ambush with .30 caliber rifles; one from about 100 yards and the other from about 50 feet. They fired nine shots into the police car and Nash Garcia. The officer managed to open the car's door and then fell out onto the ground, severely wounded. The offenders then beat him about the head with gun-butts to make certain he was dead. They loaded his body into the police car and drove another six miles into reservation land, to a spot near Sandstone Mesa where they abandoned it. They returned the following day, filled the car with brush and set it afire.

Officer Garcia wasn't missed until Sunday morning when he failed to respond to a call from headquarters. State Police Chief Joe Roach said it wasn't unusual for the officer to be out of contact for a day or so, especially if he was working on the reservation. Concern for Garcia's safety increased when officers contacted his wife and she said she had not heard from him, either. His work, she said, sometimes kept him away from home for several days at a time.

A search and an investigation were initiated. It didn't take long. A local cowboy and several other witnesses told investigators they saw Garcia in pursuit of a pickup driven by one of the Felipe brothers: Willie, 31, or Gabriel, 28. On Sunday evening, State Police officers Dick Lewis and Joe Fernandez went to Willie Felipe's house on the Acoma reservation. Felipe offered no resistance and told the officers what he and his brother had done.

"I knew they'd get me," Willie Felipe said later to an Albuquerque *Journal* reporter. "They always get them."

The next morning Willie led a seven-vehicle caravan of officers and other searchers to Sandstone Mesa. They found "...a few pitifully small pieces of charred bone in a pile of ashes on the floor [of the car]."

On Monday evening, April 14, Albuquerque motorcycle policeman Robert Olona, Nash Garcia's cousin, arrested Gabriel Felipe on North First Street in Albuquerque. Gabriel offered no resistance when taken into custody. He maintained that he took no part in the killing. He asserted that he actually tried to stop Willie from shooting the State Policeman. Officers found Garcia's service revolver in a suitcase in Gabriel Felipe's hotel room along with another gun, which belonged to the suspect.

The Felipe brothers were tried, convicted and sentenced to life in federal prison by U. S. District Court Judge Carl Hatch. One of the brothers died in prison and the other was released in the early 1970s.

Nash Garcia was the first member of the New Mexico State Police to be murdered in the line of duty. Two officers, Walter Taber in 1937 and Delbert Bugg in 1946, were previously killed in motorcycle accidents. A third State Police officer, William Speight, died as he tried to reach a radio tower near Cloudcroft in February of 1949. The State Police Department was created in 1935.

Nash Garcia, 38, was born in Torreon and reared in Albuquerque. He served two years as a Bernalillo County Sheriff's Deputy before he joined the State Police in June of 1944. He was first assigned to the Albuquerque area, promoted to captain in June 1948, and placed in command of the district. When Joe Roach was named State Police Chief in 1950, he ordered Garcia demoted to the rank of patrolman. Garcia requested reassignment to the Grants area. Nash Garcia was survived by his wife, Martha, and three daughters; Yvonne, 13, Yolanda, 11, and Yevette, 7.

WHO KILLED SHERIFF PAT GARRETT??

Former Sheriff Pat Garrett was shot to death on February 29, 1908. By then, more than a quarter century had passed since he shot and killed William H. Bonney (Billy the Kid) at Fort Sumner, New Mexico (July 14, 1881). The intervening years had not been particularly good to Garrett.

In the first place, Governor Lew Wallace, who had left New Mexico at the end of May, 1881, declined to authorize the payment of the five hundred dollar reward offered for the capture or killing of Billy the Kid. Garrett was obliged to attend the territorial legislative session the following February and plead his case by lobbying on his own behalf. His style seems to have been buying drinks for territorial solons, and he succeeded in influencing them favorably. The reward was paid, but observers generally agree that Garrett's lobbying effort made the five hundred dollars a break-even proposition.

Garrett decided not to seek reelection to the office of Lincoln County Sheriff in 1882 after serving a single two-year term. Instead he stood for Territorial Council, which was similar to the modern-day State Senate. He lost in a tough race.

He also produced a book called *The Authentic Life of Billy the Kid*[1]. Garrett didn't actually write the book—his good friend Ash Upson did—but he hoped it would make him some money. It didn't. And to make matters worse, the historical accuracy of the book's content was seriously questioned. One critic said, "The whole book can be picked to pieces from beginning to end."

By 1884, the former sheriff was operating a ranch along Eagle Creek, not far from Roswell. He may have had a margin of success at ranching, but it was a sedentary life compared to his earlier adventures, and he was soon drawn to West Texas where he organized the so-called LS Rangers. The ostensible purpose of the "Rangers"[2] was to put a stop to cattle rustling on the LS, and other cattle ranges. It soon became clear that big ranchers expected Garrett and his men to kill rustlers, rather than arrest them. Garrett declined to continue under those terms and the LS Rangers were disbanded in early 1885.

Back at the Eagle Creek ranch, Garrett demonstrated his acuity of intellect when he envisioned a vast irrigation system that could water the Pecos River valley and turn the area into a lush farming district. He participated in several companies organized to dig ditches and divert the waters of the Pecos. In the end, though, Garrett's partners forced him out and his entire investment of cash and time was lost[3].

In 1890, Garrett ran for sheriff of the newly created Chaves County, and was defeated by John W. Poe, the same man who had accompanied him when he killed

The Kid, and the same man who succeeded him as sheriff of Lincoln County. An unhappy Pat Garrett packed up and moved to Uvalde, Texas in the spring of 1891.

Life in Uvalde didn't suit Garrett. He seems to have done fairly well at horse breeding and racing, but he became restless and soon began looking for greener pastures. Dona Ana County, New Mexico, provided just such a location. On February 24, 1896 he returned to New Mexico specifically to investigate the disappearances of Col. Albert Jennings Fountain and his son, Henry. Both had vanished near the White Sands on February 1, 1896. In August 1896, Garrett was appointed Sheriff of Dona Ana County, and elected in his own right in November of the same year.

Still, Sheriff Garrett's luck didn't improve much. The main suspects in the Fountain case were Oliver Lee, Jim Gililland and Billy McNew. He arrested McNew without incident. Lee and Gililland were a different story. The sheriff and his posse trailed them to Wildy Well, a spot near the present day Oro Grande, south of Alamogordo, and a major gun battle erupted when he attempted to arrest them. When the gunsmoke and dust cleared, one of the possemen was wounded and dying and Garrett and the remaining lawmen were forced into an ignominious retreat. The outlaws remained free. Lee and Gililland were subsequently arrested, —not by Garrett—tried and acquitted.

In October 1899, Garrett and his deputy, José Espalin, went to the W. W. Cox ranch in the Organ Mountains, east of Las Cruces, in search of a fugitive named Billy Reed, AKA Norman Newman. Reed was wanted for the murder of his partner in Oklahoma. He didn't go peacefully. He slugged Garrett and ran for the meat house where his gun was stashed. He didn't make it. Deputy Espalin fired twice, one of his bullets passing through the killer's heart.

Garrett remained Dona Ana County Sheriff until 1900, but he was nearing 50 years of age and looking for some other line of work. The Federal Government beckoned.

In December 1901, President Theodore Roosevelt—over loud protests by disgruntled Republicans—appointed the former sheriff as Collector of Customs for the Port of El Paso for a two-year term. He received a second appointment in 1903. There are many reports that during this time in his life, Garrett became something of a curmudgeon and spent a great deal of time in drinking, gambling and philandering. His activities did not go unnoticed in El Paso, Las Cruces or Washington, D.C.

In 1905, Garrett and his friend, Tom Powers, an El Paso saloonkeeper and gambler, attended the Rough Riders reunion at San Antonio, Texas. Powers hoped for an introduction to President Roosevelt. Garrett obliged and introduced Powers to the President as a *cattleman* and the three men were photographed together. Garrett feared that if he introduced Powers as a gambler, it would reflect badly on his own reputation. When the president learned the truth of the matter, he was not even slightly amused. In spite of Garrett's best efforts at damage control, he learned on December 13, 1905, that he would not be reappointed.

Over the years, Garrett had acquired two small but well watered ranches in the Organ Mountain, 25 miles east of Las Cruces. They were about the only assets he had, and he didn't own them free and clear. He tried prospecting and mining on his property, but that never accomplished more than meeting expenses. He continued his drinking, gambling and womanizing ways, and his disposition became even more cantankerous. He was at odds with neighboring rancher W. W. Cox over some cattle and the Reed killing. His debts mounted and his debtors began dunning him and pursuing their claims in court.

In 1907, Garrett's son, Poe, leased one of the ranches to Wayne Brazel—a Cox cowboy—for grazing purposes. Payment was to be ten heifer calves and one mare colt per year. Little did Poe Garrett, or his father, know that Brazel intended to graze goats on his property.

Pat Garrett was in the process of trying to undo the arrangement his son had made when, on February 29, 1908, he began a ride into Las Cruces from his ranch. He rode in a buckboard with a man named Carl Adamson. Wayne Brazel joined them along the way. At a point near Alameda Arroyo, four miles east of Las Cruces, as the old lawman stood urinating, the sound of two shots shattered the cold winter air. One bullet entered the back of his head and exited through the right eyebrow and the second bullet, fired after he was down, entered the stomach and ranged upward to the shoulder. Carl Adamson said the old lawman moaned once, stretched out, and died.

Adamson's story was that he stood with his back to both Garrett and Brazel when the shots were fired. He turned almost immediately, he said, to see Brazel holding a smoking six-gun. He rushed to Garrett's side only to discover that the former lawman was dead. He covered the body with a robe and left it where it fell. Adamson and Brazel rode on into Las Cruces where Brazel surrendered himself to Dona Ana County Deputy Sheriff Felipe Lucero. Brazel claimed self-defense from the beginning.

The creaky gears of the New Mexico Territorial criminal justice system began turning. On March 3, Brazel formally entered a plea of not guilty to a charge of murder. Dr. W. C. Fields testified that Garrett had no glove on his left hand and was obviously urinating when he was shot in the back of the head (Garrett was right handed). The second shot was fired after the victim was already on the ground. Fields described the killing as cold-blooded murder. Bond was set at $10,000. Rancher W. W. Cox posted it later the same day and Brazel was freed. Brazel was indicted for murder on April 13, but he was not tried for more than a year, on April 19, 1909.

As one historian has said, "The case was prosecuted with appalling indifference and incompetence." Adamson was not called upon to testify and Brazel swore that Garrett threatened him with a shotgun and that he only fired in self-defense. He denied that Garrett had been shot in the back. The jury began considering the matter at about 5:30 p.m. and returned with a verdict of not guilty about 15 minutes later.

There were, and are, nearly as many theories about what happened that day in 1908 as there are observers. Many at the time simply could not believe that a mild-mannered young man like Brazel—he was 31 years old—would kill anyone, so they looked elsewhere. The most popular theory is that a hired killer named Jim Miller actually fired the fatal shots.

A meeting was allegedly held at the St. Regis Hotel in El Paso in 1907. Oliver Lee, Bill McNew, Carl Adamson, Wayne Brazel, W. W. Cox, Jim Miller, and several others attended it. This scenario holds that each man in attendance hated Pat Garrett for one reason or another, but W. W. Cox is said to have arranged and chaired the gathering, and to have volunteered to pay for the killing. Cox not only despised Garrett for killing Billy Reed (AKA Norman Newman)[4] on his ranch, but he also wanted access to the water on Garrett's ranch. Oliver Lee, it is said, conceived the idea of using Wayne Brazel to lease the Garrett property for grazing, then running in a herd of goats. He knew Garrett would react badly, and that would force a confrontation that might lead to a shooting which could be called self-defense. Jim Miller, who was Carl Adamson's brother-in-law, was engaged to do the deed, for a fee of $1,500.

Miller, the story goes, hid behind a low hill in a prearranged spot, and when Adamson stopped the buckboard, Miller simply shot Garrett and promptly returned to Fort Worth. According to this legend, the plan worked perfectly, and famed New Mexico lawman Fred Fornoff[5] *did* find empty Winchester cartridges on a low hill near the scene of the killing.

There were other theories. The Garrett family believed that Carl Adamson actually pulled the trigger. Another tale was that W. W. Cox ambushed Garrett, and Brazel took the blame out of loyalty to the rancher.

Pete Ross, an Albuquerque prosecuting attorney who has done considerable research into Garrett's death, believes that the murder was done out of political expediency, and that Governor George Curry, along with attorneys Albert Bacon Fall and Mark Thompson, was part and parcel of the crime. Ross argues that the investigation into the murder was short-circuited by Governor Curry and the prosecution of Brazel was so badly handled because the conspirators simply wanted the matter to go away. Ross makes a convincing argument.

It is axiomatic in criminal investigations, though, that things are usually as they seem to be, and that is probably the case in the killing of Pat Garrett.

Historian Leon Metz says this:

"That Brazel's plea of self-defense was not consistent with the facts does not mean that he was lying about killing Garrett; it simply meant that he was lying about *how* he did it. Garrett's death was clearly a case of murder, perhaps not premeditated, but murder nonetheless. Brazel feared the old manhunter and possibly had a reason to worry about his safety if the goat problem could not be settled amicably. The two men had argued bitterly, and when Garrett turned his back, Brazel took the safe way out and shot him. There were no conspiracies, no large amounts of money changing hands, no top guns taking up positions in the sand hills. It was simply a case of hate and fear erupting into murder along a lonely New Mexico back road."

Wayne Brazel married and acquired a small ranch west of Lordsburg a few years after Garrett's murder. In 1913 his wife died and he shortly sold out and disappeared.

Jim Miller killed 20 to 40 men—depending on the source—during his lifetime. The year after the Garrett affair, he killed a man named Gus Bobbitt near Ada, Oklahoma, and was shortly arrested for the crime. On the day that Wayne Brazel was acquitted, April 19, 1909, a lynch mob took Jim Miller and his three cohorts into a barn in Ada and hanged them one at a time (they only had one horse). Legend held that Miller admitted killing Garrett just before he was strung-up. A member of the mob denied that Miller said anything of the sort.

---

[1] The complete title of the book was, *The Authentic Life of Billy the Kid, The Noted Desperado of the Southwest, Whose Deeds of Daring and Blood Made His Name a Terror in New Mexico, Arizona & Northern Mexico, a Faithful and Interesting Narrative.* Its author was identified thus: Pat F. Garrett Sheriff of Lincoln Co., N. M., By Whom He Was Finally Hunted Down & Captured by Killing Him.

[2] The LS Rangers should not be confused with the Texas Rangers. Garrett had no affiliation with the Texas Rangers.

[3] The entire company, The Pecos Valley Irrigation and Improvement Company failed by the year of Garrett's death: 1908.

[4] Historian Metz says that Cox was not particularly annoyed by this affair, and in fact loaned Garrett money a couple of years later.

[5] Fred Fornoff (1859-1935) served as Albuquerque chief of police, Bernalillo County deputy sheriff, deputy U. S. Marshal, captain of the Mounted Police, and as a Santa Fe Rail Road investigator. He believed that Jim Miller did the killing, but admitted that he could not prove it.

GERONIMO: LAST OF THE WARRING APACHES

Did you ever wonder, as you drove on modern highways across the deserts and through the mountains of New Mexico, how during the 19th century, the United States Army was ever able to win a military victory over the various Indian tribes? The Indians, after all, had been around for hundreds of years, and the nomadic tribes in particular had roamed freely for all of that time. They knew the terrain, and knew it well. They knew how to live off the land and they had a tradition of unconventional warfare. The army had none of those advantages.

Among the most difficult of the tribes to bring to bay were the Apaches. While it is true that many of them had been placed on reservations in Arizona and New Mexico by the late 1860s, it is also true that several Apache bands were not finally contained until the late 1880s. Among them were the Jicarilla, Mescalero, Mimbres, Warm Springs, and Chiricahuas.

There are many reasons why the Apaches were not happy confined to reservations. The romantic notion is, of course, that they yearned for the freedom to range widely and at will, as they had done throughout history. There is probably something to that. But there is much more. Indian Agents, who were supposed to see to tribal needs, consistently cheated the Apaches, and many other reservations Indians, for their own enrichment. Corruption was the rule rather than the exception. The result was that the Indians lived without much that had been promised to them.

The Apaches also lived with the fear that at some point, either the U. S. Army, or some other government agency, would turn them over to territorial civil authorities in New Mexico or Arizona, which authorities would promptly take the Indians out and hang them for crimes associated with raiding.

The last major military effort against the Apache began in May of 1885. About 140 Apaches led by Geronimo, Mangus (son of Cochise), Nana, and Chihuahua, fled the Turkey Creek Area near Fort Apache, Arizona. They traveled well over 100 miles on foot[1] and hid in the Black Mountains of western New Mexico. General George Crook reported that reasons for the Indian's flight were pretty much as listed above.

Lieutenant Britton Davis of the U. S. Third Cavalry, however, remembered that there were two major bones of contention expressed by Apache leaders just prior to their departure. One was that they were no longer allowed to beat their wives, and the other that they were forbidden to make and drink *tiswin*, a strong, alcoholic, beer-like beverage made from corn. The Indians said it was not the government's business how they treated their wives, or what they drank.

Whatever the reason, Geronimo[2] was free again and that spread terror throughout Old Mexico, New Mexico and Arizona.

The basis for the terror was very real. The Apaches had been plundering and killing settlers—Spanish, Mexican and American—for more than 300 years, and they did so with great facility. They did not raid and kill for honor in battle. They did it for loot and for sustenance. The Apaches stole everything they needed, or wanted, beyond that which nature could provide. This included horses, weapons, and even money. It was not a common practice for Apaches to take scalps. It was of no value to them to keep accounts of how many people they killed. Individual status within the tribe had more to do with material possessions, loot and plunder, than with prowess in killing the enemy.

The style of attack was also chilling. They would carefully reconnoiter their target with an eye to observing what kind, and how much, resistance they could expect. They would then strike quickly, often at night, on foot, killing all adult males and generally, but not always, capturing all women and children. They were ferocious and cruel. Single-family farms and ranches were among their favorite targets. On one occasion, pursuers arrived at a ranch recently raided by Apaches to find a small girl impaled, yet alive, on a meat hook. On another, when Judge H. C. McComas and his family were attacked by a band of Apaches south of Silver City, New Mexico, the Judge was shot seven times, his wife brained with a club, and his son kidnapped, never to be recovered.

The Apache also had a phenomenal ability to withstand the heat of the desert and go long periods without water. One source reported that the Apache's "...water metabolism almost rivaled that of the camel." A "civilized" man would die of thirst while the Apache would just keep going.

Lt. Davis best sums up the ability of the Apache against the U. S. Army in the 1885-86 campaign.

"In this campaign thirty-five men and eight half-grown or older boys, encumbered with the care and sustenance of 101 women and children, with no base of supplies and no means of waging war or of obtaining food or transportation other than what they could take from their enemies, maintained themselves for eighteen months in a country two hundred by four hundred miles in extent, against five thousand troops, regulars and irregulars, five hundred Indian auxiliaries of these troops, and an unknown number of civilians."

By 1885, agreement had been reached between the governments of the United States and Mexico that U. S. troops could cross the Mexican border in pursuit of marauding Indians. Geronimo could no longer expect to take refuge in the Sierra Madre of Sonora, Mexico, and be safe from the U. S. Army.

In January of 1886, U. S. troops under Captain Emmet Crawford and Lt. Davis located Geronimo's main camp in the mountains about 90 miles south of Nacori, Sonora. They captured virtually all of the loot and plunder, including horses and food supplies, that the Apaches had accumulated since their flight from Turkey Creek began eight months before. Crawford and Davis did not capture any Indians, but Geronimo and his band were so demoralized by the loss that they agreed to meet with Crawford and negotiate for peace.

Unfortunately, on the day the talks were to take place, Mexican soldiers from nearby villages happened upon Crawford's camp, and the Apache who were there. The Mexicans attacked. They considered Apaches fair game, any time, any place and under any circumstances. When the shooting was over, Crawford was dead, and 15 Mexican soldiers, including the commander of the troop, were also dead. The Indians had withdrawn to a nearby hill from which they watched the Americans and the Mexicans fight. None of the Apaches, described as "interested spectators," were reported to have been injured.

It was famed scout, Indian fighter, bounty hunter—and eventually assassin—Tom Horn who was able to convince the Mexicans that they were fighting American troops.

The Apaches still wanted to talk peace, and it was agreed that they would meet with General Crook some two months later. Crook was without prejudice toward the Apaches and he'd been successful in dealing with them in the past. He did not, however, like Geronimo personally, and he told the man as much. Crook said that Geronimo was a liar who had broken his word so many times that he could no longer be trusted. Crook was also disgusted that Geronimo blamed everyone but himself for all the depredations that had occurred since the Indians left Turkey Creek.

It was agreed, however, that Geronimo and his band would surrender. General Crook departed for Fort Apache leaving a small contingent of soldiers behind to escort the Indians north. Crook had probably not reached the U. S. border before Geronimo and some of his warriors got drunk on 100 proof whiskey, said to have been sold to them by an American named Tribolet. Instead of going north, the Apaches returned south, back into the mountains of Sonora.

The escape outraged General Phil Sheridan, General Crook's commanding officer. It appeared that Crook had failed in this golden opportunity to capture Geronimo for once and for all. It was obvious to Sheridan that yet another major military effort would be required to bring the last of the warring Apaches to bay and that was problematical. In a report to President U. S. Grant in 1871 it had been pointed out that the United States had lost more than 1,000 lives and spent more than $40,000,000 in fighting the Apache, with little result. It is certain that the powers in Washington, D. C. did not appreciate the fact that some 15 years later, 5,000 troops remained ineffective in the field against a small band of Apaches. Crook was reassigned to a post on the Platte River and replaced by General Nelson Miles.

Miles was not about to take the matter of Geronimo lightly. He saw the Apache's capture as a significant step up the career ladder. He had, after all, captured Chief Joseph of the Nez Pierce in 1877 at Bear Paw Mountain.[3] One of the first things Miles did in Arizona was reorganize his command. That included the elimination of the Apache Indian scouts, without whom Lt. Britton Davis and Captain Emmet Crawford would never have found Geronimo in the first place. Miles did not trust the Indian scouts, and neither did General Sheridan.

The general also established a series of heliograph stations across the territory. Mirror signals enabled him to send messages to his troops over distances of three to four hundred miles in a matter of hours rather than days.

These preparations made, Miles took to the field in pursuit of Geronimo. By his own estimate, his troops covered more than 2,000 miles over a period of three months. No Geronimo. Miles learned that it was virtually impossible for American soldiers to locate Apache Indians in the Mexican mountains. As General Crook might have said, it takes an Apache to find an Apache.

While all of this was going on, Geronimo was able to slip back into the United States and, with a small band, conduct a series of raids. It was reported that he killed 14 people, including two soldiers, and stole horses, guns and ammunition. The public pressure on Miles was enormous to either kill or capture the Apaches, preferably the former.

Officers who had previously served under Crook finally persuaded Miles that he needed at least some Apache scouts. The general assigned Captain Charles Gatewood, along with 25 cavalry troops and 22 scouts the task of locating Geronimo. By August of 1886, they had done so. Gatewood personally delivered the message to Geronimo that General Miles wished to meet with him on the U. S. -Mexican border to discuss surrender. Geronimo agreed. On August 25, the Apaches started north.

Time had run out for Geronimo the warrior. He was more than 60 years old and his band consisted of 22 men and 14 women and children. He was being pursued by 5,000 regular U. S. Army troops. He surrendered to General Miles on September 4, 1886 at Skeleton Canyon on the Arizona—New Mexico line. Estimates are that in his final 16 months of freedom, Geronimo and his band killed ten U. S. soldiers, a dozen Indian scouts, 75 American citizens and about 100 Mexican citizens.

By then, the only Apache leader who had not surrendered was Mangus who remained in Mexico. He was no threat to anyone because he did not have a band with which to fight. When he was captured later in 1886, he had with him only two men, three women and seven children.

The United States' war with the Apache Indians was over.

So, how did the U. S. Army defeat the Indians, in spite of geography and Indian tradition? In the final analysis, they simply wore them down to the point they no longer had the will to resist. Even Geronimo, at last, got tired.[4] No Apache would again take to the field against the might of the U. S. Army.[5]

---

[1] Popular legend has it that Apaches warriors were good horsemen. Not so. As often as not, they fought on foot. Their concept of the way in which to use a horse was simply to ride it to death, then butcher and eat it. As food, horsemeat was preferred to beef or mutton. Among Indian tribes, the Comanche were probably the best horsemen.

[2] Geronimo's Apache name was Goyalka (spelled in many different ways), which translates as "The Yawner." How he came to be called Geronimo—Spanish for Jerome—is not clear. There is nothing to indicate that he was a great thinker and his priorities seemed to have changed with some regularity. At times he seemed prepared to fight the encroachment of white men to the very death. Other times he would meekly surrender and return to the reservation. He was not, strictly speaking, a chief, but he was the leader of a warring band. His main claim to fame it that he was the leader of the last significant Apache resistance.

[3] As a Major General, Miles was commander of the Division of the Missouri at the time of the Battle at Wounded Knee, South Dakota, in December 1890, the last major engagement in the Indian Wars.

[4] Geronimo was first exiled to Florida, then Alabama and finally to Fort Sill, Oklahoma where he died of pneumonia on February 17, 1909. He was never allowed to return to Old Mexico, New Mexico, or Arizona. The Apache were not released from captivity until 1914.

[5] The Apache Kid committed countless crimes—rape, murder, robbery—in southern New Mexico and Arizona from 1887 to 1894, but his depredations were addressed by civil authorities for what they were: criminal acts, as opposed to acts of war.

TERRITORIAL PRISON WARDEN JAMES GREGG FORCED TO RESIGN: IRREGULARITY IN ACCOUNTS

A story that used to be popular with University of New Mexico students had to do with the belief that the city of Santa Fe, in the 1880s, had a choice between becoming home to the University of New Mexico or home to the Territorial Penitentiary, and chose the latter. Students seem to have liked (or disliked) the notion that the capitol city would rather welcome convicted criminals than university people.

The story, though, has no historical basis. The Territorial Penitentiary was opened for business, and accepted its first prisoners, on August 21, 1885. UNM was not approved by the Territorial Legislature until February 1889.

Several communities expressed interest in becoming home to the university during that legislative session, but Senator Bernard S. Rodey of Albuquerque drafted the bill establishing the school and it was strongly supported by other Albuquerque legislators and businessmen. Other institutions went to other towns: Socorro became home to the School of Mines, Las Cruces acquired the College of Agriculture, Las Vegas got the Insane Asylum.[1] Santa Fe was not even a contender for UNM, perhaps because the prison was already located there.

New Mexico did not have a prison of its own prior to 1885. Those convicted of crimes in the territory were incarcerated in Kansas, Iowa, or even as far away as Illinois. In 1884, Governor Lionel Sheldon complained to the legislature that it was costing 20¢ per day to house prisoners in Kansas, and with transportation included that amounted to $75.00 to $100.00 per *year* per prisoner. He also argued that the existence of a prison within the territory would serve as "an ever present menace, and would prove of itself one of the strongest and most effective deterrents [to crime] which we could employ."

In April of that year, the legislature authorized the issuance of $150,000 in ten year bonds to build the facility in Santa Fe, near the present day intersection of St. Francis Drive and Cordova Road. It was to be 56 feet wide by 76 feet long, and four stories high. The wall around the structure was to be two feet thick and 20 feet high. Using convict labor, construction began in July 1884.

In February 1885, four convicts, while engaged in quarrying stone for the prison, managed to escape custody by taking guns away from their guards. Charlie Ray, Ollie Ewing and Charles Spencer[2] were serving time for cattle rustling and Gregorio Piñon was a convicted murderer. Ray and Piñon were recaptured. The other two, so far as is recorded, never returned to New Mexico. The governor fired the guards.

If that wasn't embarrassing enough, in August 1885, just one week before the facility was to be inspected and approved by the Prison Board, three more men escaped and were not recaptured. Thus, before the New Mexico Territorial Penitentiary ever officially opened, before it housed a single inmate, five men escaped from it.

Prisons of the time were designed and operated for the purpose of punishment. Rehabilitation was not a part of the program. The rules were strict. Letters could be written and visitors received by inmates only once per month. Talking was held to a minimum, and only between cellmates. Conversations with prisoners in other cells were not permitted. Guards of the time were armed and given wide latitude regarding the use of firearms to maintain order. Indications are that guards frequently shot first and asked questions later.

In the early days, once the facility went into operation, escapes were not a problem. The trouble was with the administration. One writer said, "For the first few years of its existence, more crime was committed by prison officials than by inmates."

The first warden was James E. Gregg. He lasted less than a year. He was accused of charging the territory 43¢ per day per prisoner when the actual cost was about 30¢. When the territory sued him for the difference, he resigned.

Thomas Gable was next, and he lasted less than two years. He was accused of purchasing supplies on the open market, rather than by contract, at prices 40 to 50 percent higher than necessary. Cost under his administration rose to $1.56 per day per prisoner.

Col. E. H. Bergmann was named warden in July of 1891 and for a few years the institution was free of embarrassment. But that wasn't to last. Some time around mid-decade,[3] Bergmann and his son were accused of entering into a conspiracy with a prisoner to poison Governor Miguel Otero. No motive for the crime was ever discovered and the charges were "quietly discharged" some time later.

Governor Otero appointed Holm O. Bursum of Socorro as warden. Bursum was generally well regarded, but because he was a successful rancher he was frequently away from Santa Fe and at home attending to his sheep business. At last, he too was accused of liability for a shortage of $7,500. He denied responsibility, but repaid the amount to the territory, under protest. The matter dragged on for several years, until George Curry became governor in 1907 when it finally reached a courtroom. When the dust settled, Bursum was exonerated of all charges against him, and his $7,500 was returned.[4]

The ups and downs of the New Mexico pen over the years are too many to mention. Early problems, though, may have been prophetic. In 1956, the state built a new prison south of Santa Fe. It was the site of one of the bloodiest prison riots in the history of the United States. Thirty-three inmates died at the hands of other inmates in a 36-hour period beginning early on the morning of February 2, 1980. "What was left of the prison was almost rubble," according to one eyewitness. A number of new prison facilities have been constructed in the years since.

---

[1] *Insane Asylum* is not considered to be politically correct. Today it is referred to as the State Hospital.

[2] This is the same Charles Spencer who escaped from the Grant County Jail at Silver City along with the Kit Joy gang in March of 1884.

[3] One source says it was 1895, but that could not have been since Otero did not become governor until 1897.

[4] Albert Bacon Fall, then Attorney General, prosecuted Bursum.

JUAN GUTIERREZ & EIGHT FAMILIES SETTLE ALONG LAS HUERTAS CREEK

In the late 18th century, British colonists living in what is now the eastern United States were having trouble with England's King George III over the issues of taxation and representation. Colonists living in what is now the American southwest had no such problems with Spain's King Charles III. Simple survival was challenge enough for Spanish people in the New World, and many had nothing to tax.

For want of money to pay his debts, Juan Gutierrez of Bernalillo was obliged to sell his ranch to the Santa Ana Indians in 1765. The extent of his debt and the size of the ranch are not known, but the change in ownership resulted in the displacement of eight families that had been tenants on his land. Gutierrez was not insensitive to the needs of the families and he soon petitioned governor Tomas Valdez Cachupin for a grant of land at a place called Las Huertas, east of Bernalillo.

The amount of land requested is lost to history, but it extended from just east of Bernalillo and San Felipe Pueblo well into Las Huertas Canyon. Gutierrez assured the governor that the area requested was more than adequate to support himself, his family and the eight other families. The settlement was to be along Las Huertas Creek, which would provide water for man and animal. The canyon contained open meadows suitable for grazing flocks and for cultivation of small fields and gardens. It is possible that Gutierrez and the eight families were already living in Las Huertas Canyon when the application was made. The final approval of the grant was not made until 1768, and by then twenty-one families lived there.

Settlement in such an area required the construction of a fortified *villa* to fend off frequent attacks by nomadic Apache and Navajo Indians. Houses were built side by side around a square with a corral between each and a high wall on the outer perimeter. A single heavy wood gate occupied one end of the compound. It was closed at sundown and not reopened until morning. Young boys, usually fourteen and under, tended flocks in the mountain meadows. They dug a series of holes in the ground in which they could hide when marauding Indians appeared, unless, of course, they had time to escape to the village. That the Indians would attack from time to time was simply a fact with which they all lived. Las Huertas was identified as a functional village by 1779 when it was included on a provincial map.

During the 18th century, Indian raiding all over New Spain, from California to New Mexico became so severe, and costly in life and property, that the Viceroy in Mexico City, Bernardo de Galvez, issued an order calling for drastic action. The first step was a massive war of attrition against the nomadic tribes. It began in 1786 and by 1790 was considered a success. The second step created a program that provided food to the Apaches and Navajos so they had no need to raid for sustenance. A part of the program provided for the delivery of copious amounts of cheap liquor to the Indians, too. The plan seemed to work and there was relative peace on the Spanish frontier for the following 20 years.

The Mexican Revolution against Spain began in 1810, and Spanish troops were moved from the north to fight in Mexico. At the same time, the Spanish government could no longer provide food and liquor to the Indians, so the nomads reverted to their old ways, and villages like Las Huertas were once again fair game. After Mexican Independence in 1821, the new governor admitted that he could not protect the people of Las Huertas and he ordered them to remove themselves. The village was completely abandoned by 1823. Most of the families moved down to Algodones close by the Rio Grande.

The settlers began moving back into the canyon in 1835 in ever-larger numbers. Several new villages were built at places called Tecalote, Ojo de la Casa, Rancho San Francisco, Los Alamos and Placitas. By 1848 it was estimated that Las Huertas was home to about 200 people, and by 1881, 500 lived there. The canyon seems to have become much more attractive as a place to live after the Navajos were completely subdued in 1864.

Governments had changed again with the American occupation in 1846, and land ownership was addressed in the treaty of Guadalupe Hidalgo in 1848. The treaty provided that Spanish and Mexican land grants would be honored within existing boundaries. That became a problem for Las Huertas (and many other land grants). The original boundary reference points, as established nearly 100 years before, included descriptions such as this: some red hills to the east of Bernalillo to a point in the mountains then to a water hole, and so forth.

The first claim for the Las Huertas grant was made to the U. S. Government in 1862, and it was for 130,000 acres. When the final patent was issued 45 years later, in 1907, it included just over 4,700 acres. Some of the land was lost as a result of boundary interpretations, disputes, and the like, but fully one third of the grant claimed was acquired by Thomas Catron and Mariano Otero, members of the infamous Santa Fe Ring, who took the land in exchange for assisting residents in securing their patent. What service Catron and Otero provided is certainly open to question since the claimants lost 125,000 acres of land grant.

The San Antonio de las Huertas land grant is with us yet today. Most of it is now in private hands, but there remains a governing body—called the Land Grant Board—that is made up of heirs of the original settlers. The board has authority over common land areas, cemeteries and roads. In the past it had much more authority and even operated the school system and named the superintendent. The board's authority has been eroded by the growth of municipal and county governments and today it does not have taxing authority or access to any other source of revenue. Land grant roads, those that are also school bus routes, are maintained through an agreement with Sandoval County.

Simple survival at Las Huertas, as on the rest of the Spanish frontier of 18th century New Mexico required constant toil, day after day; without respite. Homes had to be built and maintained, water had to be carried from the creek, wood had to be cut and gathered for cooking and warmth, crops cultivated and harvested, flocks tended, weaving had be done and clothing made, and all of that while fending off attacks by marauding Apache and Navajo Indians. There was no leisure time and few if any creature comforts.

A typical house of the time contained two rooms and measured, over all, 30 to 32 feet in length by 15 to 16 feet in width. One end was the kitchen/living area, which was usually the smaller of the two. It contained a fireplace called a *jogón de campana.*[1] Bins containing various grains and dried fruits and vegetables occupied one wall. The loom was kept in the living area. Most houses contained no furniture and the family gathered around the *jogón* to eat. Utensils were not used and eating was done with the fingers or a *tortilla* used in spoon-like fashion.

The other end of the building was the bedroom. It also contained a fireplace in one corner. A wooden pole, used as a place to hang blankets during the day when they were not in use, extended across the room. There were no beds and the blankets were used to make pallets upon which the family slept. A concave area in one wall of this room was home to the family's *santo*, or figure of a saint. The only other items that might have been present were wooden chests. The *cajas* were used for storing clothing and other important things. The *harineros* were larger and stronger than *cajas*, and used to store grain. These were sometimes heirlooms that had come north along the *Camino Real* with the earliest settlers.

These were single-family dwellings, and it does not appear that the size of the family had anything to do with the size of the house.[2]

The beginning of construction of such a house began with digging the floor area that was typically eight to 12 inches below ground level. Outer walls, 20 to 30 inches thick, were made of a combination of rocks and gravel held together with adobe mud. They were plastered on the outside with more mud and on the inside with white gypsum. The interior wall separating the two rooms was made of adobe bricks. The walls were low and the single door was even lower being no more than five feet high. The roof was held in place by *vigas* and *latías* covered with dried grass and dirt.

Spanish settlers of the time had few, if any, metal tools or weapons. One source indicates that as late as the 1860s, the people of Las Huertas still used arrows with flint points and stone axes. Villagers were greatly impressed in 1861 when 200 hundred, or so, Kiowa Indian scouts appeared carrying rifles. The Spanish obviously knew what guns were, but they had none.

There were no horses in Las Huertas in the early days. All travel to and from the village was done on foot. When the Kiowa scouts appeared, they too were on foot. When two Spanish men, who were actually American soldiers, arrived to lead the scouts away, they were on horseback and commanded considerable respect.[3]

Other animals were important on the frontier. Oxen were used for heavy farming chores, sheep and goats were kept and used for milk, cheese and meat, and their wool and hair were used for making clothing and blankets. The Spanish may have kept a few cows from time to time, but that was the exception and not the rule. Nothing indicates that they raised hogs but chickens were common. Archaeologists believe that most of the meat consumed was domestic rather than that of wild animals abundant in the area. Bears may have been hunted and their skins used for clothing, but that would have been difficult without firearms.

Growing crops, fruits and vegetables as well as corn and other grain, was obviously important for the sustenance of the people, but it was important for another reason, too: nomadic Indians coveted those items. There are indications that the Spanish paid a kind of extortion to the Indians by simply giving them a portion of their harvest in exchange for being spared an attack that could be very expensive in life and property.

The people of Las Huertas were generally born, lived their entire lives, and died without any kind of medical attention. The infant mortality rate was quite high, but if a child survived infancy, the chances of growing to maturity were good. When someone fell ill, traditional home remedies were used and if that failed, the *curandera* was summoned. She was a special person in the community with knowledge of herbs and other remedies. If she failed and the patient died, it was generally considered God's will and believed that nothing more could have been done in any event.

And when someone perished, it was necessary to remove the body to the closest church and *camposanto*[4] for burial and that was at San Felipe Pueblo, more than six miles away. There were rock mounds along the road between Las Huertas and San Felipe upon which the litter bearing the departed could be placed while the mourners rested. This shared religious relationship with the people of San Felipe lasted for many years. The first consecrated cemetery was not established in the Las Huertas/Placitas area until the 1870s.

In spite of it all, the Las Huertas settlers in the 18th century had something many other Spanish people did not have at the time, and that was a considerable degree of personal freedom. It was common practice in those times for the poor people who lived in the larger communities along the river, and elsewhere, to be bound to a *patrón* who could literally keep them in his service for a lifetime. This was not true of the people of Las Huertas. They may have had very little, but what they had was theirs. They only had to share a part of it with the Apache and Navajo.

Life in 18th century Las Huertas was hard, but it was better than bondage.

---

[1] *Campana* means bell and describes the shape of the fireplace. The fireplace might also be simply called a *jogón*, or hearth or *jogón de cocina*.

[2] In later years, after the threat of Indian attack ceased to be a concern and it was no longer necessary to live in fortified villages, it became a common practice to add bedrooms as children were born.

[3] The Kiowas were probably being used by the army to pursue the Navajos of western New Mexico.

[4] A *camposanto* is a cemetery.

GRANT COUNTY DEPUTY KILLED BY KIDNAPPER:TOM HALL SHOT IN THE BACK—KILLER HANGED

Grant County Sheriff James B. Woods hired Tom Hall as deputy not long after he took office in 1883. Hall, married and the father of five, lived in the village of Pinos Altos, northeast of Silver city. He was also commissioned as a deputy U. S. Marshal. The local press regarded Hall as "an honest, fearless and capable officer."

On Tuesday, March 16, 1886 Deputy Hall took a ride from Silver City to Pinos Altos. He may have been on personal business, but it is more likely that he was looking for a group of rustlers and bandits who had kidnapped a 15-year-old girl named Reyes Alvarez in the Santa Rita Mountains, east of Silver City, on the previous Friday. In their flight, the outlaws had killed a citizen named Aguilar Santiago. They had been seen on a trail northeast of Silver City.

It was nearing dark when Hall approached the Junction of the Pinos Altos and Ft. Bayard roads. He overtook a party of riders that included a young girl. He rode along with them for some distance and asked some probing questions about who they were and where they lived. One of the riders dropped back, pulled his gun, and shot the deputy, probably in the right arm. The officer, knocked from his horse, was running for his life when he was shot a second time, through the body. The outlaws left him where he fell and rode on. Hall was found later that evening and taken to Silver City for medical care. He died at about 1:00 a.m. the next day. All he could say about his killer was that he did not recognize him.

On Thursday, the 18th, young Miss Alvarez was discovered at the residence of a Mrs. Fessler in Silver City. She had been there since the evening Hall was shot, but kept her presence a secret because, she said, she feared the man who had kidnapped her and shot the deputy, a man she knew only as Pilar. She said she had been able to escape at the time of the shooting and hid in some brush alongside the road and later made her way into town. A coroner's jury could find no contradictions in her story. A posse set out in search of Pilar.

But Pilar was not to be found. Many crimes and depredations in and around Grant County were attributed to him, but he seemed impervious to capture. The fact was that he left the area soon after the fatal shooting. He went first to Socorro, then on to Albuquerque and finally west to Arizona where he worked as a sheepherder. He remained a fugitive for nearly two years before Grant County authorities learned that he was in custody in Flagstaff. He made no secret of who he was and claimed that he shot Deputy Hall in self-defense after the deputy fired first. Pilar was returned to Silver City to stand trial.

The trial took place on Wednesday, June 6, 1888. It took three hours from the time the first juror was questioned until the jury returned a verdict. Pilar continued to claim that Hall fired first, twice. He also claimed that he had not kidnapped Miss Alverez, but had "won her away with love." Her testimony refuted those assertions, and those who found Hall along the road testified that the officer's gun had not been fired. Moreover, Pilar's court-appointed attorney, J. M. Ginn, "could not say anything in favor of the defendant." Pilar was convicted of first-degree murder and sentenced to hang.

A news item at the time said this: "Pilar was only about twenty-seven years of age, rather short of stature, but fairly good looking, and by no means stupid. He joked with other prisoners, said he would return in spirit to see them hung, and remarked that as a man was not born to live always he had as well die one day as any other. He jocularly said he wanted to go to hell on a black horse."

Known as both Pilar Saiz and Pilar Perez, he was executed by hanging as Pilar Perez at 9:58 a.m. on July 6, 1888 at Silver City. The same newspaper recorded the event. "The drop was nearly seven feet. Pilar's neck was broken in the fall. Thus the law is vindicated and the death of Thomas Hall is avenged by the hanging of one of the most desperate young murderers ever known in the southwest. There was one thing remarkable about the spectators present, not a single expression of sympathy was manifested for the condemned man during the breathless moments preceding the hanging. It was evident that the murderer had no real friends among the spectators."

LUNA COUNTY DEPUTIES T. H. HALL & A. L. SMITHERS KILLED IN RAGING GUNFIGHT: OUTLAW KILLED

When the Mexican Revolution began in 1910, many North Americans went south to fight on the side of the rebels under Francisco I. Madero. Among them were brothers John and Reynold Greer and Irvin Frazier. The three of them participated in the March 1911 battle at Casas Grandes in northern Chihuahua during which rebel forces were defeated by federal troops. In the course of the fighting, John Greer received serious bullet wounds to his head and body and was left behind on the battlefield as the rebels retreated and federal troops advanced. Irvin Frazier rode to his rescue. Firing his rifle until it was empty, Frazier was able to hold off the soldiers long enough to get Greer on to his horse, and the two rode to safety. They soon crossed the border into the United States and Frazier remained with Greer in a mountain cabin until the wounded man recovered. Greer promised Frazier that he would repay the favor, with his own life if necessary.

In November of the same year, John Greer was given an opportunity to make good on his pledge.

Irvin Frazier, using the name John Gates, was arrested for burglary and held in the Luna County Jail at Deming, New Mexico. He got word to his friend, John Greer, that he needed help in escaping. On the night of November 7, 1911, a masked man climbed over the wall at the jail and held Sheriff Dwight B. Stephens and two deputies at gunpoint. He stole their guns and freed Frazier. A third man, also masked, waited with three horses outside the wall. They all made it safely away from the jail.

Sheriff Stephens and a posse made of deputies Tom Hall, A. L. Smithers, Johnnie James and W. C. Simpson took up pursuit. The chase took eight days during which the outlaws were able to provision themselves by robbing ranch houses along the way. Finally, late on the afternoon of November 18, the posse caught up with the outlaws at an adobe house on the VXT ranch in the Black Mountains of Socorro County. As the posse surrounded the place, the outlaws mounted their horses and rode out, single file, as if to meet the law officers. Suddenly, at a distance of fifty or so yards, they stopped and quickly dismounted, drawing guns as they did so, as if in a military maneuver. Then they opened fire, shooting both deputies Hall and Smithers. Smithers fell dead in his tracks, shot through the body. Hall was able to empty his Winchester rifle before he, too, fell mortally wounded from a bullet wound in the head. The killers remounted and attempted to flee.

Sheriff Stephens, who had taken a position on the opposite side of the house, hurried into the fight. He shot John Greer as bullets hit all around him, and both

Reynold Greer and Irvin Frazier again jumped from their horses and fled into an arroyo on foot, firing as they went. Deputy Simpson arrived on the scene and opened fire on Frazier with some success, and, though wounded, the outlaw made good his escape, as did Reynold Greer. John Greer, 19, died at the scene of the fight.

Sheriff Stephens and what remained of his posse abandoned the chase and took the three bodies to the railroad at Engle, 85 miles to the east.

The Deming *Headlight* eulogized deputies Hall and Smithers in this way:

> Thos. H. Hall and E. L. Smithers [sic], as truly heroes as ever went forth in the defense of law and justice have died a martyr's death. A home in Deming is desolate. A wife and mother's heart is bleeding at every pore. Five orphan children, four manly sons and a noble daughter are bowed in grief and go forth into the world to battle without the counsel, and strong protecting arm of a father.

A few weeks later, a man using the name John Gates, hungry and desperate, attempted to pawn a pistol in El Paso, Texas. Engraved on the butt of the weapon was the name of the man from whom Luna County Sheriff Dwight Stephens had acquired it. Gates was shortly arrested and identified as Irvin Frazier. He was promptly returned to Socorro where he was tried for the murders of Tom Hall and A. L. Smithers. Convicted of the crimes, he was sentenced to death by hanging.

During his time in the state penitentiary awaiting execution, he was able to smuggle out a letter to Reynold Greer in which he detailed the best way for Greer to rescue him as he was being transferred from Santa Fe to the gallows in Socorro[1]. His suggestion was that Greer board the train in Albuquerque and set up a trap at La Joya. Officers learned of the letter and took appropriate measures, but no effort was made to deliver Frazier from his date with the hangman. Reynold Greer was never captured.

Captain Fred Fornoff of the New Mexico Mounted Police, Socorro County Sheriff Emil James, Eddy County Sheriff Miles Cicero Stewart and 15 or so additional deputies, armed with rifles and shotguns, transferred Frazier and another killer, Francisco Grando, from Santa Fe to Socorro in the early morning hours of April 25, 1913. Along the way, Frazier told Sheriff Stewart that he hadn't killed either of the Luna County deputies. He said both officers were down before he ever fired a shot. The condemned men were taken to the courthouse and held there briefly before they were removed to a gallows that amounted to a trapdoor placed in the floor of a second story room in the jail. Frazier asked for a drink of whiskey. Fornoff refused. Frazier's final words were, "Get that noose tight, boys. Have as little pain to this as possible."

At exactly 5:42 a.m., the trapdoor dropped open and Frazier came to the end of his rope. A doctor declared him dead 12 minutes later. He was 26 years old.

Sheriff Dwight Stephens was himself killed by jail escapees in February of 1916.

---

[1] Each New Mexico county carried out its own executions by hanging until 1929 when the state, by law, assumed the responsibility. The state first used the electric chair in 1933.

DEE HARKEY: MEAN AS HELL

One of the most colorful New Mexico lawmen in the days before statehood was Daniel R. "Dee" Harkey of Eddy County. He said of himself that he had "...been shot at more times than any man in the world not engaged in a war." And yet he never killed anyone in the line of duty and he himself lived well into his eighties.

Harkey was born at Richland Springs, San Saba County, in central Texas in March 1866, one of 13 children. By the time he was three years old, both of his parents had died (within 15 days of each other). It fell to the eldest brother, Joe, then 17, to raise his seven younger brothers, and five younger sisters. By all accounts, Joe did a stellar job of it, but the Harkey boys seemed destined for violence. Brother John was killed in a gunfight over a woman in January 1877. Brother Jim was shot and killed in a fight over singing Yankee Doodle—not a popular tune in Confederate-leaning Texas at the time—in February 1878. A jealous husband shot brother Mose from ambush in 1887. John and Jim managed to kill their killers before they died, and another Harkey brother avenged Mose's murder.

It is interesting that the three brothers who became peace officers, Joe, Jeff and Dee, all lived to old age.

Joe Harkey was elected sheriff of San Saba County in 1880. Two years later, when he was just 16, Dee went to work for his brother as deputy. He held the job for four years. In this position he had his first encounter with a famous bad man. Jim Miller was running with the Renfro brothers and Bill White. Because one of the Renfros had been tried and sentenced to jail, Bill White attacked one of the jurors, who then made a complaint to Sheriff Joe Harkey. Five of the gang were then in a saloon in San Saba. Joe's plan for the arrest was a simple one: the two lawmen would step inside the saloon door and Joe would kill White while Dee would do the same to Miller. Dee told what happened next.

"Of course, I thought I must kill Miller, but when I jabbed my pistol in his face, he put up his hands and said, 'My god, Kid, don't kill me.' So I took his gun off him and looked around, and Joe had White unarmed, so we took the five of them and put them in jail."[1]

"Killin' Jim" Miller, famous as a hired gun and bushwhacker in later years, killed between 20 and 40 men, depending on the source of the information. Many folks believe that it was he who actually killed famed lawman Pat Garrett near Las Cruces in 1908, but it has never been proved. A lynch mob in Ada, Oklahoma hanged Miller in April 1909.[2] Harkey never mentioned how many lives he might have saved if he'd killed Miller as his brother ordered.

Dee moved to Eddy, now Carlsbad, New Mexico in 1890. By 1893 he was named deputy U. S. Marshal and deputy sheriff. Before the dust settled, he was also constable, city marshal, inspector for the Cattle Sanitary Board[3] and inspector for the Cattle Raiser's association of Texas, all at the same time!

One of Harkey's most consistent nemeses was Dave Kemp, a partner a saloon in Phenix[4] a partner in a butcher shop in Eddy and a former Eddy County sheriff. Kemp is said to have practiced corruption and cattle rustling while he served as the county's chief lawman, and he remained a thief as a private citizen. Harkey made Kemp's life uncomfortable for him. Word reached Harkey that Kemp meant to bushwhack him so he took steps to not only avoid the ambush, but to capture the would-be killer, which he did.

"I unarmed him and told him I was going to kill him. He begged me not to kill him, for he was unarmed, but I insisted I had to kill him to keep him from killing me. After an hour or two…I decided not to kill him if he would sign an affidavit that he would leave the country and never come back. Dave agreed to this…. I gave [him] back his pistol and we separated. Dave complied with his agreement for some years until he came back to kill Les Dow."

When Kemp murdered Sheriff Dow in 1897, it was Harkey who arrested him and protected him from a lynch mob by hiding the killer in his own home. Harkey didn't like Dow any more than he liked Kemp, but he believed that the law should take its course. Kemp was acquitted of the murder charge on a plea of self-defense and stayed around Eddy County afterwards. Harkey caught him at rustling again, but another man took the blame for Kemp. Harkey comments, "I never did mix much with Dave after that. His sister shot and killed him on Dave's ranch near Higgins, Texas, a few years ago."[5]

In another adventure, Harkey trailed a pair of thieves named Slaughter and Welch for 21 days from Eddy to Las Cruces, Hot Springs (now Truth or Consequences), Hillsboro, Silver City and Lordsburg. From there to Deer Spring[6] on the Mexican border, and back to Lordsburg and then to Wilcox, Arizona. From there he went to San Simon and then to Deer Creek. The outlaws had joined a cattle outfit owned by Slaughter's uncle. Eighty armed cowboys were at Deer Creek for a roundup. Harkey disguised himself and rode into the camp where he arrested Slaughter and Welch as they warmed themselves beside a fire. The wagon boss thought about stopping the arrest, but decided that two thieves were not worth the trouble it would cause. But Harkey didn't take any chances and hurried 90 miles to Wilcox where he and his prisoners boarded the caboose of an eastbound freight train.

Harkey gave up public service in 1911 and went into ranching and farming. He says this at the close of his autobiography[7]

"And so this brings me to the end of my story. The spaces are still wide and open out in our country. But the cattle stealing has gone out of fashion. We've gotten civilized. Instead of cattle thieves, bank robbers, and outlaws, we now have statesmen who practice nepotism, pad the public payrolls and graft as much as they think they can get away with (in an honorable way, of course) just like the folks back east."

―――――――――

[1] The San Saba jail, at the time, had a hole in one wall where some previous prisoners had escaped. This required either Dee or another jailer to sand guard constantly to keep the remaining prisoners from fleeing.

[2] Harkey is mistaken in his autobiography when he says Miller was hanged "about 1901."

[3] This was a law enforcement position akin to modern-day livestock inspectors.

[4] This community was located about three miles south of Eddy. Since Eddy was dry, Phenix was home to saloons, gambling houses and brothels. It only existed for about three years. It is sometimes spelled Phoenix and Fenix.

[5] Harkey is wrong about this. Dave Kemp died of a heart attack on January 4, 1935 at the age of 72. He was buried at Booker Cemetery in the Texas Panhandle.

[6] Probably Deer Creek, located 15 miles east of Cloverdale in New Mexico's Boot Heel region.

[7] Most historians consider Harkey's autobiography, *Mean As Hell*, as fanciful at best and downright dishonest at worst. His recollections are certainly subjective, his dates often confused. Of course, he was in his early 80s when he wrote it.

JIM HARSHMAN: RELUCTANT HISTORIAN

After the close of the Civil War in 1865, people migrated from east to west in large numbers. There were as many reasons for making the move as there were people who did it. Some wanted to take advantage of cheap land offered by the Homestead Act. Some saw economic opportunity in mining or timber. Some moved west because their relationship with the law in the east had not been good. And many moved west because the climate was believed to have curative powers. Such was the case with one J. H. "Jim" Harshman.

Harshman left no impression on the affairs of his time. His name does not appear in the chronicles, annuals or literature of the American West. He was not missed once he was gone. Fortunately, in 1929 he became involved in correspondence with western writer Neil M. Clark of Santa Fe. Harshman wrote some 32 letters to Clark dealing with the events of his life more than 50 years before. Clark published the letters in a book titled *Campfires and Cattle Trails, Recollections of the Early West in the Letters of J. H. Harshman* (The Caxton Printers, Ltd., Caldwell, Idaho, 1970).

James Hamer Harshman was born near Jacksonville, Illinois, in May 1858. Orphaned at a young age, he was raised by relatives. In 1875 he took sick with a severe cold that "settled on his lungs." Because of that, the following year he was sent to Colorado with $20.00 in cash. The plan was that he remain for eight weeks. He actually spent the next eight years living, working and traveling in Colorado, New Mexico and Texas. He was at various times a mailman, hide buyer, cowboy, miner, café cook and construction hand. His recollections are interesting.

Harshman was present at a shoot-out in Tascosa, Texas, in 1878 or 1879. A young man by the name of Bob Russell got drunk one day and announced that he was going to ride his horse into a store operated by one Jule Howard. Howard, a man about 50, and a friend of Russell's, said that he was not going to do any such thing. Russell insisted that he was and went to his nearby house and got his gun. Then, gun in hand, he mounted his horse and rode into the store. Jule Howard fired four shots, three of which struck Russell: one in the chest, one in the head and the third removed Russell's trigger finger. Russell managed one shot that went into the ceiling.

According to Harshman, these events occurred at about four o'clock in the afternoon. He, Jule Howard and Russell's wife nursed the wounded man until he died at about eight o'clock that evening. There was no doctor within 100 miles of Tascosa. There was also no lumber to be had in the town, so a coffin was fashioned from some packing crates Howard had out behind his store. Harshman said this about the funeral: "I was the youngest one there and supposed to have fewer sins I suppose so I was delegated to read the burial service. His wife had a small Bible and we buried him on a high bank overlooking the [Canadian] river and covered his grave with a lot of stones so the coyotes could not dig him up."

Russell was the first resident of Tascosa's Boot Hill Cemetery.

In conclusion of the matter, Harshman said, "There was no law in the country. The country was not organized and [had] no officers. Everyone said he [Russell] only got what was coming to him and so nothing was said or done. They were both likeable [sic] men and good friends. The whole thing was caused by whisky alone."

Harshman was present in Las Vegas, New Mexico, in 1879 or 1880 when young Dick Wootton and a friend got into an altercation with a dance hall bartender, and shots were fired. Wootton and his friend fled. The dance hall crowd, including Harshman, took up pursuit and caught the young men at their camp. Wootton had been badly wounded. The disposition of the matter is interesting. Wootton was not strung up, or even arrested. His goods, including his guns and saddle, were simply taken from him and divided up among those present. Harshman does not say whether he got anything, or not.[1]

Clark asked Harshman what he recalled about the death of Billy the Kid. Harshman, of course, was not involved in any way, and it is not clear where he was living in July of 1881. He was bound to have heard about it, and he did. According to Harshman, Billy had an adobe house that he used as a place to rest when he was not on one of his "expeditions." Sheriff Pat Garrett found out about it, went there and hid behind a bed and waited for the young killer to return. When Billy stepped into the doorway, which was clearly lighted, Garrett shot him without warning. Harshman was not judgmental about the way in which Garrett killed Billy. "That was the only way to get him [Billy] as he was so quick with his gun."

While reliable sources indicate that this is not exactly how it happened, it is interesting to note that this rumor tends to sympathize somewhat with the Kid. Harshman acknowledged that Billy was a "bad" man, but, "[he] ... killed only a few more men than some of the others...."

In spite of the various instances of violence Harshman witnessed, his letters point out that such events were the exception rather than the rule. While Harshman himself was frequently armed as he traveled about the west, he was never involved in a shooting scrape. He said this: "Of course there were a lot of bad men as they were called like Billy the Kid, [Clay] Allison, [Doc] Holliday, Dutch Henry[2] and many others but we do not know the circumstances that made them so and I do not think there were as many of them in comparison to the population as there are 'gun men' in Chicago today [1929].... I know I was never afraid to go where I pleased [in the west] but in Chicago there are places I would not feel safe with a big policeman on each side of me."

By 1884, Harshman's western adventure seemed to have run its course. He took a job with Wells, Fargo & Company in Kansas City. By 1890 he was stationed in Chicago. He remained with Wells Fargo until his retirement in 1920. He moved to Florida where he raised chickens and strawberries until his death in 1931. There is nothing to indicate that he ever returned to the West, and he never looked back. Not until 1929, that is, and historians should be happy he did.

---

[1] Dick Wootton went on in life to serve in the Colorado State Legislature, as Chief of Police at El Paso, Texas, and Chief Deputy Sheriff of Bernalillo County, New Mexico. He was killed when struck by a streetcar in front of the courthouse in Albuquerque in 1925 at age 74. His father was the famous Richens "Uncle Dick" Wootton (1816-1893) of Raton, New Mexico.

FIGHT OVER TURKEYS RESULTS IN GUNFIGHT: CUSTOMS OFFICER JAY HEARD SHOT, KILLED NEAR HACHITA

There are nearly as many motives for murder as there are murders. Greed, lust, jealousy, envy and downright meanness are among the most common. A flock of turkeys seems to have been the precipitate cause of a 1932 killing in southwestern New Mexico.

In the early 1930s, Claude Gatlin[1] was named foreman of the Little Hatchet ranch in the boot-heel region of southwestern New Mexico. Among other livestock Gatlin found at the ranch was a flock of turkeys which belonged to his predecessor, Tom Berkely, and J. H. "Jay" Heard who was the inspector in charge of the Hachita station of the U. S. Customs Service.[2] The birds were a considerable nuisance to Gatlin because they roosted in the ranch tack shed and left their droppings all over saddles, bridles, and other horse riding equipment. Gatlin sent word to Inspector Heard to come and get the turkeys. Heard seems to have ignored the request.

After a period of time and further annoyance, Gatlin crated up the birds and hauled them into the community of Hachita where Jay Heard lived. He proceeded to dump them over a fence into Heard's front yard. The inspector, upon hearing the racket, confronted Gatlin, and a fight soon followed. Legend holds that Heard administered to Gatlin a sound thrashing, and may have even pistol-whipped him.

"Next time I see you," Gatlin said as he left Heard's house, "I'll kill you."

Gatlin's tenure as ranch foreman at the Little Hatchet was short-lived and he was soon fired for drunkenness. He went to stay on a ranch owned by Tom Boles in the Animas Mountains on the Mexican border. Whiskey may have been the common thread in the relationship between Gatlin and Boles as Boles held his own reputation for drinking and drunkenness.[3]

At about the same time Inspector Heard developed reason to suspect that cattle and horses were being smuggled into the United States from Mexico across the Boles ranch. On Tuesday, June 3, 1932, Heard and another inspector, A. J. "Andy" McKinney, set out to investigate and interview Boles. Gatlin saw them as they drove up to the ranch headquarters in a Ford pickup. He quickly secured an automatic rifle and hid around the corner of the house. As the officers unknowingly approached the house, Gatlin stepped into the open, rifle in hand.

"What are you doing here, Heard?" Gatlin demanded.

Before the officer could respond, Gatlin opened fire. He fired four times, and all four bullets penetrated the windshield of the truck and hit Heard, two in the chest, one in the jaw and one shot away the thumb on the inspector's right hand. Even so, Heard was able to draw his own gun and get off two shots, but both went into the dirt. Inspector McKinney pulled his gun and started in pursuit of Gatlin, but the killer dashed into the house where he used Tom Boles' wife and another woman as shields. Gatlin dared the officers to shoot at him, or to try to enter the house. McKinney and Boles agreed that it would be suicide to try, and in any event, one of the women might well be injured or killed if more shots were fired. They determined that the best immediate course of action was to seek medical help for Inspector Heard. They took him by automobile to Hachita where they put him aboard a passenger train bound for El Paso. One source indicates that Heard died on the train; another that he died in the hospital.

McKinney and Boles notified peace officers from Hachita to Cloverdale in southern Hidalgo County to be on the lookout for Gatlin, and they organized a posse and returned to the Boles ranch to take up a search for the killer. As word of the shooting spread up and down the Animas Valley, other posses were mounted and took up pursuit. They scoured the rugged and desolate country along the Mexican border for miles in either direction for several days. Gatlin made good his escape and was never captured and prosecuted for the crime.

Gatlin did not disappear from history, however. He remained in Mexico, living a "squalid" life, according to one source, and returning to the United States on thieving raids. He also seems to have kept up with his drinking ways. He died from exposure one night, drunk, in a snow bank.

Jay Heard was 51 years old when he died. He'd been a Customs Inspector for about ten years, five of which he'd spent in Hachita. A wife and son, two brothers and a sister survived him.

It was all over a flock of turkeys.

---

[1] One source identifies this subject as Claude Gatliff. Probably a typographical error.
[2] J. H. Heard was a mounted Customs rider. These officers were sometimes called outriders. One source incorrectly refers to him as a Border Patrol Officer.
[3] In February, 1937, Tom Boles, while drunk, shot up the town of Hachita. Deputy Sheriff John Hall shot him in the arm when he "menaced" the officer. The bullet broke the cattleman's arm and he was later charged with resisting an officer, flourishing a deadly weapon and discharging firearms within a settlement.

CONRAD HILTON: A SON OF NEW MEXICO

What did the New Mexico State Bank of San Antonio, the Palmer House in Chicago, and the Waldorf-Astoria in New York City all have in common? What did the youngest member of New Mexico's first legislature in 1912 have in common with host of the United States Congressional Prayer Breakfast in 1956 (along with President Dwight Eisenhower)?

The answer to the first question is that the same man owned all of those properties, at one time or another. The answer to the second question is that the man was Conrad Nicholson Hilton, a native of San Antonio, *New Mexico.*

The emphasis on New Mexico is important. The very first line in Hilton's autobiography is, "I was not born in Texas." Hilton goes on to relate the story of the time he was to become a so-called "Texan of Distinction" and the Governor of Texas was somewhat dismayed to learn that there are at least two San Antonios in the United States, and one of them is not in Texas. Hilton was finally made an honorary Texan of Distinction.

Conrad Hilton was born on Christmas day in 1887, in San Antonio, New Mexico. His father, Augustus "Gus," was born in Norway and arrived in New Mexico by way of Fort Dodge, Iowa, in 1882. His mother, Mary Laufersweiler, also from Fort Dodge, married Gus on Lincoln's birthday in 1885. Conrad was the second of eight children and the oldest boy.

It would not be accurate to say that the Conrad Hilton story is one of rags-to-riches. There were never any rags. Gus Hilton was quite a successful businessman in his own right. A merchant and trader, he operated the only general store in San Antonio, and he dealt in wool, furs, and coal mining speculation. In 1904, Gus sold his mining interests for $110,000 which made him one of the richer folks in New Mexico. By 1907, most of the money was gone as a result of the bank panic of the same year. But Gus was never broke, as Conrad said; only bent.

Conrad Hilton's education covered a lot of bases. In 1899 he attended the Gross Military Institute in Albuquerque. The following year he attended the New Mexico Military Institute (NMMI) in Roswell. The year after that he was sent to St. Michael's College in Santa Fe where he made his first communion. After that he spent two additional years at NMMI. Conrad also attended school in Long Beach, California, during the time when Gus was "rich." By 1907, he was back in New Mexico attending the School of Mines in Socorro.

Legend has it, especially among Texans, that Conrad Hilton bought his first hotel in Cisco, Texas, in 1919. It is true that the Mobely Hotel in Cisco was the first one he bought, but it was not his first hotel experience. After the panic of 1907, the Hilton's were on hard times, but only from a cash-flow point of view. They had many other assets, and one of them was their house in San Antonio.

Gus and Mary had observed the practice of adding a room to the house upon the birth of each child. Since some of the children were not living at home, and since the house was not far from the railroad station, it seem logical to rent the rooms to travelers on a daily basis, with home-cooked meals thrown in. Gus re-did the house to meet this need and Conrad and his brother, Carl, met each train, day or night, to steer customers toward what was the very first Hilton Hotel. Revenues from this endeavor put Gus back on a sound economic footing.

By the time he was 21, Conrad was the manager of his father's store. This was not a particularly harmonious relationship. Young Conrad wanted to do try many new things with the business, but his parent, somewhat more conservative in his approach, did not concur. Gus also promised Conrad a partnership in the business, and that seemed slow in coming. Besides, Conrad recognized that the business was his father's, and he wanted something of his own.

The first thing Conrad did to strike out on his own was to run for the new State Legislature in 1912 at the age of 24. The effort did not improve his relationship with his father. Gus thought Conrad should stay home and mind the store. In fact, Gus actually worked for Conrad's opponent. Conrad won anyway, by a vote of 1821 to 1578, and became the youngest member of New Mexico's first legislature.

Conrad introduced several bills, most of which failed. One of them called for a prohibition against movies which depicted crime. Another called for a prohibition against depositing the state's money in what he called fly-by-night banks. Both failed badly. One that passed called for the marking of roadways to better accommodate the growing use of automobiles.

Here is what Hilton said about the first New Mexico State Legislature: "I knew real frustration from red tape and muddling, disgust at under-the-counter deals, and complete futility when I saw good bills, my own and others, defeated through self-interest, laziness or cumbersome procedure." This marked the end of Conrad's political career.

It marked the beginning of Conrad Hilton, banker. He decided to start his own bank with $2,900 of his own money, and set out to find other investors. He did it on horseback. He ranged up and down the Rio Grande Valley, begging, cajoling, and pleading, and by September of 1913 he reached his goal of $30,000. In spite of the fact that he raised the money for the bank's charter, he was not even named an officer in his own bank. The larger shareholders elected a 70-year-old business rival named Allaire.

Conrad entered into a proxy fight using the small stockholders to gain control. The problem was that Allaire started a depositors run on his own bank so that when Conrad won the proxy battle, he had nothing to take over. The bank was broke. Gus saved the day by securing deposits from El Paso and Albuquerque that totaled $6,000. Conrad became vice president and two years later the bank had deposits of $135,000. But World War I was on the horizon. In 1917, Conrad sold the bank and enlisted in the U. S. Army. His career in banking was over.

Conrad served in France until war's end and returned to New Mexico. He didn't stay long. Texas was booming with oil discoveries, and that's where he went. He bought the Mobley Hotel in Cisco in 1919. By the time the Great Depression rolled around in 1929, he owned eight Texas hotels. He almost failed during the early '30s, but managed to hold on.

The rest is business history. Conrad went on to own hotels worldwide but he never forgot his New Mexico roots. His sons, Nick and Barron, attended the New Mexico Military Institute. When Conrad married Zsa Zsa Gabor in 1942, he did it in Santa Fe, although the divorce which followed a couple of years later did not occur in New Mexico.

In 1945, Conrad set up the Conrad Hilton Foundation for the purpose of distributing a portion of his personal profits. One of the first beneficiaries was the Town of Bernalillo, New Mexico. The Catholic Church operated a school in Bernalillo. The teachers were the Sisters of Loretto, one of whom had taught Conrad the catechism. She wrote him the following letter:

"We have started a campaign to build a gymnasium which is badly needed. We have been praying quite hard for the success of the campaign. I thought perhaps you could afford a small donation."

Hilton wrote back:

"Dear Sister:
I received your letter of recent date. I am sure you have been praying extra hard, for your campaign has begun and ended."

Lalo Torres, former mayor of Bernalillo, confirmed that Hilton made a sizable contribution to the construction of the gymnasium. He said that Father Max Valdez was the pastor of the church at the time, and that Valdez was a great sports enthusiast. Torres said that many local folks also contributed to the gym, including his own family. The gym that Hilton helped pay for still stands in Bernalillo, on Camino del Pueblo, just south of Our Lady of Sorrows Church.

Conrad Hilton died in 1979.

DOC HOLLIDAY KILLS ARMY SCOUT MIKE GORDON AT LAS VEGAS: GORDON DRUNK

Dentist John Henry Holliday, better known as "Doc," is usually associated with the Earp Brothers—Wyatt, Virgil, Morgan, Warren and James—and the gunfight at the O.K. Corral in Tombstone, Arizona in 1881. But he'd probably have gained his own measure of fame in the Old West all by himself; in fact he did most of his evil deeds without the help of the Earps. Depending on which source one is prepared to believe, he killed as many as 10 men, wounded several others—with both gun and knife—and participated in the killings of several others. A couple of his shooting scrapes took place in New Mexico. He also supplemented his income by robbing stagecoaches and trains in both New Mexico and Arizona.

Holliday was born in August of 1851 in Griffin, but raised at Valdosta, both in Georgia. Legend holds that he attended dentistry school in Baltimore, Maryland in the late 1860s or early 1870s, but proof of that is lacking.[1] Most likely he learned dentistry by simply observing established dentists at work, a common practice at the time.

Dentistry in the late 19th century was not the science it is today. There were no x-rays, no high-speed drills, no local anesthetics. A dentist's primary tool was a pair of pliers. When a tooth ached, it was simply, and painfully, extracted. An itinerant dentist, who might also have been a barber or operated a medicine show, often became a source of entertainment for the citizens of any frontier community he visited. He might set up his dentist chair in the town square or other public place, and amuse the assembled citizenry with the sufferings of his patients as he ministered to their oral health. There is no evidence that Holliday practiced dentistry in this way, but there is a story about him engaging in a gunfight with one of his own patients in Dallas. The exact nature of the quarrel is not known.

There was never much chance that Doc Holliday would succeed at dentistry. By the early 1870s doctors had diagnosed him with pulmonary tuberculosis and his constant, consumptive cough could not have impressed his patients.[2] By 1875 he had moved west, to Dallas, Texas, in search of a drier climate. He opened a dental practice, but spent most of his time playing poker, dealing three-card monte and drinking copious amounts of whiskey.

In addition to the shoot-out with one of his patients, Doc also engaged in a gunfight with a Dallas saloonkeeper named Austin in 1875. Neither of the "gunfighters" was wounded, but police arrested both and they were fined for disturbing the peace. Throughout the remaining years of the 1870s, Holliday seems to have ranged widely over the American West, from buffalo camps in Texas to mining towns in Dakota's Black Hills to railheads in Kansas and boomtowns in New Mexico.

At Jacksboro, Texas, northwest of Dallas, a soldier apparently caught Doc cheating at cards. In the gunfight that followed, Holliday shot the soldier to death, and wounded two of his friends. He quickly sought safety in the cooler climes of the Dakotas. By the late 1870s, Doc was back in Texas, specifically Fort Griffin, near the present day Abilene. It was there that he met both Wyatt Earp and a woman named Katherine Elder who was also known as Big Nose Kate Fisher and Kate Bender. Kate was a career prostitute and she and Doc became an item.

Holliday must not have been a very good card cheat since he seems to have been caught at it again in Fort Griffin. This time, when Doc's foe went for his gun, the dentist went for his knife and killed his challenger with it. Doc was promptly arrested and jailed. Local folks began to organize a lynch party and the authorities didn't seem much inclined to protect their prisoner. Big Nose Kate came to the rescue. She set fire to a barn and while citizens were busy fighting the blaze, she was able to free Doc.[3] They fled north and shortly appeared in Dodge City, Kansas.

While Mr. & Mrs. J. H. Holliday registered in a Dodge City boarding house, there is no evidence that Doc and Big Nose Kate ever married. Doc hung out a shingle and practiced some dentistry in Dodge, but as usual spent most of his time gambling and drinking in Front Street saloons. Against Doc's wishes, Kate returned to prostitution, servicing the cowboys who arrived with the Texas cattle herds. By 1878 or 1879, Holliday moved on, first to Colorado, and then to Las Vegas, New Mexico. One source says he killed two men and wounded a gambler at Trinidad, Colorado around this time.

Holliday arrived in Las Vegas without Kate, and once again took up the practice of dentistry, and once again it didn't last long. He became a partner in a saloon with a man named Webb.[4] This time the gunfight was not over a card game.

A scout for the Fifth Cavalry named Mike Gordon set out to celebrate the openings of several saloons and gambling halls in East Las Vegas in late July 1879. He'd been drinking for several days, and he attempted to get his former girlfriend to leave the saloon owned by Holliday and Webb. She refused. He threatened to shoot up the place, but initially decided against it. After a while, though, while standing in the street, he fired a shot into the barroom. The bullet passed through the pants leg of a patron. No one seemed bothered by the assault until Gordon fired a second shot into the building. Doc is said to have stepped out the door and fired a single pistol shot that struck Gordon in the chest and emerged just below his shoulder blade.[5] The scout died the next day. The Coroner ruled the death a case of "excusable homicide."

For once Holliday didn't leave town immediately, and it was at about this time that he may well have taken up a new line of work: robbery. There are indications that Doc participated in the robberies of the Santa Fe to Las Vegas stagecoach on August 18 and 30, and of a train in October 1879. He did leave town late that year, or early the next and probably returned, at least briefly, to Dodge City.

He is known to have returned to New Mexico at least once, and that was in June of 1880. Holliday had feud going with a man named Charley White. Some sources believe it dated to earlier days in Dodge City, and others that it was of Las Vegas origin. Whichever it was, Doc learned that White was tending bar in a Las

Vegas Saloon, and as he and Big Nose Kate traveled through town on a train, he stopped long enough to seek out White and attempt murder.

Doc stepped in the door of the saloon and immediately began firing at White. Bar patrons scattered and ducked for cover. White managed to get behind the bar and produce his own gun, with which he opened fire. When the gun smoke cleared, White was down and apparently dead. Holliday, uninjured, calmly re-boarded the train and resumed his trip, presumably to Tombstone. Actually, Charley White was not dead, was not even seriously wounded. A bullet had merely stunned him and he was able to resume his duties a few hours later.

Doc and Kate arrived in Tombstone in 1880. Local authorities soon became convinced that Doc was practicing stagecoach robbery in addition to his activities as gambler and procurer. In fact a saloonkeeper named Mike Joyce flatly accused Doc of robbery. Doc charged into Joyce's saloon, gun blazing. He managed to wound Joyce in the hand and an innocent bystander in the foot.

Sheriff John Behan strongly suspected Doc of taking part in a stage robbery on March 15, 1881 in which the driver and a passenger were killed. Behan's case against Holliday was greatly enhanced when Big Nose Kate, at odds with Doc again, and drunk, gave the sheriff a statement in which she implicated Doc in the robbery. Holliday was arrested and jailed on a murder charge and obliged to post a $5,000 bond (history doesn't record where the bond money came from). The Earp brothers, who controlled the Tombstone Marshal's office, then arrested Kate and locked her in jail until she sobered up and repudiated her statement. Charges against Doc were dropped and Kate left town. This marked the end of the romance between Doc and Kate.

Dismissal of the charges against Doc was news that spread far and wide. The Las Vegas (New Mexico) *Optic*, recalling Holliday's days in town, said, "Doc was always considered a shiftless, bagged-legged character—a killer and professional cutthroat and not a whit too refined to rob stages or even steal sheep."

By the fall of 1881, the feud between the Earp brothers and the so-called cowboy faction was in full fettle. The gunfight at O. K. Corral—which actually took place in a vacant lot next to Camillus Fly's photography laboratory—occurred at about 2:00 p.m. on Wednesday, October 26, 1881. The participants were the McLowery brothers, Ike and Billy Clanton and Billy Claiborne on one side, and Wyatt, Virgil and Morgan Earp, and Doc Holliday on the other. There are as many versions of the gunfight as there are people who tell the story. Witnesses generally agreed that Doc Holliday killed Tom McLowery with a shotgun blast. It is said that McLowery was hit by 12 buckshot. Other fatalities that day were Frank McLowery and Billy Clanton. Ike Clanton and Billy Claiborne fled when the first shots were fired and escaped injury. Virgil Earp received a wound to the leg and Morgan was hit in the neck. Both survived. Doc received a graze to one side and some say that his holster was shot away. Wyatt Earp was uninjured. The entire affair took between 25 and 30 seconds.

A plethora of charges and counter-charges were filed in the days following the duel, but ultimately the Earps and Holliday were cleared of any wrongdoing.

Morgan Earp was murdered on March 18, 1882, at Tombstone. Two days later, Holliday participated in a party of five men who sought out the killers. They found Frank Stillwell in Tucson and shot him some 30 times. Two days later, back in

Tombstone, the same group located Florentio Cruz, better known as Indian Charley, and shot him to death, too.

The Earp gang split up after that to avoid murder charges. Doc and Wyatt went to Colorado. Arizona lawmen attempted to extradite Doc for the murder of Frank Stillwell, but the governor of Colorado declined to approve the request. Doc seems to have spent the remainder of his life in Colorado. One of his last reported shootings was at Leadville in August of 1884, when he shot a bartender named Billy Allen over a five-dollar debt. Allen survived a wound to the arm, and Doc was acquitted at trial. One source says that Doc killed one A. J. Kelly, also in 1884, and was also acquitted of murder.

John Henry "Doc" Holliday entered a sanitarium in Glenwood Springs, Colorado in May of 1887. He died there of tuberculosis on November 8. He is said to have consumed a glass full of whiskey, and said, "This is funny" just before he lapsed into oblivion. He was 36 years old.

---

[1] One source reports that Holliday graduated from the Pennsylvania College of Dental Surgery in 1872.

[2] Some of the actors who have portrayed Holliday in the movies could not have borne even a slight resemblance to the gunman: Victor Mature in *My Darling Clementine* (1946); Kirk Douglas in *Gunfight at the O. K. Corral* (1957); Jason Robards in *Hour of the Gun* (1967); Dennis Quaid in *Wyatt Earp* (1994); to name a few. Holliday stood less than five feet ten inches tall and weighed about 150 pounds. Val Kilmer in *Tombstone* (1993) probably comes closest in appearance. The actor starved himself to appear thin and consumptive.

[3] Some popular legend holds that Wyatt Earp participated in Doc's escape from Fort Griffin, but there is no historical support for it.

[4] One source says Doc's partner was John Joshua Webb, formerly of Dodge City. Another source says it was Jordan L. Webb.

[5] One source says Holliday shot Gordon with a shotgun.

THE LEGEND OF THE HUMMER: A NAVAJO RETURNED SPIRIT

The diminutive Navajo Indian was frequently seen walking on the streets of Cuba, New Mexico. The brown greatcoat he wore was far from new and one of its large pockets often contained a bottle of wine. He never looked down. His head was always back, his face ever looking upward. He was generally alone, as other Navajos would often cross the street to avoid any contact with him. Townspeople did not stop and visit with him, either. The man did not talk at all but chanted unintelligibly and endlessly. That is why he was called "The Hummer."[1]

He never harmed anyone. He was not avoided for that reason. He never insulted anyone, either. He could hardly have done so without talking, and talk he would not. Some said that sometimes, when he'd had too much to drink, he'd recite his U. S. Army serial number. Those numbers were the only words some people ever heard him speak, and most folks never heard that much.

The Hummer's problem—if indeed he had a problem—did not begin with the army, but the end of his military service contributed to the legend that surrounded him. Toward the end of World War II, a government casket arrived in Cuba. Authorities said it contained the remains of the Navajo soldier. It was appropriately interred. One day, some nine months later, the Hummer appeared, alive and well, at his home near the community of Torreon, southwest of Cuba.

No one seemed able to explain his amazing resurrection, but in some way the army acknowledged the mistake and a pension was conferred upon him. His name on a government check educated one Cuba police officer as to who the Hummer really was, but his true name is not important.[2]

If one mix-up by the army concerning the Hummer's death had been the only unusual thing to occur, there would be no legend. Many such mistakes were reported. But a previous return from death had occurred some years before he entered the army.

The Hummer and three other men were riding in an automobile when a wall of water rushed down Torreon Arroyo struck it broadside. The vehicle was swept away and it was assumed that the four men had perished. Some time later, and some distance away, the car was found partly buried in the sand. All windows and doors were closed and locked. The *three* men inside were dead. The Hummer was not one of them. About three weeks later he arrived at home, alive and well. There were those who swore they saw the man in the car when the water hit. The Hummer, of course, never said anything about it.[3]

Because of this incident, the Navajos considered the man a returned spirit.

And there is more. Remember that he harmed no one but he did drink a lot. When he was enough intoxicated to be a danger to himself, the local police would occasionally take him home to Torreon, or hold him in protective custody. The tale is told of the time an officer took him home, a point about 17 miles from Cuba. It was late at night and the officer said he never passed a car, coming or going. And yet the Hummer beat him back to town. The officer swears to it. He saw him back in town with his own eyes.

On another occasion, when the decision was made to hold him in protective custody, he was locked in a cell. As the officer who had locked him up stood talking to another officer, the second officer noticed that the Hummer was standing behind the first officer, saying nothing, doing nothing. Just standing there. The man had freed himself from a locked cell.

But often he didn't bother to free himself and remained peacefully in custody. He always had a cell to himself because no other prisoner was willing to share a room with him. Once while the Hummer was in jail, another prisoner was brought in. He told the officer in charge that he, the prisoner, would be shot before he would enter a cell with the Hummer. He was not forced to do so.

The great fear of him leads to another chapter in the legend. Through an unknown set of circumstances, he was again said to have been riding in a car with three other men. One of the men was so much afraid that he stabbed the Hummer in the upper chest and threw him out of the car. The Hummer wandered around the area, and walked some 200 feet, leaving a heavy trail of blood, before he received attention from some passers by. At the hospital, medical care personnel determined that he had no blood pressure, and his blood loss was great. And yet, the legend maintains, only a few hours later he was back walking the streets of Cuba.

To paraphrase one who was at the hospital, "I don't know if he was declared dead or not, but he should have been. He didn't have any blood left in him."

By the late 1980s, most folks believed him to be in his 70s. That would make him close to 90 at the turn of the century in 2001, if indeed he was still alive. Even a returned spirit, after all, can only return so many times.[4]

As one source said, in a different culture, a different society, the Hummer might have been worshiped as a king or god. As it was, though, he lived on the Navajo Indian Reservation near Cuba, New Mexico.

---

[1] One source, a Cuba resident, said that he'd heard the man utter a few words when he occasionally begged money for wine. He also said he'd seen the man as far away as San Ysidro and Bernalillo

[2] Another source, also a Cuba resident, said he was not aware of any military service by the Hummer, and doubted that he served in World War II. He believed the Navajo to have been in his middle 40s in the late 1980s.

[3] Another version was told by yet another Cuba resident. He said the incident involved the Hummer and another man, both of whom were riding horses when they attempted to cross Torreon Arroyo at flood stage. They were washed away and the other man was killed while the Hummer survived unscathed.

[4] Two additional long-time Cuba residents were sources of the legend. One of them said, "Don't use my name. I don't want to wake up some morning to find the Hummer standing in my front yard." The other, a former Cuba policeman, said the Hummer always made him, and other officers, very nervous.

SHOOT OUT IN CORRALES: LOUIS & LOUISA IMBERT BOTH KILLED

What is today known as Rancho de Corrales was for generations known as the Territorial House or simply as the T-House.[1] It is one of the older structures in the village of Corrales dating back to the early 19th century. History holds that it was constructed between 1801 and 1809[2]. The building was originally a residence.

Ownership of the Territorial House over the years is somewhat uncertain. Official and oral history are incomplete, contradictory and confusing. It seems reasonably certain that the building and 25 to 30 acres around it were purchased by a French grape-grower and wine-maker named Luis Emberto and his wife, Louisa, in the middle 1880s.

Florencio Garcia, a life-long Corrales resident, told the tragic Embertos tale to Robert Gilliland sometime prior to 1975. Mr. Garcia was 88 years old at the time.

In the late 1880s and early 1890s, Luis and Louisa were quite prosperous. They planted an orchard as well as grapes and Mr. Garcia said, "the fruit could not be imitated." The peaches were freestone and as large as a cup. They sold their fruit in Albuquerque. The Embertos were also popular in the Corrales community. They entertained frequently and lavishly and their home was a favorite gathering place for local residents.

But in May of 1893, things changed for them. Their son, Luis Jr., about 10 years old at the time, was playing with a rifle (perhaps a shotgun used to kill snakes) with some other boys in what is now the north end of the dining room. A lady named Dolores (Lola) Griego was busy hanging grapes from ceiling *vigas*. Young Luis Jr. at one point said he was going to kill Mrs. Griego, and then he shot her to death. Mr. Garcia said the matter was investigated, but he failed to mention the outcome except to say that the boys thought the gun was not loaded.

After that, the quality of life for the Embertos seemed to decline. Luis and Louisa frequently fought, waving guns at each other and shouting in French, threatening to kill one another. They both carried guns in holsters. One cause of their battles was a young man named John Mitchell who was rumored to have been Louisa's lover (after all, Louisa was known to have been married once before she married Luis, and divorced women at the time were indeed suspect). Mitchell lived with the Embertos. He also packed a gun.

The matter came to a head on the evening of Saturday, April 30, 1898. Based on Mr. Garcia's narrative, it is difficult to say exactly where the events took place. At one point he indicated that they took place in a nearby residence which Emberto had rented from Manuel Gonzales. At another he indicates the residence of Luis Garcia and at yet a third, the Territorial House itself.

On that evening, Luis told Mr. Garcia's father that he was going to kill Louisa later that same night. The elder Garcia did not believe him, but he did tell Louisa. She didn't believe it, either. In fact, she even took off her own gun and hung it behind a door. But Luis was serious. He showed up later in the evening and when the dogs outside began barking, he shot them (at least shot at them). Upon seeing Luis, Louisa ran for her gun, but she was too late. The two of them struggled and Luis fired three times; two bullets struck Louisa, one in the neck. She bled to death.

Mr. Garcia said it was also believed that Luis intended to kill John Mitchell and another man by the name of Ramon Gutierrez. No mention is made of what grudge he held against Gutierrez, but he failed to kill either man. Mitchell was away attending a dance at the Anesito Armijo house and when Luis went to the Gutierrez house, the family kept him out.

The story is a little vague as to where Luis spent the night after the killing, but clearly he spent it drinking. On Sunday morning he tried to get a horse from Francisco Gonzales, presumably to get away. Gonzales could not, or would not, give him one. Luis then barricaded himself in a nearby house, probably the residence of Luis Garcia.

In the meantime, the local judge was notified of what Luis had done. He ordered that several men post themselves where they could watch Emberto's activity. The judge also ordered that Bernalillo County Sheriff Tom Hubbell[3] be summoned. His instructions were that no one was to shoot at Luis until the sheriff could arrive and give orders to do so.

At one point during the day, Luis came out of hiding and asked one of his watchers, Filiberto Gurule. To have a drink with him, Gurule declined and Luis opened fire on the informal posse. No one was hurt, and no one fired back.[4]

By the time Sheriff Hubbell arrived, about 40 men, all armed, had gathered around. One of them was a Navajo Indian named Jose de la Cruz who was something of a local marksman. De la Cruz was stationed behind a wall with a clear view of the door where Luis showed himself from time to time. By then, too, Luis Emberto was quite drunk.

Hubbell approached the front door and told Luis that he had come for him. Luis said, "Take me if you're such a big man!" Luis opened fire on the sheriff, missing him completely. Hubbell ordered de la Cruz to fire, which the Indian did. His bullet struck Luis in the forehead, killing him instantly.

Mr. Garcia reported that Hubbell then fired a bullet into Emberto's chest. Hubbell later denied it, but claimed that one of his deputies did so.

Thus the matter was concluded. The local priest denied Luis and Louisa burial in the church cemetery and so, according to Mr. Garcia, they were buried about 500 feet behind the Territorial House in unmarked graves.

Luis Emberto, Jr., left Corrales one week after his parents died, for points east. He never returned. Mr. Garcia said he later became a professor at Columbia University in New York.

John Mitchell later married, but what became of him is not known.

Tom Hubbell served as Bernalillo County Sheriff until 1905.

---

[1] For many years prior to 1987, the T-House was own by Robert and Cuca Gilliland. Robert died in 1975 and Cuca sold the establishment in 1987. She retained rights to the name and the new owners, Arturo Jaramillo among them, renamed it.

[2] For a bit of historical perspective, this would have been during the presidential administrations of John Adams and Thomas Jefferson.

[3] Corrales was in Bernalillo County at the time. Sandoval County was not created until 1903.

[4] Gilliland heard another version of the story in which shots were exchanged for two hours before the sheriff arrived.

A NEW ACCOUNT OF THE 1898 CORRALES SHOOTOUT

After the previous story was published in the Rio Rancho *Observer*, Corrales native Rosie Armijo reported that an account of the events she heard from her mother, Roberta Targhetta, generally agreed with Florencio Garcia's recollections. Mrs. Armijo, however, delved further into the matter and found a news account of the killings that appeared in the Albuquerque *Morning Democrat* on May 3, 1898. It is quite a departure from the oral history provided by Mr. Garcia.

Most basic is that the names of the victims was wrong; "Emberto" according to Garcia, "Imbert" according to the news story. Since the murderer left a letter behind, signed "Louis Imbert," that version of the name would seem to be correct. In fairness it should be noted that the interviewer could have made the mistake, and not Mr. Garcia. It is also possible that correct spelling was lost in the translation from French to Spanish to English.

The basic story is that the Imberts, successful orchard farmers, had developed marital problems. Accounts agree that both of them had a weakness for brandy, and that was certainly a part of the problem. The Garcia account alludes to one John Mitchell who resided with the Imberts. The implication was that there was some kind of illicit romantic relationship between Louisa Imbert and Mitchell. The news account reports that John Michel, 22 years old at the time, was in fact Louisa's son, the product of an earlier marriage. Both agree that he was not present at the time of the shooting.

The news account is more detailed concerning the relationship between the Imberts. They were in the process of divorce and had separated. For a time they lived apart only in as much as they lived in opposite ends of the same house. During this period, Louis is alleged to have taken a shot at Louisa, missing her head by inches. She had him arrested, and prosecuted, which resulted in conviction and an 18 month jail sentence. Louis was free on appeal bond when he killed Louisa. He swore he was innocent of the charge of trying to kill her previously, and in the letter he left behind he used that affair as an excuse to murder her.

Throughout the night following the murder, Louis avoided any attempt to capture him, but he remained in Corrales, and holed up in a residence. Sheriff Tom Hubbell was summoned to the scene and arrived, according to the news account, with deputy C. E. Newcomer. The sheriff found another of his deputies, Melquades Martin, already there, along with a number of local residents. Both accounts agree that Hubbell tried to talk to Imbert, and that the Frenchman opened fire. Garcia said the shots missed completely. The news account said one of Imbert's bullets took a button off of Hubbell's coat sleeve.

According to Garcia, a Navajo Indian marksman named Jose de la Cruz was present and when the opportunity presented itself, he shot Imbert in the head, killing him. The news account says that Imbert poked his rifle out the window to take aim at the sheriff and in doing so partly exposed his head, at which time the sheriff and other possemen opened fire, killing Imbert. No mention is made of an Indian marksman. (Mrs. Armijo said the version she heard also told of an Indian man doing the shooting, but one from Sandia Pueblo. She also pointed out that de la Cruz is not a common Navajo or Sandia Pueblo name.)

In any event, the matter was closed. Garcia said that the Catholic Church would not allow the Imberts bodies to be interred in the church cemetery and that they were both buried in unmarked graves on the property, which would mean somewhere behind the present location of the Territorial House. The news account makes no mention of the disposition of the bodies.

The several accounts of this tragic affair illustrate the difficulty in getting things right. There is little doubt that Mr. Garica was sincere in telling his story, but he was a child when the events occurred and elderly when he recalled them. Perceptions can change considerably over the years. It should also not be supposed that the news account was one hundred percent objective. At the time, newspapers were openly partisan and often slanted reports in favor of their pet politicos. The reporter in this case was obviously a fan of Sheriff Hubbell. He wrote this: "Sheriff Hubbell and his deputies cannot be too highly commended for their fearlessness...."

LAS CRUCES DEPUTY JERRELL KILLED BY TEXAS STAGECOACH ROBBERS

An unusual set of circumstances led to the demise of Deputy W. L. Jerrell in February 1884.

On New Year's Eve, 1883, two men dressed in the style of miners dismounted their horses and walked into Barncastle's Store in the town of Doña Ana. They produced pistols and robbed the store of several hundred dollars. (They overlooked a safe that contained somewhere between $1,000 and $5,000.) The robbers tied up storeowner John Barncastle and warned him, upon pain of death, not to stir until they were out of sight.

Barncastle was an important man in Doña Ana County. A posse quickly organized and took up pursuit of the bandits. Barncastle offered an initial reward of $100 for the capture of the thieves. Neither pursuit nor reward resulted in an arrest. By January 26, a local newspaper reported the reward offered at $1,000 and one of the outlaws had been identified as George Hester. A man by the name of Walters had gone after the robbers. (It was agreed that expenses incurred in capturing the outlaws would come out of the reward.) Walters wired back to Las Cruces that he'd traced Hester to Seven Rivers in southeast New Mexico, but that he needed more money to continue the pursuit. H. C. Harding was sent with additional funds and assigned to assist Walters. Word got back to Barncastle that Harding went to El Paso where he pawned a pistol and overcoat the storekeeper had loaned him and gambled away the expense money.

In the meantime, word reached Las Cruces that George Hester rode out of Seven Rivers headed south to Fort Concho, near San Angelo, Texas. W. L. Jerrell, a billiard hall owner, volunteered to go after the outlaw and Doña Ana County Sheriff Guadalupe Ascarate appointed him deputy. By early February, Jerrell had reached San Angelo and apparently met with no success in locating Hester. On the morning of February 5, Jerrell boarded a stagecoach bound for Abilene, Texas. Also aboard the coach was Sgt. L. S. Turnbo of the Frontier Battalion of the Texas Rangers.

A few miles outside San Angelo, the coach met another stagecoach coming from Abilene. Its driver reported that he'd been robbed just a few miles back. The driver of Jerrell's coach elected to continue his run. Jerrell and Turnbo—the only two passengers who were armed—drew their guns and held them at the ready in the event of hold-up. Soon a gunshot was heard and the stage was ordered to stop. Jerrell immediately fired at one of the robbers who shot back. Turnbo also opened fire and a bandit clasped his hands to his stomach and fell to the ground. The horses bolted and the stage raced away from the scene of the robbery as the outlaws fired at the vehicle. Several bullets pierced the coach and two of them hit Jerrell, one in the back and one in the shoulder, breaking his collarbone. The coach returned to San Angelo where Deputy Jerrell died of his wounds later the same day.

The officer was initially buried in San Angelo, but later exhumed and returned to Las Cruces. The city of San Angelo paid all transportation and burial costs for Deputy Jerrell.

History does not record that George Hester was ever captured and prosecuted for the Barncastle robbery; nor does it record that the stage robbers who killed W. L. Jerrell were ever captured and punished.

No account of Deputy Jerrell's death reports his age, although he was described as a young man. He was married and the father of three. His brother-in-law was Jim White, the sheriff of El Paso County, Texas.

Local newspapers described W. L. Jerrell thus: "[He was] a man of nerve and brave as a lion."

———————

NEW MEXICO'S JEWISH MERCHANTS: A PEACEFUL REVOLUTION

Arthur Seligman, Governor (1931-33)
(Photo Courtesy the Albuquerque Museum Photoarchives PA 1978.050.642)

New Mexico and the American West were as much a part of the cultural melting pot as were the large cities of the eastern United States. Popular literature—as well as movies and television—have generally used white, Anglo-Saxon, Protestants generally, as the stereotypical farmers, soldiers and merchants who settled New Mexico and the west in the years after the Mexican War of the late 1840s. But there were many others, from French trappers to Black cowboys, from Mexican farmers to Indian potters, who contributed to the multi-cultural society we enjoy today.

And there was another group that made an enormous contribution to New Mexico and the American West, a group that actually fomented a peaceful revolution in Territorial New Mexico. These were the Jewish pioneer merchants. The revolution they brought about was in the area of business and commerce.

In the years prior to 1821, the economy of New Mexico was primarily agricultural and geared to the limited expectations of citizens under Spanish governance from Mexico City. What stores there were—and they were few—only operated on an irregular basis. Trade goods were only occasionally available to residents because nearly all of them were shipped north from Chihuahua and that was an arduous task. American goods were occasionally available, but they had to be shipped from the east coast of the United States to the east coast of Mexico at Vera Cruz, then hauled overland to Chihuahua, and then finally delivered to the towns in the far north of New Spain.

These shipments were sporadic, time-consuming, and expensive, but the Chihuahua merchants throughout the Spanish period had enough clout, primarily by use of corrupt officials, to maintain their monopoly and keep out trade goods from the United States.

Things began to change with Mexican Independence from Spain and the opening of the Santa Fe Trail in 1821, but really free and competitive trade did not arrive in New Mexico until after the American occupation in 1846. This was true not just because trade barriers came down, but also because of the huge demand for supplies and consumer goods by U. S. Army troops scattered all over the southwest. The local economy, able only to provide basic sustenance, could not meet the demand.[1]

It is perhaps historically coincidental that an economic depression began in Europe in 1836, and it had a profound effect on many Jewish families living in Germany, especially in Baden and Westphalia. Economic prospects for them became extremely limited so they began looking toward America where opportunity was reported to be unlimited.

The German Jews who came to the United States and the southwest in the middle 1800s had several advantages.[2] Most of them were better educated that those who had preceded them. They were often fluent in several languages while most of the English-speaking people were not. Many of them came from families with long experience in commerce and banking. These things, along with innate industry, gave them every opportunity to succeed, and most did. Some did not. Eugene Leitsendorfer, Jacob Houghton and the Goldstine Brothers all failed in the Santa Fe general merchandise business before 1850. Times changed after that.

The way Jewish merchants succeeded is the stuff upon which the old Horatio Alger's boy's books were based. They started out small, often with no more than a "pittance" according to one source. They would convert their limited funds into merchandise that they would then peddle on foot, or horseback, *villa a villa*, farm to farm, ranch to ranch. Once they had acquired sufficient capital, they would select a community and begin a general merchandise operation. Success and expansion would grow from that point. Some became army sutlers and others Indian traders.

The Jewish merchants, like the Spanish people already living in New Mexico, often had extended families. The priorities of these two groups did not really come into conflict. The Jews used their families to expand their commercial interests. Younger members were used as clerks and drummers, often going into business for themselves later. Other family connections were used as sources of credit and merchandise.

The Spanish, on the other hand, were more oriented towards agriculture and the acquisition of lands upon which to raise livestock or to farm. Their large families were often used to that end. The stories of the Perea family of Bernalillo and their vast land holdings are legendary.

Some Jewish merchants raised sheep, but only as a sideline. Some Spanish ranchers also operated businesses, but, again, generally only as a sideline. The two priorities seem to have complimented each other. The early Anglo settlers often did not have the advantage of extended families. By the 1870s, however, the Anglo hierarchy, made of political appointees, was able to form the so-called Santa Fe Ring and steal from the other groups.

When a young Jewish man left his native Germany for the new world, he generally did so with two primary goals in mind: the first was that he succeed in America, and the second that he return to his native land for a wife with whom he would return to the United States. Some did exactly that. Others, however, found that once they returned to Germany, and married, their wives had no interest in living on the frontier. If they returned to the United States at all, and many did not, they remained in the settled and civilized east.

Some young Jewish men gave up entirely on the second of these two goals. It was just not practical for them to return to Germany. In some cases the cost was simply too great. In others, the urgency of business was too important for them to take leave for a year, or more, to go to Europe. In yet others, the men themselves became so much a part of New Mexico society that it was only natural that they marry into it. Many took Spanish Catholic, Indian or Anglo wives and never returned to Germany at all.

Names of some of the early Jewish merchants remain prominent in New Mexico today: Seligman, Ilfeld, Jaffa, Soloman and Bibo, to mention a few. The stories of Nathan and Solomon Bibo are illustrative.

Isak Bibo (1807-1880) and Blumenschen Rosenstein (1822-1875) were married in Prussia in 1843. They had 11 children, eight boys and three girls.[3] All of them came to the United States and spent at least some time in New Mexico. The town of Bibo, located about 12 miles north of Laguna Pueblo in Cibola County, is named for the family. Ben Bibo, a grandson of Isak and Blumenschen, operated a trading post there until around 1920.

The oldest of the Bibo children was Nathan who was born in Westphalia, Germany, in 1844. He came to the United States in 1866 and stayed on the east coast for about a year. He arrived in Santa Fe in 1867 where he joined his brother, Simon, who'd been in New Mexico for about a year. The brothers soon learned that only 21 years after the American Occupation of New Mexico, the business community in Santa Fe was firmly established, and opportunities for them were somewhat limited.

The leading business houses in the Territorial Capital were the Staab Brothers, Elsberg and Amberg, Johnson and Koch, Simon Seligman and the Spiegelberg Brothers. It was with the latter company that Nathan first found employment. It would become a lifetime characteristic that Nathan Bibo could not be happy with long-term commitment to a place. Shortly after Nathan was hired, Willi Spiegelberg was named post trader at Fort Wingate in western New Mexico. Nathan was more than happy to accept a position as manager there on Willi's behalf.

From the Fort Wingate base of operations, Nathan had his first successes, and failures, as merchant, trader and entrepreneur. In 1869 he was named subagent for the Navajo people and charged with conducting a census and the distribution of farming supplies and equipment. Also through contacts made at Fort Wingate, Nathan bid on a supply contract for Fort Apache in eastern Arizona. He was awarded one that required delivery of 100 tons of hay and another that called for delivery of 50 tons of corn.

He met the terms of the corn contract although he was obliged to build a bridge over some swampy ground so that his wagons could pass. It is not recorded as to the profit he made after paying the additional expense, but had he known to ask, the U. S. Army would have built the bridge for him.

Nathan had problems with the hay contract. He subcontracted with two men named Howard and Leonard to deliver the hay. He soon learned that they were indeed delivering hay to Fort Apache, but they were claiming that it was their own and collecting payment for it. Nathan was receiving credit for none of it. To add insult to injury, they were using Nathan's hay-cutting machinery.

Nathan set out for Fort Apache to fulfill the contract himself. It was late in the year, though, and he was caught in an early winter storm that forced him to abandon his oxen, wagons, and equipment. He was rescued by two friendly Apaches and taken on to Fort Apache. While there someone suggested that he might be able to meet the terms of his contract if he made use of Apache labor. He purchased a gross of knives from Albuquerque and gave them to Apache women. They went into the fields and cut hay by hand. Nathan said later that each woman would deliver 60 to 100 pounds of hay to the fort each day, while they "...carried their papooses on top of the hay." They filled his contract.

While at Fort Apache, Nathan became acquainted with Thomas Ewing, the post trader. Ewing suggested that Nathan might be interested in buying a trading post he owned at Cubero, near both the Laguna and Acoma reservations. Nathan borrowed $3,000 and the deal closed in October, 1871. In less than a year he sold out to a man named Cronley and moved on to Bernalillo, just north of Albuquerque.[4]

In Bernalillo, Nathan became friends with Don Francisco Perea, the nephew of Don Jose Leandro Perea, known as the Sheep King of New Mexico. Francisco persuaded Nathan to build a store in the middle of town. To encourage the venture, he sold Nathan a strip of land 120 yards long, next to his vineyards, at a very reasonable rate. The store Bibo built still stands. On the east side of Camino del Pueblo, it is now called the Plaza though for many years it was known as The Mercantile, or simply, The Merc. Nathan also built himself a home, a large stable and the post office.

In 1884, restlessness struck Nathan again. He became convinced that without a railroad terminal, Bernalillo would not grow in any significant way. Also by that year, another of his brothers, Joseph, and a sister, Lina, were living in Bernalillo. Nathan sold out to Joseph, took his considerable resources and moved to California.[5]

He was again successful in the mercantile business in San Francisco, and it was there that he married Flora Abrams by whom he fathered two children, Ruth and Irving.

Irving later wrote that his father was an inveterate gambler who was not above losing as much as $5,000 in one night's poker game. In spite of that, he seems to have done well in California and he retained interests in several ventures in New Mexico. His California period ended after about 20 years with the great San Francisco earthquake and fire of 1906. It wiped him out. That, coupled with his incessant gambling, and, some have said, an eye for the ladies, combined to mark the end of his marriage to Flora. Nathan returned to New Mexico in 1906 or 1907, according to Irving, and spent the remainder of his life looking for gold.

There is a legend that Nathan, after his return to New Mexico, married a "native" woman by whom he had a son who became a multi-millionaire and high-ranking official in the Mexican government. Historian, and Rabbi, Floyd Fierman, says that efforts to prove, or disprove, this story have met with no success.

Nathan died in 1927 at age 83.

Solomon Bibo was the sixth child—the fifth son—of Isak and Blumenchen Bibo. He was born in Bakel, Westphalia, Prussia in 1853. Like his brothers before him, he immigrated to the United States at an early age, leaving Germany in October 1869. He joined his brothers Nathan and Simon in the merchandising business the following year.

Like his brothers, he found business opportunities more to his liking away from the territory's urban centers of Santa Fe and Albuquerque, and like them he gravitated toward west-central New Mexico. By the early 1880s, Solomon was the officially designated Indian trader for the Pueblo of Acoma in what is now Cibola County.

Acoma is located about 56 miles west of Albuquerque and the original village occupies the top of a 357-foot mesa. The name comes from the Keres language: *ako* meaning "white rock" and *ma* meaning "people." Thus, the Acoma are the white rock people. When Coronado arrived in 1540, Acoma was reported to have a population of several thousand.

Early on, the Acomas received the Spanish warmly, but they soon came to resent the newcomers. In the fall of 1598, the Indians set upon a troop of Spaniards and killed ten of them. In retaliation, the Spaniards attacked Acoma the following January. In the battle that followed, several hundred Indians were killed and many others—men, women and children—were captured and marched off to Santa Fe. All were enslaved and legend holds that all men over 25 years of age had one foot cut off.

While animosities between the two groups continued for many years, the Spanish Crown made the Acoma land grant official in 1659. The U. S. confirmed it in 1858. The arrangement was not entirely satisfactory to the Acomas. They believed that land, which should have been theirs, was taken away before the Spanish delineation of boundaries, and then confirmed by the U. S. By the 1880s, some of the land was being used for grazing by the adjacent Laguna Indians, and that caused even more resentment among Acomas.

The Acoma people in the late 19th century had a reputation for being "suspicious, distrustful and unfriendly" to outsiders. This was the atmosphere Solomon Bibo encountered when he arrived at Acoma in the early 1880s.

Solomon was a quick study. For one thing, he had a facility with languages and was soon able to speak Keres the tongue of the Acoma people. This was a great benefit to the Indian people because they had previously not had a representative who could speak their language and English and Spanish as well. Bibo, on behalf of the Pueblo, petitioned the U. S. Government several times requesting a new survey of reservation boundaries. These efforts were not successful.

In 1884, Solomon came up with an idea that he believed would at least protect Acoma from outsiders. He personally leased the entire reservation, 95,791 acres, from the tribe for 30 years. He agreed to prevent others from using the land while the Acoma people were free to continue to use the land as they saw fit. Solomon gained water and grazing rights and agreed to pay the tribe $300 for the first ten years, $400 for the second and $500 for the final ten years.

Indian agent Pedro Sanchez took grave exception to the arrangement. He accused Bibo of flimflamming the Indians. He wrote, "They [the Acomas] will come, eventually, to beg their own bread, and probably, turn out stealing, etc." Sanchez moved to have Solomon's trader's license revoked. He also accused the Acomas of stealing three cows and warned that if they were not returned, the Indians could find themselves in prison.

He held a meeting at McCarty's Station near the reservation, which, he said, was attended by about 60 Acomas. Using a Laguna interpreter he asked the Acomas if they had all agreed to the lease with Bibo. Sanchez reported that all but one of them answered no to the question. He then ordered Bibo to cancel the lease. Solomon refused.

Motives are interesting. Sanchez had previously sided with Laguna Pueblo in the land/boundary dispute. He had also sided with the Marmon Brothers of Laguna who had previously attempted to lease the Acoma reservation for ten years at a rate of one cow per year. Bibo had opposed that deal, arguing that one cow per year was far too little.

In July of 1884, Sanchez succeeded in revoking Bibo's trader's license and ordered him off the reservation. Solomon had no intention of leaving. His version of the McCarty's meeting was a bit different. He said there was no proper interpreter present, and that only about 30 Acomas attended. Sanchez, Bibo said, threatened the Indians with severe punishment if they did not repudiate the lease. Solomon also produced a petition, signed or marked by about 100 Acomas, that supported the lease and demonstrated faith and trust in Bibo.

Then on May1, 1885 Solomon Bibo married Juana Valle, a member of the Acoma Pueblo, in a tribal ceremony.[6] There were, naturally, those outside the reservation who claimed that the marriage was simply a fraudulent effort by Bibo to become a part of the tribe. That the marriage lasted nearly 50 years and produced six children ultimately contradicted that belief.

In late 1885, the Acoma people elected Solomon governor of the Pueblo. Indian agent Sanchez was removed from office. Solomon was reelected to office twice and continued to make use of the provisions of his lease with the Pueblo throughout its term. Solomon's brother, Simon, wrote this: "His [Solomon's] intentions with these Indians are of the best nature and beneficial to them—because the men, women, and children love him as they would love a father and he is in the same manner attached to them."

In 1888, the federal courts cleared Solomon of any wrongdoing whatsoever in his dealings with the Acomas.

In spite of his close ties and strong friendships with the Acoma people, Solomon remained Jewish. His father had been a cantor and Solomon wanted his children to receive Jewish educations. That was not possible in New Mexico at the time. In the late 1880s, Solomon and Juana moved to San Francisco. He retained business interests and partnerships with his brothers in New Mexico throughout his life, and he and his family spent many summer months visiting them and Juana's family at Acoma.

Solomon died in San Francisco in 1934. Juana died there in 1941.

---

[1] It should not be supposed that the Santa Fe Trail trade was the exclusive domain of the so-call Missouri Traders. Many Mexicans, prior to 1846, and Hispanic Americans after, participated in the overland trade, some in a big way.

[2] There were Jews among the much earlier Spanish who settled in both old and New Mexico. They were called *Sephardim*. These were the years of the Spanish Inquisition, 1480-1834. Because of Spain's Edict of Expulsion in 1492, Jews were not allowed, upon pain of death, to practice their religion. Many remained faithful Jews, however, and were tortured or executed for remaining so. Others converted to Catholicism. They came to be called crypto-Jews. They practiced their Judaism secretly.

[3] Floyd Fierman in *Guts and Ruts, The Jewish Pioneer on the Trail in the American Southwest*, says they had ten children, but a genealogical chart in the same book shows eleven. Other sources confirm the latter number.

[4] At some point, other of the Bibo brothers regained control of the Cubero Trading Company. According to Phil Bibo of Grants, they sold it to Sidney Gotlieb sometime after the turn of the century.

[5] Joseph incorporated the business and sold shares of it to the Seligman brothers, Sigfried, Julius, Ernest and Carl, his nephews. When he retired between 1915 and 1920, he sold his remaining shares to them and they took over operations. Thanks to Albuquerque attorney Milton Seligman for this information.

[6] They were married again on August 30 of the same year by a Justice of the Peace.

MA & PA JONES SETTLE SEVEN RIVERS (??)

Seven Rivers, located about 15 miles north of Carlsbad, New Mexico was a community looking for an identity. And now it is looking for a history.

One source claims that cowboys settled the place at the time of the Civil War (1861-65). Another claims the town was established in 1867 when a man named Dick Reed opened a trading post there, and competitor Sam Samson opened a mercantile near-by. Yet another says it was settled by "Ma and Pa Jones" who arrived from Virginia in an ox cart in 1870. It does seem certain that there was a community there by 1870, although the post office was not established until 1877.

The original settlement was called Dogtown because of the prairie dog villages in the area. At some point, probably around 1877, it was renamed Seven Rivers because of the seven streams (arroyos) that drained into the Pecos River. In 1883, the whole town moved about a mile west of the original location and came to be called Henpeck. No source identifies the origin of that name. One source also reports that the place was called Ashland at one time or another, but offers no elaboration. It was also called White City, after a rancher in the area.[1] Finally, though, the place came to be called Seven Rivers, before it disappeared from the face of the earth.

Seven Rivers was a cow town in the classical sense. It was located along the Goodnight-Loving cattle trail, and became an important stop for cowboys tending transient herds bound for the gold camps of Colorado and the grasslands of Wyoming and Montana. The trail itself was named for Charles Goodnight and Oliver Loving [2] who sought to take advantage of cattle prices that were higher in the Rocky Mountain west than they were in Texas. The trail began at Red Fork on the Brazos River in Central Texas, then northeast to the Pecos River and north to Seven Rivers and on to Fort Sumner where it broke into four different trails that continued north to four separate destinations.

The town was also surrounded by large cattle ranching operations. The southern boundary of the famed Chisum Ranch was nearby. By 1875, John Chisum claimed to run 80,000 head of cattle and employ 100 cowboys. Also nearby was the Holt Cattle Company that was much smaller with only about 8,000 head. The Eddy Brothers also ranched in the area.

Seven Rivers was originally located in Lincoln County[3] but played virtually no part in the Lincoln County War (1878-81), but many residents participated. They were mostly outlaws who referred to themselves as the "Seven Rivers Men," the "Banditti" or simply as "the Boys." Led by Jesse Evans, they were fond of stealing cattle, particularly those belonging to John Chisum, and then selling them to L. G.

Murphy, the economic dictator of Lincoln County. When Murphy needed gunmen to do his bidding, he called on Evans and the Boys. Members of this bunch murdered John Tunstall in February 1878.

Isolation made the town ideal for outlaws. There were no other towns around—Eddy, later Carlsbad, was not established until 1888—and it was 125 miles to the county seat at Lincoln. There was no rail or stage service, so if the trip was made, it was done on horseback or by use of horse-drawn conveyance.

A census of Lincoln County communities conducted in 1885 showed that Seven Rivers was home to about 300 people (most of the Boys were dead or in jail by then). There was no church, but predictably enough, several saloons. One of the latter establishments boasted "a door with easy hinges." That is, a door which could be easily removed and used to bear the body of someone too fast with his mouth and too slow with his gun.

The last Seven Rivers town site was flooded by waters of the Pecos when Brantley Dam was constructed in the 1980s.[4] Because of that, the cemetery was exhumed and the remains removed to Twin Oaks Memorial Park north of Artesia. Before being re-interred, the skeletons were studied by forensic experts. Newspaper and court documents were also studied. All of this provides an interesting picture of life in old Seven Rivers.

Here is what one source says about the study:

"Bullet or knife fragments were found in the bodies of ten of fourteen men in the 18 to 45 age group. Two had knives still in place; a third had a knife wound in the head. Although many men may have died with their boots on, none was buried in his boots. In those days, boots were too expensive to waste by burial in a grave."

Among the residents of the graveyard was K. S. Keith who was killed by Indians who then cut off his right leg above the knee. No reason is given for the amputation. John Northern was shot dead in the saloon where he worked. William Johnson was murdered with a shotgun, by his father-in-law, because he mentioned that he had been a Union man during the Civil War.

There were 14 children in the cemetery under the age of two. Their deaths were attributed to scarlet fever, diphtheria, measles, croup and other disorders considered relatively minor today. One family lost four members, grandmother, mother and two children, to dysentery, the result of bad drinking water.

One other point on the complexion of the Seven Rivers area: Texans dominated it. Chism, Goodnight, Loving, and Evans were all Texans. Many Texans of the time had a propensity for unceremoniously taking what they wanted. What they wanted most was land, and it didn't matter that people who had acquired it under Mexican or Spanish rule already owned it. The Texans held that the "Mexicans" were without rights.

So, if you were Anglo, you were allowed to live in Seven Rivers. If you survived infancy, and avoided being shot or stabbed as an adult, you might live 45 or 50 years. There was no place to worship, but plenty of places to drink.

English novelist Anthony Trollope said this about the people he met in the American West: "I found the men gloomy and silent—I might almost say sullen. They drink often and to great excess."

———

[1] This White City should not be confused with the Whites City that is located in southern Eddy County, near Carlsbad Cavern National Park.

[2] Oliver Loving died at Fort Sumner in 1867.

[3] Eddy County was not created until 1889.

[4] The dam was originally built in 1893, but was destroyed by a major flood. Reconstructed in 1906, it was incapable of holding back major floods because of silt buildup. Money for the latest structure was approved by congress in 1972.

TEXAS BANK ROBBERY GANG WRECKS HAVOC IN EASTERN NEW MEXICO: TWO LAW OFFICERS KILLED, HARVE BOLIN & TOM JONES

Ed "Perchmouth" Stanton, a Texas outlaw, he participated in the killing of Lincoln County, New Mexico, Deputy Sheriff Tom Jones in July 1933.
(Photo from author's collection)

Olton is small, dusty high-plains town located in Lamb County, Texas between Plainview and Clovis, New Mexico. At about 11:30 on the morning of July 15, 1932, three men walked into the Olton State Bank with guns drawn. Amid threats of death and violence, one of them forced two bank employees and one customer to lie face down on the floor while the other two looted the place. The robbers attempted to lock their victims in the vault as they left, but they couldn't get the heavy iron door to latch. The bolts were locked open. So, they simply fled. Witnesses said the getaway car, driven by a fourth man, was a Chevrolet sedan with yellow wheels bearing Texas license number 215,265. The thieves took $3,850.54.

This was the era of the so-called social bandits: Clyde Barrow and Bonnie Parker, Charles Arthur "Pretty Boy" Floyd, Wilbur "Tri-State Terror" Underhill, Ma Barker's murderous sons, and others. While none of these famous bandits were suspected of the Olton robbery, the search for the outlaws ranged widely around the Texas Panhandle and eastern New Mexico. For a month, all leads, searches and roadblocks came to naught.

Then on August 17, 1932, two deputy sheriffs, one from Olton and one from Plainview, arrested two men at a farm in rural Hale County, Texas. In their possession officers found tires that had been stolen from a filling station in Tahoka, Texas. Most important, though—and news accounts are not clear as to why it was so—one of the men, Henry Reed, was thought to have information about the Olton robbery, and he did. Reed provided officers with information concerning the whereabouts of the robbers: Lee Pebworth, Jack Sullivan and Glen Hunsucker. On August 19, all four men were indicted for bank robbery by an Olton grand jury.

Sheriff Bob Crim of Lamb County organized a posse made up of himself; one of his deputies, Bob Miller; the Plainview night marshal and part time Hale county deputy sheriff, Harve Bolin; and deputies Jack Howard and R. L. Hollis of Roosevelt County, New Mexico.[1] In the early morning hours of Saturday, August 20, 1932, the posse drove from Portales to Bluitt[2], a small community located between Milnesand, New Mexico and Bledsoe, Texas, in the far-southern part of Roosevelt County. They went to the Pebworth farm and hid, then waited for dawn.

Just after daylight, four men emerged from the farmhouse and walked toward the barn and corral as if to do morning chores. A Clovis newspaper reported what happened then.

> The officers walked into the open ... [and] stepping between the suspects and the farmhouse, the officers ordered, "put up your hands."
>
> Instead of obeying, the bandits reached into feeding troughs near which they were standing, drew 30-30 rifles and opened fire.
>
> The officers were armed only with revolvers.
>
> As the volley began, the bandits dropped behind the troughs for protection, but later barricaded themselves in the barn at one end of the corral.
>
> In the first exchange, Bolin and Hollis fell, Bolin dying instantly. Hollis was shot twice, once through the mouth and once through the hip.
>
> Officers said they believed one of the bandits was seriously wounded.

In the confusion that followed, all of the outlaws escaped from the scene of the gunfight. Sheriff Crim made arrangements for Hollis to receive medical care and by telephone he alerted sheriffs in all directions to be on the lookout for the killers. One man, Joe Jones, was captured at the scene, but he was Pebworth's son-in-law and claimed no part in the affray. He was later cleared of any charges.

Lee Pebworth and a man named Stanley Headrick fled the scene in a 1930 Ford two-door sedan, headed south. By the time they reached a ranch near Tatum, Pebworth was suffering greatly from a bullet wound to the stomach. Headrick left him at the ranch and drove into Tatum to find a doctor. Sheriff Bob Beverely of Lea County, New Mexico arrested Headrick there and Headrick led officers to Pebworth. He surrendered without a fight. His only comment was, "Well, I got the xxxx that got me."

In the aftermath of the gunfight, R. L. Hollis survived his wounds, and so did Pebworth, who was about 60 years old at the time.

On October 5, 1932, rather than go to trial and face the possibility of sitting in New Mexico's brand new electric chair, Pebworth made a plea of guilty to the charge of killing Harve Bolin. His prison sentence was 99 years "FLAT." He was also assessed costs of $3.75.

Headrick claimed that he took no part in the gunfight, and none of the surviving peace officers recalled seeing him with a gun in his hand. Charges against him were eventually dropped.

The other participants in the gunfight were two of Pebworth's bank robbery abettors, Jack Sullivan, 25 and Glen Hunsucker, 19. Efforts to find them were not immediately successful, but Sheriff Crim was committed to running them to ground. Harve Bolin had been a close friend of his. In early September, Crim received a tip that Sullivan might be found in Mountainair, New Mexico. The sheriff took two of his deputies and drove to Estancia, New Mexico where he enlisted the aid of Torrance County Sheriff Ramon Gallegos and Undersheriff J.J. Langham. The five of them drove to Mountainair and took up positions where they could watch the town's Main Street.

On Tuesday morning, September 13, 1932 the officers watched a two-door sedan with a man and woman inside park in front of Bill's pool hall (Bill was probably the local bootlegger). Crim said he recognized the driver as Jack Sullivan, a man he'd seen shooting at him in Bluitt just a month before. The officers also observed a .45 caliber automatic pistol in the door pocket when Sullivan stepped out of the car. The outlaw was only inside for a short time, and when he drove away, he was able to elude the officers before they could detain him. Crim and his posse took up pursuit. They confronted him a couple of blocks away. When ordered to stop, Sullivan accelerated, opened fire with his pistol and sped around a corner. Officers returned fire and hit the car 14 times, but Sullivan still managed to get out of town. The Mountainair town marshal, Thomas Cain, arrested Sullivan five miles from town sometime later. Sullivan had been hit twice in the left thigh, once in the back, near the kidneys, and several times in the right arm; his elbow was nearly shot away. His companion a woman named May Cuban, 19 was hit in the arm and both thighs. She was not believed to have been a part of Sullivan's criminal activities. Her wounds were painful, but not serious.

Sullivan survived his wounds. He was first taken to an Albuquerque hospital, and then transferred to Lubbock where he was held in the local jail on bank robbery charges while doctors tended his arm. The piece of lead bullet they removed from his arm was described as about as big around and as thick as a dime. The operation left his arm immobile and his fingers stiff. It took two months for him to regain limited use of the appendage, but that was enough. On Thursday afternoon, November 18, when the jailer brought the evening meal to the jail's hospital ward, Sullivan slipped behind him, darted out the door, and locking it shut behind him, made an escape into the street. He stole a car at gunpoint and got out of town before a pursuit could be mounted.

Sullivan's picture was widely circulated throughout the southwest, and the pressure was kept on. Officers knew he was born in southwest Oklahoma, and that he'd lived in Vernon, Texas, so they scoured those areas. Officers also believed that the wound Sullivan had received in his right arm in the Mountainair gunfight would cause him trouble so hospitals were regularly watched. For more than a month, no trace of him was found. Then, on December 21, 1932, Sheriff R. L. Rheay of Wilbarger County Texas, near the Oklahoma line, saw a young couple leaving the hospital in Vernon. The sheriff recognized the man as Jack Sullivan. The outlaw made it to his car, but after a fast and furious car chase in the business district of Vernon, the sheriff and his deputy were able arrest him. Officers reported that Sullivan was heavily armed, but he did not resist. With him, again, was May Cuban.

Sullivan was tried at Plainview on a change in venue in late January 1933 on the bank robbery charge. He attempted to mount a defense using witnesses who claimed that he'd been seen in Wolforth, south of Lubbock, on the date of the bank robbery in Olton. His witnesses, however, were all blood relatives, in-laws or friends of the family and their creditability was doubtful. A jury convicted Sullivan and sentenced him to twenty years in prison.

He was tried a second time in late February 1933 for the stealing a car at gunpoint during his escape from the Lubbock County jail. On March 1, 1933, he was given an additional 17-year sentence.

So, of the original four robbers of the Olton bank, three were now accounted for. Henry Reed, while indicted, was never prosecuted for his part in the crime. Lee Pebworth was doing 99 years in the Santa Fe pen for killing Deputy Harve Bolin in New Mexico. Jack Sullivan was doing 37 years in Huntsville, Texas. That left only Glen Hunsucker,[3] and he was likely the worst of the lot.

In his late teens when events reported here transpired, Glen was the son of A. C. Hunsucker, a sometime storekeeper and sometime burglar, and Ida Leon Hunsucker, the operator of a tourist camp at Quitaque, Texas.[4] (Ida may also have been the local bootlegger.) Glen was the oldest of five sons. How he became acquainted with Lee Pebworth and Jack Sullivan is not clear.

After the Olton robbery and the shoot-out at the Pebworth farm, Hunsucker seems to have laid low. Some suspect that he participated in other robberies, but if he did he was successful in avoiding capture or being identified with the crimes. He may have spent his time around Quitaque and Amarillo. His share of the Olton loot— nearly $1,000—would have lasted for quite a while, especially in a 1932 economy when pay for work was often only a dollar per day.

On November 30, 1932, Ed "Perchmouth" Stanton was released from the Huntsville, Texas prison after serving two years for theft. Stanton's home of record was Silverton, Texas, where his brother resided. Stanton had served a part of his sentence with A. C. Hunsucker, Glen's father. Silverton is just 20 miles up the road from Quitaque. Exactly what relationship existed between Stanton and the Hunsuckers is not known, but Glen seems to have spent much of his time with

Perchmouth even though Stanton was twenty years his senior. It is also not clear that Stanton was acquainted with Lee Pebworth or Jack Sullivan even though all four families—Hunsucker, Pebworth, Sullivan and Stanton—had roots in Oklahoma, and all four men were career criminals.

Stanton had served three prison sentences beginning in 1920, two in Texas for theft and one in the Federal Prison at Leavenworth, Kansas, for robbing a post office. He had no intention of changing his ways.

At around midnight on January 22, 1933, a Swisher County deputy sheriff named F. O. Goen caught two men and a woman trying to steal gas from a Happy, Texas, filling station. The thieves managed to escape from the officer, but he notified Sheriff John Moseley in Tulia that they were headed his way. Sheriff Moseley prepared to intercept the Ford coupe. He soon saw the car approaching, and gave chase. The suspects refused to stop, even when the sheriff fired warning shots. At last they pulled into a filling station at the south end of Tulia. The sheriff drove up and ordered the suspects to drive back into town, and he attempted to turn his car around to follow them. Unfortunately, he backed into a bar ditch and the jolt caused him to drop his gun. Thus unarmed and disadvantaged as he attempted to dislodge his car, the two male occupants of the Ford approached the sheriff, firing .45 caliber automatic pistols as they came. Bullets punctured the car; broke the windshield, and finally at least one of them hit the lawman in the head.

Glen Hunsucker then took the time to put fuel in his Ford and rob the filling station of $25 before he and Perchmouth Stanton, along with a young woman named Bernice Inman, drove away, back to Quitaque, leaving Sheriff John Moseley dead behind them.

Less than a week later, a deputy sheriff at Rhome, Texas received word that some subjects in a car had stolen five gallons of gasoline from a cotton hauling truck north of town. Deputy Joe Brown managed to stop the car and escort the occupants to his barbershop—Brown was also the town barber—where he detained them while he called the Wise County sheriff in Decatur. As he used the telephone, Glen Hunsucker pulled his gun and shot the deputy in the back, killing him instantly. The killers again drove away.

Along with Glen and Perchmouth in Rhome at the time of the Brown killing were Ida Hunsucker, Glen's mother, and Doyle Meeks, who worked for Ida. Ida fled along with the killers, but Meeks remained behind and surrendered himself to authorities. He gave officers the names of the killers. Ida dropped off Glen and Perchmouth in Dallas and drove on down to Huntsville Prison to visit her husband. On her return trip to Quitaque, near Childress, Texas, she was taken into custody.

Ida at first denied that she knew the identities of the killers. She claimed that the men, strangers named "Joe" and "Reed," showed up at her tourist camp in Quitaque and demanded that she drive them to Dallas. She asked that her hired man, Meeks, be allowed to accompany them and do the driving. They agreed, she said. After the killing, she claimed that they forced her to drive to a place near Lake Worth where they gave her $3.00 for gas and let her go. She could not maintain the falsehood for long and on January 30, she admitted what she knew and named the killers. Ida was charged with murder and warrants were issued for Glen Hunsucker and Ed "Perchmouth" Stanton[5] for the murder of Joe Brown.

Now the Texas Rangers got involved in the chase, but nothing much came of the effort. Occasional reports on the search for the killers appeared in various newspapers, and the conclusion was always the same. No trace. Trail at a dead-end. No new information. By the end of March, Ida was released from jail on bond. Still nothing.

Then Sheriff Jake Honea of Briscoe County—located between Tulia and Quitaque—noted that John Stanton, Perchmouth's brother, was no longer living near Silverton, the county seat, and he wondered where Stanton had gone. A little investigation revealed that someone named Stanton had taken up a homestead in Lincoln County, New Mexico, near a place called Ramon. Sheriff Honea wondered if Lincoln County Sheriff A. S. McCamant might be willing to look into the possibility. McCamant was indeed interested.

McCamant learned that a man named Will Stanton had taken over a dry-land homestead near Tipton's Well, between Ramon and Cornoa. People in the area reported that strange men seemed to come and go around the Stanton place, and no one knew who they were. A suspicious McCamant had the place watched beginning in May, but it wasn't until Friday, July 14 that he became convinced that his quarry was present. He took a posse of six officers and paid a visit to the place on Saturday but all he found was a woman who claimed that she didn't know where Will Stanton might be found, and she didn't know anything about Perchmouth or Glen.

The officers returned on Sunday. Will Stanton was there but he said he didn't know anything about his brother. Officers searching the area, however, discovered a set of tire tracks that had not been there the day before. This was significant since Will Stanton did not own a car. The chase was on.

The trail led to the west, toward Corona. Sheriff McCamant, his chief deputy, Tom Jones, and possemen Jack Davidson and Hubert Reynolds made up the posse. They followed dirt roads and trails for more than 20 miles. In some places, the car's tracks were easy to see. In other places they had been obscured by other traffic. Finally, the fresh tracks led into an open meadow surrounded by low hills and the car's path through the tall grass was clearly visible. The terrain offered the killers an ideal place for a bushwhacking. The officers spread out as they carefully advanced. Jones was some distance to the right of the sheriff's car, and McCamant was to the left. Davidson and Reynolds were with the car.

"Look out, Jones!" Davidson yelled. "There's a man over there!"

A barrage of shots then poured in and Deputy Jones was hit and went down, killed instantly by a bullet to the head. Hunsucker began advancing on the remaining officers, firing a rifle rapidly as he came, until he fell, riddled with bullets, and dead. Gunfire from the ambuscade stopped then, and the remaining officers advanced on the position that Stanton had held. But Perchmouth was gone. Only his car remained, and it was out of gas.

Deputy Reynolds took the bodies to Corona while McCamant and Davidson stayed in the meadow over night. The next day an enlarged posse scoured the area and soon enough found Stanton, wandering around and lost. He was armed with a

Winchester rifle and a .45 caliber automatic pistol. He did not resist arrest and in a matter of a few days, he was back in Texas.

In September 1933, Stanton was tried for the murder of Sheriff John Moseley. The .45 automatic he carried when he was arrested in New Mexico was the same gun that killed the sheriff. A jury shortly convicted him and sentenced him to death in the electric chair. But that was not the end of the story. During the appeals process, Stanton was housed in the Lubbock County jail, and like Jack Sullivan, Stanton escaped on June 25, 1934. He returned to New Mexico where he managed to hide out for nearly two months. On August 23, Sheriff G. R. "Boots" Fletcher of Colfax County, New Mexico, arrested Perchmouth Stanton for the last time near Therma.[6]

Texas authorities didn't waste any time. Less than five weeks later, on September 28, 1934 Stanton was strapped into a large chair at Huntsville prison and electrocuted. His only regret, he said, was that he wouldn't be able to participate in the prison rodeo a week later.

On March 7, 1935, the state of New Mexico dropped its charges against Stanton for the murder of Lincoln County Deputy Sheriff Tom Jones.

The final score:
On one side, four peace officers shot and killed in two years.
On the other:
Jack Sullivan sentenced to 37 years for robbing the Olton Bank and breaking jail. He was never charged in the killing of Harve Bolin. He actually only served about eight years, being released from Huntsville Prison in 1941.

Lee Pebworth sentenced to 99 years for killing Harve Bolin. He also served only eight years before being released from the New Mexico Penitentiary.

"Perchmouth" Stanton executed for killing Sheriff John Moseley. He was never charged with killing Joe Brown or Tom Jones.

Ida Hunsucker sentenced to two years for accessory to killing of Joe Brown; the only one prosecuted for Brown's murder.

Glen Hunsucker shot to death after killing Deputy Tom Jones.

Henry Reed, free as a bird for turning states evidence.

A sad chapter for two states.

---

[1] Some sources include the District Attorney from Plainview, Mead Griffin, in the posse.

[2] Bluitt was a very small farm and ranch community. In 1927, school enrollment was about 47. The town's post office closed in 1944, and today nothing remains but the cemetery.

[3] This name is variously spelled Hunsacker, Hansacker, Honeysuckle, and others. Hunsucker seems to be correct.

[4] The name of this town is pronounced *Quit-a-quay.*

[5] At various times, Ed Stanton was referred to as John, Henry or Taylor Stanton. He was also called "Parrotmouth" as well as "Perchmouth."

[6] The name of *Therma*, New Mexico, was changed to *Eagle Nest* in 1935.

KIT JOY BANDIT GANG BITES THE DUST: SILVER CITY MERCHANT KILLED

A headline and story in the Albuquerque *Morning Journal* for March 11, 1884 read:

WILL ROB NO MORE

The Whole Gang of Train Robbers Bite the Dust.

Mitch Lee, Kit Joy, Frank Taggart

And Geo. Cleveland Gone Where

The Woodbine Twineth and

The Wicked Cease from

Troubling.

Silver City, N. M., March 10—Four of the train robbers and Carlos Chavez, the murderer and Charles Spencer, the horse thief…broke jail this morning at 9 o'clock. A large posse of our citizens immediately followed them to the foothills of the Pinos Altos range which is some six miles north of town, where they overtook them, and in the desperate fight that ensued one of our most estimable citizens, J. W. Laffer[1] was killed, as was also George W. Cleveland, the negro [sic] train robber, and Carlos Chavez, the murderer of the Chinaman at Fort Bayard, Mitch Lee was wounded and captured and Frank Taggart was also captured. Both of these men were hung one half mile from where they were captured by a party of determined citizens. Kit Joy, another of the train robbers, is still at large. He is the man who murdered Joseph W. Laffer…. A party of three started in pursuit of Joy, and it is believed that he was overtaken and killed as his pursuers are very reticent about the matter. In any event, he is badly wounded and his escape is simply impossible.

"John W. Laffer [sic] was one of our foremost and most enterprising businessmen, esteemed by all who knew him and that he should meet his death at the hands of such a gang seems almost unbearable.

"The negro [sic] Cleveland was captured by Sheriff Whitehill and brought here by Socorro county officers, he is the man who gave the officers a clue by which all the others have been arrested. Taggert is the man captured near St. John, [sic] Arizona, and brought back here via Albuquerque by Sheriff Whitehill and his son. Mitch Lee was taken in the American Valley country not a great while ago while Kit Joy has only been in custody a short time. This is the gang that threw the Southern Pacific train off the track at Deming, and then shot the engineer. This death for the desperadoes is a fitting one and nobody in the Territory will regret the fact that they are gone never to return. There seems to be no doubt, but what Kit Joy has gone beyond."

Christopher "Kit" Joy may have been born in Texas about 1860, but his parents and a sister lived at Hillsboro, New Mexico in the middle 1880s. He is known to have spent some time around Tombstone, Arizona before he arrived in the Silver City, New Mexico area where he worked as a cowboy. One of his employers was none other than Sheriff Harvey Whitehill. One reporter said that Joy rode with Billy the Kid at one time, and while they would have been about the same age, sources consulted do not support the contention.

The train robbery mentioned above took place on November 24, 1883 at Gage, NM, about 15 miles west of Deming. The robbers were Kit Joy, Mitch Lee, Frank Taggart—all cowboys—and George Cleveland. Mitch Lee shot and killed Engineer Theopholus C. Webster after the train was derailed. Investigators located the bandit's camp nearby. The outlaws had fled, but they left behind a recent edition of a California newspaper.[2] The detectives located a Silver City saloonkeeper who hailed from California and subscribed to the paper. While he had no specific recollection of that particular issue, the officers became convinced the robbers were from Silver City.

Further investigation led officers to Frank Taggart, and he was known to associate with the other three men. Whitehill learned that Cleveland was in Socorro, and arrested him in a hotel there. By means of a ruse, he got Cleveland to confirm the identities of his companions. Kit Joy and Mitch Lee were captured by ranchers near Horse Springs, New Mexico in January 1884. Taggart was captured in Apache County, Arizona the same month. All were jailed at Silver City.

And they all escaped on March 10, taking Charlie Spencer and Carlos Chavez with them. One source reports that the posse overtook the outlaws about three miles north of Silver City, and a running gunfight developed from there, which covered some five miles. During this time, Cleveland and Chavez were killed. Some believe that the posse did not kill Cleveland, but that Kit Joy, or one of the other train robbers, did the deed in revenge for Cleveland's cooperation with Sheriff Whitehill. One source, many years after the fact, indicates that the hanging of Frank Taggart was "unjust."

So the tally for the day was one posseman, Joseph Laffer, dead; four outlaws dead, two shot (Chavez and Cleveland) and two hanged (Lee and Taggart); and one escapee (Kit Joy). Only Charlie Spencer was returned to jail that evening.[3] And contrary to the wishful thinking displayed by the writer of the above news item, Kit Joy was not wounded or killed by his pursuers, or soon captured.

Joy managed to get to the Gila River country in northern Grant County where he stole food to survive. A group of local ranchers formed an *ad hoc* posse for the purpose of capturing the outlaw. On the morning of March 21, the searchers spotted Joy. Rancher Erichus "Rackety" Smith opened fire. His second shot took the outlaw in the left leg, just below the knee. The wound required amputation of the limb. Joy was tried at Hillsboro in November 1884 for the murder of railroad engineer, T. C. Webster. Convicted of second-degree murder, he was sentenced to life in prison. He was released some years later and retired to Bisbee, AZ. He was never tried for killing Joseph Laffer.

Harvey Whitehill was one of the better-known peace officers in Territorial New Mexico, but he was not Grant County sheriff when these events took place, even though he did participate in them.[4] He was elected sheriff in 1874 and served until 1882 when he was elected to the territorial legislature. He served a final term as sheriff in 1889-90. He is probably best known for being the first lawman to arrest William H. Bonney, AKA Billy the Kid, for petty thievery, in 1875; but he was involved in many adventures as a peace officer. Sheriff Whitehill died at Deming in 1906 at the age of 69. He was buried at Silver City.

---

[1] Another source identifies this citizen as Joseph N. Lafferr.

[2] A second source claims the newspaper was from Kansas and the subscriber did remember who received the page from him.

[3] Charles Spencer escaped from the New Mexico State Penitentiary in 1885 and was never recaptured.

[4] James B. Woods was Grant County sheriff from 1883 to 1887. Woods was active in capturing the train robbers, but he was visiting in Arkansas when the jailbreak occurred.

FORMER EDDY COUNTY SHERIFF DAVE KEMP KILLS CURRENT SHERIFF LES DOW

James Leslie "Les" Dow, Sheriff, Eddy County, January 1, 1897 to February 18, 1897.
(Photo from author's collection)

The *Pecos Valley Argus* for February 19, 1887 reported the following incident. (Note that the town of Eddy became Carlsbad in 1899.)

SHERIFF J. L. DOW ASSASSINATED

Yesterday evening, about 6:45 p.m., Sheriff J. L. Dow was assassinated on Fox street in Eddy.

He was coming from the bank building, and when almost in front of The Argus office was shot by one of two men who were concealed in the doorway and who had evidently been waiting for him. Two shots were fired, only one taking effect. The ball entered the left corner of the mouth, shattered the jawbone and passed out at the back of the neck.

The pistol was held quite close and his face was severely powder burned. Immediately after the shooting the parties ran past the post office and turned down into the alley.

Mr. Dow staggered across the street ditch, finally sinking down in front of the E. K. restaurant, from where he was carried into Blackmore's drug-store, his wound dressed and later removed to his home.

It was not thought at the time that the wound was fatal, but he only survived till early this morning, dying about 7 o'clock.

While nothing positive has been announced, it is thought the men were recognized by Mr. Dow, and are also known to the officers, and that arrests will follow very soon.

Sheriff James Leslie "Les" Dow, 37, had only replaced Eddy County's second sheriff, J. D. Walker, seven weeks before his death.

Eddy County's first sheriff, elected in 1891, was David Kemp, a killer, rustler and gambler from Hamilton, Texas. Exactly how he came to be elected is open to debate, but suffice it to say that there was a good deal of ballot box stuffing and other Election Day chicanery in those days. Sheriff Kemp, in partnership with one Ed Lyle, operated a saloon, house of prostitution and gambling den in the small community of Phoenix, about a mile south of town, on the Pecos Road. During his term in office, he functioned in the best interests of his outlaw friends and Eddy County became "quite rowdy."

Dow, a former Chaves County deputy sheriff, deputy U. S. Marshal and range detective, had a strong record in support of law and order. It was Dow, in fact, along with famed lawman Ben Williams, who had put the Socorro rustler gang, led by Slick Miller, out of business. Dow and Williams also developed the evidence necessary to indict another bunch of rustlers led by Oliver Lee of Alamogordo.[1]

Some time after Dave Kemp left office, he got into a confrontation with Eddy town constable Dee Harkey, and Harkey threatened to kill Kemp if he didn't leave town, never to return. Kemp agreed and lived up to the terms of his banishment for two or so years, until just after Les Dow took office. Constable Harkey again approached Kemp who said he had a couple of days of business to attend to and then he would leave town peaceably. Harkey was aware that Sheriff Dow was away from town, and not expected back for three days. Harkey told Kemp to tend his business and leave. Les Dow came back to town a day early.

Authorities became quickly convinced that Kemp and a second man, Will Kennon, had killed Sheriff Dow. Harkey even claimed that Kemp admitted the murder to him, but Harkey didn't like Les Dow any better than Kemp did and he helped Kemp avoid a posse led by Dow's Deputy, Bob Armstrong. Harkey arrested Kemp later the same night and held him at his own house rather than the local jail for fear he'd be lynched.

Kemp was later tried at Roswell. Harkey wrote in his autobiography that Kemp paid a man named Bill Smith $50.00 to give perjured testimony. Smith swore the shooting was a matter of self-defense. He testified that Dow called Kemp a "damn son-of-a-bitch" and pulled his gun first. Kemp was acquitted. Harkey also said this:

> Dave Kemp and Les Dow were both considered dangerous men,
> and Les's reputation helped Dave in his defense. After the trial, Dave
> left a note on [Bill] Smith's door to leave the country, and Smith did so.

Dow was born in DeWitt County, Texas, south of San Antonio, in 1860. He became a deputy U. S. Marshal in Texas at a young age and in the middle 1880s was hired by the Southwestern Livestock Association to put a stop to cattle rustling in southern New Mexico and west Texas. Along with his wife, Molly, he moved to Seven Rivers, New Mexico, in 1885. He acquired a ranch in the area, and operated a saloon in Seven Rivers. Les Dow was the father of four sons, two of whom survived to adulthood. Both of them—Hiram and Robert—became lawyers and ranchers in southeastern New Mexico, and their descendants still reside in the area.

---

[1] The indictments of Oliver Lee, Jim Gilliland and Bill McNew on evidence provided by Les Dow and Ben Williams, began a series of events which led to the murders of Prosecutor Albert Jennings Fountain and his son, Henry. Before the matter was concluded, many famous New Mexicans would be involved: Pat Garrett, Albert Bacon Fall, Thomas Catron, and George Curry among them.

DEPUTY KENT KILLED BY HORSE THEIVES NEAR FOLSOM: JAMISON BROTHERS ARRESTED

Among those who care about such things, there has long been a debate concerning the date upon which the "Old" West stopped being wild and woolly. Some argue that the introduction of barbed wire in the middle to late 1870s effectively closed the open ranges and the frontier days ended. Others maintain that the last fight in the so-called Indian Wars, the Battle at Wounded Knee, South Dakota in December, 1890, marked the end and there are those who set the date at the close of the 19th century 1901. The following story illustrates that there were still wild goings-on some years after that date.

A band of horse thieves busily plied their trade in northwestern Union County, New Mexico in the spring of 1909. In one case alone, they stole 28 head from the ranch of John King near Folsom, but many other ranchers suffered losses of riding stock. In early June, Sheriff D. W. Snyder learned that some of the stolen horses had been sold to farmers around Richland in southwestern Kansas, and he immediately sent his deputy, Jim Kent, to Kansas to see what he could find. Kent located and recovered many of the horses and learned that others had been traded for mules and other horses. He picked up a trail in Richland that took him to Trinidad, Colorado. There Kent learned that a man named Clarence Hamilton had sold the mules and horses to a Colorado farmer.

When Hamilton went to a Trinidad bank with the farmer to close the deal and collect, he found Deputy Kent waiting for him. It didn't take long for Hamilton to tell Kent that the Jamison brothers actually stole the animals. The Jamisons maintained a "camp" in eastern Colfax County, near the Union County line, only about five miles from the King ranch.

Sheriff Snyder dispatched Deputies Kent, H. M. Williams and Gay Melon to arrest the Jamison brothers. The posse reached the King ranch on the evening of July 1 and spent the night there. It was still dark the next morning when the posse took the trail to the Jamison place, and the officers took positions of concealment outside the small adobe before daylight. Shortly, one of the Jamisons exited the house to gather kindling and firewood for use in preparing breakfast. Deputy Kent followed him back inside and at gunpoint ordered, "Throw up your hands!" Kent's demand was immediately answered by a gunshot from an adjoining room. Kent, shot in the neck, fell to the floor, mortally wounded. Deputy Williams then approached the door and he too was shot and severely wounded. Deputy Melon hurried away from the scene and back to the King ranch for help. Williams, in great agony from a stomach wound, was able to reach his horse and mount, and he too started for the King ranch. His strength failed him, however, and he collapsed along the road. A posse from Folsom found him there, unconscious from loss of blood.

News accounts of the time reported that the Jamisons stepped over and around Kent's body as they finished preparing and eating breakfast. Then they mounted up rode west, toward Raton, but apparently not in great haste.

Meantime, Melon reached the King ranch, and John King rode to Folsom where he sent a telegram to Sheriff Snyder:

> July 2, 9:00 a.m.
> Sheriff:
>   J. I. Kent killed at Jamison ranch. Take along posse from there overland at once.

Sheriff Snyder and a three-man posse set out from Clayton immediately and by riding hard overtook the killers about midnight at the George ranch, only 20 miles from the scene of the killing. One story is that the Jamisons surrendered themselves to Mr. George, who was a Justice of the Peace. Other accounts are less clear as to what the outlaws were doing at the George place.

The officers and their prisoners began the trip back to Clayton at once, and arrived there at noon the next day. The Sheriff and his posse had covered a distance of more than 200 miles in about 29 hours.[1] The Jamisons were locked in jail, and when another brother, and their father, arrived from Raton to visit them, they were arrested, too. There was talk of lynching, but no effort was made to do so.

Deputy Williams survived a long wagon ride in the hot sun to Folsom where a local doctor dressed his wound. The morning train then took him to Trinidad where the bullet could be removed.

Local newspapers reported that James I. Kent was born in Bartols County, Texas in 1875. Maps contemporary to the times, as well as modern references do not show any such county in Texas.

Kent's obituary said this:

> He was a highly esteemed citizen, doing right by his fellow man for the sake of doing right, a friend to those for whom he professed friendship. His untimely death we greatly deplore and realize that one has been called from our midst whose place in our community will be hard to fill.

Complete details regarding the prosecutions of the Jamison brothers are not known. It is known that George Jamison was convicted of manslaughter for killing Deputy Kent, and sentenced to five years in the Penitentiary.

---

[1] Simple arithmetic reveals that the posse averaged nearly seven miles per hour, which was pretty speedy traveling in those days. A ride of 50 to 60 miles per day on horseback was generally considered a day's work.

WHISKEY & GUNS DON'T MIX; DRUNK COWBOY SHOOTS, KILLS SILVER CITY MARSHAL & CONSTABLE

Five cowboys from the Victorio Land and Cattle Company ranch rode into Silver City, New Mexico on Saturday afternoon, August 27, 1904. Fall roundup was scheduled to begin the following week and there'd be no opportunity to get back to town until the work was done. Drinking in the Club House and Palace Saloons was the order of the day and two of the cowboys, Howard Chenowth[1] and Mart Kennedy far over-did it. At one point during the evening, the two engaged in a loud quarrel along a city street and Victorio ranch foreman Pat Nunn intervened. And before August 27th became August 28th, Chenowth tried to ride his horse into the Palace Saloon, only to be stopped by Nunn and deputy sheriff Elmore Murray.

It was close to two o'clock on the morning of the 28th when Nunn and Murray encountered the two cowboys on the street. One version of the story goes that Chenowth and Kennedy were fighting and Nunn interceded. Another version holds that Nunn simply told the two men to return to the ranch because both were drunk. Chenowth agreed to go and mounted his horse. Kennedy, angered at being ordered to cease his revelry, refused to go. He said he'd quit the Victorio and he took his saddle off the company horse. He called Nunn an "ugly" name. The ranch foreman resented the remark—whatever it was—dismounted his horse, removed his gunbelt and placed it on the curb before he engaged Kennedy in a fistfight.

The fight didn't last long. Nunn was a bigger man, physically, and he was sober. He knocked the cowboy to the ground and stood over him as Chenowth removed Nunn's gun from its holster and announced that he would not allow anyone to harm his friend. Chenowth fired. The first bullet hit Nunn in the chest, exactly were he carried a watch in his shirt pocket. The timepiece was ruined but Nunn was not otherwise injured. The second bullet grazed the foreman's forehead removing both eyebrows.

Deputy Murray struggled to get the gun away from Chenowth. An elderly man named H. A. McGowan tried to help the deputy as Precinct Constable Perfecto Rodriguez approached the scene. He'd been visiting a nearby saloon, heard the shots and ran into the street to learn the cause of the disturbance.

"Get the gun!" He yelled at Murray.

"That is just what I am trying to do," the deputy responded just as Chenowth shot the constable in the chest, knocking him down.

Chenowth broke free and he and Kennedy fled north on Texas Street with Deputy Murray close at hand, still trying to get Nunn's gun away from Chenowth and trying to prevent Kennedy from drawing his own gun. Sources at the time reported that Deputy Murray had been friendly with the two cowboys, which may account for the fact that they didn't shoot him.

Town Marshal William Kilburn, who lived only two blocks away, hurried to the scene and came upon the three men. Murray told Kilburn to get Chenowth's gun, but before the marshal could take any action, Chenowth shot the lawman in the neck rendering him immediately unconscious. The two cowboys broke away again and fled the scene on foot.

A sizable crowd gathered. Constable Rodriguez was found to be dead from his wound and Marshal Kilburn, severely wounded, was removed to Ladies' Hospital. He was not expected to survive. Neither of the lawmen had been armed. Officers and citizens soon developed a plan to search Silver City for the killers. About then, Mart Kennedy walked into the Palace Saloon and ordered a drink. He announced that he'd done nothing wrong and shouldn't be arrested. He was quickly taken into custody. A Justice of the Peace had already issued murder warrants for both of the offending cowboys.

A jailer named Gill and three deputies, Charles Williams, John Burnside and John Collier, escorted Kennedy to jail, keeping a careful lookout for Chenowth. As the party passed Samuel Lindaner's dry goods store, Collier spotted Chenowth hiding behind some boxes on the sidewalk. He said nothing for some distance and then told Burnside. The group shortly encountered a citizen who provided Collier with a shotgun. Unfortunately, it was not loaded and the deputy was obliged to return to the Club House Saloon for ammunition. Then he moved carefully along the street until he stood in front of Lindaner's store, in the middle of the street.

Collier ordered Chenowth to surrender, several times, and Chenowth refused every time. At Burnside's warning, Collier took cover behind a tree in front of the Silver City Mercantile. Collier again ordered Chenowth to give up. Chenowth refused and advanced toward Collier, gun in hand. The cowboy stopped behind a signpost and started to take aim at the deputy, and as he did, Collier fired. Half a load of number 6 birdshot splintered the post and the other half hit Chenowth in the side of the head. It didn't kill him but he went down immediately and was arrested. [2]

Constable Rodriguez, 45, was well known in Grant County and Southern New Mexico as he had been active in politics for many years. He'd previously served as deputy U. S. Marshal in addition to several terms as constable. A wife and six children survived him. The local newspaper said, "...[his] remains were followed to their last resting place by a large number of friends."

Marshal Kilburn, 40, died of his wound a week later. He was born in Missouri but spent most of his adult life in Colorado and New Mexico. Kilburn served as a Grant County deputy under Sheriff Harvey Whitehill[3] before becoming Silver City Town Marshal in 1888. He served until 1891 and was reelected to the post in 1895 and again in 1903. His wife, Emma, was Whitehill's daughter. Kilburn left four children behind. The local paper said this about Marshal William Kilburn: "As a peace officer he was especially gifted. He was absolutely fearless in the discharge of his duties and at the same time exercised such good sense and judgment that even those whom he was compelled to exert his authority upon were his friends."

Howard Chenowth was tried and convicted of the murders of both Marshal Kilburn and Constable Rodriguez. Sentenced to 50 years in prison. He was held in the jail at Silver City pending the outcome of an appeal. On Christmas day, 1905, with he help of several accomplices, said to be family members, he escaped custody. He successfully avoided capture by hiding on his father's ranch in Arizona. Later, he and his brothers traveled to the American Northwest and into Canada. Finally he fled to Brazil. He married there and fathered seven children before his wife died. At that point, he sought a pardon for past crimes, and Governor Richard Dillon granted his request on March 5, 1927. He moved his family back to New Mexico and spent the remainder of his life working on ranches in New Mexico and Arizona. He died in Tucson in 1947 at the age 65.[4]

----

[1] The name is spelled variously as Chinowth, Chenowth, Chinoworth, and others. Historian Bob Alexander as done the most comprehensive research into this case and he spells it Chenowth.

[2] Another version of the story, which appeared in an Albuquerque newspaper, was that Deputy Murray shot Chenowth. The above retelling is based on detailed accounts reported in the Silver City newspapers of the day.

[3] Grant County Sheriff Harvey Whitehill was the first lawman to arrest William Bonney—Billy the Kid—in 1875.

[4] Historian Alexander in *Lawmen, Outlaws, and S. O. Bs.* paints a positive picture of Chenowth in the years after the killings.

JOHN KINNEY: NEW MEXICO'S PREMIER CATTLE RUSTLER

There were several gangs of outlaws that roamed and rustled cattle on the ranges of the Old West. Best known is that of William H. Bonney (Billy the Kid). Others included those led by Oliver Lee, Jim Greathouse, Eli "Slick" Miller, and the Stockton brothers. But by far the largest of them all was led by John P. Kinney. One historian described his gang as the "most dangerous band of rustlers ever to operate in New Mexico."

Kinney was born in Hampshire, Massachusetts in 1847. He enlisted in the U. S. Army's 3rd Cavalry at Chicago, Illinois in 1867 and served until 1873 when he was discharged, as a sergeant, at Ft. McPherson, Kansas.[1] He arrived in the New Mexico's lower Rio Grande Valley, near Mesilla in 1875.

By early 1876, he was already in trouble with the law. He is reported to have participated in shooting up a New Year's Day party at Fort Selden in which two soldiers were killed. No account tells the outcome of this incident, but in November 1877 Kinney was indicted by two Doña Ana Grand Juries, once for assault and once for assault with intent to murder. In June 1878 he was indicted for the murder of Ysabel Barela. He was tried at Silver City acquitted.

In December 1877, he recruited and organized a band of gunmen to go into Texas to assist the Rangers in the so-called Salt War at San Elizario, near El Paso. There exists serious question as to how much he helped. Lt. J. B. Tays, the ranking Ranger, said "Neither myself or my men had anything to do with them [Kinney's people]. I knew a great many of them were bad men [and] they were acting badly." Kinney reportedly killed four "Mexicans" during this involvement.

His gang was reported to have increased in size to 70 men, and he let it be known that he wanted another 30 to join his ranks. Few, if any, outlaws ever commanded so many gunmen, but of course there is no confirmation that these numbers are accurate.

Within six or so months, Kinney arrived in Lincoln County with 16 men and joined the Dolan-Riley faction in the Lincoln County War. He was there, ostensibly, to assist Sheriff George "Dad" Peppin. In an engagement at San Patricio, Kinney participated with 11 men. The reward "Colonel"[2] Kinney and his men anticipated for their participation was the herds of cattle and other plunder to be taken from the other side in the war, namely Alexander McSween and John Tunstall's estate. During the Five Day Battle, the major engagement of the Lincoln County War, Kinney is believed to have participated in the killing of Alex McSween, and afterwards, he and his men broke into and looted Tunstall's Store in Lincoln. He was subsequently indicted for this offense, but never tried.

Frank Angel, an investigator for the U. S. Department of Justice who probed the Lincoln County War said this: "After Kinney and his party have accomplished their mission of murdering McSween and robbing and stealing all they can, they retire and return whence they came."

Back in Mesilla, Kinney operated a butcher shop that was a front for a massive cattle-rustling operation. He was also a bully who kept the community in a state of fear. Here is an account of one of his caprices: "He [Kinney] pistol-whipped his crony, Frank Emmons, in broad daylight in front of the Thorn Hotel. The attack left deep cuts all over Emmons' skull, his face was bruised and blackened in every feature, his lips and ears were slashed open, his jaw broken and several teeth and a piece of jawbone completely knocked out. Kinney had the town so thoroughly intimidated that the sheriff and other local officers did nothing."

But there was one man in southern New Mexico at the time who was not at all intimidated by John Kinney, and that was Major Albert Jennings Fountain. As a military man, attorney and prosecutor, Fountain had been fighting marauding Indians and rustlers for 20 years. By the use of undercover operatives, Fountain learned that Kinney's main base of operations was in Lake Valley, south of Hillsboro, where he maintained a gang of 30 to 40 gunmen/cattle thieves. Kinney had set up a sophisticated system whereby stolen livestock would be relayed from one group of rustlers to another, which made pursuit difficult.

In addition to using stolen stock to provide meat for his own butcher shop, cattle were also in demand in mining camps, by railroad construction crews, and to fill contracts with Indian agencies in the area.

Major Fountain, at the direction of Governor Lionel Sheldon, reorganized the First Regiment, New Mexico Volunteer Militia, and began drilling on weekends. On February 13, 1883 Fountain received arrest warrants and orders from the Governor to "act in every way upon his [Fountain's] best judgment." The chase was on.

Soon four Kinney gang members were arrested north of Las Cruces: Mariano Cubero, Leonardo Maese, Gaspar Montenegro and Juan Bernal. Then in the village of La Mesa, six more were arrested including Doroteo Sains who was believed to be Kinney's number two man.[3] Seven more were captured at Rincon on March 3. In all, about 25 rustlers were arrested, but not Kinney.

But then on March 5, Fountain received word that Kinney was in Silver City and he rushed a courier to Capt. Black of Company F who was able to pick up the outlaw's trail. On March 8, the soldiers surrounded Kinney, his brother, Mike, and his mistress at Ash Springs, just west of the New Mexico line in Arizona. Kinney is reported to have said he would "as soon be sent at once to hell as to be taken to Las Cruces."

Fourteen charges were filed against Kinney and in spite of every trick in the book employed by his attorney, W. T. Thornton,[4] it took a jury just eight minutes to convict him on all counts. Kinney was sentenced to seven years in the federal penitentiary at Leavenworth, Kansas. A. J. Fountain accompanied Kinney to prison, but the term was cut short through legal maneuvering.

Kinney appears to have given up his life of crime after he got out of prison. He moved around the west, dabbling in mining claims and for a time he operated a feedlot in Kingman, Arizona. At last he settled in Prescott and died there of Bright's Disease in 1919. He is reported to have been married once and to have fathered one daughter. One source says, "He died respected by people who did not know his background."

New Mexico was a better place for his departure.

---

[1] One source says that Kinney arrived in New Mexico as a member of the 8th Cavalry and served at several Rio Grande posts. Another says he was discharged at Camp Bowie, Arizona, in 1873.

[2] Kinney was also occasionally called "Captain."

[3] Fountain subsequently killed Sains when the outlaw attempted to escape.

[4] Thornton served as Territorial governor of New Mexico from 1893-1897.

OLIVER LEE OF THE TULAROSA COUNTRY: GOOD GUY OR BAD???

Oliver Milton Lee was certainly as well known in southern New Mexico as William Bonney (Billy the Kid), and he probably killed just as many men, justifiably and otherwise. But Oliver Lee had many friends in high places who aided and protected him in times of trial and tribulation. Among them were Albert Bacon Fall, who became one of the first United States Senators from New Mexico (1912-21) as well as Secretary of the Interior under the Warren G. Harding presidential administration (1921-23) and George Curry who served as Territorial Governor (1907-10) and as the first Congressman (1912-13) from New Mexico.

And Oliver Lee wasn't killed early in life like The Kid. He was 75 years old when he died in 1941.

Oliver Lee was born near Buffalo Gap in central Texas in 1865 or 1866 the son of Mary Hendrick Lee and a man from New York.[1] Young Oliver Lee and his half brother, Perry Altman, first arrived in the Tularosa Valley of south-central New Mexico in 1884. He was so taken with the place that in early 1885, he journeyed back to Texas and returned to New Mexico with his entire clan, hired hands and a heard of cattle. Oliver Lee envisioned a ranching empire in the arid far-reaches of desert west of the Sacramento Mountains and he was not inclined to let anyone get in his way, even those who were there before him.

Many chroniclers of the time felt called upon to emphasize one particular attribute Lee possessed: his ability with a six-gun and rifle. On one occasion he is reported to have ridden his horse around a cedar post at a full gallop, firing his pistol as he rode. All six shots are said to have hit the post. Another tale is that he could hit a half-dollar tossed into the air, without aiming.

The most fantastic tale of Lee's marksmanship is told of a July 4, 1885 shooting competition in which he participated. As the story goes, he handed a young boy a pine board (dimensions unknown) and told him to ride out one mile and plant it firmly in the ground. Lee is said to have hit the board five times out of six with a rifle.

As his life evolved, the chroniclers may have been right. Lee's ability with firearms, and his willingness to use them, may have been his most important characteristic.

A young man named George McDonald had accompanied the Lees from Texas to New Mexico in 1885. In 1888, he became involved in a dispute over some livestock at the spring roundup. A cowboy named Benito Montoya found McDonald's body on June 13 of that year. He'd been shot in the head as he sat beside a water hole near his home. The bullet passed completely through McDonald's head and flattened out when it hit the rock behind him. Oliver Lee retrieved the slug and carried it attached to his watch fob. The killing was attributed to one Walter Good, a member of a family that ranched on land that Oliver Lee coveted.

Searchers found what was left of Walter Good on August 28, 1888. He'd been dead for a couple of weeks, shot in the head with his own gun. A few days later, a coroner's jury concluded that Good had been killed by a group of four men, one of whom was Oliver Lee. Folks at the time believed Lee actually did the shooting because of his close relationship with George McDonald.

Lee went to Las Cruces in December 1888 and surrendered himself and was admitted to a bail bond of $10,000. He returned home. One source says that Albert Fall defended Lee in this matter, while another says that Fall and Lee didn't meet until 1889. Whatever the case, prosecution was delayed a couple of times and in 1889, the venue was changed to Socorro County where the matter disappeared into the limbo of lost legal causes.

John Good, Walter's father, sold his holdings in the Tularosa country not long after Walter was killed, but Oliver Lee didn't get them, at least then. Some years later Lee would control virtually *all* the land between Tularosa and El Paso.

In early 1893, Lee later alleged, some of his cattle which grazed on land near the south end of the Sacramento Mountains turned up missing. He and one of his hired hands, Billy McNew, set out in pursuit of his stock. Along the way they rode into a hunting camp occupied by George and Carl Gaither, father and son of El Paso. They asked the hunters if they'd seen a cattle herd. They had not. Oliver Lee borrowed a .44 caliber rifle from the Gathers, fearing, he said, that he might have to fight. Why he was hunting rustlers without a gun is not explained.

At a point east of El Paso, about where the airport is now, Lee and McNew overtook the herd. Two men, Charles Rhodis and Matt Coffelt were pushing it along. Both were known to Lee and McNew, and both had roots in the Tularosa Valley, and neither were reputed rustlers.

According to Lee, he announced to the men that he would ride into the herd and cut out his own stock. As he did so, Charlie Rhodis took a shot at him. Lee immediately shot and killed Rhodis, at which time Coffelt fired a shot. Lee killed him too.[2]

One source goes so far as to state flatly that Rhodis and Coffelt were not rustlers. Another indicates that the killings were "near-murders." Lee surrendered himself to authorities in El Paso and wired Albert Fall to come to Texas and take over the case. Fall did, and there were no indictments.

Lee returned the .44 caliber rifle to the Gaithers the same afternoon he used it to kill Rhodis and Coffelt.

Oliver Lee established his main ranch just west of the Sacramento Mountains, near the mouth of Dog Canyon.[3] But he was not alone there. A Frenchman by the name of Francois "Frank" Jean Rochas[4] had established a farm, orchard and ranch up in the well-watered canyon. Against all odds, Rochas—who was not surprisingly called Frenchy—had no trouble with the Apache Indians who'd used the canyon for centuries, but he did have problems with the Texans who'd moved in beginning in the 1880s. They were jealous of his control of the water flowing through Dog Canyon and they didn't appreciate him wasting the precious stuff by irrigating apple, peach, pear, and cherry trees. Rochas, a solitary man who developed and maintained no friendships, held on for ten years.

The day after Christmas, 1894, three horsemen rode up to the door of Frenchy's one room stone cabin. No one knows, of course, what the exchange of words between them amounted to, but one of the riders pulled his gun and shot Rochas. The Frenchman made it to his bed and lay down before he died. He was 51 years old. A local cowboy found the body a couple of days later and reported the matter to authorities.

Once again, many folks at the time believed that Oliver Lee was responsible for the murder. It seemed no coincidence that a year before, in November, 1883, Lee had dug a ditch more than a mile long to capture the water flowing out of Dog Canyon. But once again, legal action fell short of justice. The coroner's jury that looked into the matter ruled that Rochas had died of a gunshot wound, but the panel failed to indicate that a human being had fired the gun that caused his death. One observer said this:

> "There was no mourning and no thought of going after the killers. After all, Frenchy had not gone out of his way to make anybody love him, and his relatives were far away."

Rochas farming operations went into disuse and the irrigation system he'd built was dismantled. Lee continued to use the water, and in 1905 he laid claim to all the water flowing out of Dog Canyon.

Frenchy Rochas was not the only burr under Oliver Lee's saddle blanket. Another was a Las Cruces attorney named Albert Jennings Fountain. In March of 1894, a group of about 20 ranchers, including Oliver Lee, created the Southeastern New Mexico Livestock Association. W. C. McDonald, who would become New Mexico's first governor after statehood, was elected president and Albert Fountain was appointed the Association's lawyer. Fountain was assigned the task of eliminating the large rustling operations that troubled ranchers all over south-central New Mexico.

By the end of 1894, Fountain prosecuted and imprisoned about 20 rustlers, most of them members of a loose group known as the Socorro gang. Among them was one Eli "Slick" Miller, sentenced to ten years. Fountain then turned his attention to what was called the Tularosa gang, and that included Oliver Lee and Billy McNew.

Among Fountain's investigators were Ben Williams and Les Dow. Dow uncovered evidence that implicated Lee and McNew in cattle rustling. By late January 1896, Albert Fountain had presented his evidence to a grand jury in Lincoln. Thirty-two indictments against 23 individuals were returned, including Lee and McNew. On January 30, Albert Fountain, traveling with his eight-year-old son, began the trip home to Las Cruces from Lincoln. The two of them were last seen alive on February 1, 1896.

A massive search was undertaken, but no trace of Fountain or his son was found, although their buggy, horses, and many of their possessions were located. One set of tracks that lead away from the area, to the east. A man named Carl Clausen followed them until he reached Oliver Lee's ranch at Wildy Well. Lee was there.

"We are looking for Colonel Fountain and his boy—or their bodies," Clausen said to Lee. "Could you come out and help us?"

"No, I haven't the time. And that ___ is nothing to us," Lee replied.

More than $10,000 in rewards—a huge amount at the time— were offered for recovery of the bodies and arrest of the perpetrators. They were not claimed. The Dona Ana County Sheriff at the time, Guadalupe Ascarate, seemed unwilling or unable to conduct an effective investigation; but it should be noted that he was a political ally of Albert Fall who was the archenemy of Albert Fountain and often represented Oliver Lee. The Stock Growers association hired the Pinkerton Detective Agency to conduct an investigation, and their operative soon concluded that the suspects in the crime were Oliver Lee, Bill McNew and Jim Gilliland. Then, through the good offices of Territorial Governor William Thornton, famed lawman and man-hunter Pat Garrett was brought into the case as Sheriff of Dona Ana County. He, too, was convinced that the killers were Lee, McNew and Gilliland.

The law, at least at this early stage, was not about to give Lee another pass. Albert Fountain was not some obscure cowboy or a hermit foreigner. He was an important man in his time. He'd served in both the Texas and New Mexico legislatures. He'd been an Indian fighter and he'd pursued and prosecuted dozens of outlaws over the years. He also published a newspaper and participated in theatrical productions. There would be much more indeed to the Fountain case, and Oliver Lee's participation in it.

The investigation took many curious twists and turns.

It was rumored that Albert Fall was present at his mine holdings near Gold Camp, about seven miles from the Chalk Hills where the Fountains were last seen alive. Jack Fountain, Albert's son, even publicly accused Fall of planning the murders, and Pinkerton detective J. C. Fraser reported that he was "… not satisfied that he [Fall] was not a party to the conspiracy." Fall, for his part, claimed at one point that Fountain wasn't even dead, and that he would turn up in Cuba. Others among Fountain's detractors agreed that he wasn't dead and reported that he'd been seen alive in Mexico and in Denver, Colorado. The rumor was that he'd run off with a younger woman.

The same Pinkerton Detective interviewed Slick Miller, the Socorro rustler, in his Santa Fe prison cell. Miller described a conspiracy hatched in 1894 that called for the murders of Fountain and Southeast New Mexico Cattle Growers Association president W. C. McDonald. He claimed that Billy McNew and others were assigned the duty of killing Fountain at the Chalk Hills. Fraser reported to Governor W. T. Thorton that he believed "…the entire matter will come home to Oliver Lee, and that McNew…and others are implicated in the matter."

But the wheels of the justice system stopped turning by the autumn of 1896. The Pinkerton agents pulled out and left the matter in the hands of Pat Garrett, but he was busy running for election to sheriff of Dona Ana County. Lee and McNew walked the streets of Las Cruces and Tularosa openly armed and in defiance of anyone who might attempt to molest them.

Governor Thorton resigned in 1897 and acting Governor Loren Miller appointed Albert Fall to the office of Solicitor (Attorney) General. That didn't last long. When Miguel A. Otero was appointed governor later in 1897, one of the first things he did was dismiss Fall. Otero also let it be known that he expected officials in Dona Ana County to do something about the Fountain case.

In early 1898, before any warrant was issued, Oliver Lee and Pat Garrett came unexpectedly face-to-face. Lee, Albert Fall, George Curry, Tobe Tipton and one other man were playing poker in Tipton's saloon in Tularosa. Garrett joined the game. After a few hands, George Curry remarked that he'd heard that someone at the table was about to be indicted in the Fountain case, and that a lawyer who might also be involved was also present. Lee picked up on the remark.

"Mr. Garrett, if you wish to serve any papers on me at any time, I will be around here or out to the ranch" he said.

"All right, Mr. Lee," Garrett politely replied, "if any papers are to be served on you, I will mail them to you, or send them to George Curry here to serve on you."

The next meeting between the two men was not nearly as amiable.

Garrett arrested Billy McNew in early April 1898 and lodged him the Dona Ana County jail without bond. But Garrett didn't seem anxious to go after Lee and Jim Gilliland, who had also been charged in the Fountain case. History does not record that Garrett ever went to the Dog Canyon ranch or to the town of Tularosa.

In early July of that year, two of Garrett's deputies, Clint Llewellyn and Jose Espalin, discovered Lee and Gilliland at the W. W. Cox ranch on the east side of the Organ Mountains. The two officers took no action, but as they rode away, Espalin whispered "*cuidado*" (be careful) to Lee.[5] Garrett promptly mounted a posse made up of Llewellyn, Espalin, Ben Williams and a former schoolteacher named Kent Kearney. They followed the fugitives east across the Tularosa Basin to Lee's Wildey Well ranch and arrived early on the morning of July 13.

Lee's version of events that day is largely undisputed. Garrett and Kearney opened fire first as Lee and Gilliland slept on the roof of the ranch house, and in the return volley, Kearney was struck twice, shot once by each of the fugitives. Lee later said he aimed to kill Garrett, but missed when the sheriff ducked. The fight became a standoff. The posse couldn't move without exposing itself to rifle fire from the roof.

"You got yourself in a hell of a close place," Lee said to Garrett.

"I know it. How are we going to get away from here?" The sheriff asked.

"I don't know," Lee replied and fired several shots through a shed where Garrett had concealed himself.

Lee at last allowed a humiliated Pat Garrett and his posse to withdraw. Kent Kearney was taken to Tularosa for treatment, but died soon afterwards. Lee and Gilliland were subsequently charged with his murder, too.

Lee and Gilliland went into hiding after the fight a Wildey Well. Lee claimed that he was convinced that Garrett meant to kill him before the gunfight, and afterwards he was sure of it. Garrett, for his part, didn't seem to be in a hurry to go after the fugitives. But Lee, of course, had an ally in Albert Fall.

Fall came up with a solution to Lee's problem, and that was to create a new county which would encompass the Chalk Hills, thus taking jurisdiction away from Garrett and giving it to the sheriff of the new county. Through some neat wheeling and dealing, Otero County was carved out of Dona Ana, Socorro and Lincoln counties and came into existence on January 30, 1899. Governor Otero appointed George Curry as the county's first sheriff.

Soon after the new county was created, Lee and Gilliland made arrangements through Sheriff Curry to surrender themselves. On March 13, 1899, they appeared before Judge Frank Parker in Las Cruces. Part of the deal was that the fugitives would not be housed in the Dona Ana County jail, and the brand new Otero County didn't have a jail. Judge Parker ordered Lee and Gilliland confined in the Socorro County jail.

All that remained was the trial.

Judge Frank Parker agreed with attorneys on both sides of the Oliver Lee case that a fair trial could not be held in either Dona Ana or Otero counties. Grant and Socorro counties were considered, but Sierra County actively lobbied for the privilege of holding the trial in its relatively new courthouse (built in 1892). The Sierra *Advocate*, in March of 1899 took Judge Parker to task for failing to hold sessions of court in Hillsboro[6] in the past, and said this: "The very least he can do now is to give us the Oliver Lee trial." So Hillsboro was selected and the trial scheduled for late May. Lee and Gilliland would be tried for the murder of little Henry Fountain.

Hundreds of people poured into the small town and news reporters from all over the west arrived in droves. A telegraph wire was strung 20 miles from Lake Valley so that trial news could be broadcast in a timely way.

This would be no ordinary murder trial and the principals, victim Henry Fountain and defendant Oliver Lee, became almost of secondary importance. The trial was to be a political struggle between two of New Mexico's most powerful factions. Albert B. Fall, the primary defense attorney, was a legislator and leader among the territory's Democrats. Thomas Catron, acting as lead prosecutor, was the leader of New Mexico's Republicans and the famed Santa Fe Ring.

Three other men attended the trial, men whose names have been lost to history. They were cowboys and they sat daily in the same seats in the rear of the courtroom. Each had a gun concealed in his clothing. They also saw to it that a saddled horse was tied up not far from the courthouse and that there were fresh mounts waiting a various points along a route to the Mexican border. It was generally believed that Lee would be acquitted, but if that was not to be, then the resources were available to take him from authorities before any sentence could be executed. Both Lee and Fall claimed to have no knowledge of this plan.

The main plank in the defense platform was that since the body of Henry Fountain could not be found, the prosecution could not prove that murder had been committed. The Territory would be compelled to make a case based on circumstantial evidence.

Catron called former Territorial Governor W. T. Thorton to testify. The governor said that he had received bloody dirt and horsehair from one of the searchers and analysis proved it to be human blood. Fall was able to discredit the testimony of the doctor who tested the blood by casting doubt on the method used.

Sheriff Pat Garrett testified that he'd found a pool of blood in the Chalk Hills, near where the Fountain buckboard was located, and it looked to him as if someone had been killed there. Major H. S. Van Patten of Las Cruces testified that he too had found a pool of blood, and in it some silver coins. This testimony was generally unrefuted. Yes, blood had been found. But where were the bodies?

Jack Maxwell had been Garrett's prime witness and the prosecution put great stock in his testimony. But his memory of events at the Dog Canyon ranch at the time of the Fountain's disappearance seemed vague and contradictory. Maxwell's creditability was further eroded when defense lawyers forced him to admit that he had an agreement with Garrett by which he would be paid $2,000 for evidence to convict Lee. This was not verbal pact. It was a written contract signed by the parties involved, and Garrett was compelled to produce the document and read it to the jury.

The first defense witness was a rancher named Albert Blevin who testified that he had been at the Dog Canyon Ranch with Oliver Lee at the time the Fountains disappeared. Lee's mother testified to same thing. Oliver Lee took the stand in his own behalf. He said that he did not learn of the Fountain's disappearance until several days after it occurred. He also said that when he heard that he was being implicated in the matter, he went to Las Cruces and offered to surrender to authorities who refused to take him into custody. He said that when he learned that a posse was being organized, he believed that its purpose was to kill him rather than take him to trial. He said he "...hurried out of Las Cruces." The prosecution was unable to cast any serious doubt on any of this testimony.

When both sides had rested their cases, Albert Fall faced the jury for his closing statement. "Gentlemen of he jury, the prosecution of Oliver Lee is the result of a conspiracy to send an innocent man to the gallows. The District Attorney is involved in the conspiracy; the Honorable Thomas B. Catron is involved in that conspiracy. His honor on the bench is involved in that conspiracy."   Judge Parker did not take kindly to the accusation. He banged his gavel and said, "Mr. Fall, unless you withdraw your remarks about this court from the jury immediately I shall send you to jail for contempt."

Fall replied, "Your honor will not send me to jail for contempt until I am through addressing this jury. When I finish my argument you may do whatever you wish."

Judge Parker did nothing. He knew that there were many more of Lee's friends in the courtroom than there were of Catron's and the territorial lawyers. He also knew that any effort to silence Fall could have resulted in a blood bath right then and there. Fall concluded his remarks and walked out of the courthouse unmolested.

The jury was out about as long as it took them to elect a foreman and take a vote. They returned in eight minutes with a verdict of not guilty for both Lee and Gilliland. The trial had lasted 18 days. No one else was ever prosecuted in the matter of the disappearance of the Fountains, nor for the killing of posse member Kent Kearney.

There is no record that Lee was involved in any killings after the turn of the century although he was involved in a shooting scrape in 1907 over a fence in Dog

Canyon. There are those, too, who believe that Lee was involved in the murder of Pat Garrett in 1908.

Lee continued to acquire land and in 1914 an El Paso company bought out his Circle Cross ranch for $800,000 with the proviso that Lee continue as general manager of the company. In a matter of few years the Circle Cross controlled all the land between the Mescalero Apache Reservation in New Mexico and Isleta, Texas. The ranch failed a few years later, but Lee survived and continued to live in Alamogordo. He served as director of the Federal Land Bank and was elected to terms in both houses of the New Mexico legislature in the 1920s. He was noted for always packing a gun, even when he sat at his legislative desk.

Lee died in bed, of a stroke, on December 15, 1941. Whether he was a good man, or bad, depends on who you care to believe. George Curry and Albert Fall held him in high esteem. The Fountain family and Pat Garrett certainly had a different opinion.

---

[1] No source provides the first name of Oliver Lee's father. He is identified as a "New Yorker" and a "forty-niner" who was somewhat older that Lee's mother.

[2] Charlie Rhodis had a girlfriend in El Paso. She placed a headstone on his grave. It read:

Charles Rhodis
Died Feb. 12, 1893
Age 33 Years
She stoops and gently plants a flower of sweet perfume
To blossom forth in beauty upon a cowboy's tomb

[3] Oliver Lee Memorial State Park, located about 10 miles south of Alamogordo, is made up of parts of Lee's ranch and Dog Canyon.

[4] Many believe that Rochas was the mysterious stranger who constructed the miraculous staircase inside the Loretto Chapel in Santa Fe in 1873. The stranger is generally described as an old man, but Rochas would have been in his early 30s at the time.

[5] Another source says that Espalin said, "Look out, there are strangers in the country."

[6] Hillsboro was the seat of Sierra County until it was moved to Hot Springs (now Truth or Consequences) in 1938.

SHERIFF KILLED IN TAOS UPRISING: S. L. LEE KILLED AT HIS HOME

On May 13, 1846, the United States declared war on Mexico after Mexican troops crossed the Rio Grande and killed 11 Americans in west Texas. On August 18, 1846, The Army of the West under the command of General Stephen Watts Kearny captured Santa Fe—without firing a shot—and thereby occupied New Mexico for the United States. Committed to a smooth transition from Mexican to American rule, Kearny appointed civil officials to run the new government. Charles Bent of Taos, a trader and the brother-in-law of Kit Carson, was named Governor and Donaciano Vigil of Santa Fe was named Secretary. General Kearny and the main body of his army left Santa Fe for California in late September. Colonel Sterling Price stayed behind with a garrison-sized contingent of troops.

By the late fall of 1846, Col. Price heard rumors of a conspiracy to kill and/or expel all the Americans in four northern New Mexico counties: Santa Fe, Rio Arriba, Taos and San Miguel. He was able to forestall a cabal in Santa Fe on December 21, but major uprisings against Americans occurred at Taos, Rio Colorado and Mora in January 1847. On the 19th, a mob made up of Mexican nationalists and Taos Pueblo Indians attacked the Taos jail and demanded the release of three Taos Indian prisoners held there for theft. Faced with an armed and hostile mob, Sheriff Stephen Lee complied and then fled to his house. The mob chased him there and shot him to death.

Before the day was over, several others were killed: Governor Bent, Circuit Attorney James Leal, Prefect Cornelio Vigil, along with Narciso Beaubien and Pablo Jaramillo who were Taos residents. Josefa Jaramillo Carson, wife of Kit Carson, was present at the Charles Bent home, visiting her sister, Ignaicia, Bent's common law wife, when the attack occurred and Bent was killed. She was not injured. Carson was not in Taos at the time of the uprising.

Seven Americans were also slain at Rio Colorado and two at Arroyo Hondo.

Col. Price, advised of the massacre on January 20, started north on the 23rd with about 350 troops including a detachment of 79 mountain men recruited by Cerán St. Vrain, Charles Bent's business partner. In spite of deep snow and bad weather, the Americans quickly defeated a rebel force of about 1,000 men at La Cañada on January 24 and a force of 700 to 800 at Embudo on January 27. The American troops reached, and surrounded, Taos Pueblo on February 4. The rebels awaited them inside the fortified mission of San Gerónimo. Price ordered the church bombarded with cannon and it was nearly destroyed. When the battle at Taos was over, about 200 rebels were dead, either killed in battle or quickly tried for murder or treason and executed afterwards. About 35 Americans were killed. On February 12, Donaciano Vigil, who became acting civil governor of New Mexico upon the death of Charles Bent, announced a "triumph" over the rebels.

Sheriff Lee, a native of Kentucky, reached New Mexico in 1824 and tried his hand at trapping before he became a trader and merchant based in Taos with interests in both Chihuahua, Mexico, and cities in the United States. Gov. Bent appointed Stephen L. Lee to the office of Taos County sheriff in spite of the fact they were business rivals. The exact date of Lee's appointment is not known, but history records that he was busy collecting taxes by October 1846.

———————

SAM KETCHUM WOUNDED IN WILD GUNFIGHT AT TURKEY CANYON: COLORADO SHERIFF KILLED

Colorado and Southern passenger train Number 1 was on its regular run from Denver to Fort Worth on the evening of July 11, 1899. At about 10:30 p.m. a gang of bandits made up of Sam Ketchum, Harvey Logan and Elza Lay stopped it near two cinder cones called Twin Mountain, about five miles south of Folsum in Union County, New Mexico. Sam Ketchum, about 45 years old at the time, was the older brother of Tom Ketchum who was one of several New Mexico outlaws who used the name "Black Jack." Harvey Logan and Elsa Lay were both regular members of Butch Cassidy's Wild Bunch, but Cassidy did not participate in the Twin Mountain robbery.

The thieves blew the safe in the express car and made their escape without any difficulty. The railroad claimed the thieves got nothing, but other accounts at the time reported that they made off with about $70,000 in cash. The latter assertion is supported by the effort lawmen put into catching the bandits.

W. H. Reno, a special agent for the railroad, accompanied by Sheriff Ed Farr of Huerfano County, Colorado, soon arrived in Cimarron, New Mexico. On Sunday, July 16, officers learned that three men who fit the descriptions of the robbers had been seen entering Turkey Canyon, about eight miles north of Cimarron. Reno and Farr organized a posse that included cowboys Henry N. Love and Perfecto Cordova of Springer, a young fellow named F. H. Smith of New York, who went along for "the fun of it", and several others.

Different sources include different posse members. One source says Deputy U. S. Marshal Wilson Elliott was a part of the posse, and in fact led it. Two other sources fail to list Elliott as a posse member. Two sources list Miguel Lopez and a Captain Thacker as posse members, while a third omits them. One source says the posse was seven strong, another says eight. The first news reports named six possemen. Some reporters seem to confuse the posse that fought in Turkey Canyon with posses that took up pursuit of the bandits after the battle.

At about 5:15 that afternoon, the posse came upon the outlaw camp. Bullets began flying at once. Lay was hit first but remained able to return fire. Ketchum, hit in the arm was put out of action. Unwounded, Logan laid down a withering fire on the lawmen. Sheriff Farr took a bullet in the wrist. He calmly bandaged the wound with his handkerchief and continued the fight. Smith was hit in the calf of his leg and Farr was hit again, this time in the chest. He fell on top of Smith. "I'm done for," the sheriff said, and died. Love was badly wounded in the thigh. Firing died down, then. It was nearly 6:00 p.m. and beginning to rain. Early news reports indicated that one of the bandits had been killed in the fight, but that was in error. The posse remained in Turkey Canyon throughout the rainy night as all three outlaws managed to escape.

There arose a dispute after the battle as to who did what. U. S. Marshal Creighton Foraker claimed that deputy marshal Elliott was in charge at Turkey Canyon. Other reports said that Sheriff Farr had discretionary authority, and W. H. Reno claimed he was personally in charge. The argument got even more acrimonious when Foraker claimed that Reno deserted the posse when the first shots were fired. There were also hard feelings because Sheriff Farr's body remained at Turkey Canyon over night in the rain. Large posses searched the mountains for the outlaws the following day, but an almost continuous downpour hampered them considerably.

Sam Ketchum, his upper arm badly shattered by a bullet, made it to the Ute Creek headquarters of the Lambert ranch, about three miles west of Turkey Canyon. Ketchum told cowboys there he'd been shot in a hunting accident. They had not heard of the gun battle and believed him. A ranch hand in Cimarron for supplies the next day learned of the gunfight and told authorities that a wounded man had appeared at the ranch. W. H. Reno and others arrested Ketchum later that day without incident. Transferred to the Territorial Prison at Santa Fe, Ketchum died of blood poisoning on July 24, 1899.

Logan and Lay rode all night and all the next day putting as much distance between themselves and Turkey Canyon as possible. One source says Logan left Lay with a man named Red Weaver who nursed the outlaw back to health. Another source says Logan paid a young Hispanic family a large sum of money to minister to Lay's wounds. Whichever it was, Lay recovered and joined Logan at the Virgil Lusk Ranch, near Eddy (now Carlsbad), in mid August.

Lusk managed to get word to Eddy County Sheriff Cicero Stewart that the outlaws were at his place. The sheriff and two deputies, J. D. Cantrell and Rufus Thomas, hurried to the ranch. In a brief gunfight, Lusk, Thomas and Lay were all wounded and Lay was captured. Under the name McGinnis, Lay was convicted of second-degree murder and sentenced to life in prison for killing Sheriff Farr. On July 1, 1905, New Mexico Governor Miguel A. Otero commuted the sentence to ten years. Elza Lay was released on January 10, 1906.

Harvey Logan, also known as Kid Curry, was considered the most violent member of the Wild Bunch. He escaped from the gunfight at the Lusk ranch, again unwounded. He was never prosecuted for the murder of Sheriff Farr although he was arrested in Knoxville, Tennessee in 1901. He escaped from jail there and made his way back to the West. Logan committed suicide in July 1903, near Glenwood Springs, Colorado, after a train robbery near Parachute, rather than submit to arrest.

Posseman Henry Love died of his wound on July 20, 1899. The rifle bullet that struck him in the leg drove the blade of his pocketknife into his flesh. Love had used his knife to treat cattle sick with blackleg—a form of anthrax—and the contaminated knife blade infected the cowboy with the disease and caused his death four days later at Springer.

Posseman F. H. Smith recovered from his wound.

Edward Farr was born at Kerrville, Texas and moved first to New Mexico, and then Walsenburg, Colorado, about 1887. He was elected sheriff of Huerfano County in 1898. A special train took his body from Trinidad to Walsenburg for burial on July 20, 1899.

UNARMED ALBUQUERQUE OFFICER ALEX KNAPP
KILLED BY DRUNK PRISONER

On the day New Mexico became the 47th state of the Union, January 6, 1912, Police Officer Alex Knapp and Police Chief Tom McMillan stood talking on First Street in downtown Albuquerque. At about 3:00 o'clock on that Saturday afternoon, a passing citizen told Officer Knapp that a drunk had passed out near the First National Bank at Central Avenue and Fourth Street. By the time Knapp arrived, the man in question was up and walking away. The officer approached and asked the man where he lived, saying that he would escort him home. The man apparently refused to say and Knapp told him he was taking him to jail. The man didn't resist as they walked along, but when the two of them were in front of Goff's Blacksmith shop on Copper Avenue, between Second and Third Streets, the stranger fired a .25 caliber pistol from his overcoat pocket. The bullet struck Officer Knapp in the chest, above the heart, punctured his lung and lodged in the back muscle.

Though severely wounded, Knapp wrestled the man to the ground and choked him into unconsciousness. Help arrived. Bystanders took Knapp to his home on Central Avenue before doctors ordered him removed to St. Joseph's Hospital. Other officers and citizens took Knapp's assailant, initially identified as Fred J. Watson, and still unconscious, to jail. Doctors were obliged to take "heroic" measures to save the man's life. Chief McMillan was anxious to take Watson to the hospital so that Knapp could identify him as the attacker. Officers carried an unconscious Watson to Knapp's hospital room on a litter and held him in a sitting position while Knapp made a positive identification.

Watson regained consciousness later that night at the county jail. He became surly and refused to talk to anyone. Some of the jail personnel believed that he had been faking unconsciousness. They also said he appeared to be a "foreigner."

For more than a week the Albuquerque *Morning Journal* provided medical updates daily. First reports called Knapp's wound "fatal." A day later, after a restful night, hope returned that he might survive. Then recovery seemed likely, baring any setback. But on January 15, Knapp succumbed to pneumonia, brought on by his wound.

Immediately after the shooting, more than a week before, Chief McMillan had began investigating the matter and learned that Fred J. Watson had arrived in Albuquerque from Flagstaff, Arizona, the day before the shooting. He'd spent his time drinking heavily, according to witnesses, in several First Street saloons. McMillan also learned that Watson was in fact Theodore Goulet, 25, an ex-convict from Minnesota who was wanted there for a parole violation. His father, Joseph Goulet, had served as a Minneapolis police officer for about 10 years. Joseph Goulet sent Chief McMillan a check for $150 to be applied to his son's defense. "Judge" William C. Heacock agreed to represent Theodore.[1]

Goulet was charged with first-degree murder for the killing of Officer Knapp.

Watson/Goulet attempted to break jail by using a tin cup as a saw even before Knapp died but was foiled in the effort. On Sunday evening, April 28, 1912, he succeeded in freeing himself. A second killer being held in the Bernalillo County jail, Sam Lyle, had hacksaw blades smuggled into the lockup. Lyle cut the bars in an effort to effect his own escape, but he failed to make the hole large enough to accommodate his great bulk. Goulet, however, smaller in stature, was able to flee. He left Lyle behind.

Goulet was captured two days later as he walked along the railroad tracks south of McIntosh in Torrance County. He did not resist arrest. Goulet was taken to the state penitentiary for safekeeping until his trial.

On September 26, 1912, Goulet went on trial for murder. Judge Heacock claimed that at the time he shot Officer Knapp, he suffered from "mental aberration" brought on by over indulgence in liquor; that he had no memory of firing the shot that took the officer's life. One of the witnesses to the crime who testified at the trial was Will Keleher, then a newspaperman who later became an attorney and the author of numerous books on New Mexico history.

It took the jury only one hour and twenty-five minutes on the evening of September 27 to find Goulet guilty of second-degree murder. His sentence was set at 10 years to life in prison.

Alex Knapp's obituary read:

> Patrolman Knapp had been a member of the Albuquerque police force ten years. His record was a splendid one. He was known for his attentiveness to duty, fearlessness and kindness. He seldom carried a gun and on the day he was shot was unarmed.
>
> The dead officer was about 50 years old. He was born on a farm in Indiana. Early in life, after he had grown to manhood, he was a river man on the Ohio [River]. Later he was engaged in the grocery business in Jeffersonville, Ind. He came to Albuquerque eleven years ago [1901] and a year later became a member of the police force. Mr. Knapp was twice married. His first wife died about a year ago after having been an invalid for almost ten years. The widow who survives is a bride of but a few months.

---

[1] Judge Heacock was a noted gambler who could be found most evenings in one gambling hall or another playing monte.

THE LACKEY—TESSIER MURDERS AND THE DEMISE OF THE SANDIA MOUNTAIN DESPERADO

Buffalo Springs[1] in the Estancia Valley, east across the mountains from Albuquerque, was the scene of an infamous murder in March of 1887. Near there, two elderly immigrants operated a large sheep ranch running as many as 20,000 head of woollies. Joseph Lackey was a native of Ireland and Julian Tessier a native of Switzerland. Both bachelors, they lived quietly and tended their flock and their own business.

In the early spring of 1887, Lackey traveled to Las Vegas to sell a load of wool. He returned home on March 4th and late that afternoon neighbors noticed smoke rising into the clear sky from the direction of Lackey and Tessier's place. No one bothered to check on them until the next day when other ranchers found both men dead. Tessier's bullet-riddled body—he'd been shot in the head, chest and hips—was found a little distance from the cabin, as if he'd been fleeing his attackers. Lackey's charred body, found in the burnt remains of the cabin. He'd been shot in the back. Neighbors reported seeing three or four men riding away from the area.

Albuquerque newspapers reported that Lackey and Tessier were well liked and respected in the Estancia Valley. Neither had a known enemy. Many folks did know, though, that they kept the cash proceeds from their ranching activities in the cabin at Buffalo Springs. It wasn't much of a secret, either, that Lackey returned home with considerable cash from the wool sale in Las Vegas.

According to one newspaper account, Lackey met three men in Las Vegas, one of whom was known to authorities. All of them were present when the rancher sold his wool and received payment. They therefore became suspects.

Also, shortly after Lackey and Tessier were found dead, two ranchers, named Carroll and Metcalf, followed tracks made by the riders seen leaving the scene of the crime. They led north, toward Las Vegas. Carroll and Metcalf lost the trail on the second day, but they continued on to Las Vegas. After prowling the saloons and *cantinas* of the town for a day or so, they identified two men they considered suspects. Santa Fe County Sheriff Francisco Chavez was summoned and he promptly arrested the two: Porfrio Trujillo, described as a "worthless vagabond" and Ricardo Valdez, a coal wagon driver. Trujillo was carrying a brand new revolver and $80.00 in cash. Valdez had $300.00 cash in his pocket.

Sheriff Chavez believed that Trujillo and Valdez were guilty of the crime, but he was also convinced the third killer was Marino Leyba, known as the Sandia Mountain Desperado. Leyba had been released from New Mexico's brand new prison in the summer of 1886 after serving a term for assault on Constable Lorenzo Sanchez of Puerto de Luna in 1881 and horse theft in 1882. And while he was never convicted, many believed Leyba to have been responsible for the murder of Col. Charles Potter in Tijeras Canyon in October 1880.

Also in 1880, at Puerto de Luna, Leyba engaged in a gunfight with famed lawman Pat Garrett before Garrett became sheriff of Lincoln County in January of 1881.[2] Leyba was feared by residents of central New Mexico, Hispanic and Anglo alike. One of his favorite pastimes was riding through villages at a full gallop, shooting chickens as he went. The desperado was described as six feet tall, 180 pounds, with black hair and blue eyes. He wore a sweeping mustache, reddish in color. Historian Marc Simmons described his disposition as "surly."

A reward of $1,200 was offered for Leyba's arrest. In late March 1887, two Santa Fe County sheriff's deputies, Joaquin Montoya and Carlos Jacome, set out in search of the killer. Near Golden on the east side of the Sandia Mountains, they found him. The deputies first saw him riding along a trail in some timber about seven miles south of town. Personally acquainted with Leyba, Jacome rode ahead and engaged the bandit in conversation. Leyba became suspicious when he saw Montoya approaching and he jumped from his horse and stood facing the officers, his hand on his gun.

"What are you doing here?" he said.

"Don't draw your gun," Montoya said. "Give me your right hand. We shall not harm you, but you must consider yourself our prisoner."

Leyba wasn't having any of it. He drew his gun and fired, the bullet grazing Montoya's head and making a hole in his hat. Both deputies drew and fired, and the Sandia Mountain Desperado fell dead in the trail. He had not yet reached his 30th birthday.

Accounts of the Lackey-Tessier murders do not report the fate of Trujillo and Valdez, but New Mexico was well rid of Marino Leyba.

---

[1] The exact location of this particular Buffalo Springs is difficult to determine although one source says it was about 40 miles east of Albuquerque in Santa Fe County. There is a Buffalo Springs near the east end of the Chilili Land Grant in present day Torrance County, but it is not likely the scene of this crime since it is too far south to have been in Santa Fe County. It should also be noted that one source says the Lackey-Tessier ranch was actually near a place called Antelope Springs.

[2] Pat Garrett had captured two escaped prisoners at the Dedrick ranch and was escorting them to jail in Las Vegas when he stopped off in Puerto de Luna. He was accosted there by Leyba who is reported to have said, "No *cabron* like Pat Garrett can take *me*!" whereupon he drew and fired. He missed. Garrett drew and fired, but his first shot missed, too. The lawman's second shot, however, hit Leyba in the shoulder. The outlaw dropped his gun and fled. He was later captured and tried for the attempted murder of Pat Garrett, convicted, and fined $80.

DEPUTY HAWKSHAW LEONARD KILLED IN ROSWELL GUN BATTLE

Barney Leonard, known as "Sarge" and "Hawkshaw," cannot be easily categorized as a lawman. What made him unique was the fact that his left arm was missing below the elbow, the result of military action in Cuba during the Spanish American War in the late 1890s. He arrived in Roswell—employed by the New Mexico Military Institute as a firearms instructor—in 1909 and stayed for the remainder of his life. At various times he served as Roswell police officer—he was the city's first traffic cop, patrolling the streets on a Harley-Davidson motorcycle with a specially rigged handlebar to accommodate his missing left hand—game warden, constable and sheriff's deputy. Acting in the latter capacity cost him his life.

July 1933 was a costly time for the New Mexico sheriffs. A Lincoln County gunfight on July 16 between lawmen and Texas bank robbers took the life of Deputy Sheriff Tom Jones. Outlaw Glenn Hunsucker was also killed. Hunsucker's partner, Ed "Pearchmouth" Stanton escaped and Deputy Leonard rode to the neighboring county to assist in the manhunt. Stanton surrendered to officers near Ramon on Monday the 17th.[1]

Leonard returned to Roswell in time to go to an address on McGaffey Street in the southeast part of town where Sheriff John Peck and Police Chief Frank Young and an eight-man posse had cornered Frank Wallace, an Oklahoma fugitive.

In addition to robbery charges in Oklahoma and Colorado, the Albuquerque Police wanted Wallace for the kidnapping of Officer Jack Craig on the previous Friday, July 14. Wallace left Craig in a hotel room, bought a used car for $35.00 and headed out of town. The Torrance County sheriff reported seeing the car, a Ford Coupe, in Estancia, heading south. On Sunday, the same car was spotted in Roswell, at the residence of one of Wallace's relatives. Officers watched the house, hoping to nab Wallace when he came out. By late Monday afternoon, they had not seen the fugitive, and impatient officers decided to move in.

With the house surrounded, Sheriff Peck ordered all inside to come out, and three women and two children emerged from the back door. The sheriff then ordered Wallace to come out with his hands up. Instead, Wallace opened fire with two .38 caliber revolvers. Barney Leonard was hit as he rushed toward the door. The bullet broke his spine. All other officers opened fire and continued shooting until it was quiet inside the house. Sheriff Peck ordered one of the women, Catherine Faris, back into the house. He told her to bring out the killer, or his guns. She came out with the guns. She said Wallace was dying. Bystanders counted 43 bullet holes in the house and doctors found seven bullet wounds in Wallace, but he was not dead.

"I should have given up," he said to Sheriff Peck.

"I gave you every chance," the sheriff replied.

"It will be over with soon enough." Wallace, 30, didn't utter another word before he died later that evening at St. Mary's Hospital.

Leonard also died later that evening.

Local newspaper headlines declared that, "Sarge Leonard has joined his final posse."

---

[1] Deputy Sheriff William Meador, 21, of Torrance County was also shot and killed in July 1933. He died after a gunfight at Mountainair when he, and other officers attempted to arrest fugitive Jack Layman.

GEORGE LUFKIN DISCOVERS SILVER AT LAKE VALLEY

"Lake Valley is the toughest town I've ever seen. I'm satisfied a man died with his boots on every night."

So said a surveyor named Parker as quoted by old time Hillsboro resident George Meyers.[1] While there is little doubt that Lake Valley was a violent place to live in the late 1870s and 1880s, Parker's assertion is probably a bit exaggerated.

There are a couple versions of the town's origins, but they both agree that George Lufkin made the first silver discovery in the area in 1878. One source says the place was originally named Daly for George Daly who had been killed by Apaches. Another says that Lufkin sold his find to George Daly, a member of a Colorado syndicate, and that marauding Apaches killed Daly in the early 1880s. In any event, the name Daly did not stick and some folks called the place Sierra City. Because there was a small lake nearby, the name Lake Valley was officially adopted when the Post Office was established in 1882.

The silver deposits found in the Lake Valley district were the richest in all of New Mexico. One of the earliest mines was the Sierra Grande, which produced more than $700,000 worth of bullion in six months. The largest of them all was named the Bridal Chamber. So large was it that a railroad spur line was built directly in to the mine to facilitate removal of the ore and to keep production costs low. One source says there was so much exposed silver that one could hold a candle to the wall and it would actually melt.[2] Another source reported that the walls of the grotto were almost pure silver. Three million dollars was extracted from the Bridal Chamber.[3]

There was indeed trouble with the Apaches, Victorio, Nana and Loco in particular. George Daly was killed when the troop of cavalry he accompanied was ambushed by the Apaches. Five others were also killed, including the officer in command of the soldiers. Indians never attacked the town Lake Valley, but several ranches in the area were set upon by the hostiles. One source reported that of the 33 graves at Lake Valley, Indians had killed 28. (Hardly an indication that a man per night was being killed in the community.)

Lake Valley and other towns in the area—Kingston and Hillsboro—also became centers for rustler gangs. Probably the most significant outlaw bunch was led by John Kinney. According to the Santa Fe *New Mexican*, the thieves were "running off oxen of farmers in the Mesilla Valley so they cannot plow and the country is a wasteland." Major Albert Jennings Fountain was charged with putting a stop to the depredations. He implemented a multi pronged attack and soon began arresting rustlers and by March 1883 he had many of them in custody, including John Kinney.

But that was not an end to the problem. Members of the Kinney gang were seen in and around Lake Valley.

Fountain wasted no time in moving his troops from Las Cruces, first to Nutt Station, and then north to Lake Valley. He ordered another company of his troopers, under Francisco Salazar, to head for Kingston. Both companies were successful in rounding up the remaining rustlers before they rendezvoused back at Nutt Station. This effort finally broke the back of the criminal organization.

Just over two years later, in May 1885, Fountain, by then promoted to colonel, was back in Lake Valley. He established regimental headquarters there as troops under his command sought out Apaches, many of them under Geronimo, who had been raiding in the area. One source says this about that effort: "Almost at once, the number of reports of killings and property losses began to drop, and after June 30 no casualties due to Indians raids were reported in the entire protective zone patrolled by his First Regiment."

And while all this was going on, legend holds, efforts were made by townspeople to put a lid on the violence by hiring Timothy Isaiah "Longhaired Jim" Courtright as town marshal.[4] One source says this; "hired as town marshal, [Courtright] engaged several law breakers in gun battles and things began to settle down." The problem is that no other historian reports that Courtright was ever marshal in Lake Valley. He was an ore guard for the American Mining Company, and he did kill a couple of would-be robbers, but that was the extent of his efforts toward law and order. He later murdered two squatters for a rancher, and former Union General, named John Logan. He left New Mexico with the law on his heels.[5]

Courtright is only interesting to western history buffs because on February 8, 1887 he engaged in a gunfight with gambler Luke Short in Fort Worth, Texas and came up wanting. The two guns he habitually carried did not prevent Short from putting three bullet holes in him.

Historians generally agree that at its peak, Lake Valley had a population of 3,000 to 4,000 souls, although one claims only 1,000. Whatever it was, as the silver mines played out, the population dwindled until the place became a classic ghost town. What remains of it today is on private property, but some of the ruins can be observed from State Road 27, about 18 miles south of Hillsboro.

---

[1] This quote is taken from *Ghost Towns of New Mexico, Playthings of the Wind* by Michael Jenkinson with photos by Karl Kernberger. Unfortunately, references are not provided and so the date of the comment is not reported, nor is further information about the surveyor.

[2] Silver melts at 1764° so it is unlikely that a candle would do the job.

[3] A single chunk of silver ore from Lake Valley, valued at $7,000, was displayed at Denver in 1882.

[4] Courtright's hair was really not very long, especially for his times. It did not reach his collar. Wild Bill Hickok's hair was much longer.

[5] Courtright returned to New Mexico a couple of years later, faced trial on the murder charges, and was acquitted.

EDITOR MAGEE SHOOTS JUDGE LEAHY! INNOCENT BYSTANDER KILLED

Carl C. Magee, newspaper editor, he killed a bystander after he was assaulted by a district court judge.
(Photo Courtesy The Albuquerque Museum Photoarchives, PA 1978.050.497)

The newspaper business in New Mexico today is somewhat different than it was 80 or so years ago. In times gone by, papers were often *openly* partisan, *openly* committed one or the other of major political parties. It was also not unusual for editors to attack the leadership of their own parties if the people in charge weren't to their liking.

Carl C. Magee was just such a journalist. Magee arrived in Albuquerque from Oklahoma in 1917 and purchased the *Albuquerque Morning Journal* in 1920. The paper was Republican in its orientation and had the largest circulation in New Mexico at the time. Magee came to dislike some members of the Republican Party leadership and soon took them to task on the pages of the *Journal*.

Specifically, he did not like San Miguel County District Court Judge David Leahy and that county's political boss, Secundino "Sec" Romero. San Miguel County, Magee wrote, is "the worst boss-ridden county in New Mexico. It is the Kingdom of King Sec Romero. [It] has the worst county government in the United States of America." Judge David Leahy, Magee added, "is the political right bower of Sec Romero." Leahy and Romero, in turn, didn't care much for Magee's editorial stance. Judge Leahy said that Magee was a "lying, unamerican [sic], political harlot, fatheaded imbecile, remittance man, dirty cowardly reprobate, wicked, wanton, false, malicious, dishonest, corrupt, unscrupulous, [and] worse than the assassin of President McKinley."

In 1921, Magee was obliged to sell the *Journal*. Some said that was so because Leahy, Romero, and others, convinced Magee's financial backers to withdraw their support. By 1923, Magee was back in the news business as editor of the *New Mexico State Tribune*. He continued his campaign against Leahy and Romero.

Leahy attempted to retaliate by filing libel and criminal contempt charges against the editor. Magee was tried on such charges several times, in Leahy's court, and convicted, only to be pardoned by Governor James Hinkle. Magee said, "[I have] no more chance in Leahy's court than a lamb [has] with a butcher." It was rumored that Leahy had arranged for Magee to be shot and killed, but no attempt is known to have been made on the editor's life.

The Magee/Leahy feud came to a head on August 9, 1925. On that evening, Magee sat in the lobby of the Meadows Hotel in Las Vegas talking with a reporter from the *Las Vegas Optic* and a man named John Patterson. Former Judge Leahy happened to walk past and someone pointed out that Magee was inside. Leahy seemed to have felt that the time was right for him to square matters with the editor. He approached Magee and demanded that he put up his fists and fight. Witnesses reported that Magee's hands remained at his sides when the former jurist began to pummel him about the face. Magee when down under the onslaught and Leahy began kicking him. As the beating continued, Magee pulled a gun—a .25 caliber automatic pistol—from his pocket and fired three times. Two shots struck Leahy in the arm.

The third shot, unfortunately, went astray and struck a young highway engineer named John Lassetter, who died within a matter of a few minutes. Lassetter's involvement in the altercation had been limited to trying to pull Leahy off Magee, along with several other men.

After the shooting, which left Leahy with a broken arm, the judge demanded a gun from any of the bystanders for the avowed purpose of killing Magee right then and there. No one offered him a gun and he left the hotel without any effort being made to stop him. He went to a local doctor's office to have his arm set. Magee was taken to the hospital suffering from injuries to his face and ribs. He was served there with a warrant charging him with first-degree murder in the death of John Lassetter.

By the time the matter went to trial in June of the following year, the charge had been reduced to manslaughter. Leahy testified that he acted as he did because Magee had previously challenged him to fight, man to man. Magee denied it saying that he had only challenged the judge to step down from the bench and become a plaintiff in a suit so that their differences could be considered, man-to-man, by an impartial judge.

Few people in Las Vegas at the time believed that Leahy went into the hotel with the limited intention of thrashing Magee and Magee himself said he only fired when he believed that Leahy was bent on kicking him to death. His statement was buttressed by the fact that Leahy was a large and powerful man. Judge Luis E. Armijo directed a verdict of not guilty. The jury complied and then wrote a letter to Judge Armijo commending him for his decision.

That ended the matter. No one was ever punished for the death of young Mr. Lassetter. Leahy had been voted out of his position on the bench and he returned to the private practice of law. Magee, who had changed his political affiliation from Republican to Democrat, ran for the United States Senate, and lost. Not long after that he returned to Oklahoma where he became editor of the Scripps-Howard newspaper.

There he continued to write his vitriolic editorials, and once again got into trouble. In 1933, the Chief Justice of the Oklahoma Supreme Court threatened to kill Magee for editorial comment. It should be noted however, that Magee gets credit for the motto of the Scripps-Howard Newspapers: "Give Light and The People Will Find Their Own Way."

And aside from his journalistic career, Carl C. Magee has another claim to fame. He is the man who invented parking meters. The first of them were installed in Oklahoma City in 1935. It is said that he made, and lost, a great deal of money with this enterprise. He had sold more than 140,000 of them by 1941.

Seems like Carl Magee was bound and determined to make people mad.

———————

CONSTABLE JUAN MARTINEZ KILLED: THREE OTHERS DIE IN LINCOLN CO. GUNPLAY

Sam, Mart, Merritt, Tom, John and Ben were the Horrell brothers of near Lampasas in central Texas.[1] Some of their neighbors called them "fun-loving cowboys" who regularly shot up the town. They were also the leading members of a group "...whose occupation was the branding, killing and skinning of other people's cattle." On March 14, 1873, in the Matador Saloon in Lampasas, Tom, Mart and Merritt, along with their brother-in-law, Bill Bowen and several other outlaws were confronted by Captain Thomas Williams of the Texas State Police who sought to arrest Bowen. In the gunfight that followed, four State Policemen, including Williams, were killed. Mart Horrell and three other men were later arrested and housed in the jail at Georgetown, Texas, between Austin and Waco. On the night of May 2, 1873 the remaining Horrell brothers, and about 30 other riders, stormed the jail and freed Mart and his friends. After that, the brothers rounded up their cattle, sold them and headed northwest to New Mexico.

The Horrell bunch arrived in Lincoln County in the fall of 1873. They bought a homestead/ranch and settled on the Rio Ruidoso not far from the present day village of Hondo. Other relatives and hangers-on also settled in the area. The county seat at Lincoln was the local hub of activity.

On December 1, Ben Horrell, along with Dave Warner and former Lincoln County Sheriff Jack Gylam rode into the town of Lincoln. Some said they "undertook to run the town." Others said they simply wanted to carouse in the saloons and brothels. Whatever the reason, they were armed and soon enough they were drunk and shooting their guns. Constable Juan Martínez demanded that they surrender their weapons, and they did. It wasn't long, though, before Horrell, Warner and Gylam were again armed and shooting up a brothel. Constable Martínez and four members of the police guard, accompanied by an interpreter, again confronted the miscreants. As the interpreter began to explain the situation to Horrell and his friends, Dave Warner—who had a long-standing grudge against Juan Martínez—suddenly pulled his pistol and shot the constable, killing him instantly. Warner was killed on the spot by return fire and Horrell and Gylam fled, only to be chased down and also killed by the police guard.

The Horrells considered the death of brother Ben as murder, and retaliation was swift. A few days after the gunfight in Lincoln, two prominent Hispanic citizens were found murdered on the Horrell ranch. Efforts by Sheriff Alexander Hamilton "Ham" Mills and a posse to arrest the Horrells failed when they discovered that the

Texans had "forted up" in their house on the Rio Ruidoso. On December 20, the Horrells returned to Lincoln and shot-up a wedding *baile*, killing four Hispanic men and wounding one woman. Again, efforts to capture the Horrells were unsuccessful, and other clashes between the Texans and Hispanic citizens occurred. Toward the end of January 1874, a Horrell outlaw associate, Edward "Little" Hart, murdered Deputy Sheriff Joseph Haskins for no reason other than that Haskins was married to an Hispanic woman.

The Horrells, no longer welcome in southeastern New Mexico, began a retreat in early 1874, heading back to Texas. About 15 miles west of Roswell, they encountered five Hispanic freighters and killed all of them. Estimates are that a total of more than a dozen Hispanic citizens were killed by the gang during the course of the so-called Horrell War of 1873-74.

But Texans were no longer hospitable to the clan, either. Citizens of Lampasas took pot shots at them when they returned to town, but none of the Horrells were killed. By 1876, the Horrell brothers were engaged in a feud with cattleman/gunman John Pinkney Calhoun "Pink" Higgins. Higgins shot Merritt Horrell to death in the Matador Saloon that year. In 1878, Mart and Tom Horrell were arrested for robbing and killing merchant J. F. Vaughn at a place called Rock School House on Hog Creek in Bosque County. A mob of masked citizens, estimated at 100 strong, stormed the jail at Merridian and killed both outlaws in their cell on December 15, 1878. Only Sam Horrell, the oldest of the brothers, managed to avoid a violent death. It is reported that he returned to New Mexico in 1880 and died peacefully at an unknown place, on an unknown date.

History records nothing of a personal nature about Constable Juan Martínez. One writer refers to his "hardihood" in taking the initiative to disarm the drunken gunmen. Given the character of the times, there is no question that he showed considerable devotion to duty.

---

[1] John Horrell was killed in a gunfight in Las Cruces, New Mexico, before the events described here. The family name is also spelled *Harrell* or *Harrold*, depending on the source.

MYSTERIOUS DAVE MATHER: KILLS ONE, WOUNDS TWO, IN SALOON SHOOTING

Many western history buffs consider Mysterious Dave Mather one of the most enigmatic characters in the history of the Old West. Within the context of the times it was rather easy for him to foster a shadowy image by reticence and even deceit. He was, after all, as much a con man as a gun hand. Most western history writers have something to say about Mather, and with some exceptions, they generally agree about his exploits. In his own time, lawmen in Arkansas, Texas, Kansas and New Mexico knew him all too well. The only real mystery about Mather has to do with what became of him.

Dave is said to have been a direct descendent of the 17th and 18th century Puritan preachers Increase (1639-1723) and Cotton (1663-1728) Mather. One source says he was actually descended from Timothy Mather, Cotton's uncle. This source reports that Mysterious Dave—David Allen Mather—was born in Connecticut on August 10, 1851 to Ulysses W. Mather and the former Lydia E. Wright.[1] His brother, Josiah "Cy", was born in October 1854. A third brother lived less than a year.

In 1868, "Davey" and Cy ran away to sea, but that didn't last long. They both jumped ship in New Orleans in 1870 and went their separate ways. No one seems to know exactly what happened in the interim, but "New York" Dave—as he was called early on—was involved in cattle rustling with two other men in Arkansas, in 1873: Dave Rudabaugh and Milt Yarberry.[2] Lawmen chased all three of them to Texas for thievery and alleged participation in a murder in Sharps County. For a short time, it appears that Dave Mather hunted buffalo on the plains of West Texas.

He appeared in Dodge City some time in 1874 and was soon involved in an altercation with a gambler that left him with a severe knife wound to the stomach. Few folks around town expected him to survive, but a Dr. McCarthy, using a pool table for an operating table, and whiskey for an anesthetic, sewed Mather up. After Dave became a Dodge City policeman, he'd "persuade" gamblers, prostitutes and others to visit Doc McCarthy for the purpose of a physical examination, the cost of which was five dollars. McCarthy acknowledged some years later that the practice wasn't exactly ethical. He also noted that he needed the money.

In 1878, Mather showed up in Mobettie, Texas with another former Dodge City policeman named Wyatt Earp. The two of them were selling "gold" bricks they claimed had been found in an old Spanish mine. The scam might have worked had they not sold one of the phony bricks to the sheriff. He discovered the fraud and escorted the bunko artists out of the county. Mather may have killed a man in Mobettie, but that is not confirmed.

Dave returned to Dodge City, but it wasn't long before he became a mercenary gunman for the Santa Fe Railroad in the so-called Royal Gorge War in Colorado. Among the other hired guns in that dispute was his old friend Dave Rudabaugh, as well as Doc Holliday and Bat Masterson. Nothing much came of the matter and Dave appeared in Las Vegas, New Mexico in 1879 where he soon became a deputy marshal.

His reputation as a gunman really took root in Las Vegas. His first shooting, in November, was of a soldier who attempted to flee custody. Dave shot him in the thumb and shoulder. In January 1880, Mather was present in the Close and Patterson Saloon when four young toughs shot deputy marshal Joe Carson nine times. Mather pulled his guns and opened fire. When the smoke cleared, one of the killers was dead, another badly wounded. The other two were less seriously injured.[3] Mather is believed to have led the lynch mob that took the killers out of the jail a week or so later. All three were summarily executed.

Also in January of that year, Dave killed a railroad worker named Joe Castello in a street gunfight. He resigned his lawman position in March.

Mather returned to Dodge City but didn't stay long. Early the following year he was arrested in San Antonio, Texas, for passing counterfeit money. He was acquitted of that charge and was next in Dallas where he was arrested for stealing jewelry from a prostitute. He spent three months in jail before he was tried and acquitted of those charges, too.

He next appeared in El Paso. One source says he served as a deputy marshal under Dallas Stoudenmire. Another says he served under Marshal Jim Gillett. Both appointments were unlikely and in any event, he did not make any name for himself in West Texas.

By mid 1883 Mather was back in Dodge City where he was appointed both deputy town marshal and Ford County deputy sheriff. He was also a partner in the Opera House Saloon. Nothing was to last with Dave. In the spring of the next year, a new city administration took office and one of the first orders of business was to replace Dave Mather with Tom Nixon, an old buffalo hunter and competing saloonkeeper. To complicate matters further, word around town was that Dave and Nixon's wife had an intimate relationship. One night, in an alley near the Opera House Saloon, Nixon took a shot at Mather, and missed. Dave declined to press charges so Nixon went free. Three days later, Mather came upon Nixon on the street. Nixon tried to pull his own gun, but before he could, Mather shot him, four times. Mather was acquitted of murder charges.

After 1885, Dave drifted out of the public eye. He turned up briefly in New Kiowa, Kansas and then again in Long Pine, Nebraska. A body matching his description was found along a railroad in Texas in 1886, but it was never positively identified. Some believe that he moved along to Canada where he joined the Royal Canadian Mounted Police and lived until 1922. The RCMP denies that he was ever a member.

Most absurd is the story about Mather being part of a posse that pursued an unidentified flying object from Arizona to Mexico in 1889. Mather, the story goes, rode his horse to a spot where the spaceship had landed and never came back. The UFO lifted off and disappeared over the horizon.

The final mystery of Mysterious Dave Mather will probably never be resolved.

---

[1] Some sources claim Mather was born in 1845, and in Massachusetts.

[2] Rudabaugh was later sentenced to death for murder at Las Vegas, New Mexico, and Yarberry, who became Albuquerque's first marshal, was hanged there for murder in 1883.

[3] Some sources indicate that two of the killers escaped unharmed, only to be hanged later. Some sources also omit Mather from this fight entirely. There is little doubt, however, that he was there.

RAILROAD OFFICER J. A. McCLURE KILLED:
KILLERS SHOT-DOWN IN TEXAS

A 249-mile railroad line known as the Belen Cut-off, between Belen, New Mexico and Texico, on the New Mexico/Texas border, opened in 1907.[1] One unforeseen result of the new line was that it offered thieves an opportunity to rob freight cars as slow-moving trains crawled up the 1¼% grade east-bound on the 25 mile stretch between Belen and the Abo Pass. Often the criminals would board the slow-moving train, enter the cars and throw cargo off to the side of the railroad right-of-way where accomplices in wagons would gather it up. They would also break into and steal from any rail cars left unattended along sidings. This went on for a long time until railroad officials grew weary of the practice, and the accompanying losses.[2]

On Wednesday, January 25, 1911, two railroad officers were sent to investigate the thefts. They boarded an eastbound train at Belen. One of the agents—unnamed in news reports of the day—got off at a flag stop to send a telegram before they reached the Abo Pass and the train went on without him. Agent J. A. McClure continued on alone. He was never seen alive again.

When McClure failed to return the following day, the chief of the railroad police, Ben Williams, took personal charge of the investigation, though due to an injury he could not take part in the actual chase. He immediately suspected homesteader Frank Howe and his two sons, Robert and Guy, who lived near the railroad tracks at Abo. They were leading members of a loosely organized group known as the Abo Pass Gang. Williams also believed that McClure was already dead at that point.

On Friday, January 27, a posse of heavily armed officers headed by Billy Olds, a railroad special agent and former Arizona Ranger, and Lt. John Collier of the New Mexico Mounted Police,[3] reached Abo to conduct a thorough search for McClure. The search was futile the first day. One rancher reported that he'd heard shots on Wednesday, but feared to investigate and remained indoors the remainder of the day. Other area residents also refused to cooperate with the posse members. Local folks feared the Howes, father and sons.

On the afternoon of the second day, Agent McClure's body was found, head down, in a deep well on property belonging to Frank Howe. Also found close by were several large caches of goods stolen from railroad cars, including five wagons laden with corn, dried fruit and chop feed for animals.

Investigation revealed that McClure had been shot from ambush. He had apparently discovered that thieves had stolen corn from a boxcar, and by following a trail of kernels left by a leaking grain bag, he located the outlaw camp. As he neared it, the thieves opened fire, hitting the officer in the wrist, arm and stomach. After he fell,

Officer McClure was shot a fourth time, in the top of the head, the bullet exiting at his chin. His body was robbed of all valuables, including a gold watch and a semiautomatic pistol, before it was thrown into the well. The Howes and four of their horses were gone.

By Sunday, several posses were in pursuit of Howe and his sons, and the Santa Fe Railroad offered a $500 reward for arrest and conviction. Ben Williams believed that the outlaws would head for Mexico, and he was right.

The Howes traveled southeast to Gallinas, an El Paso & Rock Island Railroad stop south of Corona. They stole a saddle from a rancher along the way. They boarded a southbound freight and rode all the way to Fort Hancock, Texas, about 50 miles south of El Paso where they were thrown off the train. When they attempted to cross into Mexico on foot, Tom L. O'Connor, a United States Customs guard, and M. R. Hemly, a Justice of the Peace, attempted to stop them. The outlaws had rifles hidden in the bedrolls they carried, and they opened fire at once. O'Connor fell, mortally wounded with a bullet in the lung, and Hemly received a bullet wound to the arm. The Howes then fled east, toward Sierra Blanca, Texas. (Why they did not continue into Mexico is not known.)

At that point, four Texas Rangers from Ysleta joined with the New Mexico lawmen in pursuit of the killers. At about 9:00 p.m. on Tuesday, January 31, the posse overtook the Howes. A gunfight erupted immediately and Robert Howe, the younger of the brothers, was wounded in the leg with the first volley. His older brother and father abandoned him to the posse and fled into a thicket, firing as they ran. Officers surrounded the undergrowth and prepared to stand siege until the morning's light.

In only an hour or so, though, Frank and Guy Howe emerged from the brush, rifles in hand and firing as they ran toward the law officers. Officers returned fire and both outlaws fell, shot dead. Ben Williams said later that about 500 shots were fired in the two gun battles with the Howes. What ever became of Robert Howe is not known except that he was not killed in Texas.

J. A. McClure was about 40 at the time of his death. He'd been employed by the railroad for many years serving previously as a conductor, brakeman. A wife and child who resided in Texas survived him.

---

[1] Construction actually began in 1903 but economic hard-times held it up for several years.

[2] It was widely believed that a railroad employee was involved and tipped the thieves as to which cars contained them most desirable loot. This was not proved, however, and no arrests were ever made.

3 The New Mexico Mounted Police, existed from 1905 to 1921. It should not be confused with today's Mounted Police organization that is made up of civilians who act in support of the New Mexico State Police. John Collier was a Grant County deputy who participated in the arrest of Howard Chenowth for the murders of Constable Rodriguez and Marshal Kilburn.

OUTLAWS KILL MARSHAL McGUIRE & DEPUTY HENRY IN MARTINEZTOWN GUNFIGHT: KILLERS ESCAPE

On Saturday night, November 20th, 1886, Marshal Bob McGuire and his deputy, E. D. Henry, went to Martíneztown, northeast of Albuquerque's new town, to arrest outlaws, John "Kid" Johnson and Charlie Ross. The two were members of a gang of robbers and rustlers who had been plying their trade in the area in recent days. The officers held arrest warrants for both, though the specific charges against the two are not known.

Marshal McGuire had received word that the desperadoes could be found hanging around Pasqual Cutinola's dance hall. A search of the establishment was fruitless, but the officers continued looking around Martineztown. They soon found the two outlaws holed up with two young women—Simona Moya and Tercita Trujillo—in a one-room adobe house not far from the dance hall. As the officers made ready to dash through the door, Miss Moya opened the portal and stepped outside for a pitcher of water. McGuire, Henry and the woman fell into a confused heap. The outlaws quickly realized what had happen, grabbed their guns and opened fire. The lamp went out as the officers returned fire and the women took cover under the bed. McGuire was hit in the chest, abdomen and right arm. Deputy Henry was hit twice in the chest and once in the right leg. When a lamp was lit and the smoke cleared, Henry lay dead on the floor. Marshal McGuire was badly wounded, but alive. The outlaws were gone.

Charlie Ross was hit, too. One bullet struck his shoulder and lodged against his shoulder blade and another one grazed his head. He managed to get to his horse but he only made it a short distance before he collapsed and sought shelter with a woman who lived nearby. A Santa Fe Railroad detective (and former Albuquerque city police officer) Carl Holton and Police Officer Pete Isherwood tracked Ross to the house which was located in an area of Albuquerque called Hell's half-acre ("…the very worst part of the town—a rendezvous for third rate harlots and first class cut throats and horse thieves," according to the *Albuquerque Morning Journal*). The officers arrested the killer without incident.

Ross claimed later that McGuire and Henry started shooting first, and that he didn't fire his own gun until he had already been shot three times and was flat on the floor with Henry standing over him. Ross also claimed that he had no idea why the officers were after him and Johnson.

Marshal McGuire died of his wounds on November 26, but he remained lucid to the end and was able to tell his version of the gunfight to District Attorney Harvey Fergusson and four witnesses. McGuire, the second Albuquerque City Marshal,[1] was 40 years old at the time of his death. Newspapers of the time said his death was "...a loss to the town of an honest, effective, and fearless officer and respected citizen." The Marshal's brother took his body back to his native Oswego, New York, for burial. Henry, a native of Ohio, was buried in Albuquerque.

Charlie Ross recovered from his wounds. On January 3, 1887, he escaped from the Bernalillo County jail. One source says Ross' girlfriend slipped him a key; another says that Ross and jail inmate Peter Trinkaus of Gallup, a convicted murderer, bribed a guard.

Ross left a note addressed to the editor of the Albuquerque *Daily Democrat*:

> County Hotel, January 3, 1887, to Mr. Roberts of the Democrat: Please say in your paper that hearing there is a reward offered for my partner, Johnson, that I have gone to find him. Tell the boys not to feel uneasy about my absence, and as the weather is such that they might take cold, it may be better for their health to stay at home. We'll turn up in time, and don't you forget it.
>
> /S/ C. Henry Ross, with his hair parted in the middle.

Ross was recaptured on January 27 after an attempted train robbery west of Grants and returned to jail in Albuquerque. He escaped again in July 1887, and was never recaptured.

Kid Johnson, described as "...full of cowboy swagger, wears a Chihuahua hat and wears his pants in his boots," received wounds to the neck and foot in the gunfight. He got to his horse and left town, crossing the Rio Grande near Isleta. At the Rio Puerco he joined up with an ox train and train's captain doctored his foot until he was able to put a boot on and continue his flight. Johnson was later arrested in El Paso on charges of killing the two Albuquerque officers. It was decided that not enough evidence against him existed to justify trial on those charges, and they were dropped. Never tried for the murder of the two officers, Ross and Johnson both lived to old age.

As a result of the Martíneztown gunfight, the Albuquerque Morning *Journal* for November 23, 1886 reported thus:

> The city council are going to give the policemen latitude hereafter in the use of firearms in making arrests. They have had orders never to use their arms except in case of being fired on. Hereafter any criminal may be shot by the police if he makes a show of his arms or attempts to use them.

---

[1]   The first Albuquerque Town Marshal was Milt Yarberry. He was hanged for murder on February 9, 1883.

BLACK COWBOY GEORGE McJUNKIN DISCOVERS PREHISTORIC BONES

George McJunkin was a Black man who earned his living by working as a cowboy. Like many others of his time, his surname was taken from the east Texas family who owned him when he was born into slavery in 1856. As a young man he migrated to west Texas where he did ranch work until he joined a cattle drive heading north. By 1877 he was working on the Crowfoot ranch near the town of Folsom in Colfax County, New Mexico. He worked his way up to foreman and remained employed there for the rest of his life.

McJunkin was much more than a working cowboy. For one thing, he could read and write which was remarkable at a time when literacy was the exception rather than the rule among all races. Not only *could* he read, but he *did* read, and extensively. He studied geology and astronomy and was at least passing familiar with anthropology. He was so curious about the natural world that he carried a telescope on his horse so he could study the nighttime sky. He also played the violin.

There were not many Black people in McJunkin's corner of the American West, the area near where New Mexico shares common boundaries with Colorado, Oklahoma and Texas. He seems to have been well liked and greatly respected as a cowhand and ranch foreman. One story McJunkin himself told was about the time he and a group of white cowboys went into the Eklund Hotel in Clayton, New Mexico, for a meal. McJunkin was refused service and one of the white cowboys asked why.

"That's our policy," the manager said.

The cowboy removed his pistol from its holster and placed it on the table. "Your policy has just been changed," he said.

McJunkin was served his meal along with his friends.

His preoccupation, however, with things which had no immediate practical value, things like fossils, old bones and constellations, made McJunkin at least a marginal outsider to folks as generally pragmatic as cowboys. Famed New Mexico writer Tony Hillerman noted that McJunkin "...[was a] misfit more by mind than by color."

At about midnight on August 27, 1908, the town of Folsom was nearly washed away by a gigantic flood of the Dry Cimarron River. Thirteen inches of rain fell that afternoon in an area where about that much total rain falls in most years. At least 17 people died in the disaster. The Crowfoot Ranch was some miles upstream from the town and not long after the flood, McJunkin and another cowboy found themselves riding the rugged country along the rim of Dead Horse Arroyo, just north of Cimarron Creek.

The arroyo was considerably washed out making it much deeper than it had been before the flood. McJunkin noticed animal bones exposed on the arroyo floor; bones he had not seen there before. These were not just old cattle or buffalo bones, either. They were much too large. There was something unusual about them being there. It was about 14 feet from rim to floor of the arroyo and it occurred to the cowboy that for the bones to have been buried so deep would have required many years of sedimentation. McJunkin knew he'd found something truly unusual.

He studied his find more closely. The bones were somewhat mineralized and the skeletons were intact. Then the cowboy saw something even more extraordinary. Within the same layer of soil which held the bones were objects which appeared to be man-made: hide scrapers and finely crafted points which were nothing like the arrowheads used by 19th century plains Indians. As he continued to examine his find and to consider what it meant, he became convinced he had found evidence that a different kind of man hunted a different kind of animal in the American West thousands of years before 1908; thousands of years before anyone thought possible.

He was the only one excited by what he had found.

Scientific gospel of the time held that the first North Americans crossed the Bering Strait in their migrations and they could not have done so until ice-free passage was possible about 4,000 years before. The gospel held that man had simply not been present in North America during the Pleistocene era, or the late Ice Age, and therefore McJunkin's conclusions were wrong. His "credentials" were lacking, too, of course.

From 1908 to 1921 the cowboy did everything he could think of to interest the scientific community in what he had found. In 1919 a scientist from the Denver Museum poked around a bit in Dead Horse Arroyo, but nothing came of it. McJunkin took sick in 1921 and died at Folsom in the spring of 1922.

Eighteen years after McJunkin made his original find, the Colorado Museum at last sent a serious expedition to examine Dead Horse Arroyo.[1] What the Johnnies-come-lately "discovered" in 1926 was exciting enough that a second party was sent the following year and another the year after that. They called it Folsom Site and what they uncovered proved that George McJunkin had been right all along. Twenty-three huge, prehistoric, long horned bison had been killed, skinned, cooked and eaten by man about 11,000 years before. (Radiocarbon dating has since shown that the Folsom Site bones were deposited there between 8900 and 8000 BC.) Scientific gospel was revised and allowed as how man had been able to cross the Bering Strait from Asia to North America on numerous occasions before and during the Ice Age.

The scientific community ignored George McJunkin during his lifetime. Sad to say, he is ignored yet today. Many chronicles that refer to the Folsom find make no mention of him. Others make no more than passing mention of the Black cowboy. Some sources date the find from when the scientific community acknowledged it. *The Random House Dictionary* says the Folsom Site was discovered in 1925, and *Webster's New World Encyclopedia* says 1926. Neither mentions McJunkin or 1908.

Too bad. It took more than twenty years but McJunkin was proven right while dozens of scientists were proven wrong. He was a remarkable man who deserves a better place in the history of the American West.

---

[1] Mrs. N. H. Click in *Us Nesters in the Land of Enchantment* cites a 1967 article in the Raton *Range* by editor Fritz Thompson which says that the bones in Dead Horse Arroyo were rediscovered in 1921 by a cowboy named Ernie Brandt. Brandt, the story goes, passed a sample along to a man named Carl Schwachheim, and that led to further study by archeologists. Brandt was acquainted with McJunkin and acknowledged the Black cowboy's earlier discovery.)

SUSAN HUMMER McSWEEN BARBER: THE CATTLE QUEEN OF NEW MEXICO

By the 1890s, Susan McSween Barber[1] was known as the Cattle Queen of New Mexico, an appellation that had some merit. She is reported to have operated an 8,000 head cattle ranch at Three Rivers on her own, and to have driven a herd across the mountains to Engle for transshipment by rail. The Cattle King of New Mexico, John Chisum, said this of her: "This courageous woman was ... a successful rancher in her own right."

There is little doubt, though, that her earlier life on the Western Frontier was somewhat more exciting than the day-to-day tedium of cattle raising.

Susan was born in Gettysburg, Pennsylvania in December of 1845. As a young woman she moved to Kansas. She lived at Atchison for a time, and married 30-year-old Alexander A. McSween there on August 23, 1873. The two of them moved to Eureka, Kansas, but did not tarry there for long. They moved on to New Mexico in the autumn of 1874 and arrived in Lincoln on March 3, 1875. Penniless when they arrived, Alex soon established a law practice that afforded them an adequate income.

Alex also soon became embroiled in the dispute that would evolve into the Lincoln County War. Historian Robert Utley has suggests that McSween may have been *the* major player in that bloody conflict. "McSween," Utley wrote, "contributed decisively to its origin and progress."

The Lincoln County War's major battle was fought in Lincoln in July 1878. On one side, William H. Bonney (Billy the Kid) and his cohorts holed up in McSween's house. On the other side were a sheriff's posse and a detachment of soldiers from Fort Stanton. Susan made several attempts to negotiate a cease-fire, or, failing that, safe passage out of the house for her husband, with Colonel Nathan Dudley. She was not successful, and when the gun smoke finally cleared after the final fight on July 19, Alex and several others were dead.

Susan did not visit her husband's dead body, nor did she attend his funeral. No one seems to know quite why, but few historians fail to mention it.

Susan was not one to sit idly by and let matters stand. She made her contempt for those responsible for her husband's death, Dudley in particular, well known. The result was numerous threats against her life. By September, she packed what little she had left in the world and moved to Las Vegas, New Mexico for her own safety.

There she met a young one-armed attorney named Houston Chapman[2] whom she retained to represent the estates of both her late husband and John Tunstall, a business associate who had been murdered the previous February. Chapman was aggressive and immediately went after Col. Dudley by filing a lawsuit against him.

Dudley retaliated by alleging that Susan was a promiscuous woman many times over. He provided Governor Lew Wallace and General Edward Hatch with eight different affidavits that alleged firsthand knowledge of the same number of adulterous relationships. One of them, offered by Francisco Gomez, even said that Sheriff George Peppin was an eyewitness to the assignation. The oddity was that all of those submitting affidavits were members of the faction that opposed McSween and his associates. In spite of repeated demands from Susan, Chapman and Susan's brother-in-law, David Shields, also an attorney, they were not provided copies of the affidavits.

Then on February 18, 1879, the first anniversary of Tunstall's murder, Chapman was also shot to death. His murder occurred on Lincoln's main street.

According to one source, an outlaw named Billy Campbell shot Chapman in the chest, the bullet exiting his back. Then J. J. Dolan shot him again, just to make sure, one supposes. Campbell then poured whiskey on the inert body and set it on fire. Another source reports that Dolan accidentally discharged his rifle, which startled Campbell into firing his pistol that just happened to be aimed at Chapman's chest. The second source makes no mention of the fire.

After Houston's death, Susan took control of her own affairs and became administratrix of both her late husband's estate and that of John Tunstall. She acquired title to Dick Brewer's ranch[3] by foreclosing on a note her husband held on the place. She may also have received a small herd of cattle from John Chisum. She married George Barber in June 1880 and the two of them began acquiring ranch land near Three Rivers. Barber practiced law in both Lincoln and White Oaks while she ran the ranch. She divorced Barber in 1892 alleging that he had never supported her. She continued running the ranch until 1917 when she sold it to Albert Bacon Fall of Tea Pot Dome scandal fame.

She moved to White Oaks where she resided for the remainder of her life. She was regarded as a generous hostess who frequently entertained her guests by playing the piano and singing. She died there in 1931.

Her modest tombstone in the Cemetery at White Oaks simply reads "Susan McSween Barber."

She may have been the Cattle Queen of New Mexico, but you have to look hard to find her grave marker.[4]

---

[1] Dan L. Thrapp in his *Encyclopedia of Frontier Biography* spells her maiden name in this way. Will Keleher in *Violence in Lincoln County* spells it *Homer*. She was often referred to as Sue or Susie. Some sources indicate that her middle initial was E, but no source indicates what that might have stood for.

[2] George Curry in his autobiography mistakenly cites Chapman's first name as William. Chapman was a native of Portland, Oregon. His arm was lost in a youthful accident, but sources do not indicate which arm was lost.

[3] Brewer was one of the so-called Regulators of the Lincoln County War. He, along with Buckshot Roberts, was killed on April 4, 1878 in a gunfight at Blazer's Mill.

[4] Another famous New Mexican interred at White Oaks in the state's first governor, William C. McDonald.

KILLING SPREE IN RATÓN: SALOON KEEPER MENTZER LYNCHED (TWICE)

Gus Mentzer, 24, worked as barkeeper for William "Billy" Burbridge, a gambler who owned and operated the Bank Exchange Saloon[1] in Ratón, New Mexico. Burbridge fired Mentzer for drinking and carousing and Mentzer left town for a time. On the evening of Monday, June 26, 1882, he came back. Mentzer, drunk and armed with pistols provided by another gambler, named Turner, approached Deputy Sheriff Pete Dollman on the street in front of the Bank Exchange Saloon. He pulled one of the guns and jammed it against the deputy's ribs.

"Give up your gun," Mentzer demanded.

"Oh, no, I could not do that," Dollman replied.

"But you must!"

About then a citizen named Johnson got close enough to knock Mentzer's hand downward and the gun discharged harmlessly into the dusty street. Mentzer ran to the front door of the saloon. Deputy Dollman fired several shots in his direction, all of which missed except the one that struck a citizen named W. H. Harris who just happened to be hurrying along the sidewalk. Mentzer escaped into the saloon, then fled out the back door.

Dollman and a group of citizens searched the town, but Mentzer was not to be found. At about 9:00 p.m. the young gunman appeared at the Bank Exchange Saloon and ordered a drink. Whether he got it or not is unrecorded. Deputy Dollman was present in the saloon and he and other citizens chased Mentzer into the street and began shooting at him. The fugitive fled toward the railroad depot where he shot and wounded J. H. Latimer in the leg and breast. He jumped aboard a railroad engine that had its steam up, but he couldn't make the giant vehicle move. Citizens S. H. Jackson and Hugh Eddleston approached the engine.

"There he is," Jackson shouted an instant before Mentzer shot and killed him. Eddleston was killed a few seconds later.

Deputy Dollman and another deputy, William Burgen, were then able to capture Mentzer whose gun was empty. They took the prisoner to the Little Brindle Saloon where he was left in the charge of Deputy Burgen behind a locked door. Burgen went about putting leg irons on the prisoner while Dollman went to the telegraph office to wire the bad news to S. H. Jackson's widow.

One of Mentzer's victims, Hugh Eddleston, had been a business partner of Justice of the Peace Harvey Moulton, and the judge soon arrived at the saloon where Mentzer was being held. He banged on the door, but Burgen would not let him in. Moulton kicked the door opened and entered, gun in hand.

"Give up the son of a ----- to be hung!" he ordered, according to a witness.

Burgen refused, citing his duty to protect the miscreant.

As Moulton made a grab for the prisoner, Burgen fired and the judge only lived long enough to fire a single shot into Burgen's stomach. Mentzer escaped and fled to the Williams and Frick butcher shop where Deputy Dollman arrested him yet again. The young killer begged Dollman to protect his life and the deputy said he'd do his best, but Dollman must of have known his efforts would be futile. The butcher, Williams, provided a rope and the crowd took Mentzer away from Dollman and told the killer to "say his prayers."

Someone threw the rope over a sign in front of the Raton Bank and the noose was put in place around Mentzer's neck. He "fought like a tiger" as citizens hoisted him up. Then a brace broke and the sign and Mentzer both came tumbling down to the board sidewalk. The crowd was not to be dissuaded. A young boy was boosted up and he placed the rope over the top of a signpost at the corner of Clark Avenue and First Street, and Mentzer was again strung-up. That time it worked. His body was left hanging until Tuesday morning. Later the same day a coroner's jury ruled that "Gus Mentzer came to his death by being hung by the neck by unknown parties."

Deputy Burgen, was taken to the offices of the Ratón Coal and Coking Company where he suffered great agony until he died at 10 o'clock on Tuesday morning. Not a great deal is known about Burgen. A local newspaper described him as an Irishman—a fine looking man, according to the editor—who lived in Canada for ten or twelve years before he arrived in Ratón in the spring of 1882. Colfax County Sheriff Allen C. Wallace appointed him deputy sheriff for the coal mining community of Blossburg, five miles northwest of Ratón, less than a week before Moulton killed him. Burgen was only present in Ratón on the day of the Mentzer affair because he'd come to town to visit with his brother who lived there. He was buried at Blossburg on June 28, 1882. "His funeral was largely attended."

The coroner's jury reported thus:

We ... find that William A. Burgen came to his death by a pistol shot wound received while in the exention [sic] of his duty, fired from a pistol in the hands of Harvey Moulton, Justice of the Peace.

Ratón's citizens were so irate at four killings, two woundings, and one lynching in one night that a mass meeting was held the very next evening. "Ten or twelve hundred" attended according to the local newspaper. A committee of eleven was named to prevent further disturbance. They issued a report that read in part:

...all professional gamblers, footpads, thieves, cappers, dance hall men, bunko men, and all these [sic] who have no visible means of support, as well as all dance house girls and prostitutes generally, are hereby notified and publicly warned to leave this town within 48 hours from 12 o'clock at noon on the first day of July, 1882, and never return under penalty of incurring the just wrath of an indignant and outraged people.

It was never made clear why the gambler, Turner, provided Gus Mentzer with the guns he used to do his evil work. Turner was arrested in Las Vegas during the first week in July 1882, and removed to Springer where he was tried on unspecified charges. The court fined him $20 and costs and set him free. A Ratón newspaper commented: "Turner will not be likely to show his elegant frame in Ratón again very soon."

---

[1] Some sources indicate that Burbridge and Mentzer were partners in the Bank Exchange Saloon.

L. G. MURPHY: THE RISE AND FALL OF HIS LINCOLN COUNTY EMPIRE

The ordinary perception of outlaws in the Old West is that of stagecoach and bank robbers, horse and cattle rustlers, gunfighters and killers; men rough-hewn and unpolished. But then—as now—there were outlaws who committed their crimes while sitting in offices behind desks, decked out in the fashion of the day. To paraphrase an old-time songwriter, *some men will rob you with a six-gun, some with a fountain pen.*[1] L. G. Murphy was of the latter ilk.

Lawrence Gustave Murphy was born in Wexford, Ireland in 1831. Not much is known about his youth except that he graduated from Maynooth College, a Roman Catholic institution that prepared young men for the priesthood. Murphy was no priest. He arrived in the United States as a young man and joined the U. S. Army and served in the 5th Infantry for about ten years, attaining the rank of sergeant. He arrived in New Mexico about 1860 and in 1861 he joined the 1st New Mexico Volunteers at Fort Union as a lieutenant.[2]

He served under Col. Kit Carson in the western New Mexico campaign against the Navajo in 1863-64 and after the Indians surrendered and were relocated to Bosque Redondo, near Fort Sumner, he served there briefly as Indian agent. By 1866 he was the quartermaster at Fort Stanton, near the town of Bonito,[3] and held the rank of major. He left the army the same year.

In 1867, Murphy and another former army officer, Lt. Col. Emil Fritz, were in business together as sutlers at Fort Stanton, and Murphy also served as Postmaster. Their business, L. G. Murphy & Company, went far beyond selling notions and incidentals to soldiers. The basis of the enterprise was contracts with the army for supplies of all kinds. This was a natural for Murphy. One source says, "Supplies and logistics were his [Murphy's] specialty."

Records indicate that the company did well from the beginning. For 1867, Murphy reported sales of $22,000, upon which he paid $22.00 in taxes. Since barter was used as often as cash money in commercial transactions, it is impossible to determine the amount of business the company really did. In September 1867, Murphy received a "supply as needed" contract with Fort Stanton for the delivery of beef on the hoof. Such contracts called for payment of top dollar, but no record survives showing how much beef was actually delivered, or how much the army paid for it.

The following year, Murphy & Company received a contract for well over $9,000 to supply lumber to the fort, and in 1869 another for nearly $8,000 for the delivery of 250,000 pounds of corn. Murphy and Fritz also served as subcontractors for other Fort Stanton suppliers, and indications are that Murphy, using his old Quartermaster connections, siphoned off military supplies to his own inventory. He was accused of taking 26 sacks of flour that had been consigned to the fort commissary. Nothing came of the allegation.

During the two or three-year period from 1867-69, Murphy and Fritz built a store building on land belonging to Fort Stanton. It amounted to 7,000 square feet of floor space and contained some 18 rooms. Murphy offered to sell it to the army for $12,000 in 1870. The army declined. Observers can only speculate as to how much of the lumber, mentioned above, went into construction of the store.

In 1869, with the creation of Lincoln County, Murphy was elected probate judge, an important position at the time, as a Democrat. Indications are, however, that he maintained a close working relationship with Thomas B. Catron, one of the Republican leaders of the so-called Santa Fe Ring.

Even so, Murphy had problems along the way, not the least of which was that his authority as post trader at Fort Stanton was not renewed in 1870. He did the logical thing: he took control of the situation. Some of those who were awarded the position never showed up at all, and those who did were promptly bought out by Murphy & Company. Murphy may not have been the *de jure* post trader, but he owned the building and remained the *de facto* man in charge. Besides, in the same year, he had seven contracts, worth more than $40,000 for supplies to Fort Stanton, and in the following year the value of them increased to about $45,000.

By 1871, Murphy was responsible for delivering provisions to the Mescalero Apache Indian Reservation and for actually issuing them to individual tribal members. The original estimate of the number of Indians to be supplied—as provided by A. J. Curtis, the Mescalero Indian agent—was 325. Using Murphy's accounting methods, that number increased to 2,679 in just 16 months! Murphy's billings increased accordingly. His first voucher, for June 1871, was for less than $160.00. His voucher for May to July, 1872, was for $12,418.42. Average monthly billings for the sixteen-month period from June 1871 to September 1872 reached nearly $3,500.

Indian Agent Curtis didn't seem to be bothered by the exponential growth of the Mescalero population. During his tenure in that office—something less than two years—government purchases from L. G. Murphy & Company amounted to around $125,000.

During this time, Murphy & Company branched out. Sam Wortley's hotel and restaurant in Lincoln became Murphy properties. Murphy owned the Rio Bonito beer brewery located near Fort Stanton. Murphy & Company also served as the bank for Lincoln County. The company erected a large store building in Lincoln. It came to be known as "The House," as in "The House of Murphy."[4]

Murphy also consolidated his power, political and otherwise. Politically, Major William Brady, with whom Murphy had served in the army, was elected Lincoln County Sheriff in 1869 and 1877. Murphy also took on J. J. Dolan as bookkeeper. Time would show that Dolan was nearly as ruthless as Murphy himself.

The result of all this effort was that Murphy literally ruled Lincoln County. Because he held the supply contracts with Fort Stanton, he was the only market for livestock and other agricultural commodities produced by area farmers and ranchers.

Because he controlled mercantile and banking interests, and held all the paper on outstanding credit, he controlled the economy. As probate judge, he was the highest-ranking elected official in the county, and Sheriff Brady was indebted to the House of Murphy.

So self-assured was Murphy that he said this to one of his political opponents, for all the public to hear: "You might as well try to stop the waves of the ocean with a fork as to try and oppose me!"

Here is what one woman wrote about those times:

"The firm of L. G. Murphy & Co.... not only supplied the whole of Lincoln County with the necessities of life, but it held the population in what was approximate peonage.... Only those who have experienced it can realize the extent to which Murphy & Co. dominated the county and controlled its people, economy and politics.... All Lincoln County was cowed and intimidated by them."

Murphy's method of dealing with any political or economic opposition was to simply eliminate it. In 1875, a rancher by the name of Robert Casey had become a thorn in Murphy's side, politically speaking. Murphy hired a local cowboy named William Wilson, who'd once worked for Casey, to kill the rancher for payment of $500 and a promise that, even if caught, he'd be protected. Wilson did that for which he'd been hired, shooting Casey twice and killing him.[5] In a display of utter cynicism, Murphy officiated at Casey's funeral—he had, after all trained to be a priest—and then did everything he could to get Wilson off the hook. He failed and Wilson was sentenced to hang. The execution took place on December 10, 1875. Asked if he had any final words, Wilson turned to Murphy who stood nearby on the scaffold, and said, "Major, you know you are the cause of this. You promised to save me, but..." He never finished the sentence because Murphy tripped the lever that opened the trapdoor beneath Wilson's feet, sending the man to oblivion.[6]

Into this Lincoln County environment rode Alexander McSween in 1875 and John Tunstall in 1876. McSween was a Scot and an attorney and Tunstall was an Englishman with vast financial resources supplied by his family. A young man of 23, Tunstall set out to supplant Murphy & Company. He said, "I propose to confine my operations to Lincoln County, but I intend to handle it in such a way as to get the half of every dollar that is made in the county *by anyone* (emphasis added)." Certainly no modest goal.

Both McSween and Tunstall were Protestants. Some historians have hypothesized that at least part of the conflict in Lincoln County was religious in nature, pitting the Catholic Irishmen—Murphy, Dolan, Riley, Brady and others—against the Protestant newcomers.

McSween, after doing some legal work for Murphy, joined Tunstall and so did famed cattleman John Chisum. Chisum got involved because cattle rustlers in the Seven Rivers area frequently stole his cattle and then sold them to Murphy (or, later on, to J. J. Dolan and John Riley), who in turn used the livestock to fill contracts with the army at Fort Stanton or the Indians at Mescalero. Tunstall went into the ranching business and with McSween and Chisum and opened a general store and a bank in

Lincoln. This effectively put an end to the monopoly L. G. Murphy had previously enjoyed.

By this time in his life—he was 46 years old—Murphy was enjoying very little and he was not a well man. In 1877 he sold the House of Murphy to J. J. Dolan. It was largely a paper transaction and Murphy continued to have a great deal to say about business matters, not that he was any great help. By January 1878, J. J. Dolan & Company was insolvent, but not ready to give up.

To Murphy and Dolan, it was logical that Tunstall had to go. His death would leave McSween alone in the opposition mercantile since Chisum tended to stay away from Lincoln, back at his ranch on the Rio Pecos. McSween had little or no money of his own and, because of some of Murphy's chicanery, he was embroiled in a legal controversy surrounding the will of Emil Fritz that held the possibility of landing the lawyer in jail.[7]

On February 18, 1878, John Henry Tunstall was shot to death while en route from his ranch on the Rio Feliz to Lincoln. His killers were deputies of Sheriff William Brady, but they were also notorious outlaws, members of the Jesse Evans gang of thieves and killers. This event led to the violence that has come to be called the Lincoln County War, which reached its climax with a five-day gunfight in Lincoln in July of the same year.

But Murphy was not around Lincoln when the fighting took place. He moved out, bag and baggage, to Santa Fe in May of 1878. Jimmy Dolan helped him move. Murphy was ill beyond rehabilitation. It was said of him throughout his life that he was much given to indulgence in strong drink, and it was catching up with him. He was admitted to the hospital in Santa Fe and he died there on October 20, 1878.

One source says he died "apparently of cancer." Other sources are less charitable. The Santa Fe *New Mexican* declared that he suffered from "bilious fevers" and died from "general debility." Lincoln County resident Frank Coe said this: "[He] was sick and was put in the hospital and the Sisters of Charity would not let him have whiskey, and that cut his living off. He died in a short time and everybody rejoiced over it."

And so it is that L. G. Murphy, the villain who can be credited with causing countless deaths in the Lincoln County War, died and faded into relative obscurity. Certainly his renown was over-shadowed by that of Pat Garrett and Billy the Kid. There are those among his defenders who say that he didn't do anything more than many others of his time. If that is so, it is a sad commentary. And even so, it is unlikely that many of his contemporaries caused the violence, death and discomfort that L. G. Murphy did.

----

[1] This ditty was penned after the events described here. The fountain pen was not invented until 1885.

[2] Another source says Murphy was commissioned a captain.

[3] Bonito was first called Las Placitas, then Lincoln when the county of the same name was created in 1969.

[4] This building still stands in Lincoln. It later became the county courthouse and it was this structure from which Billy the Kid escaped in 1881, killing two deputies as he did so.

[5] One version of the story went that the argument was over $8.00 in wages that Casey owed Wilson, but there was no fight. Wilson simply shot Casey, twice; once in the hip and once in the face. It took the rancher a day to die.

[6] Actually the hanging was badly botched, and it was necessary to hang Wilson twice. The shock of the first hanging, however, rendered him unconscious, and he did not awaken before he died some 30 minutes later. Murphy's secret was safe.

7 Fritz died in Stuttgart, Germany in the summer of 1874. One of McSween's first cases after he arrived in Lincoln was the probate of Fritz's will. Murphy accused McSween of misappropriating the proceeds of a $10,000 life insurance policy.

MASS MURDER AT BONITO CITY: MARTIN NELSON GOES BERSERK

The valleys of the Sacramento Mountains, in the area between Carrizozo and Ruidoso, are among the most beautiful places in New Mexico. In the early 1880s a town sprang up in the well-watered Bonito Valley and for obvious reasons it assumed the name Bonito, or Bonito City. Farming along Bonito Creek was the town's major economic enterprise, but a great deal of prospecting for precious metal in the surrounding mountains was also important.[1]

By 1885, Bonito City amounted to three general stores, a church, a blacksmith, a school, a saloon, a lawyer, and a two-story log hotel. By all accounts it was a quiet town, never noted for rowdiness. Residents boasted of the fact that in the first few years of the town's existence, sheriff's deputies were never summoned from the county seat at Lincoln to the deal with any breach of the peace. Justice of the Peace Charles Berry reported not a single killing in his precinct.

All of that changed in the early morning hours of May 5, 1885.

Mr. And Mrs. John Mayberry operated the hotel, which also served as a restaurant, and they resided there with their three children: Johnny, 17, Eddie, 8, and a daughter, Nelly. Dr. R. E. Flynn, recently arrived from Cincinnati, Ohio, occupied one of the upstairs guest rooms and a twenty-four year old prospector named Martin Nelson[2] occupied another.

Sometime in the early morning hours of that Tuesday, Martin Nelson rose from his bed and, with a rifle in hand, knocked on the door of the room shared by the Mayberry brothers. When Johnny opened the door, Nelson shot and wounded the boy. But Johnny grappled with his assailant and was knocked to the floor where he was shot again, and killed. Nelson then shot and killed eight-year-old Eddie as the child screamed in terror.

Dr. Flynn, awakened by the commotion, rushed into the room, only to be shot in the head and killed instantly. As John Mayberry hurried up the stairs, Nelson shot him in the heart; he fell back, dead.

Mrs. Mayberry followed her husband, and Nelson shot her, too, in the breast, but he failed to kill her. Bleeding profusely, she retreated down the stairs, tracking her own blood as she did so, and out the door and down the street seeking help, all to no avail. Nelson shot daughter Nelly in the side, and believing her dead, he left her where she fell on the hotel floor and then he followed her mother into the street. He soon overtook Mrs. Mayberry, shot and killed her, and then threw her body into an irrigation ditch.

The town became alarmed at the shooting in the dark of night, and citizens remained indoors, peering carefully through curtained windows. At last, saloonkeeper

Pete Nelson—who was in no way related to Martin Nelson—ventured into the street. He was able to seize the killer and he attempted to wrest the gun away from him. He failed, and Martin Nelson shot him to death, then beat him severely with the gun's stock and left his body in the middle of the street.

Grocer Henry Beck stepped into the street to see what was going on, only to be shot to death for his trouble.

The shooting stopped then, and Martin Nelson disappeared for a time. Residents stayed inside, waiting for the dawn. When sun-up came, groups of heavily armed men emerged and searched the streets for the killer. Then, as three men, Charles Berry, Rudolph Schultz and Don Campbell, stood talking, one of them spotted Martin Nelson walking down the mountainside, coming toward them. Just then, Nelson spotted the men, and he raised his rifle to fire, but Charles Berry fired first, his bullet hitting the young killer in the chest. Martin Nelson fell dead on the spot.

Nelly Mayberry alone survived the carnage Martin Nelson left behind. She left the town a couple of years later, and never returned. The seven victims were buried side by side, and Nelson was interred some distance away.

No motive for Nelson's actions was ever determined. He had been in no previous trouble with the law and was well enough liked in the time leading up to the killings.

The Mayberry Hotel remained unmolested for fifteen years. A. L. Burke wrote this about it:

"They [residents of Bonito City] claim to have seen strange things, heard agonizing groans, seeing lights pass from one room to another, and heard muffled shots from within, as they would pass the old hotel at night... People who would venture near the old log building and peep through the windows could still see the bloody footprints of bare feet on the steps of the stairway. At one time, a newspaper reporter was sent to investigate the mystery and write it up for a certain eastern paper. He gained admittance to the old hotel and watchers had but a short time to wait before they saw him running from the place as though being chased by a band of spooks from the infernal regions."

Floy Skinner said that the murders "killed" Bonito City. The town grew not at all after 1885, but remained occupied for more than twenty years. By 1910, when only two people remained in the town, the post office closed. Bonito City was a ghost town until 1930 when the Southern Pacific Railroad dammed up Bonito Creek to capture water for use in steam engines. All of the town's buildings, including the hotel, were dismantled before seventy-five feet of water covered the scene of the mysterious Mayberry Murders.

---

[1] Several sources indicate that silver mining was the reason for the town's existence. Floy Skinner, who was born in Bonito City, is quoted as saying that if there was any gold in the area, no one ever found it.
[2] One source indicates that Nelson was town constable. A. L. Burke, who wrote the most definitive description of the tragic events related here makes no mention of this.

EVA POE NEWKIRK AND THE BLIZZARD OF 1957: 14,000 HEAD OF LIVESTOCK PERISH

Northeastern New Mexico was spared the worst of a blizzard that hit West Texas in January of 1956 and the weather during the winter of 1956-57 wasn't anything out of the ordinary, but the early spring of '57 was something to remember, especially by those who lived between Raton and Clayton.

On Friday, March 22nd, the Albuquerque *Journal* predicted thus: "Partly cloudy weather, rising temperatures and moderate winds Thursday signaled the departure of one storm—and the approach of another.

"The new storm, shoving in from the west, is expected to bring scattered showers today in the western and northern portions of the state." The prediction was a little off, and just a little late.

Eva Poe Newkirk and her husband Tom lived on a ranch north of Folsom, New Mexico in 1957. What follows is her edited account of the blizzard of that year as she told it in a long letter to her family. She began writing on March 23.[1]

"March 22, 1957: A day that will go down in history.

"We have a real old-fashioned blizzard. It hit yesterday afternoon about 3 o'clock. It blew all night, and [is] still blowing hard. There seems to be a lot of snow. It's hard to tell, though.

"Tom got sick yesterday morning.... I hope and pray I don't have to get out in this awful storm to take him to the doctor. It is ten minutes after 10, and the storm is much worse. The radio has quit. I listen every time I hear the phone ring. We don't have electricity (as you know, we burn butane). So many heat their houses with electricity and do their cooking with it. The store has closed—no heat and no water.

"It must be terrible out here on those flats. I just wonder how many cars are stalled on the highways, and how many poor old cows and calves will die in this! Will write more later.

"Well, it is twenty minutes of two, and it is worse than it has been yet. A train went by, but we couldn't see it at all. Oh, Olive, this is serious.... Can't hear anything on the radio. More later.

"It is now 3:00 PM. And this wind is worse, and it gets so dark at times with the dust that you can hardly see. Can you imagine dust mixed with snow like this? I was just talking to May Mobley at Des Moines, and the line went out. Now, no telephone. I'm wondering how many lives will be lost in this. We still have the roof over our heads, but at times I wonder how much longer we will. We have heat and plenty to eat, and I feel right now that that is more than some have, so I am thankful. We can hardly see through any of the doors or windows for the mud packed on them.

"It is now 4:00 PM, and no change. It's just awful. I have seen a lot of bad storms since I came here in 1912, but this is the worst I have ever seen. I hope we will be able to hear something on radio (as you know, it is a battery radio) tomorrow. No doubt, by this time, there are hundreds of cattle buried alive. Not to mention calves, horses, sheep, or what not. At times, it is so quiet, you can't hear anything; then it strikes with such force, I just tremble. Tom has been in bed all day yesterday and today.

"Well, it is 7:30 PM and still raging. The trap door on the east end of the house to the attic is open and banging. Snow is drifting into the big bedroom. The north side of the floor is white with snow. This has never happened before in the whole time Tom's folks have lived here.

"Sunday A.M. March 24, 1957. Yes, this is the Lords' Day, but His children will not be able to meet for worship today. And He knows they can't. The storm is still raging. No telephone, no radio, a sick husband and three miles from a living soul. We still have heat, and the roof is still on. But, no doubt, the attic is full of snow. It is starting to leak now. I do pray that everyone is as well off as we are....

"Monday A.M., March 25. It is now 9:00 AM, and still raging. The sun is trying to come out, but oh! This wind is drifting the snow terribly. I am wondering about poor old Mr. And Mrs. Dickerson out there just this side of Des Moines. He is 91, and she isn't far behind in age. They are so alone. No children or grandchildren near at all. They have no phone and are burning coal oil. I pray they are warm and have plenty to eat.

"It is now 10:15 and still raging. The sun isn't as bright as it was. It got worse in the afternoon yesterday, but oh, I hope it clears this afternoon. 3:20 PM. Well, it is still raging, and more dust than snow. I went to the barn to see if the chickens were all right and to get water and feed to them. The drift in front of the coop is was eight or nine feet high. The wind isn't quite so strong, I believe. Tom is up and about, but so weak.

Well, this is Tuesday, March 26, and I am so thankful to say the sun is shining, and it never looked so good to me in my life. We still have some north wind, and it is cold. We heard the radio some last night, and this morning.... Pat and I will start shoveling the road open.

"...It is now 6:00 PM. Pat and I just came in.... We finally got the car out of the garage. We put the chains on, and started out with shovels. We got to Buffalo Head before we got stuck.

"I am so sore from shoveling snow. We shoveled our last drift about 11:00 this morning. A friend of ours, Felix Chavez, saw us up the hill this side of Folsom. He got his shovel and came up and helped us. I was so glad to have his help. I went in this afternoon; got another supply of groceries and chicken feed. Tom is much better."

By Friday, Mrs. Newkirk was able to get into Folsom. What struck her most was the number of dead cattle she saw, and the final pages of her letter enumerated livestock losses for each rancher in the area. In all, an estimated 14,000 head of New

Mexico cattle perished during the storm, most of them in the Raton-Clayton area of the state.

The blizzard of 1957 produced winds of up to 80 miles per hour and snow that accumulated in drifts up to 30 feet deep. A total of 30 people died in the storm, but only one New Mexican. P. L. Ward of Raton froze to death after being inadvertently locked out of his own house wearing only his undershirt.

Spring weather resumed in April.

[1] The complete text of Mrs. Newkirk's letter can be found in *Us Nesters in The Land of Enchantment,* which was compiled by Mrs. N. H. (Cora) Click and privately published in 1980.

"LAS VEGAS, NEW MEXICO HOTTEST TOWN IN COUNTRY" SAYS GOV. MIGUEL OTERO

Miguel A. Otero, Governor 1897-1906
(Photo Coursesy the Albuquerque Museum Photoarchives, PA 1978.050.404)

Many towns on America's western frontier acquired reputations for lawlessness, for being "wild and wooly." Some such reputations were well deserved while others were more the product of myth and legend. Dodge City, Kansas was probably the most famous even in its own time. Any lack in notoriety was corrected with the long running television series *Gunsmoke*. Dodge City was a railhead—shipping point—for cattle driven north from Texas in the years after the Civil War. That meant that hundreds of armed Texas cowboys arrived in town with pockets full of wages and cravings for whiskey. Much of the violence can be attributed to those two factors.

Ellsworth, Hays and Newton, Kansas, were also high on the list. In fact, one of the bloodiest gunfights in the history of the west took place in Newton in the fall of 1872. A Texas cowboy named Hugh Anderson undertook the revenge killing of town marshal Mike McCluskie.[1] When the shooting was over, eight bystanders and the marshal lay dead or wounded on the floor. The event became known as the "General Massacre."[2]

But what about New Mexico? The territory was home to no cattle shipping points comparable to the Kansas cow towns, but the arrival of the railroad did bring with it an element of the population that eschewed law and order. Probably the wildest of New Mexico towns was Las Vegas.[3] Here is what Governor Miguel A. Otero said about the town—he lived there at the time—in his memoirs:

"For more than a year after the entry of the railroad, it can be stated without fear of contradiction that Las Vegas was the 'hottest' town in the country. Such a statement would be substantiated by the record, for one month, which the … files of the [Las Vegas] *Daily Optic* establish. They show that twenty-nine men were killed in and around Las Vegas, either murdered outright or shot in self-defense or hung by the well-regulated Vigilance Committee. Such a record, I am certain, would be hard to parallel in the history of any of the wild towns of the West."

Because of Fort Union to the east of Las Vegas, and the Santa Fe Trail, violence was nothing new to the community. In fact, just a month before the railroad arrived in town, a drunken teamster named Manuel Barela shot and severely wounded an elderly gentleman named Jesús Morales. When Morales' equally elderly friend, Benigno Romero, asked Barela to explain himself, Barela killed Romero. A vigilante group settled matters with Barela by means of a short rope and a long drop from the platform of the village windmill.

The railroad arrived in Las Vegas in early July 1879 by which time famed gunman John Henry "Doc" Holliday was operating a saloon and gambling parlor on Centre Street. A former army scout named Mike Gordon became enamored of a woman who was associated with Holliday's establishment, but she rejected him. Gordon came calling with a gun in his hand. He fired several shots into the barroom but before he injured anyone, Holliday shot him. He died later in the day. A Coroner's Jury ruled the matter excusable homicide.

It was around this time that one Hyman G. Neill was elected Justice of the Peace in East Las Vegas, the new town that sprang up with the arrival of the railroad. Neill was better known as Hoodoo Brown. Neill created the first police department and manned it with some of the most notorious gunmen and robbers of the time: Mysterious Dave Mather, Dave Rudabaugh, J. J. Webb, Tom Pickett, and Joe Carson, among others. When some of them were not busy enforcing the peace in town, they were out in the country robbing trains and stagecoaches. Even Doc Holliday and Wyatt Earp seem to have been associated with Neill.

Dave Mather disappeared from the scene, as mysteriously as he had arrived. Dave Rudabaugh, later one of Billy the Kid's gang, was eventually assassinated by vigilantes in Parral, Mexico.

In February 1880. J. J. Webb murdered Michael Keleher in the Goodlet and Roberts Saloon for the purpose of stealing about $2,000 from him. This was the case that led to the demise of Hoodoo Brown's gang. A West Las Vegas grand jury reviewed the matter and indicted Webb for murder and Brown for theft. Webb was arrested, but Brown (H. G. Neill) had disappeared. Webb ultimately escaped from jail and died a few months later of smallpox.

Pickett was arrested with Billy the Kid in December 1880. He managed to bail out of jail and disappeared for a time. He was a practicing outlaw until he became a deputy sheriff in Arizona in 1912. He died of kidney disease in 1934.

Carson may have been the exception in this bunch. He was a 40-year-old married man with a 14-year-old daughter. While he was suspected of participating in a stagecoach robbery with Neill's bunch, he was never charged. On January 22, 1880, Carson, functioning in his job as marshal, approached a group of four men in the Close and Patterson Saloon: Tom House, Anthony Lowe, John Dorsey and William "Big" Randall. He asked them to comply with an ordinance that required them to check their guns with the bartender. Tom House probably fired first, two of his bullets hitting the marshal in the arms. The other three scofflaws began firing and Carson went down. He may have got off two shots—he carried two guns, one in a holster and one in his hip pocket—before he died with eight bullets in his upper body and one in his leg.

Dave Mather happened to be in the saloon at the time, and his aim was true. He killed Randall with two bullets to the chest. He put two bullets into Lowe's body and another two into House's leg. House and Dorsey escaped only to captured two weeks later. They joined the badly wounded Lowe in jail.

In the early morning hours of February 8, 1880, a group of vigilantes took the three outlaws out of the lockup and led them to the windmill in the middle of the plaza, the same spot where Manuel Barela met his doom. The lynchings, though, were not run-of-the-mill. The mob undertook to hang Lowe first, but neglected to tie his hands and he grasped the rope around his neck as he swung. While that was happening, Joe Carson's wife, who was in the crowd, grabbed a gun and began firing. Instantly, it seemed, everyone in the crowd with a gun began shooting at the killers. There was no need of further hangings that night.

By the early spring of 1880, Hoodoo Brown's rule of East Las Vegas was at an end and H. G. Neill (Hoodoo Brown) was on the run. That did not mean an end to violence in the San Miguel County community. For one thing, J. J. Webb remained in jail for the murder of Michael Kelliher.

On April 2, Dave Rudabaugh, a former policeman for Hoodoo Brown, and John "Little Allen" Llewellyn, a housepainter, went calling on the jailhouse. The jailer, Antonio Lino Valdez, recognized both and admitted them. As they approached Webb's cell, they drew their guns and demanded the keys. When Valdez refused, they shot him. One of them tossed the keys to Webb, and the two of them fled the scene in a waiting hack.[4] Webb declined to flee and remained in his cell.

Valdez died later in the day of bullet wounds to the chest.

The killers fled south, acquiring saddle horses somewhere along the way. Llewellyn, it is said, suffering greatly from both consumption and rheumatism, begged Rudabaugh to kill him and put him out of his misery. Rudabaugh obliged and buried the body along the trail. Whether the story is true or not has always been in question. What is known for sure is that Little Allen was never seen in Las Vegas again.

Rudabaugh next showed up riding with Billy the Kid. Nine months after killing Valdez, Deputy U. S. Marshal—and Lincoln County sheriff-elect—Pat Garrett arrested him, along with The Kid, Tom Pickett and Billy Wilson, at Stinking Springs, east of Fort Sumner. Garrett took the prisoners to Las Vegas where they could board a train to Santa Fe.

A crowd of citizens confronted Garrett and demanded that he turn Rudabaugh over to them, presumably for the purpose of meting out justice as they had for the killers of Marshal Joe Carson less than a year before, that is, a quick hanging. Garrett refused.[5] He faced down the mob as the train hurried out of town.

Rudabaugh was sentenced to life in prison on the federal charges and then returned to Las Vegas to face charges in the Valdez killing. He was sentenced to hang. He and J. J. Webb and five others escaped from jail on December 3, 1881. Neither he nor Webb was ever recaptured.

Less than ten years after the departure of Hoodoo Brown, there appeared in Las Vegas another criminal with a flair for organization. His name was Vicente Silva. He had actually operated the Imperial saloon and gambling parlor since 1875, but in the late 1880s he entered into criminal enterprise in a big way. He soon led a band of 40 killers and thieves, three of whom were Las Vegas policemen.

Silva himself maintained a façade of respectability and the community did not connect him with the extensive acts of cattle rustling, robbery, rape and murder that seemed to be epidemic in the region, as far to the east as the Texas Panhandle. He was much smarter than Hoodoo Brown and operated successfully for nearly five years, but he too finally made a mistake; actually a series of mistakes.

In 1892 he ordered his criminal minions to rustle cattle from a rancher named José Esquibel. Esquibel did not take the matter lightly. He was first able to recover his stolen animals and he soon learned that Silva was responsible for the crime. He filed the appropriate charges against the saloonkeeper with a San Miguel County court. For the first time Silva was exposed as the criminal he was. He fled to a hideout in the mountains, but was able to slip back into Las Vegas on a regular basis. Silva blamed a gang member named Patricio Maes for betraying him to Esquibel. He convened a kangaroo court in October of 1892. With generous portions of whiskey for each juror, a guilty verdict was quickly returned and Maes was hanged from the Gallinas River bridge.

After this event, Silva seems to have gone mad. He came to believe that his brother-in-law had somehow betrayed him, too. But Gabriel Sandoval, a meek and mild man who had tended bar for Silva, had not done so. No matter. Silva stabbed him to death and had his body disposed of in a privy. Silva also became convinced that his wife, Telesfora, had consorted with the law. In the spring of 1893, he enticed her to join him at his hideout. He promptly robbed her of what little money and jewelry she had, and then he stabbed her to death.

That act was too much, even for his hardened followers. Telesfora had been popular among them, and they could see no reason to rob her when Silva already had so much money in ill-gotten gains. Silva ordered her body buried in an arroyo. When the chore was complete and Silva and his cohorts walked back toward the hideout, an outlaw named Valdez pulled his pistol and shot Silva in the head at close range. The bandit chief died instantly. He was 50 years old.

It was some time before it became generally known that Silva was dead. The gang continued to operate for a couple of years, but it was essentially leaderless, and finally fell apart. Many of the outlaws were arrested, prosecuted and hanged. Others were sentenced to long prison terms. One source says that the last surviving member of the gang died in 1940.

For many, those who called Las Vegas "Our Lady of Sorrows of the Meadows" had the name right.

_____

[1] One source says that McCluskie was a mining foreman and makes no mention of any service as town marshal.

[2] Anderson was killed two years later by McCluskie's brother, who also died in the duel.

[3] Local folks called the area *Las Vegas Grandes en el Rio de las Gallinas* or the big meadows on Turkey River. The town itself was called *Nuestra Señora de los Dolores de Las Vegas* or Our Lady of Sorrows of the Meadows.

[4] This was an odd means of escape, but as the story goes, they forced the driver, at gunpoint, to take them to East Las Vegas where they dumped him and stole the vehicle which they used to continue their flight.

[5] Garrett claimed that Rudabaugh was wanted on federal charges of mail theft, and those charges took precedence over territorial charges.

JOSÉ LEANDRO PEREA OF BERNALILLO: SHEEP KING OF NEW MEXICO

José Leandro Perea, The Sheep King of New Mexico.
(Photo from a painting, Courtesy Sandoval County Historical Society)

José Leandro Perea was born in Bernalillo, New Mexico, in 1822, the son of Pedro José Perea and Barbara Romero. He was a third generation New Mexican as his grandfather, Pedro Acencio Perea, had arrived in Corrales in 1780 and his father was born there in the same year. By his death in April 1883, he was one of the richest—if not the richest—man in the territory. He was known as the Sheep King of New Mexico.

While yet in his 20s, José Leandro had occasion to travel east to the United States where he took careful note of the "Americans" he observed. He may or may not have foreseen the annexation of New Mexico to the United States, but he certainly understood that trade with the States would become a significant economic factor within his lifetime. After Col. Stephen Watts Kearny and his Army of the West captured Santa Fe in 1846, Perea traveled there to take the measure of people he would be dealing with in the future. His reactions were mixed, but his attention at the time was focused on agricultural and mercantile efforts.

In 1847 he took a caravan of 20 wagons loaded with dry goods to the Mexican city of Durango and sold them at a good profit. In 1853 alone, the Perea family sent about 50,000 sheep to California.[1] At one point, Perea had so many sheep that the sheering operation went on the year around. In the spring of 1877, José Leandro made a sale of 17,000 sheep to a Kansas City company. It was the largest single sale of sheep up to that time. Perea's wealth in the 1870s was estimated at $2,000,000, a staggering amount at the time.

In the early days of the "American Occupation" José Leandro seems to have been cautious in his approach to the new government. One source identified him as among the anti-American faction, and yet the same historian reports that he lent money to the territory for the purpose of paying the expenses of the legislative assembly.[2] He also actually favored statehood because he believed that the result of it would be "home rule" by the Hispanic population. Many of the Anglos who arrived soon after Kearny's army favored territorial status because they were most interested in the political patronage that would be doled out by Washington under federal governance.[3]

By the time the Civil War arrived, the entire Perea clan was committed to the Union cause. This was no secret, and when the Confederate forces under the command of General Henry Hopkins Sibley arrived in Bernalillo, they undertook to appropriate José Leandro's money. Legend holds that Rebel troopers destroyed several houses looking for the treasure, but never found it. The money is said to have been buried in the ground, covered with hides and then covered with dirt over which many hundreds of sheep passed, concealing it completely.[4] The Confederates were soon defeated and José Leandro resumed his business activities.

The beginnings of education in Bernalillo can also be traced to José Leandro. In 1872 he convinced St. Michael's College in Santa Fe to provide instructors for a school, and two brothers were so assigned. José Leandro provided space in his own home for the classes, and 92 boys attended the first year. In 1874 he gave a ten-room building to the Sisters of Loretto to start a school for girls. In 1877, when the community built a school, José Leandro donated the land and lumber for its construction, and he paid the workmen who built it.

But none of these things brought the fame, and the place in New Mexico history that did an event in early 1878. The railroad had not yet traversed the Raton Pass into New Mexico, but advance work was being done to secure rights-of-way and land for marshaling yards, round houses and maintenance shops. Two of the advance men arrived in Bernalillo in February 1878 on Concord coach. Their mission was to secure the land necessary for a division point, and that would include all those things mentioned above. José Leandro Perea owned the land. The two men, in the company of Perea's nephew, Francisco Perea, called on the town's patrón.

The meeting, according to later reports, was not cordial from the beginning. Don José Leandro was cool to his visitors as they produced and explained several maps that showed what land the railroad would need. They pointed out that the land they desired was selling for $2-3 per acre and they were prepared to negotiate a fair price and to make the necessary purchase. José Leandro replied that the price *he* required for the purchase of the land was a staggering $425.00 per acre, and nothing less. The negotiations ended at that point. The railroad men simply moved on down the line to Albuquerque where local merchants greeted them with open arms.

Why José Leandro did it remains a mystery. Some said he simply did not want to live with the disruption that the trains would cause in the community. Others said he viewed the coming of the railroad as another invasion, not so much different from Sibley's rebels, but one that he could stop. And yet another believed that he was angry at the railroad because it would put his freighting company out of business. Whatever the reason, it was a done deal. Albuquerque would become New Mexico's metropolitan center and Bernalillo would remain a village.

José Leandro Perea died on April 2, 1883. He was the father of 13 children, 12 by his first wife, Maria Dolores Chaves, and one by his second wife, Bibiana Guadalupe Perea. Many of his descendants continue to reside in Bernalillo and Sandoval County.

---

[1] Richens "Uncle Dick" Wootton, then of Taos, opened the sheep trade with California in 1852 when he drove 9,000 woolies to Sacramento.

[2] The money was repaid in 1853.

[3] Patronage resulted in the corrupt activities of the Santa Fe Ring some years later.

[4] This incident is not mentioned by Don E. Alberts in either of his definitive books on the Civil War in New Mexico (*The Battle of Glorieta* and *Rebels on the Rio Grande*). Marc Simmons in *Albuquerque, A Narrative History* says the money was not even there as it had been previously disbursed and the Pereas had fled the town. The story as told above may be more legend that fact.

J. Y. PEREA: AN ICONOCLAST IN HIS TIME

Jose Ynez Perea[1] was nearing 60 years of age when he wrote the following letter to Reverend Norman Skinner in early 1897. It speaks for itself. The numerical designations are Mr. Perea's and are probably responses to specific questions asked by Rev. Skinner. It is presented here just as it was written.

1.   I was born in Bernalillo, N. M.

2.   Date of my birth, April 21st, 1837.

3.   Places where early life was passed. My father whilst I was yet an infant, built and moved to La Rinconada, a large ranch south of the Sandia Indian Grant and north of Alameda.[2]

4.   In 1842 I was sent to school to Peralta, N. M. to Fr. Becerra. In the spring of 1844 I was taken to Chihuahua in Old Mexico. I attended Dr. Guadalupe Miranda's school, a man who had become somewhat renowned as an educator. The studies were reading and writing, ancient and sacred history which took place in the Bible, geography and arithmetic, drawing and … Catechism. It was there I made my first communion and was confirmed in 1846. I was there during the war of the United States and Mexico.
       In 1849 I went to New York and attended Mons. Peugnet's French School. There I studied French, English, Spanish and Latin, ancient and modern history, algebra, mathematics and drawing.
       It was there I made my second and last confession, after which I took up the Bible as my guide in the way of life, refusing positively the confessional though threatened with many hardships.
       My father had written to me [as to] whether I would like to go to West Point Military Academy. I took advantage of this offer to flee from my Catholic teachers who seemed turned against me.
       Early in the spring of 1851 my father sent me to Dr. Pingry's Collegiate Institute to prepare me for West Point. In the fall of the same year I passed my examination and entered the Military Academy.[3]
       In the fall of 1852 I became so disgusted with military life that I tendered my resignation which was accepted. I went to a school in Guilford, Conn., but the teacher died so I waited my father's wishes at Hoboken, attending a French School. At that

time my brother in law, Dr. Juan Montoya, arrived from New Mexico and took me home.

On my return my father treated me with severity and fearing my influence with the family, took me to St. Louis to Wilson Copper & Co.'s dry goods store as clerk. Fearing my parents continued and growing opposition, I thought the better part of valor would be to flee, so that in 1855, July 4th, I took a steamer for New Orleans and went to sea for five years.

In 1860, toward the fall, my father wrote to me [in] Boston to come home and I would be tolerated in religion. I went to California until after the [Civil] war in 1864, when I returned to New Mexico.[4] My father died in Santa Fe in 1865, not one of the family attending his death but me. He appointed me administrator from among eleven brothers and sisters. I married Victoria Armijo, daughter of Dr. Ambrose Armijo of Old Albuquerque, in 1867. She died in 1868. That same year I invited friends and founded the village of Salazar on the Rio Puerco.[5] In 1869 I moved to La Cinta, on the Canadian River, which became another village.[6]

5.   Date of residence in Las Vegas: In 1871 [I] went in partnership with Tuckerber and Myers, took a room and boarded at Rev. John A. Annin's. My store failed in 1872. I was two years on the Pecos River keeping cattle and sheep, and two on the Rio Puerco after which I met a committee appointed by the Presbytery of Santa Fe at Santa Fe to find out if I would enter the work as an evangelist. In 1877 I went to Las Vegas to study with Bro. Annin. Brother Rafael Gallegos went with me visiting and preaching in every village and ranch of both San Miguel and Mora Counties. We were often a month in each tour before we came back to Las Vegas, the centre [sic] of our labours [sic]. In 1878 I went with Rev. Taylor Ealy to Zuñi were I married Miss Susie Emma Gates on the 25th of December. Mrs. P. came from Schellsberg, Pa. Having been ordained in 1880 at Presb. held in Jemez Pueblo, I was sent to Los Corrales. My field was in both sides of the Rio Grande, on the west it reached to San Rafael around the San Mateo Mts., embracing 27 villages. Now the field is divided in two. There are six organized churches now in my original field: Two Congregational, one Methodist and three Presbyterian, but I was the "John the Baptist, preaching in the wilderness, preparing the way of the Lord" for all of them.[7]

Now my brother, if I have been too profuse, abbreviate this just as much as you please. You are at liberty to do as you wish with it.

Cordially yours
J. Y. Perea

Genealogical charts of the Perea family do not show any information about J. Y. except his year of birth. No source mentions his year of death or any children he might of fathered and he does not mention any offspring.

His older brother was Col. Francisco Perea, born in 1830. Francisco married Dolores Otero in 1851 and before her death in 1866 she bore him 18 children. He then married Gabriella Montoya in 1875, and before he died in 1913, he fathered an additional 18 children.

J. Y. and Francisco were nephews of the famed Jose Leandro Perea, the "Sheep King of New Mexico."

This letter was found in the files of the Sandoval County Historical Society in Bernalillo, New Mexico.

----

[1] Genealogical charts show the name as Jose Inez Perea and the transcriber of the above letter mistakenly shows it as signed by J. A. Perea. Given his stated parentage and date of birth, there is little doubt about who J. Y. was.

[2] Modern maps do not show exactly where La Rinconada might have been.

[3] Note that Mr. Perea would have been 14 years old upon his entrance to West Point.

[4] It is interesting to note that Mr. Perea does not mention what he did for the four years in was in California (1860-64).

[5] Casa Salazar, today a ghost town, is located about ten miles—as the crow flies—south of Cabezon along the Rio Pureco.

[6] La Cinta (the ribbon or strip) is located near the modern Bell Ranch in San Miguel County. Modern maps do not show the exact location.

[7] It is also interesting to note that Mr. Perea does not count the Catholic churches in his "field."

AMERICAN ZEBULON PIKE GETS A LOOK AT
SPANISH SANTA FE

By the first years of the 19th century, some of the movers and shakers in Washington D.C. were casting covetous eyes on the trans Mississippi American West. France posed no obstacle to western expansion by the United States. Napoleon sold Louisiana—an ill-defined area estimated at 828,000 square miles that extended from the Gulf of Mexico to Canada, and from the Mississippi River west to what is now Idaho—to the Thomas Jefferson administration for $15,000,000 in 1803.

Spain was not so accommodating. She kept her doors securely closed to interlopers from the eastern part of the continent. The Spanish government allowed no trade or other intercourse between themselves and the Americans, British or French.[1] But the barriers began to fall in 1806 when a young U. S. Army lieutenant named Zebulon Pike entered the Spanish Territory.

Pike, born in 1779, was a contemporary of Meriwether Lewis and William Clark who were assigned the task of exploring the Missouri River to its headwaters and opening a route to the Pacific Ocean in 1804. In 1805 Pike was assigned to the exploration of the Mississippi to its mouth, a task he completed the following year. His next assignment was to trek to the headwaters of the Arkansas, then on to the source of the Red River and back to Louisiana, following that stream. The Red River was thought to be the boundary between Louisiana and New Spain.

In July 1806, Pike and with a party of about 22 headed west. His route took him to the banks of the Republican River near what is now the Kansas-Nebraska line, then southwest into Colorado. He is said to have "discovered" Pike's Peak on November 15.[2] He and his men suffered greatly during the winter months because they were equipped for a warm climate, not the freezing cold they encountered. In early 1807 they crossed the Sangre de Cristo Mountains and reached the confluence of the Rio Grande and Rio Conejos in what is now southern Colorado. The expedition was well within Spanish territory.

For reasons known only to himself, Pike ordered the construction of a small blockhouse. When it was complete, he raised the flag of the United States and settled in. On February 26, 1807, a troop of Spanish soldiers arrived and took the Americans into custody. They were escorted to Santa Fe where Pike was interrogated at length before they were sent on to Albuquerque and finally Chihuahua. They were ultimately released and they returned to Louisiana in July 1807.

There is, of course, much more to the story and the people involved.

Zebulon Pike was an ambitious young man, the son of an Army major. He aimed to make a name for himself and in seeking ways to do that he came to the attention of General James Wilkinson. Wilkinson was one of the great villains of early United States history. He had an enviable military record in the young country and had risen to the rank of brevet brigadier general during the Revolutionary War. He left the army after the war, but returned to it in 1792 and in 1797 he was named commander of the U. S. Army which position he still held in 1806. For many of those years he had received an annual stipend of $4,000 from the Spanish government and many believe that he even swore an oath of allegiance to Spain.

Wilkinson was also a part of the so-called Burr Conspiracy, if not the instigator of it. Aaron Burr had served as Vice President of the U.S. from 1801-04.[3] The goal of the Conspiracy was the partition of North America into two distinct entities, the western half of which would be governed by Burr and Wilkinson. It was said that Wilkinson avoided the appearance of wrongdoing because his own personal aims were so much the same as those of the U.S. government that it seemed what he was doing was what he *should* be doing.

It is unlikely that Pike was a part of, or even aware of, Burr and Wilkinson's grandiose scheme. He was never accused of complicity in the conspiracy. He was aware, however, that his expedition was expected to do more than simply map the headwaters of the Arkansas and Red Rivers. The reason he built his blockhouse and ostentatiously displayed the American flag may have been to attract the attention of the Spanish. There was no other practical reason for it. And he didn't simply build it and wait for results, either.

One member of his party was Dr. John H. Robinson. Robinson had arrived in St. Louis just before Pike was to depart for the west. He hounded General Wilkinson until he was allowed to go along. His reason for doing so was not to serve as surgeon for Pike's troops but to collect a debt owed to an American named William Morrison by one Baptiste LaLande who lived near Santa Fe. Shortly before Pike's entourage reached the Rio Conejos, Dr. Robinson announced that he would leave the group and trek to Santa Fe. He told Pike that he would not mention that he was part of a U. S. Army expedition and that he would rejoin the group in time for the march back to civilization. He went south on foot.

Pike had to have known that Spanish officials could not ignore a lone American arriving in Santa Fe on foot. This was especially true because Robinson would be required to present his authority to collect the debt to the Spanish Governor, Don Joaquin del Real Alencaster.[4] Robinson was true to his word. He did not say that he had traveled with an army expedition. He claimed he'd lately separated from a group of hunters. The distinction was lost on Real Alencaster. The Spanish border was closed to *all* Americans.

Robinson left Pike in late January 1807. On February 26, 100 Spanish soldiers captured Pike and his men.

The first question seems to be this: Why, specifically, did Pike stop and build a blockhouse so far inside Spanish territory? He claimed it was a simple matter. He was lost and mistook the Rio Grande for the Red River. Most historians believe, however, that he knew he was inside Spanish territory, and that he wanted the Spanish to know he was there. He had, after all, allowed Dr. Robinson to leave his party and go to Santa Fe. His reason for all this was that he wanted to get a good look inside

Spanish-governed Santa Fe, and what better way than as a guest of the Spanish themselves.[5]

His plan worked very well. The Spanish soldiers more escorted Pike and his men to Santa Fe, than took them as prisoners. The Americans were not confined to jail, and were allowed freedom of movement in Santa Fe, later in Albuquerque and finally in Chihuahua. Pike was allowed to retain his personal possessions, including his sidearms. He even dined lavishly with Father Ambrosio Guerra in Albuquerque during March of 1807 while being escorted south.

There could be a couple of reasons why the Spanish treated Pike with such hospitality. Very possibly they did not wish to provoke a situation that could lead to serious problems with the United States. They already had enough problems with the French. Another reason was that the Spanish people living on the northern frontier of New Spain were actually looking to the east for expanded trade. At the time they were at the mercy of the Chihuahua merchants for all of their supplies and trade goods. Many believe that it was the Chihuahua merchants using political leverage who maintained Spain's isolationist policy toward its neighbors to the east.[6]

The next question has to do with who called the shots regarding what Pike's expedition would actually do, as opposed to its ostensible assignment. It is unlikely that Pike himself, as a lowly lieutenant, conceived of the plan, although some thought so. It is more likely that he was simply obeying orders he'd received from General Wilkinson. And there was no reason for him to think that he was operating in anything but the best interests of the United States government.

So, it is possible that Pike was on an information-gathering mission for Wilkinson and Burr. It is also possible that the young lieutenant really thought he could lay claim to the Spanish west with his small force. Some of the Spanish thought so. It was reported that Pike, as he crossed the plains, told the Indians he met that the territory they occupied belonged to the United States. It was also reported that papers Pike carried, which were seized by the Spanish and examined by Governor Real Alencaster, indicated Pike's intention to claim the territory for the United States. These papers, it is said, were the cause of Pike being sent to Chihuahua instead of being released directly from Santa Fe.

The Burr Conspiracy, of course, did not succeed. Wilkinson double-crossed Burr and Burr was arrested on orders of President Thomas Jefferson in 1807. He was charged with amassing an army for the purpose of capturing New Orleans in an effort to create his nation in the west. That was treason, but he was acquitted of the charge. Burr was found guilty of the much-reduced offense of "proposing" and invasion of Mexico. He shortly left for Europe where he tried to get the French to foment a revolution in Mexico. Napoleon wasn't interested.

Whatever Pike's orders were, whatever motivated him to behave the way he did, he is generally considered responsible for attracting eastern Anglo-Americans to the Spanish Southwest. In 1810, he published an account of his adventures in New Spain along with descriptions of the land and its people. It is said that Pike's tales of New Mexico did for eastern Americans what Fray Marcos de Niza's tales of the Seven Cities of Gold did for the Spanish in Mexico 170 years before.

As a footnote to Pike's adventure, General Wilkinson evaluated it thus: "The principle object of your expedition up the Arkansas was to discover the true position of the sources of the Red River. This was not accomplished."

The criticism did not interfere with Pike's military career. He was promoted to captain while he was in New Mexico and received regular promotions up to the rank of brigadier general. He was killed on April 27, 1813 during the War of 1812 near York, Ontario when a powder magazine exploded causing a rock to strike him in the back.

General Wilkinson, for his part, was relieved of command during the War of 1812 for poor military performance. He failed at cotton farming in Mississippi and went to Mexico to in the hope of securing land from the government. But after 1810, Mexico was in the throes of a fight for independence from Spain, which it won in 1821. There didn't seem to be a place for Wilkinson. He died in Mexico City in 1825 at the age of 68.

---

[1] It is interesting that the Spanish Crown supported the American Revolution, and then continued to forbid commercial intercourse with Mexico's neighbors to the east.

[2] Pike did not name the peak after himself. John C. Frémont named it Pike's Peak many years later.

[3] Aaron Burr killed Alexander Hamilton in a duel at Weehawken, New Jersey on July 11, 1804.

[4] This appears to have been a legitimate debt. One source says Pike himself confronted LaLande about repayment. LaLande pled poverty and the debt was not repaid. LaLande died in Santa Fe in 1825, quite wealthy.

[5] The Spanish sent Dr. Robinson to Chihuahua where he asked for political asylum. He offered to become Catholic and explore the north of New Mexico and the Rocky Mountains for Spain. The Spaniards declined the offer and Robinson was returned to the United States.

[6] The Santa Fe Trail would open only 14 years later.

RED PIPKIN: OUTLAW

The life of Daniel "Red" Pipkin—an outlaw who falls into the "lesser known" category—is a classic example of the way in which the criminal justice system worked in New Mexico late in the 19th and early 20th centuries.

Red was born in Arkansas[1] in 1876 and raised in Apache County, Arizona and Valencia County, New Mexico. By the time he was 12, he'd abandoned his father's farm near Ramah, New Mexico and returned to Apache County. He promptly fell in with a bunch of other youngsters who busied themselves with deviltry[2] and he first came to the attention of the law. As a teenager he fled the area and is known to have worked for ranchers John Slaughter and later Joe Hampton.

It was at the Hampton ranch that Red became associated with a band of real outlaws. George Musgrave and his brother, Van, were primarily horse thieves, but they soon became acquainted with the High Fives gang, a well known, but not very successful band of robbers. The Christian Brothers, Will and Tom, led the High Fives. Before Red could get into a real trouble with this bunch, the gang fell apart after a posse shot and killed Will Christian in eastern Arizona in April 1897. Most of the gang fled to Mexico.

Red remained behind and began recruiting his own band of criminals from among the ne'er-do-wells with whom he become acquainted in his younger days. This bunch hit its stride when it was joined by an older outlaw, William "Bronco Bill" Walters. The gang's first effort at robbery was an utter flop.

They attempted to rob a Santa Fe Railroad passenger train near Grants in March 1898. The authorities had been tipped off, though, and all the robbers got was a fusillade of lead from express guards. One of the gang was wounded and they all fled, empty-handed. The effort did serve to annoy the railroad, which put a $500 reward out for the bandits, dead or alive. Red fled to Mexico.

He didn't stay away long. In May of the same year, he joined Bronco Bill and another thief, William "Kid" Johnson, in robbing another Santa Fe train, this one just south of Belen. This one was a bit more successful in that the robbers got about $25,000. Much of it was in silver that was too heavy to carry and had to be abandoned. They fled west, back toward the rugged country of eastern Arizona.[3]

The authorities were really annoyed. At least two posses set out in pursuit of the outlaws. One, made up of Socorro County Sheriff Holm Bursum and deputy U. S. Marshal Cipriano Baca started northwest and another made up of Valencia County Chief Deputy Sheriff Frank Vigil and Deputy Dan Bustamente headed southwest. Bursum and Baca turned back, but Vigil and Bustamente arrived at the Alamo Navajo community, northwest of Socorro on May 24th. They camped there and set out early the next morning accompanied by a group of Navajo Indians. The Indians knew where the outlaws had camped.

The posse arrived at the outlaw camp on Alamosa Creek at about six in the morning. Some of the Navajos were able to get close enough to lead off the bandit's horses. At a range of about 100 yards, Vigil called out for the men to surrender, and initially they seemed to comply. The outlaws stood with their arms at their sides, their rifles leaning against a tree about ten feet away. The officers approached. At a range of about 35 yards, the outlaws suddenly grabbed their rifles, ducked behind some cottonwood trees and opened fire. Vigil and Bustamente both fell, mortally wounded. One of the Navajos, Vicente Guerro, opened fire but he was promptly killed, too, by a bullet to the head.[4]

Walters, Johnson and Pipkin fled west again, and reached Datil where they stole horses and rode on to the small Arizona town of Geronimo. They lived there openly and spent money freely. On July 4 they likely had a bit too much to drink, and shot up a dance. This brought them to the attention of Deputy U. S. Marshal Jeff Milton and he, along with Wells Fargo agents George Scarborough and Eugene Thacker, and a local cowboy named Bill Martin set out on July 13. The posse reached a horse camp on the Double Circle ranch near the Black River on July 29. The gang was believed to be hiding nearby. The officers took over the horse camp and determined that they would simply detain each rider as he arrived at the camp, and hold them there so they could not warn the outlaws.

On the morning of July 30, 1898 three riders appeared on a ridge about 400 yards from the camp and began descending the trail. Along the way, two of them stopped and began shooting at a rattlesnake. The third man, Bronco Bill Walters, rode on into the camp and was ready to dismount when he realized that he'd ridden into a trap. He pulled his pistol and began shooting. So did Scarborough, Milton and Thacker. Walters was knocked out of his saddle. Pipkin and Johnson quickly took cover behind a rock and began firing at the officers. Johnson didn't conceal himself well, leaving his posterior exposed and Scarborough put a rifle bullet through it. Pipkin recognized that his friend was badly hurt. He took the time to remove the Kid's money belt, said to contain $6,000 in cash, before he disappeared into the brush.[5]

Johnson died and Walters survived, to be sent to prison in New Mexico. Pipkin made good his escape. He managed to steal a horse and was soon back in New Mexico, picking up where he'd left off. On August 14, he and several others once again stopped a Santa Fe train near Grants, and once again they got nothing when the express guards held off the attack.

Red seems to have retuned to Arizona where he stole some horses, and then headed north to Moab, Utah. There he joined up with a posse that was in search of a gang of cattle thieves. He alone, shooting from ambush, managed to kill four of the five rustlers. It wasn't long, though, before Utah authorities found out who Pipkin was, and in spite of his heroic standing in the community, he was arrested and returned to New Mexico to face charges.

There followed a legal squabble—Red's attorney was the estimable Bernard S. Rodey of Albuquerque—between the federal courts and those of the territories of New Mexico and Arizona. Federal charges were found insufficient and dropped. Then Pipkin managed to get himself removed to Arizona. He was tried there on charges of grand larceny and sentenced to ten years in the territorial prison at Yuma. He served seven years, and was released in April 1907. He was never prosecuted for killing the New Mexico officers.

For the next ten or so years, Red wandered around Arizona and New Mexico, working in a slaughterhouse and at other menial jobs. He may have married, but if so, it didn't last long. One source reports that he married and his wife died within a few years.

In 1917, the old train robber became a deputy sheriff under Bob Roberts in McKinley County, New Mexico. But even so, he couldn't entirely give up the old ways. In September 1918, he shot and wounded Pat Lucero, the Gallup night marshal. The exact nature of that altercation is not known, but the dispute may have been political (Pipkin was a Republican, Lucero a Democrat). Red was tried in Bernalillo County on charges of assault with a deadly weapon, convicted and sentenced to prison. He served 18 months before being pardoned.

He returned to Gallup in 1920 and went to work as a watchman for the Gallup-American Coal Company, a job he held until 1937.

Red had been a heavy smoker his entire life, and he contracted cancer of the mouth, which was diagnosed early that year. He left his job in August. A little less than a year later he shot himself to death. He'd indicated that he didn't want to wait for the cancer to kill him. He left his pistol to a man to whom he owed money.

Thus Red Pipkin, involved in gun-play numerous times over a period of 40 years, died by his own hand.

---

[1] Another source says Red was born in Texas.

[2] Today we'd call them juvenile delinquents.

[3] Some modern writers wonder if Red really participated in the Belen robbery. Authorities at the time certainly believed that he was there.

[4] Some sources state that at least one, and maybe two, of the outlaws were wounded in this affray. Others do not mention any wounds at all.

[5] One source claims that Pipkin turned the money over to Johnson's sister. One wonders why he would have done that.

POPÉ AND THE PUEBLO REVOLT

Rare it is in New Mexico history that newcomers have been turned back en masse. Anthropologists believe that people began arriving in what is now the Land of Enchantment sometime between 10,000 and 20,000 years ago, and at varying intervals they have been coming ever since. But on two occasions, the newcomers were driven out.

In the most recent instance, an invasion of New Mexico by Texas Confederate troops during the Civil War began and ended in a matter of months in late 1861 and early 1862.

But in the earliest instance, the Pueblo Indian Revolt, there had been a long-term occupation by the Spanish, and while they were driven out, they would return a few years later, and stay forever.

By 1680, it had been 140 years since the first Spanish explorers arrived in the region. Francisco Vásquez de Coronado spent the winters of 1540-41 and 1541-42 near the present town of Bernalillo. It had also been 70 years since Pedro de Peralta established Santa Fe as capital of New Mexico.

Coronado sought riches in New Mexico just as Hernán Cortés had in Mexico in 1519 and Francisco Pizarro had in Peru in 1531. He found no mineral wealth, of course, but he did make contact with some of the indigenous people, the Pueblo Indians, and that experience was a harbinger of things to come. Coronado and his troops engaged the Indians in what was called the Tiguex War. Many of the out-gunned Pueblo people were killed. Then New Mexico was largely ignored for more than 50 years. The Spanish were busy colonizing the land to the south.

In 1595, Juan de Oñate was appointed governor and directed to colonize the region to the north. By August, 1598 he, along about 130 men, their wives and children, horses and other livestock arrived at what he called San Gabriel, near the present Española.[1] The relationship between the Spanish and the Indians in the late 16th century seemed to be one of mutual curiosity. That did not last.

In December 1598, a group of 31 Spanish soldiers under Juan de Zaldívar, Oñate's nephew, was attacked at the Pueblo of Acoma. Only five survived. Zaldívar returned to Acoma in January 1599 with 72 soldiers, and reasserted Spanish military supremacy. This is the incident in which it has since been alleged that the Spanish, as punishment, cut the feet off Acoma men. Some historians argue that while this extreme punishment was ordered, it was never executed. Others claim the order was to cut off the toes, not the feet. After all, the vanquished Acomas were also enslaved, and how much work could a man do with only one foot?

The San Juan Pueblo also rebelled against Spanish rule in 1599, and Oñate used force to establish his domination of the natives.

A goal as important to the Spanish as riches and colonization was the conversion of the Indian population to Christianity, and some conversions were made. But the converts became virtual slaves who were forced to toil for both the priests and the civil/military governors.

The Spanish soon learned that the land in New Mexico was not rich. It would not produce adequate crops on a regular basis. No gold or silver was found. King Phillip III of Spain even considered abandoning the entire colony in 1607, but finally continued his support because of the Christian missionaries. He considered their work important.

Life was hard for the Spanish settlers, and more than half of Oñate's original followers returned to Mexico after taking a look at what life offered them in New Mexico. But life was most difficult of all for the Pueblo Indians. They were over-worked and under-fed. They were the frequent victims of raids by the nomadic Apache Indians who stole crops and livestock when there was a good year. The Spanish soldiers could not seem to protect them. And, worst of all, the Pueblo medicine men were no longer allowed to practice the ancient rites of the Indian religion. Those who were caught doing so were severely punished or summarily executed.

By 1680, the Indians had had enough, and the time was right for a change. There were two primary reasons why the prospects for a successful uprising seemed good. One was that the Spanish governor, Captain General Antonio Otermín, was at odds with church leadership and his garrison at Santa Fe was undermanned and poorly maintained. Morale among the troops was bad. These things did not go unnoticed by the Indians.

The other reason was a San Juan Pueblo Indian, then residing at Taos Pueblo, named Popé (pronounced Poe-pay´).[2] He was a natural military leader with his own axe to grind. He'd been flogged by the Spaniards for practicing Black Magic in 1675. Popé had two major obstacles to overcome: the virtual non-existence of a system of communication between pueblos and the simple fact that there had never been any real unification between various tribes.

The communication problem had solved itself. In earlier times, it would have been difficult for the various pueblos to communicate among themselves because they did not speak the same tongue; each spoke one of five languages: Keresan, Tewa, Tiwa Towa or Zuñi. By 1680 many of them had learned Spanish, thus providing them with a common language.

Legend has it that Popé solved coordination problem by sending out runners carrying knotted ropes to all of the Pueblos. Leadership in each Pueblo was given a cord and instructed to untie one knot each evening, and when the last was loosened, it would mean that the following day marked the beginning of the revolt. The Indians were to kill the all the Spaniards in their own Pueblos and then go to Santa Fe to join with the warriors from the other Pueblos.

Popé solved the unification problem by simply taking advantage of the mutual hatred the various Indians shared of their conquerors.

The plan worked flawlessly. On August 10, 1680, the Indians rebelled. They killed more than 400 settlers and priests and they converged on Santa Fe. The Spaniards were quickly routed and retreated south, first to Isleta, and then on to Socorro and finally to what is now Juarez.

But there was a problem: The plan didn't go beyond the act of driving out the Spanish. Popé did not set up defensive parameters to keep them away. He hoped that without the Spaniards, life among the Pueblos would return to the way it had been more than 100 years before. But historical disunity among the tribes returned and quarrels and feuds became problems. Popé became something of a tyrant and is said to have killed those who disagreed with his leadership. There was a drought and, again, there was not enough food to go around. They were yet plagued by Apaches and Utes. Popé was deposed and died in 1690.

But the Spanish had not given up on New Mexico. In 1692, Don Diego de Vargas, with about 1700 soldiers and settlers returned to the north. He promised that the Indian leadership would not be punished for the 1680 rebellion and he met little resistance along the march.

Some of the Indians still in Santa Fe did not trust de Vargas and when he arrived, they denied him admission to the city. He attacked, captured the capital and promptly executed about 70 Indians and enslaved their families. He then sent troops to surrounding Pueblos and reestablished Spanish rule by force of arms.

The church missions were reoccupied and the settlers resumed farming. The Spanish would have no further major problems with the Pueblos. Their rule of New Mexico would last for the next 130 years.

----

[1] San Gabriel was New Mexico's first capital. After Oñate was deposed and replaced by Peralta, the capital was moved to Santa Fe in 1610.
[2] Popé is usually credited with leading the Pueblo Revolt, but there were other Indian leaders who were similarly significant, among them Tupatú of Picuris Pueblo and Catití of Santo Domingo Pueblo.

JUSTIN JEROME DE PRASLIN AND THE GHOST TOWN OF HAGAN

The New Mexico town of Hagan came into existence in 1902 when large deposits of coal were found near Una del Gato Arroyo, southwest of Santa Fe.[1] The neighboring town of Coyote, three miles northwest, appeared in 1904. The New Mexico Fuel and Iron Company was formed to operate the coal mines. Hagan was sufficiently populated in the same year that a post office was established and by 1909 the community's population was around 60 and it boasted a general store. There were high hopes for the future and the railroad was on the way.

The original idea for the construction of a railroad to Hagan and Coyote was born in 1905, and died the same year. The town survived and in 1909 the idea was reborn and construction actually began. The plan was that the rails would run north from the Bernalillo County community of Tijeras, along the east side of the Sandia Mountains, then west through Hagan and Coyote and on to the Sandoval County town of Algodones where they would connect with the Atchison, Topeka and Santa Fe Railway main line. Construction of the line stopped three and one half miles before it ever reached Hagan.

The town again managed to survive, freighting coal out by the wagonload. About ten years later there were renewed rumors about the completion of the railroad, but it never happened, either. The Albuquerque and Eastern Railroad never completed the project. The tracks reached about half way between what is now New Mexico State Road 14 and Hagan. It was, in fact, a railroad to nowhere.

Hagan continued to survive, but Coyote was not so fortunate. Without rail service, the smaller community died after a few years and all that remains today are a few adobe walls.

There were two important events in 1924. For one, the railroad finally arrived, from the west, from Hagan Junction on the main AT&SF line between the "towns" of Nueve and Elota. The Rio Grande and Eastern Railroad built the 12-mile spur.

The other event was a change in management of the mines. A New Orleans promoter named Dr. Justin Jerome de Praslin took charge. He envisioned a model city—actually a showcase community—economically supported by coal production. He hired a Bernalillo master stonemason named Abenicio Salazár to build 300 structures within three years. Salazár and his crew of about 60 *adoberos* went to work. They built houses that were extremely modern for the times. Each had a stone foundation, electricity, plumbing, coal stoves and wood flooring, and on six different floor plans. About 20 of the homes were actually completed.

Interestingly enough, the workmen did not live in the town proper. They lived in tents and other temporary quarters in the hills nearby.[2]

Salazár's crew also built the largest adobe building in the state. It housed the Hagan Mercantile, the Post Office, a pool hall, barbershop, company offices and even a ballroom. The town also boasted of the Orange Hotel, a power plant, school, railroad weigh station and Tonque Clay Products, maker of tiles and bricks, operated nearby. The town had all it needed: mining and manufacturing, transportation, a service industry and enough citizens—the population was about 500 in 1925—to be substantial. After nearly a quarter century, Hagan was alive and well.

It didn't last long. By 1930, only two trains per week were able to haul out the total production of the coalmines and Tonque Clay Products. Miners had discovered in the meantime that the coal deposits were broken up by faults and laced with layers of shale. It reached the point where more shale was being removed from the ground than coal. Coal mining became quite difficult and very soon unprofitable. The 1930 census showed Hagan with a population of 191.

The mines closed the following year and the Interstate Commerce Commission gave the railroad permission to abandon the rail line from Hagan Junction. The Post Office also closed in 1931, with mail service moved to Placitas. The mining and powerhouse equipment, including the power line that ran east to the town of Golden, was sold to a machinery company in El Paso in 1932 for $40,000.

But even then Hagan did not die completely. It clung to a tenuous existence until 1939 when a new effort at coalmining was made. It only lasted a short time, and when the mines closed that time, they closed for good. What few people remained in the town were left with nothing to do, and little by little, they moved on. By 1950, the last of them were gone. Hagan was a ghost town.[3] Many of Abenicio Salazar's houses were demolished and the materials used elsewhere.

Today what is left of Hagan—mostly empty shells, reminders of failed dreams—is on private property and not open to the public.

---

[1] *Una del Gato* means cat's claw in English. The name is a reference to the thorny black locust bush that grows in the area.

[2] The late Lorella Montoya Salazar of Bernalillo, New Mexico, sister to the political Montoya brothers of the recent past—Tom, Joe, Alfonso and Ted—and a political activist in her own right, was born in Hagan in 1925. Her family lived in a building with wooden plank walls and a canvas roof. According to her birth certificate, her father, Tom, was a teamster at the time. Her family moved back to Bernalillo in 1927. Mrs. Salazar died in December 2002.

[3] No one seems to know the origin of the town's name. T. M. Pearce in *New Mexico Place Names* does not mention the source of the name and Robert Julyan in *The Place Names of New Mexico* says the origin of the name has been lost. None of the Sandoval County old-timers interviewed for this item area know the source of the name, either.

CHAVES CO. DEPUTY RAINBOLT SHOT, KILLED AT ROSWELL: ASSAILANT ESCAPES

Chaves County sheriff Fred Higgins was out of town on February 8, 1901, visiting El Paso, and his chief deputy, and brother-in-law, twenty-three year old Will Rainbolt was in charge. The young deputy received information that one Oliver Hendricks, a young cowboy from the Eight Mile outfit west of town, was packing a six-gun at a dance being held in the southwestern part of Roswell at a place called Rag Town.[1] Rainbolt, along with his brother, Mody, drove his buggy to the party and soon located Hendricks who was engaged in a dance. The officer waited patiently until the music stopped before he approached Hendricks. Rainbolt asked the young man to give up his gun, which Hendricks did. Rainbolt then told Hendricks to get into his buggy so that he could take him to jail.

At about that time, Oliver Hendricks' brother, Nathan, appeared and attempted to talk Rainbolt out of arresting his younger brother. Rainbolt was not persuaded, whereupon Nathan drew his own gun and shot the deputy before the officer had any chance to draw his own gun. The bullet hit Rainbolt in the right arm, passed through or near his heart, and lodged under the skin on the left side.

"Mody, they have killed me," Rainbolt said to his brother, and he died.

The Hendricks brothers mounted a single horse and rode out of town, toward Eight Mile. There they secured two fresh mounts and continued their flight, to the west. A posse soon took up pursuit of the killer, but was unsuccessful. The local newspaper said the posse's failure was due to ineffectual leadership since the sheriff was away and the chief deputy was dead.

A young wife and child, as well as his parents, survived Deputy Rainbolt. His funeral was held on Sunday, February 10, and the officer was interred at the South Side Cemetery in Roswell. The tragic affair was "largely attended."

Rumors circulated that there was more to the affair than met the eye. Some said there was bad blood between Rainbolt and the Hendricks brothers that resulted from an altercation two years previous in which Rainbolt shot both of the McElroy brothers, killing one of them. It was said that the McElroys and the Hendricks' were friends and the Hendricks brothers went about armed for the purpose of settling the score with Rainbolt at the best opportunity.

It was also rumored that Will had been drinking whiskey on duty the night he was killed. Mody was mute on the subject.

Sheriff Higgins returned to Roswell in time for his deputy's funeral, and began a pursuit of the killer, but it was too late. The trail had gone cold. It would be two years before Higgins was able to trace Nathan Hendricks to North Dakota—where he was using the name Clayton—and return him to Roswell for trial.

High-priced legal talent represented Nathan. He didn't deny that he shot and killed Rainbolt, but claimed he did so in defense of his brother, Oliver. Prosecutors wanted to know why, if in fact he was innocent of murder, he had fled the territory and changed his name. Fear, he said, of Rainbolt's brother-in-law, Sheriff Fred Higgins.[2] The jury seems to have been confused by all of this—Oliver Hendricks did not testify—and convicted Hendricks of murder in the 3rd degree. His lawyers immediately filed and appeal and Nathan was released on $15,000 bond.[3] The Supreme Court ruled, two years later, that a lot of mistakes were made with jury instructions. A new trial was ordered.

This time brother Oliver came out of hiding—he'd been in the Pacific Northwest living under the name Tom Patterson—and testified on his brother's behalf. The defense also produced a new witness, one Lige Shipp, who testified that he'd shared a half-pint bottle of whiskey with Will Rainbolt only minutes before the fatal shooting. This supported other testimony that the young lawman had been drunk at the time, and physically abusive to Oliver.

On Sunday morning, June 10, 1906, the jury returned a verdict of "not guilty." Nathan Hendricks is said to have returned to North Dakota.

The local newspaper editorialized thus:

"The tragic death of Deputy Sheriff Will Rainbolt is another proof that heavy fines for carrying concealed weapons are not entirely successful in preventing the practice. In the absence of something better it would be a good thing to make the fine an even $100 and see how that would work. The time has long passed in this country when it is necessary for anybody to go armed, and as long as they do, murder is at our elbow all the time. The pernicious habit of carrying a gun is responsible for more murders than either whiskey or women, the two great prompters of crime."

---

[1] One source suggests that Rainbolt was attending the dance and observed Hendricks packing a gun.

[2] Fred Higgins had a reputation as a no-nonsense lawman. He is reported to have killed outlaw Bob Hays in Arizona's San Simon Valley in August 1896 while serving as a deputy sheriff and deputy U. S. Marshal. He also participated in the shooting death of William "Black Jack" Christian in April 1897.

[3] No mention is made of where Nathan Hendricks got the money to pay for his lawyers, or to post such a large bond.

DICK ROGERS: SHORT-LIVED GUNFIGHTER

Not much is known about gunfighter Dick Rogers, and that is probably because his career didn't last long. He did manage to get himself involved in a couple of violent confrontations in Colfax County, New Mexico in the mid 1880s.

That was the time of the so-called Maxwell Grant troubles, early in 1885. The "troubles" stemmed from a dispute between those who supported the Maxwell Land Grant Company in its efforts to dispossess "squatters" who had taken up residence on company property[1] over the years, and those who supported the alleged rights of the unauthorized settlers. The Company, to bolster its position, brought in a well-known gunman named Jim Masterson from Dodge City, Kansas, by way of Trinidad, Colorado, to head up a company of "Malitia."[2] Supported by Territorial Governor Lionel Sheldon, Masterson was authorized to raise a force of 35 gunmen for the purpose of serving ejection orders that local officers refused to enforce. Militia Company "H" was made up of "gunmen, killers, thugs and bums from places outside of New Mexico."

Masterson and his group seem to have gone about their work with a little too much enthusiasm. A petition was soon circulated condemning the actions of the militia, and a group of prominent citizens took the train south to Santa Fe for the purpose of "interviewing" the Governor. When faced with a bit of political pressure, Sheldon backed down and disbanded the militia unit on March 1, 1885. Masterson was in Cimarron when he received word that he was out of work. He and some of his cohorts rode back to Raton where they proceeded to assault some of the petition signers, including Mr. D. F. Stevens, Chairman of the Board of County Commissioners.

Feelings ran high in Raton. A vigilante group made up of settlers and cowboys as well as local citizens was organized. Dick Rogers was elected captain. One source describes him as "a fearless cowboy" and another as "a daring young cow puncher." A third was not quite as charitable. He said this: "[Rogers was] a nasty Texan who had reportedly laid at least four men to rest within the [previous] year." Yet another source called Rogers an "outlaw-vigilante." It seems likely that the reason he was elected captain was that the previous January, he and some of his friends were able get the drop on Masterson and some of his friends in a Raton saloon. It is said that Rogers made Masterson dance by shooting holes in the floorboards at Masterson's feet.

With the vigilantes in place, Masterson and some of his associates holed up in the Moulton Hotel. A young fellow named George Curry[3] had lived in Dodge City as a boy and was casually acquainted with Jim Masterson. He arranged for a peaceful resolution. All of Masterson's men were rounded up, fed a noon meal, and marched— that is to say escorted—by 300 vigilantes to the Colorado state line. They were ordered to never return to New Mexico. Curry said later that he believed that none of them ever did.

But the violence was not over. John Dodds, a cowboy from the Cow Creek outfit and a member of the vigilantes, drove a wagon into Springer, the Colfax County Seat, on March 15, to get a load of corn. He ran into deputy sheriff Jesse Lee, former member of Company "H" and they exchanged words. Later in the day Dodds got drunk and shot up the town and got into an altercation with a constable named Carter. He was arrested and pleaded guilty to disturbing the peace. He paid a fine and started for home with his wagon full of corn.

Lee and Carter overtook Dodds a mile from town and attempted to arrest him for assault on Carter. He drove them off with gunfire, but decided to return to Springer on his own. The first thing he did was send a wire to Dick Rogers in Raton. Jesse Lee then arrested him. Dick Rogers hurried to Springer, rounding up John Curry (George's younger brother), Red River Tom Whealington and Bob Lee (no relation to Jesse) at the Cow Creek ranch, along the way.

Jesse Lee received word that Rogers meant to "deliver" Dodds from custody, and he and other deputies forted up in the courthouse. A deputy U. S. Marshal named Jack Williams thought he might help avoid violence by negotiating with Jesse Lee. Williams and Dick Rogers approached the courthouse. Lee and deputies Kimberly and Hixenbaugh immediately opened fire, killing Rogers instantly. Red River Tom rode up on his horse in an effort to get to Rogers, and Jesse Lee killed him, too. John Curry rushed forward, rifle in hand, and Lee shot him down. He died the next morning. Gunfire aimed at the courthouse became general, but no one inside was injured.

The army had to be called into Springer before order could be restored, and this incident marked the highpoint of violence in the Maxwell Grant troubles.

Dick Rogers was 28 years old at the time of his death. He was probably native of Texas. One source claims that he participated in the Lincoln County War five or six years earlier, but highly regarded sources on that event make no mention of him. Neither do many other sources, but then, he wasn't around long. Gunfighting was a dangerous business.

---

[1] The Maxwell Land Grant in northeastern New Mexico, at its peak, covered 1,714,764 acres, or 2,679 square miles. The State of Rhode Island, by comparison, covers 1,545 square miles.

[2] Jim was the younger brother of Bat and Ed Masterson. One source says he was Colfax County Undersheriff at the time of these events. Many sources skip this entire incident, preferring to show Jim in the good-guy mode. He died at age 40 of "quick consumption."

[3] Curry served as territorial governor (1907-1910) and became New Mexico's first congressman after statehood in 1912.

SEBOYETA, THE MOTHER VILLAGE: SAVED BY DOÑA ANTONIA ROMERO

As the crow flies, it is fewer than 50 miles from Albuquerque west to the village of Seboyeta.[1] It is located in what is now the far northeast corner of Cibola County, close to the confluence of that county's borders with those of Sandoval and McKinley counties. Seboyeta, at the base of Mt. Taylor, was an important community in the early development of western New Mexico.

Sources disagree on exactly when the first effort to settle the area was made. Abe Peña, probably the most astute historian on the region, says that a Father Menchero attempted to establish a Franciscan Mission there in 1746. Other sources say the priests didn't arrive until 1749. Whatever the year was, the purpose of the mission was to accommodate the Navajo Indians, who had agreed to support it.

There were many problems. The Navajos soon lost interest, for one thing. An interpreter at the time is said to have been told by the Indian people that they "could not become Christians or stay in one place because they had been raised like deer." Another Navajo said this: "I know all these people well, for they are my people and my relatives, and I say that neither now nor ever will they be Christians. They may say yes in order to get what is offered them, but afterwards they will say no."

The Spaniards, it seems, had made a tactical mistake. They used Laguna Indians as slave labor to build the mission, and the Navajos feared they would end up in the same kind of servitude. They withdrew their support by 1750 and the mission was soon abandoned.

The area was ignored for about 50 years. In early 1800, the Spanish Governor, Don Fernando de Chacón gave possession of the area to thirty families which had previously resided near the Rio Grande in Albuquerque. The names of some of those settlers remain familiar today: Aragon, Baca, Chavez, Gallegos, Garcia, de Herrera, Jaramillo, Marquez, Perea, Peralta, Romero and Santillanes.

Abe Peña describes what the trip might have been like. "Imagine more than 30 carts, each pulled by a pair of oxen, lumbering and squeaking up Nine Mile Hill…. Some of the men rode horses. Sheep, goats, and milk cows followed the train herded by boys and some of the older women."

The original plan called for the trip to take four days. It actually took five. The settlers officially took possession on March 16, 1800. Alcalde Don Jose Manuel Aragon, representing Governor Chacón wrote in his official report: "Today the colonists received the grant in community and the *suertes* (lots) as individuals and acknowledged same by throwing stones in the air, pulling weeds and shouting, 'God save the King' three times, wherefore they hold and enjoy all the ownership over said tracts which I have districted for such is the will of his Majesty the King."

The settlers immediately set about two important tasks. The first was to establish a church, which they called Our Lady of Sorrows. The next was to build a fortified village. Ten foot stone walls were constructed and houses were built up against them with no windows facing outward. Two entrances, one facing south and one east, were protected by hand-hewn ponderosa pine board gates which were each a foot thick.

The Spanish settlers and the Indians of nearby Laguna got along well, but the Navajos in the area felt threatened, and were justified. The settlers often engaged in raiding Navajo villages for the purpose of kidnapping children, primarily females, which would be sold into slavery in Albuquerque for about 500 pesos each.

In 1804, the Navajos laid siege to Seboyeta. They attempted to burn the village and to breach the walls. Doña Antonia Romero was one of the heroines of this event. She climbed to the roof of a house to take a look around and saw that a Navajo warrior had managed to climb over the wall and was in the act of removing the huge bar that held one of the gates closed. "Swarms" of Navajos waited outside. "Snatching a heavy stone *metate*, Doña Antonia lifted it above her head and brought it down with all her strength on the head of the warrior, killing him instantly." (No mention is made as to why a *metate*, a stone used for grinding corn and nuts, was on the roof of the house and available to Doña Antonia. On the other hand, maybe she had climbed down from the rooftop before she slew the invader. The narrative of the event is not clear on the point.)

By the following year, the settlers had suffered about all they intended to. They made a plea to the governor to be released from their promise not to abandon the village. Their request seemed to have been ignored, and they pulled out for Albuquerque. Along the way, though, they encountered a detachment of about 30 soldiers, and the settlers returned to their homes. Trouble with the Navajo subsided after that and the village flourished.

Seboyeta became the so-called Mother Village from which settlers founded other villages in the region. Among them were San Mateo in 1862, San Rafael in 1865, and El Concho, Arizona, in 1869.

Ruins of the walls that were so important 200 years ago remain in place yet today.

---

[1] The name of the village was originally spelled *Cevolleta*. Later that was changed to *Cebolleta*. The current spelling, *Seboyeta*, was adopted to meet requirements for postal service. The word means, "place where onions grow."

RUSTLERS STRIKE NEAR CABAZON: RANCHER JUAN ROMERO KILLED

In late March of 1884, a gang of outlaws led by brothers Candido and Manuel Castillo rode north from the villa of Cebolleta[1] for the purpose of stealing cattle near the town of Cabezon. The Castillos were desperate men. They were believed to have killed a man named Mariano Larragoite in Colorado in 1879 and Jose Apodaca in Cebolleta the in 1883. Colorado authorities offered a $1,000 reward for the Larragoite killing.

These lawless men operated in a lawless land. The town of Cabezon was 70 miles by trail from Albuquerque, the county seat of what was then Bernalillo County.[2] The sheriff rarely visited the community and he stationed no deputy there. The town had no marshal, either.

The Castillo gang succeeded in stealing some cattle in the area, but local folks didn't give up the livestock without a fight. The result of the gun battle that followed was that the outlaws managed to make good their escape, and Juan Romero of Cabezon was shot dead.[3]

Killing Romero was a serious mistake on the part of the Castillos. Within a short time, rewards totaling nearly $3,000 were offered for their arrests. Merchants Rudolph Haberland and William Kanzenbach offered $500, Governor Lionel Sheldon offered $500 out of territorial funds, Jose de Baca of Cabezon offered $200 and Romero's widow offered another $300. The people of the nearby village of Casa Salazar offered additional reward money, as did Albuquerque resident Charles Lewis.

At first, the posses had no luck. The country back toward Cebolleta and Mt. Taylor was rugged with few people and lots of canyons and arroyos. The outlaw brothers seemed to have disappeared, but for the princely sum of $3,000 the pursuers could afford to be tenacious, and they were.

A posse headed by Bernalillo County deputy sheriff Jesus Montoya, which included men from Casa Salazar and Cabezon, along with a Navajo Indian tracker, followed the brothers north, past Santa Fe and on to Espanola. There, on April 11, 1884, the posse engaged the Castillos in a gunfight at Amado Lucero's store. Both Castillos were wounded and their horses killed. Manuel died later the same night of his wounds.[3]

Candido escaped yet again, and was reported to have joined another outlaw gang at the town of Abuquiu. He was subsequently captured near Walsenburg, Colorado and returned to Albuquerque where he stood trial. He was convicted of 2nd degree murder and sentenced to prison. He was released in July 1890 and returned to Colorado. He was shot and killed in a gunfight with the Park County, Colorado, sheriff in 1891.

Cabezon is today a ghost town. From 1918 to 1940 it was estimated to have had a population of three to four hundred souls who were served by several stores and saloons. It was completely abandoned by 1950.

Sources vary on when the town was first settled. Church records show that a young couple, Francisco Montoya and Juliana Montes Vigil, were married at El Puesto del Cerro Cabezon on March 19, 1772. T. M. Pearce in *New Mexico Place Names* indicates that Juan Maestas first settled the town in 1826. James and Barbara Sherman in *Ghost Towns and Mining Camps of New Mexico* state that Cabezon was settled in the 1870s.

The town was named for the volcanic plug, Cabezon Peak, which is located nearby. The place has also been called Porteria, La Puesta, La Posta and Cerro de la Cabeza. Pearce credits Oliver Perry Hovey with changing the name to Cabezon in 1891. Cabezon Peak rises about 2200 feet above the surrounding plain. It is located about 45 miles northwest of Bernalillo. Cabezon was a main stop on the stagecoach line from Santa Fe to Fort Wingate, near Grants, until 1912.

The Navajo Indians ranged widely in the area, and the first European settlers were Spanish, their names still prominent today in Sandoval County: Montoya, Vigil, Gonzales, Salazar and Baca. Later ranchers also had familiar names: Leyba, Chavez, Valencia, Armenta, and others.

Later too came the Anglo merchants. Haberland and Kanzenbach as mentioned above were cosigners on the reward for the Castillo brothers. Other included O. P. Hovey, John Pflueger, Charles Holman and Richard Heller. Heller operated a store in Cabezon from 1889 until his death in 1947. His wife continued to operate the business until the town itself died in 1950.

And what caused the demise of Cabezon? The specifics vary, but in general the town was a victim of the times. The coming of the railroad meant the end of the stagecoach line to Fort Wingate. Navajos Indians, once a major economic factor in the area, moved further west and no longer traded in Cabezon. The land around the community became severely over grazed and ranching profits fell. The Great Depression came with the 1930s and many residents left in search of work elsewhere. Paved roads[5] and automobiles meant that marketing could be done in larger communities. In the final analysis, there just ceased to be a reason for the continued existence of Cabezon.

The town could, and did, fight back against the likes of the Castillo brothers, but it could not protect itself against the encroachment of time.

(NOTE: The remains of the town are on private property and those who own it do not allow visitors.)

---

[1] Cebolleta is spelled Seboyeta these days. It is located in what is now Cibola County, just north of the Laguna Indian Reservation. *Cibola* means buffalo and *cebolleta* means onion, or place where onions grow.

[2] In 1884, Bernalillo County extended west to the Arizona Territorial boundary. Sandoval County was not created until 1903.

[3] One source identifies Romero as a deputy sheriff. Other sources make no such assertion.

[4] Another source says it was Candido who was killed in the Espanola gunfight.

[5] State Road 44 was paved in 1934.

SALLY ROOKE: HEROINE OF THE GREAT FOLSOM FLOOD

Certainly one of the biggest news stories in New Mexico during the first decade of the 20th century was the great Folsom flood of 1908. It was a disaster of the first order, but the loss of life might have been much greater had it not been for the heroic acts of a single person, Mrs. Sarah "Sally" Rooke.

It rained a little in the late afternoon of August 27, 1908, but it was nothing out of the ordinary for a summer shower. The wind kicked up a bit after sunset and dark clouds formed to the northwest. Then it began to rain hard on Johnson Mesa and at the headwaters of the so-called Dry Cimarron River. The sheer volume of the downpour exceeded anything in memory and it became obvious that the downstream community of Foslom was in grave danger of flooding.

Mrs. Ben Owen, the wife of a rancher, had seen earlier floods and she said later that this was the worst she had ever seen. She telephoned the central switchboard at Folsom. Sally Rooke answered the phone.

"It's raining so hard up here the wash tubs are running over with water. You better get out before you're swept away!" Mrs. Owen reported. She also asked Mrs. Rooke to warn her sister, Lucy Creighton, who lived in Folsom, of the impending peril.

But Mrs. Rooke didn't run. She knew how devastating a major flood might be. She had about a half hour before the flood would crest and she began cranking the telephone and warning those who lived in the path of the deluge. "Pack up and leave at once. A flood is coming down the valley," she said time and time again.

She reached more than 40 families before a wall of water, carrying boulders, uprooted trees and other debris, struck the small cottage that housed the telephone facility. Mrs. Rooke was engaged in a three-way conversation with the local telegraph operator Allcutt McNaghten and his mother when "a terrific crash of lightening was heard and Sally's voice ceased."[1]

No one will ever know how many lives Mrs. Rooke saved that night, but it is certain that the number of fatalities would have been much greater than the 17 who are known to have perished. Twelve of those who died were from two related families, the Wheelers and the Wengers, substantial members of the community, who were in their respective homes when the water hit. Bystanders heard their screams of terror and supplications for help. One of those who died was Lucy Creighton who had been visiting at the Wenger home. Others who perished either could not, or would not, move out of the flood's path.

And that path was considerable. One source reported that the wall of water was 13 feet high and a mile wide before it spent itself. Another says that when it hit the town it was a half-mile wide and five feet deep with "high, rolling waves... and rushing along with a mad torrential velocity that picked up houses and floated them off like chips."

One witness south of town said, "The houses that came down, seemed to drag on the ground until they got about a mile out of Folsom. Near the Dan Dorherty home, there was a fall, and they were torn to pieces there—the Wenger home, the Wheeler home, telephone office, lumber yard, that I recall." Indeed, nothing of the Wenger house was ever found except for half of a door.

Recovery of the victims was a grim business. Survivors found many of them partially buried in the silt the water left behind. Many of the bodies had been stripped bare by jagged rocks and many of the women had been virtually scalped when their long tresses were caught up in tree branches as their bodies tumbled along on the flood. Clothing was found in tree limbs as high as 30 feet above the ground in the aftermath of the tragedy.

But among the recovered bodies, Sally Rooke's was not to be found. It wasn't until February of the following year that her remains were discovered.[2] A rancher found them some 16 miles south of town in a drift of debris left by the flood.[3]

And what of the heroine of this story? Sarah Rooke was something of an enigma. She had lived in Folsom for about three years at the time of her death. Believed to have been a native of Preston, Jackson County, Iowa, she'd arrived in New Mexico to visit a friend, Virginia Morgan, and so liked the area that she stayed. She may have taken up a homestead, but it is unlikely that she worked it. She was in her mid-sixties at the time, and crippled with severe curvature of the spine.[4] No husband or children ever resided with her in Folsom, and no one came forward to claim kinship after her death.

Mrs. Rooke's story of heroism made national headlines at the time, but was soon forgotten. It was not until the mid 1920s that interest in her was rekindled when telephone workers began donating small amounts of money—actually nickels and dimes—to construct a monument to her memory. A granite marker was installed at her gravesite in Folsom on May 15, 1926. It reads:

In Honored Memory of
SARAH J. ROOKE
Telephone Operator

WHO PERISHED IN THE FLOOD WATERS OF

THE DRY CIMARRON AT FOLSOM, N. M.,

AUGUST 27, 1908,

WHILE AT HER SWITCHBOARD WARNING
OTHERS OF THEIR DANGER

———

WITH HEROIC DEVOTION SHE GLORIFIED HER

CALLING BY SACRIFICAING HER OWN

LIFE THAT OTHERS MIGHT LIVE

"Greater Love Hath No Man Than This"

———

ERECTED BY HER FELLOW-WORKERS

———

[1] Quoted from *Folsom, 1888-1988: Then and Now*, prepared by the Centennial Book Committee, 1988.

[2] One reporter claimed that Mrs. Rooke's body was recovered the following Saturday, 12 miles down the canyon, her headset still in place and the telephone cord broken. This was patently untrue, and there was no real reason to artificially enhance the true tale of her heroism.

[3] Some bodies were found as far as 20 miles down stream.

[4] It was this unfortunate characteristic that allowed searchers to identify her body.

NM GOVERNOR EDMUND ROSS: A FORGOTTEN NATIONAL HERO

"In a lonely grave, forgotten and unknown, lies 'the man who saved a President,' and who as a result may well have preserved for ourselves and posterity constitutional government in the United States—the man who performed in 1868 what one historian has called 'the most heroic act in American history, incomparably more difficult than any deed of valor upon the field of battle'—but a United States Senator whose name no one recalls: Edmund G. Ross of Kansas."

So wrote John F. Kennedy in *Profiles in Courage.*

That "lonely grave" is located in the Fairview Memorial Park in Albuquerque, New Mexico and the way in which Ross came to be interred there is an interesting story.

Edmund G. Ross[1] was born in 1826. A strong abolitionist, he participated in the rescue of a slave in Wisconsin in the early 1850s and by 1856 he'd joined the movement of abolitionists to Kansas. He engaged in the newspaper business there until he joined the Union Army in 1862. He attained the rank of major by war's end in 1965. In 1866 he was elected to the United States Senate after famed Jayhawker—and U. S. Senator—James H. Lane committed suicide. It was then that his troubles really began.

The issue facing Ross, and the nation, had to do with the conflict between the U. S. Senate and President Andrew Johnson. The discord centered on what was to be done with the Confederate states in terms of reuniting the nation. Johnson, like Abraham Lincoln before him, favored a charitable approach that would return the errant states to the Union as quickly as possible. The so-called radical Republicans in the congress, in the Senate in particular, believed that the south should be punished before reconciliation was allowed.

On what history would show to be very tenuous charges, the House of Representatives impeached President Johnson for "high misdemeanors." The leaders in the senate needed a two-thirds majority—36 votes— to convict, and thereby oust, the president and to thus install themselves, and the congress, as preeminent in power. Recall that Johnson had no vice president since he, as vice president, had ascended to the presidency upon the assassination of President Lincoln in 1865. That meant that Senator Benjamin Wade of Ohio, a radical Republican and President Pro Tem of the Senate, would move to the White House. Wade had been the co-author of the 1864 Wade-Davis Manifesto that condemned Lincoln's program and called for congressional, rather than executive, control of the Reconstruction process.

When Ross arrived in the senate, most of his colleagues believed him to be a radical Republican, and in many ways he was. Because he so ardently opposed slavery, he believed the south should be punished for embracing the institution and thus causing the Civil War. He had led the opposition to Senator Lane because Lane had supported the Lincoln/Johnson policy toward the south. Ross also personally disliked Andrew Johnson. But Ross placed nation above party.

And Ross was at the center of the storm because he alone among Senators would not make a commitment. He said this: "So far as I am concerned, though a Republican and opposed to Mr. Johnson and his policy, he shall have as fair a trial as an accused man ever had on this earth." The Republican leadership thus considered Ross "shaky" on impeachment and enormous pressure was brought to bear. He was bombarded with letters and telegrams, threatened by folks at home in Kansas. He was even threatened with persecution and prosecution on spurious charges. The New York *Tribune* said that he was "mercilessly dragged this way and that by both sides, hunted like a fox night and day and badgered by his own colleagues..."

Through it all, Ross kept his own counsel. He knew that a vote against Johnson's conviction was political suicide, and yet that is the way he voted. The President was saved by his single vote. Ross explained: "If the President must step down a disgraced man and a political outcast upon insufficient proofs and from partisan considerations, the office of President would be degraded, cease to be a coordinate branch of the government, and ever after be subordinated to the legislative will. It would practically have revolutionized our splendid political fabric into a partisan Congressional autocracy."

But nothing he said helped him back in Kansas. He served out his term, but his own party repudiated him and he was forced to run for reelection as a Democrat, and was soundly defeated. He remained in Kansas for a time, but facing ostracism and poverty, he moved to New Mexico in 1881. He resumed his newspaper career with the Albuquerque *Morning Journal*.[2]

Ross continued to dabble in politics and in 1885 President Grover Cleveland appointed him Territorial Governor of New Mexico. He was considered a "reform" governor from the beginning. He favored women's rights at a time long before it was popular. He supported the temperance movement and would not allow liquor in the Palace of the Governors. And he opposed the Santa Fe Ring and its land dealings. He wrote to the Secretary of the Interior:

"It is notorious that possession of large quantities of the public lands [in New Mexico] has been obtained under the form of preemption laws through the boldest perjury, forgery and false pretense, and that in some instances, this has been done, if not with the connivance, at least through the inadvertence and the carelessness of public officials."

Thus he became a thorn in the side of the existing political structure, and that made it difficult for him to accomplish much during his tenure. The one lasting memorial to his term in office was the creation of the University of New Mexico. It is also significant that he appointed an Hispanic, Mariano S. Otero to the Board of Regents. Otero became the first president of the UNM regents.[3]

Ross left Santa Fe and returned to Albuquerque after surrendering office in 1889. He farmed and did a bit of job printing. Not long after the turn of the century, he received a sheaf of documents from his former foes in Kansas that essentially exonerated him of having done any wrong deed. They admitted, nearly 40 years after the fact, that he'd made the right decision in 1868.

Ross died on May 8, 1907. A small item appeared in the Albuquerque *Tribune* in October, 1971: "When the State of Kansas started looking for the grave of one it is *celebrated statesmen* (emphasis added), Edmund G. Ross, it discovered the site in Albuquerque."

Times do change.

---

[1] A photograph of Ross' tombstone shows that his middle name was Gibson. Historian Will Keleher says that his middle name was Gilbert.

[2] George Curry in his autobiography says that Ross first moved to Deming and edited a newspaper there.

[3] One source says that it was actually Ross' successor, Gov. Bradford Prince, who made the appointment.

THE CRIMES AND DEATH OF DAVE RUDABAUGH: A NEW MEXICO VILLIAN

Dave Rudabaugh is a name not famed among the thieves and killers of the Old West, but it should be. He was one of the most ruthless and otherwise despicable of western outlaws and he was certainly well known to the citizens New Mexico in the late 1870s and early 1880s.

No photograph of the outlaw is known to exist. One source described him as "thick set and athletic in build. He [was] suave and very gentlemanly in his deportment. He [had] brown hair, hazel eyes and a heavy mustache a shade of brown lighter than that of his hair." Such an attractive image of him was not universal. Another source suggests that Rudabaugh had a mighty reputation for "uncleanliness." "The few friends that he managed to acquire said that he had taken his last bath at a very early age…. From that time forward he would not even drink water but stuck strictly to whiskey, tequila and sotol."[1]

Rudabaugh was born in Illinois in 1854. As a teenager after the Civil War, he moved on west, first to Iowa then Kansas and Arkansas. During the early 1870s, in Arkansas, he associated with a gang of cattle thieves that also included Mysterious Dave Mather and Milt Yarberry.[2] By 1875 Rudabaugh is believed to have been in Ft. Griffin, Texas where he became acquainted with John H. "Doc" Holliday and his friends.

On January 27, 1878, young Dave was a part of a gang of six that badly botched the robbery of a train near Kinsley, Kansas. The entire gang was soon rounded up and arrested by a posse led by Ford County Sheriff Bat Masterson, who had taken office only two weeks before. J. J. Webb, who would play a significant part in Rudabaugh's future, was a member of the posse.

No believer in the Code of the West, Rudabaugh quickly agreed to turn state's evidence. The Kinsley *Graphic* newspaper reported thus: "Rudabaugh testified that he was promised entire immunity from punishment if he would 'squeal,' therefore he squole [sic]. Someone has said there is a kind of honor among thieves. Rudabaugh don't [sic] think so." Four of the other five would-be train robbers were convicted.

Rudabaugh left Kansas shortly after this affair concluded. He appeared next in Las Vegas, New Mexico, where he became a member of the East Las Vegas police department. This was not a law enforcement agency in any conventional sense. It was more akin to criminal conspiracy. It was created and headed by H. G. Neill, who was also known as Hoodoo Brown. Neill was elected justice of the peace and coroner even before East Las Vegas was incorporated. He paid his police officers with money he collected—extorted many said—from local merchants. Others of his "policemen" were Dave Mather, J. J. Webb, and Tom Pickett.[3]

In 1879, Rudabaugh was accused of train and stagecoach robbery, and many believed that he was the leader of a gang of thieves, most of whom were also members of the East Las Vegas police force. For then, nothing came of the charges against Rudabaugh and the local newspaper even defended his "energy and honesty."

In Mach, 1880, J. J. Webb shot and killed a visiting Wyoming cattleman named Michael Kelliher in the Goodlet and Roberts Saloon in East Las Vegas. Hoodoo Brown, as justice of the peace, did what he usually did in such cases, which was to impanel a jury and quickly exonerate his henchman. That time it didn't work. Investigation revealed that the killing was in cold blood and that Brown had stolen the bulk of $2,000 young Kelliher had been carrying. Webb was locked in jail and Hoodoo Brown fled in the dark of the night.[4]

On April 2, 1880 Dave Rudabaugh and John "Little Allen" Llewellyn walked into the San Miguel County jail and asked to see prisoner J. J. Webb. Since Rudabaugh had visited with Webb previously, and since both men were former East Las Vegas policemen, jailer Antonio Lino Valdez allowed the two visitors inside. History is not clear as to who did exactly what, but one of the visitors demanded that Valdez give up the keys to Webb's cell. The jailer refused and one or the other of the visitors shot him. Webb declined to escape and remained in his cell. Valdez died later the same day.

Rudabaugh and Llewellyn fled in a hired hack. They only stopped long enough to rob a hardware store of guns and ammunition. A small impromptu posse gave chase, shooting at the outlaws until their ammunition was exhausted and then they returned to town. A larger posse later took up the pursuit but Rudabaugh and Llewellyn were not found. Llewellyn, in fact, was never seen again at all.

The story goes that Little Allen was not a well man and suffered greatly from tuberculosis and rheumatism as he and Rudabaugh fled to the south. As no medical care was available, he begged Rudabaugh to put him out of his misery. Rudabaugh is said to have obliged by shooting Llewelyn in the head and burying him in some sand along the trail.[5]

By June of 1880, Rudabaugh had taken up with William H. Bonney—Billy the Kid—and his gang of thieves and killers.[6] He was with Billy at the Greathouse and Kuch road-ranch in November when Lincoln County deputy sheriff James Carlisle was murdered. He was with Billy at Fort Sumner in December when the gang was ambushed by Sheriff Pat Garrett's posse and the outlaw Tom O'Folliard killed. Rudabaugh, in fact, had his horse shot out from under him in that fight. Rudabaugh was also with Billy when Garrett's posse killed Charlie Bowdre and captured the gang—including Rudabaugh—at Stinking Spring on December 21, 1880.

The posse took the outlaws first to Fort Sumner where a blacksmith chained Bonney and Rudabaugh together. From there they were taken by wagon to Puerto de Luna and then on to Las Vegas where they were jailed while Garrett made arrangements for train transportation to Santa Fe.

The stopover in Las Vegas was not good news for Rudabaugh. He was well aware that local folks were not likely to have forgotten that he'd killed Deputy Valdez the previous April. Local folks made no effort to take Rudabaugh out of the jail, but when Garrett arrived to take custody of his prisoners, the sheriff only delivered three of them: Bonney, Wilson and Pickett. Garrett demanded that Rudabaugh be turned over to him, but local authorities claimed jurisdiction for the Valdez killing. Garrett held a commission as a deputy U. S. Marshal and claimed that since Rudabaugh had confessed to stage robbery, during which he rifled mail sacks, that made him a federal prisoner, and that took precedence over local charges, even if they were for murder. Garrett acknowledged that Las Vegas could have him back once he'd been tried in Federal Court. The jailers grudgingly released Rudabaugh.

But the fight was not over. Garrett got his prisoners aboard the Santa Fe train, and it began to pull out when several armed citizens jumped into the engineer's cabin and halted the engine at gunpoint. Garrett and his deputies, Frank Stewart and Barney Mason, prepared for a fight. Garrett stepped out onto the rear platform of the rail car his prisoners occupied just in time to run face to face into Sheriff Desiderio Romero[7] and four or five other men.

"Let's go right in and take him [Rudabaugh] out of there!" one of the crowd yelled.

Garrett drew his pistol. "They [the citizens] slid to the ground like a covey of hardback turtles off the banks of the Pecos," he said later.

The train was at last allowed to depart and arrived in Santa Fe without further incident. The prisoners were locked up in the Santa Fe County jail.

None of the outlaws had any intention of staying in jail any longer than necessary. They went right to work on digging a tunnel by which to effect an escape. The sheriff discovered the plan on March 1, 1881 and foiled it.

Rudabaugh was soon tried in the court of Judge Bradford Prince, convicted and sentenced to 99 years in prison on the federal charges. He was then released to San Miguel County officials to face murder charges for killing deputy Valdez. Officials realized, however, that he could not receive a fair trial in Las Vegas, so they changed the venue back to Santa Fe. Rudabaugh faced Judge Prince for a second time. This time the sentence was death by hanging. The date was set for May 13, 1881 but a stay of execution was granted while the case was appealed. Rudabaugh was returned to the Las Vegas jail to await his doom. One of his cellmates was none other than his old friend J. J. Webb.

While many in Las Vegas were anxious to see Rudabaugh dangling from the end of a rope, others remained friendly to him. On September 18, 1881, someone smuggled a gun into the jail, specifically to Rudabaugh. He attempted escape that night, but failed. One of the other prisoners in the jail, Tom Duffy, was killed in the effort. J. J. Webb had taken no part in the escape attempt.

Rudabaugh would not acquiesce to the hangman's rope, however. On the morning of December 3, 1881, guards discovered that seven prisoners had escaped during the night, and Dave Rudabaugh and J. J. Webb were among them. All of them had managed to squeeze through a hole in the wall that measured seven inches wide by 19 inches long. One source reported that the fit was so tight that the prisoners had to remove their clothing to get through the hole. A witness reported seeing Rudabaugh and Webb walking away from town along the railroad track. They soon parted ways, though: Webb went to Arkansas[8] and Rudabaugh to southern Arizona and Mexico.

Rudabaugh was never recaptured. Reports filtered back to New Mexico from time to time that he'd been seen along the Mexican border. One source reported that he managed a Mexican cattle ranch for a period of time, but ultimately moved on. Then, early in 1886, he became embroiled in a conflict—some said it was over a card game—with some Mexican citizens at Hidalgo de Parral, Chihuahua. The *Albuquerque Evening Democrat* for January 16, 1886 reported what happened: "Dave Rudebaugh [sic], a former wicked and lawless character of Las Vegas was killed at Parral, Mexico, a short time ago. He killed two men in the fracas that settled his own hash." The people of Parral then cut the outlaw's head off and paraded it about the town by torchlight on the end of a pike.

Thus did Mexican justice succeed where the U. S. version failed, and the world was well rid of Dave Rudabaugh.

---

[1] *Sotol* is a highly alcoholic drink akin to *mescal* and *pulque*, all of which were made of distilled agave cactus juice.

[2] The careers of Mather and Yarberry are detailed elsewhere in this volume.

[3] Pickett was an outlaw in his own right. He rode with Billy the Kid from time to time.

[4] Neill was arrested in Parsons, Kansas a couple of weeks later, but released on a writ of habeas corpus. He never returned to Las Vegas and disappeared from history after 1880.

[5] Not much is known about John Llewelyn. One source describes him as "a pint-sized carpenter and house painter from Georgia."

[6] One source says that Dave Rudabaugh was the only man Billy Bonney feared. Another source says that Jesse Evans was the only man the Kid was afraid of. Billy seems to have been the measure by which "badness" was measured, for whatever it was worth.

[7] Garrett in his book, *The Authentic Life of Billy the Kid*, says that Desiderio Romero was a deputy sheriff, and brother to the Sheriff, Hilario Romero. Actually, Hilario didn't take office until January 1, 1881. Desiderio was the sheriff at the time of the events described here.

[8] J. J. Webb died four months later, in April 1882, of smallpox, at Winslow, Arkansas.

ON THE DEATH OF RUSSIAN BILL: HE CHOKED TO DEATH, GRANT CO. SHERIFF REPORTS

Here are the known facts: two men were hanged at Shakespeare, New Mexico,[1] sometime in 1881. Just about everything else about the matter is in some dispute.

One of the honored guests at the necktie party was Waldemar Tethenborn, also known as William Rogers Tettenborn or Russian Bill. He is said to have been born in Russia around 1850 to a subject of the czar and the daughter of a Scottish sea captain. He went to sea at an early age but left the salt air behind in San Francisco and migrated east to Fort Worth, Texas where he was soon wounded in a gunfight. He then traveled to Denver where he was again wounded, that time with a knife. By 1880 he had arrived in Shakespeare, New Mexico, a small collection of adobe buildings in the arid reaches of what was then Grant County in the southwest corner of the territory.

Accounts at the time describe Russian Bill as tall and gangly—above six feet—with shoulder-length blond hair and a moustache. He wore high boots with gaudy spurs and a large sombrero. He packed a pistol on his hip, maybe two of them along with a knife in his boot. Some described him as a braggart and a drunkard who boasted of his violent past, deeds of daring-do and his activities as a thief and cattle rustler. Others discount all that and point out that he was involved in the legitimate business of mineral speculation and mine ownership. He also served as an official claims recorder. It may be that the only criminal act he ever committed was stealing a horse, and that led him to an impromptu gallows.

The other guest on that cruel occasion was known as Sandy King, but his real name might have been Luther King, or Red Curly, or Sandy Ferguson. If he was Luther King, he was involved in some of the thievery that led up to the shootout at the OK Corral in Tombstone, Arizona on October 26, 1881. He would not have been around at the time, though, because he seems to have disappeared from Arizona after March 1881 when he walked away from the Tombstone jail. In any event, Sandy King was loitering around Shakespeare in the fall of 1881 after having spent a few months in the jail at Silver City. He seems to have become friends with Russian Bill, probably a saloon pal.

One day in early November 1881, King got drunk in a Shakespeare saloon before he wandered into Smyth's Mercantile and took possession of a red neckerchief for which he declined to pay. When the store clerk demanded payment, King pulled his pistol and, drunk as he surely was, he nearly missed, but managed to shoot off the clerk's index finger. One source says the sound of the shot drew immediate attention and the malefactor was promptly arrested. Another says he managed to get to his horse and flee the town, only to be captured by Deputy Sheriff Dan Tucker a short time later. Whatever the case, with King in custody, Russian Bill decided that he had best leave town, an act of which the townsfolk would have generally approved, except that the horse he rode out on did not belong to him, and its owner, Al Parker, particularly disapproved.

Russian Bill made it to Deming where he aimed to spend the night in an empty boxcar that had been shunted to a siding. He was arrested there, some say, by that same deputy Dan Tucker. Others say it was deputy Jack Rutland who made the arrest. Yet a third source says it was a hastily formed posse made up of Shakespeare townsmen who rode him down. Whoever captured him, he was soon returned to Shakespeare where he was locked up in a room at the Grant Hotel; the same room which housed the prisoner Sandy King.

Deputy Rutland, apparently somewhat indifferent to his responsibilities, guarded them. The prisoners were allowed to shout threats from windows to the townsfolk passing by, warning that they would dance to the outlaw's music within a day. Local citizens took the threats seriously. In the wee hours on the morning of November 9, 1881[2], a group of citizens—some referred to it as the Law and Order Committee, and others as the vigilantes—broke into the room. They threw deputy Rutland into a corner and covered him with a mattress while they removed the prisoners.

The two outlaws were then hanged in either the Grant Hotel or the Shakespeare Hotel—sources cannot agree—in either the barroom or the dining room. One source says that King asked only for a drink of water and "died game" while Russian Bill begged for his life. Another claims Bill calmly asked for a drink of whiskey and remarked that he didn't think there was any whiskey where he was going. What is known for sure is that they were strung up to the rafters and their bodies left where they were hanged.

As the story goes, a stagecoach arrived early the next morning and the passengers walked into the room and encountered the gruesome scene. When asked about the cause of the executions, the bartender is said to have pointed to Sandy King and said, "he was a horse thief, the other one—a damned nuisance." Of course, other sources claim the reverse, that King was the nuisance. One source claims the stage passengers cut down the bodies and buried them before breakfast. Another reports that one of the passengers stole Russian Bill's boots, and they all ate breakfast with the bodies in place.

Some months later, Grant County Sheriff Harvey Whitehill received an inquiry from a lady of means in Russia in which she inquired of the whereabouts of her son, Waldemar Tethenborn. Legend is not clear as to exactly what the sheriff replied, but various sources offer these possibilities: "he choked to death," "he died from a shortage of breath due to a sudden change in altitude," "your son died of throat trouble," "your son committed suicide," and, finally, "your son met with a serious accident."

One thing is for certain: Sandy King and Russian Bill did not again molest the citizens of Shakespeare.

---

[1] Shakespeare is located about two miles south of Lordsburg. Originally a watering stop on the Butterfield stagecoach line in the late 1850s, it was earlier known as Mexican Springs, Grant and Ralston. Today it is on private property.

[2] One source, the *Encyclopedia of Western Lawmen & Outlaws*, gives the date of these events as January 1, 1881. It is the only source found to do so. Newspaper accounts of the time indicate the date as more than ten months later.

THEIVES MURDER OTERO CO. SHERIFF BILL RUTHERF0RD: ESCAPE HANGMAN'S NOOSE

In early February 1923, two young thieves named William G. LaFavers, 19, and Charles Hollis Smelcer, 21, stole a saddle and other tack from a rancher in northern Lincoln County. Soon arrested, they were taken before a magistrate in the village of Corona and sentenced to jail at the county seat in Carrizozo. Lincoln County deputies A. S. McCamant and Graciano Yrait took custody of the two and started for Carrizozo.

McCamant rode in the back seat of the Ford touring car with LaFavers and Yrait drove. Some distance from town, on a rough road, LaFavers made a grab for McCamant's pistol which the officer carried in his pocket. The two men struggled until McCamant kicked open the car door and both fell out onto the roadway as the car came to a stop. The deputy's gun fell into the dirt and LaFavers was able to grab it before McCamant could retrieve it. Smelcer grappled with Yrait, too, but he was getting the worst of the fight until LaFavers took charge of the situation at gunpoint. The outlaws debated killing the deputies but finally forced the officers to walk away and they covered them with a rifle until they were out of sight. LaFavers and Smelcer took the car and fled. The officers had to walk 12 miles to the closest telephone.

LaFavers and Smelcer headed south. They stopped in Carrizozo and bought .30-30 caliber ammunition for the rifle they'd taken from the officers and then continued on to Tularosa. They had some trouble with the Ford and stopped there to have it repaired. Then they headed for Alamogordo.

Sheriff Bill Rutherford of Otero County returned to Alamogordo on February 13 from a trip to Santa Fe. At about 8:30 that evening he received a phone call from Harry Straley, a deputy to Lincoln County Sheriff Ed Harris. Straley told Rutherford about LaFavers and Smelcer, described them, and warned that they were armed and "desperate characters." A short time later, Sheriff Rutherford stepped out of the Warren Drug Store at the corner of 10th Street and New York Avenue and saw a vehicle matching the description of the Lincoln County car pull to the curb. Two men occupied the Ford; one behind the wheel and one in the rear seat. Sheriff Rutherford walked up to the car.

"If you have no objection, I would like to search this car," a witness heard the sheriff say.

The car suddenly lurched backward, and then shot ahead. Rutherford stepped up on the running board and reached inside. Witnesses believed that he tried to turn off the gas. A loud **BANG** filled the air and witnesses thought a tire had blown up but the sheriff fell away from the car and was left lying in the street as the Ford ran over a curb and sped away. A citizen named O. M. Smith soon knelt at the sheriff's side, but there was nothing he could do. The bullet hit Rutherford in the neck, killing him almost instantly. Witnesses and bystanders were puzzled about what became of the sheriff's hat. It was nowhere to be found and yet he'd been wearing one when he approached the Ford.

Word of the sheriff's murder spread around Alamogordo quickly. A "fast car" occupied by former sheriff Howard Beacham and car dealer Shorty Miller headed south out of town on the Orogrande Road. A second car, occupied by Deputy sheriff H. M. Denny and a citizen named Louis Wolfinger, headed southwest along the Las Cruces Road. District Attorney J. Benson Newell directed much of the search and sent out word to authorities in all directions. Thirty minutes after the shooting, a tourist car arrived in Alamogordo from the south and the driver reporting passing a southbound Ford touring car driving at a high rate of speed. All concerned believed it to be the fugitive car.

Shorty Miller's Buick ran out of fuel north of Orogrande and he and Beacham were obliged to walk into the little town for gas. By midnight officers learned that Lincoln County sheriff's Ford had been located abandoned near Orogrande. Bloodhounds were ordered and a large posse was on hand to follow the dogs, but they were unable to go beyond the railroad track, for some unknown reason. A detachment of troops from Fort Bliss arrived at early morning and an airplane took up a search of the area. A train with a railroad carload of horse-mounted possemen also arrived from Alamogordo and a second train made up of an engine, boxcar and caboose stopped in Orogrande with deputies from Lincoln County.[1]

As the day progressed, one of the posses searching south and east of Orogrande discovered a sheep-lined coat taken from one of the Lincoln County deputies when the outlaws escaped custody. The manhunt centered in that area and in the early afternoon posseman M. L. Bradford, riding horseback, spotted the fugitives as they saw him and opened fire with the rifle. Bradford was hit in the leg and returned fire, emptying his pistol without hitting either of the wanted men. The killers retreated behind a small hill and soon saw two other mounted possemen riding in their direction, and then a posse of men on foot approached. The killers raised a white cloth of surrender and put their guns down.

In their flight, the two had covered about 15 miles from the point where they abandoned the car. They had circled and were returning to the El Paso road where they intended to steal a car when they were caught. By 6:45 p.m. on February 14, LaFavers and Smelcer were locked away in the Otero County jail. Smelcer was wearing Sheriff Rutherford's hat.

A grand jury convened on February 26 and indicted the outlaws on charges of first-degree murder. The two were tried at Alamogordo and on Thursday, March 1, 1923, just 23 days after they killed the sheriff. The jury took 35 minutes to convict them of the crime. On Saturday, March 3, LaFavers and Smelcer were sentenced to hang on April 6, the penalty to be executed in the Otero County jail yard.

Defense attorneys appealed the convictions but before a higher court could hear the case, Governor James Hinkle commuted Smelcer's sentence to 40 to 50 years and LaFavers' to life imprisonment. Smelcer was paroled to Glendale, California on

April 10, 1931 and Governor Arthur Seligman pardoned him on April 21, 1932.
LaFavers was paroled to Amarillo, Texas, on December 23, 1936 and pardoned by
Governor John E. Miles on April 13, 1939.

Bill Rutherford, 40, was a well-known and prominent stockman in southern
New Mexico. He served two terms in the New Mexico legislature before he was
elected sheriff in 1922. He'd been a lawman for six weeks at the time of his death. His
mother and father, who lived at Marshall, Missouri, survived him. He was buried
there.

---

[1] Howard Brooks was a member of one of the foot posses that pursued LaFevers and
Smelcer. He incorrectly stated that the State Police brought in bloodhounds. The
New Mexico Mounted Police force was disbanded in 1921 and the modern State
Police Department was not created until 1935. His recollections were preserved on
oral history tapes, Alamogordo Public Library, September 1975. Murray E. Morgan
(1906-1988), Report on the Rutherford affair prepared in 1976 and presented to the
Alamogordo Public Library in June 1981. Morgan called the Rutherford murder "One
of the major tragedies in the history of Alamogordo."

SANDIA PUEBLO: A PEOPLE PERSECUTED

Sandia Pueblo lies just east of the Rio Grande and north of the Bernalillo County line in Sandoval County. It is a part of what was called Tiguex Province in ancient times. In area, it is one of the smaller pueblo reservations in New Mexico, but it is large in history.

Anthropologists, historians and the Sandia people generally agree that the pueblo was established about 1300 A. D. It was not called Sandia, or anything akin to it, back in those times. Since the Spanish *sandia* means watermelon, and since watermelons were not native to the desert southwest, it could not have been so. The Spanish didn't arrive in New Mexico until 1540.

Sandia Pueblo is a member of the Tiwa language division of the Tanoan language group, along with the Pueblos of Taos, Picuris and Isleta. In the Tiwa language, Sandia pueblo is called *Nafiat*, which translates roughly as "a dusty place." So where did the name *Sandia* come from?

Dr. T. M. Pearce in *New Mexico Place Names* suggests several possibilities. Even though watermelons were not native flora, it is likely that the Spanish explorers were familiar with them, and they may have made the comparison between the color of the fruit's pulp and the nearby mountains under particular conditions of sunlight, and the pueblo was then named for the mountains. Pearce also says that a report made in Spain indicated that the mountains were known locally as *El Corazon de la Sandia*, or "heart of the watermelon."

Pearce offers a final possibility. In a 1689 document, the pueblo was referred to as *San Dia* which suggests that the name could be related to *El Dia Santo* which means "The Holy Day."

How ever it came to be, the place is known to us today as Sandia Pueblo, except by the people who live there and they still refer to it as Nafiat.

An elder of the pueblo told a researcher in the early 1930s that his people lived in peace and prosperity for several hundred years before the coming of the Spanish. That appears to be true except that we don't know what happened to the approximately 40 villages of the Tiguex Province between 1300 and 1540. Only about 16 of them remained occupied when the Spanish arrived.

The elder was certainly accurate in saying that his pueblo had problems with the Spanish. Sandia was very much involved in the so-called Tiguex revolt that occurred in 1541-42. The explorer Francisco Vásquez de Coronado and his troops took so much from the Indians—food, shelter and even their women—that the behavior could not be tolerated. The Indians fought back but being greatly outgunned, and afoot against mounted soldiers, they lost. About 200 Indians—not all from Sandia—were killed and the village of Nafiat was put to the torch, though not completely destroyed.

The Spaniards departed in 1542 and the pueblo was left in peace for about 40 years. In 1581, three priests, Fray Rodriguez, Francisco Lopez and Juan de Santa Maria, arrived at Tiguex from Mexico. They were accompanied by a group of soldiers under the command of Captain Francisco Sánchez Chamuscado. Their mission was the conversion of the Indians to Christianity. Indians killed all three of the missionaries. Sánchez Chamuscado died of age and infirmity before he reached home.

The unfortunate result of the Fray Rodriguez missionary effort was another expedition in 1582. It was organized for the stated purpose of "rescuing" Padres Rodriguez, Lopez and Santa Maria. More accurately it should have been called a punitive expedition. Many Indians fled at the coming of this group under Antonio de Espéjo.[1] The Spaniards tried to lure the Indians out of the mountains, but the Indians said that while they wanted to be friends, they would not provide the Spanish with food, nor would they return their women to the pueblo.

Espéjo then set Sandia Pueblo afire, again, and executed, by garrote, 16 Indians who had not fled. Several others died in the fire. The Spaniards returned safely to Mexico.[2]

After the arrival of Juan de Oñate in 1598, the Sandia people, as well as all other New Mexico pueblos, were "colonized and Christianized" by the Spanish. The Indians were no longer allowed to practice their ancient religious rites. They were frequently sold, or traded, into slavery. And where that was not the case, they were still obliged to turn over large portions of the bounty of their fields to Spanish soldiers and church officials. They were allowed no participation in the governance of their own lives.

That era ended in 1680 with the Pueblo Revolt under the leadership of the San Juan Indian, Popé. In a coordinated attack by the separate Indian pueblos, all Spaniards were either killed or driven out of New Mexico, down the Rio Grande from Santa Fe to Isleta, then to Socorro, and finally on to El Paso. Even so, Sandia was again to get the worst of things.

Late in 1681, Antonio de Otermín, the Spanish commander who had been driven out of Santa Fe and *Nuevo México*, returned with a force of 146 soldiers and 112 Indian allies. He sent his lieutenant, Juan Dominguez de Mendoza, north from Isleta to determine the strength of the Indians along the road to Santa Fe and to punish as many of the insurgents as possible. Mendoza got as far north as Cochiti where he came to believe that he was being lured into an ambush. He also believed the Indian strength too great for the military force commanded by Otermín. He hurried south, but stopped long enough to burn Sandia Pueblo, yet again. Mendoza rejoined Otermín and together they returned to El Paso in early February 1682.

For the next 10 years, the Sandia people lived in relative peace.

In 1692, the Spanish were again on the march north. This time the people of Sandia were not going to be subjected to the pain of the invasion and the rule of the Europeans. They had long considered migrating elsewhere and the re-conquest gave them the impetus they needed to do so. They determined to remove themselves to the Hopi lands of northeastern Arizona.

They walked there: men, women and children. It was a terrible journey upon which many became ill and died. They traveled by way of the Pueblo of Zuñi where they left their sick behind. Finally they reached the pueblo of Mishongnovi near Second Mesa in what is now Navajo County, Arizona. The Hopi welcomed them because they were, as usual, having trouble with the Navajo and needed good fighters. Their hosts helped the Sandia people build their own village, which they called, not surprisingly, *Nafiat*.[3] They would remain there for 52 years.[4]

The Sandias, for the most part, got on well with the Hopis. There were differences, of course. The Sandias were used to farming in the watered valley of the Rio Grande. The Hopis were acclimated to farming in the arid desert. Their respective religions were oriented to those differences, and the Sandias found it necessary to appeal to the Hopi gods. While life was not easy for the Sandia people, they survived. As in years past, when the Sandias never lost hope that the Spanish would leave them alone forever, they now believed that the day would come when they could return to the valley of the Great River.

Their chance came in the early 1740s when two Spanish Padres, Delgado and Pino, arrived in the Hopi country to tell the Sandias that they would be welcomed back to the Rio Grande Valley. The clergymen asked that the Indians *try* Christianity, but did not demand slavish allegiance to the church. The Padres said the Sandias would be treated well and allowed to rebuild and farm in peace. Well, maybe. The real reason the Spaniards wanted the Sandias back was that they needed strong Pueblo Indian allies to help them fight against the nomadic tribes: the Navajo, Apache, Ute, and Comanche.

About 400 Sandias returned to the banks of the Rio Grande. Their village, a total ruin after so many years, was rebuilt and crops were again planted. In 1748 the Spanish governor, Codallas y Rabal, confirmed the land grant.

The problems they faced after their return were largely internal, and religious in nature. They, of course, continued to observe their traditional Tiguex religious practices, but the rituals had been altered by the assimilation of the Hopi religion and its practices, and Christianity tempered both. Some of the younger Sandias were only familiar with Hopi religious practice because they had spent their entire lives among the Hopi. All of this set the Sandias apart from other Tiguex pueblos, some of which began to shun the Sandias. This was hurtful socially, but also had practical consequences. When Apaches or Comanches attacked Sandia, the other pueblos would not come to their aid.

There also remained some resentment toward the Spanish over their meddling with marriage rituals and other legal and tribal matters. The main thing the Sandias wanted was to be left alone, to be left to their own devices, left to worship in their own way and to live in the way they felt best. But that could not be, then or now.

In 1858, the U. S. Congress confirmed the Sandia land grant, and even that was improperly drawn. The Clements survey of 1859 ignored grant documents and the boundary drawn by the survey deprived the Sandias of the main ridge of the Sandia Mountains, and the land that led up to it. This area had had important practical as well as religions purposes for more than 500 years. Virtually none of the Sandia people spoke English at the time and there was little money for lawyers. What modest protest was made proved unsuccessful.

Even so, most of their traditional land was not molested until into the 1960s and 1970s when the growth of Albuquerque, specifically the development of Juan Tabo Canyon, deprived the Indians of access to some of their religious shrines. The west side of the Sandia Mountains also became attractive to hikers and mountain climbers who, it was feared, would tamper with Indian religious sites. There was, and is, great concern among the Sandia people about maintaining the sanctity of their places of worship and the integrity of their land.

Today, the people of Sandia make good use of their reservation land. Much of the rich bottomland along the Rio Grande is under cultivation by members of the tribe. And certainly, the Sandia Casino has contributed to the economic solvency of the pueblo.

Nafiat nowadays is much more than just "a dusty place."

---

[1] According to historian Paul Horgan, Espéjo was a fugitive from justice in New Spain where he was accused of killing one of his ranch hands.

[2] Historian Rubén Sálaz Márquez says that Espéjo was the first to use the term *Nuevo México*—New Mexico.

[3] Another source says the name of the Sandia village in the Hopi country was Payupki.

[4] A large number of Pueblo refugees migrated from the Rio Grande to the Hopi country in the period from 1680 to 1879.

LORDSBURG CONSTABLE C. B. SCHUTZ KILLED BY ESCAPEES

According to news reports from the mining town of Pyramid, south of Lordsburg, a man by the name of U. Sierra got drunk one day in early May of 1893 and went after Constable C. B. Schutz with a "heavily loaded quirt." He intended to kill the lawman, but instead got arrested for his trouble. A local judge named Medbury sentenced Sierra to sixty days in the Grant County jail at Silver City.

On Sunday evening, May 7, two men, Celso Analla and David Ramires, burglarized T. R. Brandt's store at Stein's Pass of $50.00 while the storekeeper was at home eating supper. Suspected of the crime, one of them confessed and a Judge McGrath bound them over to the grand jury at Silver City.

On Thursday, the 11th, C. B. Schutz and another constable named Ownby set out from Lordsburg to Silver City with the three prisoners in tow. Ramires and Sierra, shackled hand and foot, rode in the front seat of the wagon beside Schutz who drove the team. Analla, also handcuffed, rode in the rear seat with Constable Ownby who sat on his pistol, presumably so that he had quick access to it. As the wagon crossed Cactus Flat, about nine miles south of Silver City, Analla suddenly pushed Ownby off the wagon and grabbed the lawman's pistol. Hearing the scuffle, Schutz turned to see what the matter was just as Analla shot him in the head. Schutz fell from the wagon and Analla shot him twice more, once between the shoulder blades and once in the right shoulder.

Ownby attempted to get back on the wagon, to recover his gun, but was repulsed. Analla ordered him to run for his life and Ownby complied as the outlaw fired shots at him, none of which took effect. After the constable was gone, Analla realized that Ownby had the keys to the shackles they all wore. He ordered Ramires and Sierra to pursue Ownby but it was a useless effort. The two, chained together, soon gave up. Analla robbed Schutz's body of gun and watch before the three outlaws got back up on the wagon and set out for Silver City.

They encountered an old man south of town and paid him five dollars to get them a file and some whiskey. Later that evening, Ramires and Analla went on into town and purchased food and more whiskey, and then they disappeared. Sierra spent the night with the old man and next morning, still wearing one handcuff, surrendered himself to Grant County Sheriff Andrew Laird. Sierra reported the murder of Schutz and claimed that Analla and Ramires put him off the wagon about eight miles from town and forced him to walk. It took him the better part of the night, he said, to make the trek to town in a pouring rain, and he walked the streets until dawn. The flaw in his story lay in the fact that his boots and clothing were free of mud.

Telegrams were sent to all points asking authorities to be on the lookout for the killers. Sheriff Laird and another man rode south and encountered Ownby a mile or so from town. The constable was very ill, suffering from pneumonia induced by exposure to rain and cold the nightlong. They found Schutz's body and subsequently the abandoned wagon. Posses were sent out in every direction but to no avail. The rain had obliterated any tracks they might have left.

History records nothing of a personal nature regarding C. S. Schutz.

---

1 Lordsburg was in Grant County until Hidalgo County was created in 1919.

DEMING SHERIFF DWIGHT STEPHENS KILLED BY JAIL ESCAPEES: OUTLAW KILLED IN GUNFIGHT

Things were astir in Deming, New Mexico, on Sunday morning, February 20, 1916. Members of the New Mexico Cattle and Horse Growers Association were beginning to arrive for their annual convention and the Great Council of the Improved Order of Red Men would also meet in town during the following week. Dr. Fred Stephens and his wife were in town visiting his brother, Luna County Sheriff Dwight Stephens and his family.

Things were astir over at the Luna County jail, too.

One cell in the lock-up housed three prisoners: Jesse O. Starr and C. Schmidt, burglars who'd robbed the Palace Saloon, and W. F. Dashley a forger and embezzler. Jailer Emzie Tabor opened the cell door so Schmidt could empty the chamber pot. The burglar waited until Tabor turned his back to re-open the cell door then he grabbed the jailer and pinned his arms to his sides. Starr and Dashley helped out. They took Tabor's guns and keys and robbed him of his watch and five dollars in cash. The three outlaws were in control of the jail.

They locked Tabor in their former cell and unlocked all the other cells. Two prisoners elected to join the little gang in escaping: Francisco Acosta, accused of a murder at Spalding, New Mexico, and Joe Cranston, a vagrant. (The story goes that Cranston was reluctant to participate, but the others persuaded him to go along by promising that he could drive the getaway car.) They broke into the jail's armory and took rifles, handguns and a large supply of ammunition before they crossed the jail yard and broke into the office where there was a telephone.

Dashley called Del Snodgrass, owner of the Park Garage and Ford Dealership. He ordered that a car be brought around to the jail so that a sick prisoner could be taken to Faywood Hot Springs, northwest of Deming in Grant County. Dashley requested a full gas tank and extra tires. He also asked Snodgrass to bring change of a twenty-dollar bill so he could settle up for use of the car right away.

Busy getting ready to provide garage space and automotive services to arriving cattlemen and conventioneers, Snodgrass didn't suspect a thing. He arrived at the jail only to be confronted by five men pointing guns in his direction. He, too, was robbed and locked up with Emzie Tabor. The bandits cut the phone lines, threw the jailhouse keys into a gopher hole, and set off to the northeast, toward the town of Rincon, 50 miles away.

Tabor and Snodgrass set up a racket to attract attention to their plight, but no one could hear them. Half an hour passed. Then the wife of one of the prisoners who'd elected to remain in jail arrived for her weekly visit. She freed Tabor and Snodgrass who soon sounded the alarm.

Sheriff Dwight Stephens first assumed the outlaws would head for the Mexican border, thirty miles south. He alerted all crossing points by telephone. Then he set about assembling a posse. Witnesses reported seeing the Ford with five men heading northeast, and the six-man posse gave chase in their own machine (automobiles were called *machines* in 1916). The escapees had more than an hour head start, but it wasn't enough. The Deming *Headlight* for February 25, 1916, reported what happened next:

> ...[T]he posse took the trail, finally running on their quarry in a narrow cañon where they had stopped to eat lunch. Deputy sheriff[s] John T. Kelley and Wayne Estes, who had dropped off the car and had tried to outflank the outlaws, scrambled to the top of the hill overlooking the cañon where they were seated. At the same time Sheriff Stephens, Buck Sevier and [Deming town] Marshal Tabor came up the cañon, walking to within a few feet of the men before they saw them. Sevier immediately ordered them to throw up their hands, but the only reply was a fusillade of shots. Sheriff Stephens dropped at the first exchange of shots, dying instantly, and Sevier received a scalp wound that stunned him, and that came within an ace of taking off the side of his head. From the top of the bluff overlooking the cañon deputy sheriff Kelley, Marshal Tabor, Jack Arnold and Wayne Estes poured a hot fire into the outlaws, wounding Starr and killing Cranson. The other three men, Dashley, Schmidt and Acosta broke for the brush and made their escape.

What followed was a manhunt of gigantic proportions. Several carloads of men arrived from Deming along with a U. S. Army detachment under Lt. Clyde Earl Ely. Since the gunfight actually took place in Doña Ana County, Sheriff Felipe Lucero and his posse became very active in the search, too.

W. C. Simpson, a cattle inspector, and Fred Sherman, both of Deming, joined Marshal Tabor in the search for Schmidt. They found him at 7:00 o'clock the following morning. He'd made it just sixteen miles, to the east and south of Rincon. He offered no resistance when officers arrested him.

Three days later, late in the afternoon, Sheriff Lucero and Las Cruces city marshal Adolfo Sainz caught Acosta's trail on the Flat Lake Ranch, northeast of Rincon. They trailed the fugitive throughout the night, across the San Andres Mountains and into Otero County, a distance of 35 or 40 miles. At noon the following day they located Acosta on the J. B. Baird Ranch. Suffering from hunger and exhaustion, the killer submitted meekly to arrest. He joined Schmidt in the Doña Ana County jail.

Newspapers speculated that the fifth outlaw would be soon captured. One even speculated that W. F. Dashley would be back in jail within 48 hours. It wasn't to be.

In March 1916, J. O. Starr, C. Schmidt and Francisco Acosta were tried for the murder of Sheriff Stephens. Starr admitted firing shots and seeing Stephens and Sevier fall. He claimed he fired in self-defense after the officers fired first. The jury didn't buy it. Starr was convicted and sentenced to hang. Schmidt was convicted of second-degree murder and sentenced to life in prison. Acosta was acquitted of killing Stephens, but was immediately arrested by Luna County authorities for the killing at Spalding the year before. He was tried and sentenced to 20 years in prison on that charge.

W. C. Simpson succeeded Dwight Stephens as Luna County Sheriff. He and Doña Ana County Sheriff Lucero kept up the search for Dashley in the weeks and months that followed. At one point, Simpson traced Dashley to Venice, California, but police there failed to act in a timely way and the fugitive escaped. The same thing happened in San Francisco. On August 26, Dashley's luck ran out. Authorities in Reno, Nevada, arrested him and held him for Sheriffs Simpson and Lucero who happily escorted him back to New Mexico.

Dashley, whose real name was A. B. Smith, generally considered the leader of the gang and the brains behind the escape was convicted of murder in March 1917 and sentenced to death. Neither he nor Starr were executed, however.

After Dashley's arrest and conviction, the *Deming Headlight* commented:

"The perfect understanding which exists between the peace officers of Luna, Doña Ana and Grant counties is a powerful aid in the ferreting out of criminals who may be tempted to operate in the southwestern portion of the state, and is an assurance that there is no twilight zone in these parts where outlaws can operate with impunity and feel secure from capture."

A word is in order about Sheriff Dwight Stephens. A 43-year-old native of Ohio, he'd lived in Deming for about 25 years at the time of his death. First appointed sheriff by Governor Miguel A. Otero in 1904, he served continuously, except for two years, until his death. Sheriff Stephens participated in a gunfight with jail escapees in November of 1911 in which his deputies Tom Hall and A. L. Smithers were killed.

Well liked and respected, the Albuquerque *Journal* reported that Stephens' funeral was the largest in Deming history, attended by the entire community.

Fred Fornoff, former captain of the New Mexico Mounted Police said this: "Sheriff Stephens was not a gunman in any sense to which odium might attach. The Luna County Sheriff was a fearless man and had a high sense of duty."

Dwight Stephens was survived by a wife and four children, aged three to 12 years. He was also survived by his parents who resided with his family in Deming.

_____

COL. EDWIN V. SUMNER ORDERS CONSTRUCTION
OF FORT UNION ON SANTA FE TRAIL

As a place to do military service in the last half of the 19th century, Fort Union, New Mexico had very little to recommend it. Here is what one military wife said:

"Many ladies greatly dislike Fort Union. It has always been noted for severe dust storms. Situated on a barren plain, the nearest mountains…three miles distant, it has the most exposed position of any military fort in New Mexico. The hope of having any trees, or even a grassy parade-ground, had been abandoned long before our residence there.…"

Built in 1851 in the broad expanse of the Mora Valley of northeastern New Mexico, Fort Union was intended protect commerce over the Santa Fe Trail, which had opened in 1821. There were two branches of the trail. The northern route was called the Mountain Branch and it extended into Colorado and offered a stopping point at Bent's Fort on the banks of the Arkansas River. The southern route, called the Cimarron Cutoff, traversed the Oklahoma Panhandle. The latter was shorter, but far more dangerous for the lack of water and the possibility of attack by marauding Indians. Fort Union was built on the Mountain Branch near the confluence of the two trails.

During the early years of the trail's existence, New Mexico was under the rule of the Republic of Mexico and the U. S. had no role to play in protecting travel over the route once it entered what was then Mexico. That changed with the American occupation of New Mexico in 1846.

The original concept of defending the newly acquired territory was a series of small, widely scattered, forts. By the time New Mexico became officially a Territory of the U. S. in 1851, it was clear that this was not an effective system. In that year, Lt. Col. Edwin V. Sumner was ordered to "…revise the whole system of defense" in his area of responsibility (New Mexico). The creation of Fort Union was his first step in that direction.

Construction began in 1851 by use of soldier labor. Sumner moved his headquarters and supply depot from Fort Marcy in Santa Fe to the new post the same year. This was done for more than strictly military reasons. The Colonel disliked Santa Fe and believed the town had a debilitating effect on his troops. He said, "My first step was to break up the post at Santa Fe, that sink of vice and extravagance.…"[1]

The original cost of building Fort Union was about $300,000, and there were actually three forts built on the site in its 40-year history. The first was not much more than a collection of log buildings which served as headquarters for the 9th Military District. That lasted from 1851 to 1861. No trace remains of it today.

The second fort was built for defense against the invasion of Confederate forces from Texas during the Civil War. It is referred to as the Star Fort because earthwork parapets were constructed in the shape of a star. The Confederates, under General Henry Hopkins Sibley, were stopped at the Battle of Glorieta, in March 1862, and no battle was ever fought at Fort Union. Ruins of the Star Fort remain visible today.

Construction of the third fort began in 1863. It included a large Quartermaster depot, an arsenal and the largest hospital on the western frontier with 36 beds and two doctors. The fort, too, was the largest on the frontier and it took six years to complete. It was designed to accommodate four companies or either cavalry or infantry soldiers. The ruins of it yet remain.

The logistical supply function of the fort was somewhat greater than the military mission. All supplies consigned to forts throughout the southwest were funneled through Fort Union. Many of the storage buildings remain today as evidence of the magnitude of that operation. Most of the employees of the Quartermaster depot were civilians.

Even so, military operations were important within the context of the times. Soldiers provided protection to commerce by patrolling the Santa Fe Trail, and they waged aggressive war against Apache, Cheyenne, Arapahoe, Kiowa, Comanche and Ute Indians. By 1875, the U. S. Army's war with the Plains Indians was pretty much over and the role of the fort became almost entirely that of supply depot. But even that would not last long. When the railroad arrived in New Mexico in 1879, the need for the supply depository was effectively eliminated. The fort lasted for another dozen years. It was closed for good in 1891.

There are a couple of historical footnotes regarding Fort Union and some of the people who served there. For one thing, the fort, like most forts in the southwest, was never surrounded by a stockade. There was no need for one. Indians rarely, if ever, attacked forts. Why would they attack a point of strength when with a little patience, they could attack out in the open, at a point of weakness?

The father of Fort Union, Lt. Col. Edwin Vose Sumner, later a Major General, is said to have ordered and led the only saber charge ever against a body of Indians by U. S. Cavalry troops, on July 29, 1857 at Solomon's Fork on the Kansas River. Four Cheyennes were killed, along with two soldiers. When a fort was constructed south of Fort Union, along the Pecos River, in 1862, General James Carlton ordered it named it for General Sumner. It was at Fort Sumner, of course, that Billy the Kid met his death 19 years later.

Confederate General Henry Hopkins Sibley who led the Texans invasion of New Mexico in 1862 had previously served in the U. S. Army, participating in the Mexican War, the so-called Mormon War, and the 1860 campaign against the Navajos in western New Mexico. As a major, he was second in command at Fort Union when the Civil War broke out. Sibley was a native of Louisiana and he along with the famed James Longstreet, went over to the South, as a brigadier general, on June 17.

Another colorful commander at Fort Union was Lt. Col. Nathan A. M. Dudley, appointed to the job in 1876. Subordinates described Dudley as "petty and contentious" and he was said to have had a strong affection for the bottle (as had H. H. Sibley). He was so outrageous in his behavior that he was arrested, court martialed and convicted of defaming one fellow officer, vilifying and prejudicing another, and of conduct prejudicial to good order and military discipline.

Because he had good political connections, President Rutherford B. Hayes did not affirm Dudley's convictions and he was returned to duty in 1878, this time at Fort Stanton, near Lincoln, New Mexico. It was Dudley who, against orders, involved the U. S. Army in the violence of the Lincoln County War. He was court martialed again, for conspiracy to commit murder and arson. Again his friends came to his rescue and he was acquitted and again transferred, this time to Fort Cummings, New Mexico. He retired as a Brigadier General in 1889, and died in 1910.

Fort Union has been a National Monument since 1954. It is located about 28 miles northeast of Las Vegas and eight miles north of Interstate 25 at Watrous. It is open for self-guided tours the year around.

---

[1] The village of Loma Parda, located about six miles southwest of Fort Union, soon became everything Col. Sumner hated. It was called "Sodom on the Mora" and offered soldiers every manner of entertainment, licit and otherwise. Today Loma Parda is a ghost town on private property.

IKE AND PORT STOCKTON: OUTLAWS

There were three armed clashes in late 19th century New Mexico that came to be called "Wars:" The Colfax County War (1875-76), the Lincoln County War (1878) and the San Juan County War (1881).[1] Few Old West characters can be said to have participated—to a greater or lesser degree—in all three, but Ike and Port Stockton are the exceptions.

The Stockton brothers were both born in Johnson County, Texas, Ike in 1852 and Port in 1854. Legend holds that Port killed his first man when he was only 12 years old. At 17 he shot another man and was charged with attempted murder. Ike is said to have broke Port out of jail, and the brothers fled to New Mexico, by way of Dodge City, Kansas. One source indicates that the two of them operated a saloon in the town of Lincoln. Another reports that the saloon was solely Ike's.

Discrepancies like this may be the reason so little has been written about the Stockton brothers. For instance, one source says that Port murdered a man named Antonio Archbie in Colfax County in January 1876. No other source mentions this killing. It is documented, however, that in October 1876, Port got into an argument with one Juan Gonzales in the town of Cimarron, in Colfax County. The Texan drew his pistol and killed Gonzales. Gonzales was not armed and Port was jailed.

One source says that Ike came to the rescue again, and helped Port escape to Trinidad, Colorado. Later the same month, Port was captured by the sheriff of Conejos County and promptly returned to New Mexico. Sketchy sources report that the younger Stockton was acquitted upon a plea of self-defense. Nothing explains how that could be, since Gonzales was unarmed.

What is known for sure is that in December Port murdered another man in Trinidad after an argument over a card game. His victim was, again, unarmed. And, for a third time, Ike engineered an escape from jail. Again, sources are not clear. Ike may have been with Port up to this time, and have gone to Lincoln in late 1876 when Port moved on to Animas City, Colorado, near the present Durango.

In Animas City, Port served a short time as town marshal. While getting a shave one day, the barber, a black man, accidentally nicked the Texan. Port pulled his gun and chased the man down the street, shooting as they ran. Local folks took a dim view of the altercation. Port was not only fired from his job as marshal, but run out of town. He then went to Lincoln, New Mexico—by way of Rico, Colorado—and rejoined Ike.

At some point along the way, Port married and fathered two daughters.

Exactly where Port was in 1878-79 is unclear, but he may have gone back to northeastern New Mexico. One source says he killed a man named Ed Withers at Otero in June of 1879.

Brother Ike was definitely in the town of Lincoln, New Mexico on April 1, 1878. When William Bonney—Billy the Kid—and seven or eight other cowards shot Sheriff William Brady and Deputy George Hindman from ambush on that date, it was saloonkeeper Ike Stockton who ran into the street to help Hindman, only to be driven off by rifle fire. By later the same year, both of the Stockton brothers are known to have been in northwest New Mexico/southwest Colorado. Port lived near Aztec and Ike at Durango. Both were active in cattle rustling and assorted other criminal activity, but it does not appear that they necessarily worked their thievery together.

Port ran with two other undesirables named Harge Eskridge and Jim Garret. On New Year's Eve, 1880, the three of them got drunk at a party, and were ejected. They returned and shot up the place. One source says that hard feelings from this event marked the beginning of the end for Port Stockton.

Again, reports on the event don't agree. One says that on January 10, 1881, a rancher named Alfred Graves tracked some stolen cattle to Port's ranch, and in the gunfight that followed, Port was killed. Another says that Graves and Stockton had a "difference of opinion" and as Graves rode past Port's house, Port grabbed a rifle and yelled for Graves to come back and talk. Graves dismounted and walked up to the rustler. He put five bullets into Port before Port could put even one into him. Both sources agree that Port's wife, Irma, grabbed a gun and took a shot at her husband's assailant. Graves is said to have placed a shot into a wagon spoke near Irma's head, which drove splinters into her face and eyes, ending the fight.

Some believe Port's killing touched off the San Juan County War inasmuch as Ike swore revenge upon those who'd killed his brother. Ike stepped up his rustling activities, and is said to have killed at least one New Mexico rancher, Aaron Barker, in March of 1881.

On April 11, a "posse" of New Mexico ranchers, —among them Alfred Graves—cowboys and gun hands invaded Durango for the avowed purpose of ridding the region of rustlers led by Ike Stockton. What followed became largely a fiasco. The New Mexicans took a position on a mesa overlooking Durango and the firing commenced on April 12th. Each side fired hundreds of shots, but when the smoke cleared, no one had been killed, and the New Mexicans withdrew.

Ike seems to have got the point, though, and shifted his attention to stagecoach robbery. Even so, his days were numbered. New Mexico Governor Lew Wallace posted a reward for his arrest in the amount of $2,250. One of his cohorts, Burt Wilkinson, was captured and promptly lynched at Silverton in August. Another, Bud Galbreth, was arrested and charged with murder, rape, arson and stock stealing in September. Sheriff Barney Watson went looking for Ike. On September 26, 1881, he found him, on a street in Durango. In the gunfight that followed, Ike took a bullet in the leg (one source says the knee, another the thigh) and was captured. Doctors determined that amputation was necessary and went to work cutting off a sizable portion of his leg. Ike would not have to suffer life as a one-legged man, though, because he died the next day from loss of blood.

Thus ended the careers of the Stockton brothers, neither of whom had reached the age of 30. Western historian Ramon Adams said this: "[Ike and Port were] bad men of the first order."

----

[1] An incident of violence in Lincoln County in the early 1870s is sometimes called the Horrell War, but it wasn't a war in the sense the other three were. The Horrells were simply criminals.

PROHIBITION AGENT RAY SUTTON MISSING:
FOULPLAY FEARED

The 18th Amendment—The Volstead Act—became the law of the land on January 18, 1920. It made the manufacture, transportation, and sale of alcoholic beverages illegal in the United States. To enforce the act, the Prohibition Bureau was created within the U. S. Department of the Treasury.

One of the first agents appointed in 1920 was rancher, banker, and former sheriff of Union County, New Mexico, Raymond Sutton, Sr., of Clayton. His territory covered the five northeastern New Mexico counties. He maintained his headquarters at his home, but he often stayed overnight in towns across his assigned area. He was staying at the Seaberg Hotel in Ratón on August 28, 1930. He told his wife he expected to meet with Trinidad, Colorado, Police Officer Oscar Vanderberg that evening. The two of them planned to work in the Ratón Pass area searching for rumrunners.

On that Thursday afternoon, Agent Sutton drove south out of Ratón, toward Cimarron. At a point about seven miles from Dawson, he pulled off the road and parked. Colfax County Undersheriff G. R. "Boots" Fletcher saw him parked there, waved, and drove on. Fletcher was among the last people known to have seen Agent Sutton alive.

A week later, the district director of the Prohibition Bureau in Albuquerque, Charles Stearns, became concerned about the agent. His last report had been filed on August 27, and Sutton had uncharacteristically failed to appear for a district court hearing in Clayton. Stearns contacted Colfax County Sheriff Al Davis. Sheriff Davis discovered that all of Sutton's belongings remained unpacked in his hotel room and some reports upon which the agent had been working seemed undisturbed. The sheriff called Mrs. Sutton in Clayton and asked if she knew her husband's whereabouts. She had not heard from him in several days.

By Friday, September 5, Stearns, Davis and Sheriff A. W. Turner of Union County headed up a party of about 100 men and a search in the mountains around Ratón began. The Colorado National Guard sent an airplane to help out and a posse of horsemen joined in. Other law enforcement agencies also participated: Mora County Sheriff's Department, the sheriff from Trinidad, Colorado and federal agents from across the Rocky Mountain states. Several groups offered rewards that totaled more than $500. By September 18, when no trace of Agent Sutton, or his car, had been found, the search was all but called off.

But the case took on a new dimension on September 19 when a subject by the name of James Caldwell was arrested. He'd cashed Sutton's last paycheck some four days after the agent disappeared. Caldwell used Sutton's Masonic membership card as identification. Specifically, Caldwell was charged with passing a false check and forgery.

Then, on October 18, 1930, a cowboy named Rafael Zamora found Agent Sutton's car in a deep arroyo some 18 miles southwest of Raton. Lodged between two piñon trees and covered with brush, the Pontiac was so well concealed that drivers of cars on the Taos-

Ratón highway passing by only ten yards away could not see it. Search parties had also covered the area without seeing it. Fingerprint experts went over the car with care, but rain had done much to wash away usable prints. The ominous thing about the car was the discovery of blood in the back seat. Investigators surmised that Agent Sutton had been killed outside the car, and then the vehicle used to haul his body away. Searchers hoped the body would be found near the car.

It was not.

A federal grand jury indicted James Perry Caldwell in December 1930, and he was tried at Pueblo, Colorado, in January 1931. The witness who originally saw him cash Sutton's check suddenly could not identify Caldwell as the culprit. The charge of passing a false check was dismissed. The trial continued on forgery charges. Expert witnesses testified that the signature on the check was not Ray Sutton's. They asserted that Caldwell had forged Sutton's name. The jury, nonetheless, took 20 hours to acquit Caldwell.

Agent Sutton had been very active in enforcing the Volstead Act, in raiding stills and disrupting liquor traffic. Speculation at the time was that one of the major bootleggers in the area was responsible for Sutton's death, and James Perry Caldwell was involved in it. There were countless theories concerning where the body had been disposed of but none were ever proven because the body was never found. There was little doubt, however, among those familiar with the case, that Ray Sutton was murdered, and most likely on the afternoon of August 28, 1930. No one else was ever prosecuted in the case.

The 18th amendment was repealed on December 5, 1933.

Ray Sutton was born in Woodward County, Oklahoma in 1873. In 1910 he was appointed the first sheriff of Ellis County, Oklahoma, and two years later elected to the position and reelected in 1914. He moved to New Mexico after leaving office in Oklahoma and in 1916 he was elected sheriff of Union County. He was reelected in 1918. He joined the Prohibition Bureau after leaving office.

ALBUQUERQUE MAYOR/GOVERNOR CLYDE TINGLEY: A DIAMOND IN THE ROUGH

Clyde and Carrie Tingley, Albuquerque and New Mexico's first couple in the 1930s. He served as governor from 1935 to 1938. The children's hospital was named for her.
(Photos Courtesy the Albuquerque Museum Photoarchives, PA 1978.152.210 & PA 1986.004.109.)

Certainly one of the most colorful, interesting and enduring politicians in the history of New Mexico was Clyde Tingley. He served on the Albuquerque City Commission continually from 1916 to 1934. He was governor from 1935 to 1938, after which he returned to the city commission where he continued to serve until 1953. There are not many folks in the state's annals who held public office continually for more than 35 years, not even former Governor Bruce King.[1] Interestingly enough, many texts and other histories of New Mexico fail to even mention Clyde Tingley.

Tingley accomplished a great deal during his years of service, but he did not do it with much in the way of polish and grace. He was inflexible and demanding in his approach to public affairs, he was unschooled and he was a machine politician. All of that stirred considerable resentment against him, except among voters.

Upon the occasion of being told that he was setting a bad example for the youth of Albuquerque by the way he talked, Tingley is reported to have said, "I ain't goin' to quit sayin' ain't!" He was undaunted by charges that he was undignified and a disgrace.

Tingley was born near Springfield, Ohio, on January 5, 1881. He arrived in Bowling Green, Wood County, Ohio, sometime after the turn of the century where he worked as a machinist for the Graham Motor Car Company. It was in Bowling Green that he met and courted Carrie Wooster, the daughter of a prominent farming and oil rich family.

That the Woosters were prominent is demonstrated by the fact that the main east-west thoroughfare in the town is called Wooster Street. The Wooster home was located on the east side of Bowling Green on about seven acres of land. There were two Wooster farms located nearby totaling move than 300 acres (at a time when the average Ohio farm amounted to 80, or fewer, acres). Oil was discovered on one of the farms, and that contributed to the family's wealth.

Carrie Wooster's father died of tuberculosis in the early 1900s, and Carrie herself contracted the disease. She and her mother moved to Albuquerque to seek treatment in 1910 and Clyde followed in early 1911. Clyde and Carrie were married in Albuquerque on April 24, 1911. But they did not sever their ties to Ohio.

The farms in Wood County fell to the ownership of Clyde and Carrie, and in fact became known as Tingley Farms. The crops were cultivated on shares by local farmers.[2] Clyde made frequent trips to Ohio and was remembered in Bowling Green as a friendly man, down to earth, and a great talker.

The Wooster money, and the Wooster Farms, provided Clyde with the financial resources necessary to pursue a career in politics. He began by being elected to the Albuquerque City Commission in 1916. He was consistently reelected until 1934 when he ran for, and was elected, governor. While Albuquerque did not have a mayor in those days, Clyde, as chairman of the commission, bestowed the title upon himself.

As mayor, Clyde, and Carrie too, could often be found at the railroad station where they would greet all manner of celebrities who stepped off the train to stretch their legs. They ranged from Charles Lindbergh and Albert Einstein to Mary Pickford, Rudolph Valentino and Ronald Reagan.[3] It was not uncommon for the Tingleys to be photographed with the famous of the day. No modest shrinking violet was Clyde Tingley.

His lack of modesty is demonstrated by the number of monuments he named, or had named, for himself: Tingley Coliseum on the State Fair Grounds, Tingley Drive in southwest Albuquerque, Tingley Beach on an artificial lake, also in southwest Albuquerque, and Tingley Field, Albuquerque's baseball stadium from 1938 until 1968. A grove of trees on old U. S. Route 85, north of the town of Bernalillo, used to be called Tingley Park.[4] Clyde had a reputation for getting things done, and he was more than willing to take the credit.

As Governor, Tingley maintained a close relationship with President Franklin Roosevelt. Because of it, he was able to secure large amounts of Civilian Conservation Corps (CCC) and Works Progress Administration (WPA) money for New Mexico, but mostly for Albuquerque. With these funds Tingley was able to assist the University of New Mexico in its rapid growth during the late 1930s. The airport terminal was built, as were buildings at the State Fair Grounds and the railroad overpass on Albuquerque's Central Avenue. It was also during this time that a number of federal offices were established in Albuquerque and the old Federal Building was constructed in the downtown area at 5th and Gold. Tingley was also instrumental in the alignment of old Route 66 through Albuquerque.[5] Clyde and Carrie were also responsible for the creation of the Children's Hospital at Hot Springs (now called

Truth or Consequences) in 1937. In this case, the people of Hot Springs voted to name the facility for Carrie Tingley. The Tingleys had no children of their own, and Carrie spent much of her time raising money for the Children's Hospital, and collecting toys that she delivered to the children at Christmas time.

The rapid growth of Albuquerque and New Mexico following World War II led to the closure of the Tingley era in politics. By 1947 his brand of power-brokering and machine politics was repudiated and his influence was broken. He continued in public life for a few years, but his dominance was at an end. Clyde Tingley died in 1960, less than two weeks shy of his 80th birthday. Carrie died the following year. But as long as Tingley Coliseum and Carrie Tingley Children's Hospital exist, the Tingleys will be with us.

----

[1] Bruce King's public career spanned the years 1954 to 1994. He began as a Santa Fe County Commissioner, then moved on to the House of Representatives before being elected governor in 1970, 1978 and 1990. There are, however, gaps during which he did not hold public office. King reports that he first met Clyde Tingley in 1936, when he, King, was 12 years old. He credits Tingley with inspiring him to become governor.

[2] Farming on shares meant that the farmer who did the work shared the farm's profit with the landowner. In many cases it was a 50-50 split. In others it was 60-40, depending on who purchased the seed and fertilizer.

[3] Carrie Tingley was a movie buff. She spent many of her afternoons in Albuquerque's movie theaters.

[4] Neither *New Mexico Place Names* by T. M. Pearce nor *The Place Names of New Mexico* by Robert Julyan have even one entry for Clyde Tingley

[5] Route 66 originally went through Santa Fe. Tingley was an ardent supporter and promoter of New Mexico's tourist industry.

PANCHO VILLA INVADES NEW MEXICO: 17 U. S. CITIZENS KILLED, 100 MEXICANS ALSO DIE

Some pedants have attempted to draw comparisons between the September 11, 2001 Attack on America in New York and Washington D.C. by terrorists and the March 1916 raid on the town of Columbus, New Mexico by Mexican revolutionaries under the direction of Francisco "Pancho" Villa. There are really very few comparisons.

-   The Attack on America resulted in the deaths of more than 3,000 civilians. Villa's raid resulted in the deaths of 17 Americans, nine of them civilians.
-   The Attack on America was unprovoked. It can be argued that Villa's raid was specifically provoked, even though his motive has been debated from that day to this.
-   The Attack on America was unconventional. Villa's attack was surreptitious, to be sure, but it was conventional in the context of the times. The Americans had the chance to fight back, and did so successfully. They killed more than 100 of Villa's soldiers.

It seems worthwhile to review the chronicle of the Columbus raid.

About 400 Mexican revolutionary troops crossed the border into the United States in the early morning hours of March 9, 1916 and rode about three miles to the town of Columbus, New Mexico. They immediately set about looting the place. A detachment of the 13th U. S. Cavalry, camped nearby, was taken by surprise and responded in some disorder before soldiers and citizens alike effectively repelled the invaders. One source claims the Villistas took more than 100 Army horses and mules and many guns as they retreated south. Another source reports that the Mexicans actually left behind so many of their own horses, that an auction was held to sell them, along with their saddles. Such is the confusion about what happened that day, even so many years after the fact.

Most historians believe that Villa was not present at Columbus. One writer reports that the Mexican commander was Pablo López who was wounded in both legs during the fighting. He was subsequently captured near Satevó, Chihuahua by Mexican regular troops, tried and executed by firing squad at Chihuahua City.

A Rio Rancho, New Mexico man, Enrique Garcia, argues that Villa *was* present during the raid. Garcia's grandfather, Alejandro Garcia, was a colonel in Villa's army.

Alejandro claimed that he participated in the Columbus raid, and that he rode at the head of the column with the famed revolutionary.[1]

Garcia said that the raid was the result of a business deal that went bad. His story was that Villa delivered a herd of cattle to some Columbus businessmen who refused to pay. He also said that the Villistas only took from Columbus banks the money that was due them. Another alleged motive frequently cited is that Villa had paid Columbus merchants for delivery of guns and ammunition. They had taken his money and then failed to deliver the weapons. Yet another conjecture is that the raid was simply meant to steal guns and ammunition from the cavalry detachment camped there.

There may also have been a political motive. Villa remained at war with the Venustiano Carranza government in Mexico City in 1915-16[2]. He had managed to get along with the Americans up until 1915 and he hoped that the United States would recognize him as the legitimate leader of Mexico. Instead, the Woodrow Wilson administration recognized Carranza. And it went beyond that. The Wilson administration also placed an arms embargo on trade with the Villistas, which closed the munitions traffic in places like Columbus, New Mexico.

And militarily, Villa was on hard times. He'd suffered several humiliating defeats by Carranza's army and his troops had been reduced in number from thousands to hundreds. He had been declared an outlaw in Mexico. In late 1915, the United States allowed a force of about 4,000 Mexican soldiers to cross into Texas at Eagle Pass, and to take a train to Douglas, Arizona. There they reentered Mexico and attacked Villa's forces at Agua Prieta, winning a telling victory. Villa blamed the United States for his defeat and his hatred for Mexico's neighbor to the north grew considerably.

None of this, of course, serves to justify the murder of American civilians, or soldiers either. And Pancho Villa's days as major force were numbered. The United States Army sent a so-called Punitive Expedition—about 12,000 strong—under the command of General John "Black Jack" Pershing, into Mexico to exact retribution from Villa. After 11 months of searching the deserts and mountains of northern Mexico, Pershing gave up and withdrew. Villa had simply dispersed his troops into small groups, and he himself hid out in a cave in the Sierra Madre until summer.

Villa reemerged with a small army in September 1916, and captured the city of Chihuahua. He departed with a large supply of arms, only to return in November and do the same thing all over again. He was defeated on the plains of Horcasitas in early December, and later the same month he captured Torreón, but lost it back to Carranza's forces by New Year's Day, 1917.

One historian of the Mexican Revolution said this: "The centaur of the North [Villa] was becoming a minor character in a drama that was becoming more political than martial.... In the years [after] the Punitive Expedition he continued to fight a war peculiarly his own. Much of the time it seemed to be a war for war's sake."

In July of 1920, Villa quit fighting altogether. He had about 700 men left in his "army." The Mexican government gave him a 25,000-acre rancho in the state of Durango. He stayed out of politics after that, but he had made many enemies over the years. It all caught up with him on July 20, 1923 when he was assassinated in the town of Parral, shot 13 times by eight gunmen. The identities of his killers have never been proven, but a man named Jesús Salas Barraza claimed to be the "intellectual author" of the assassination plot.

The final distinction that must be made between the Attack on America and the Columbus raid is this: A park commemorating the 1916 raid was dedicated in 1959. It was not named for any of the citizens who were killed there, or even for General Pershing. It was named for Pancho Villa. No park in New York City will ever be named for Osama Bin Laden.

---

[1] Alejandro Garcia lived in Las Cruces for many years. He died in 1983 at the age of 113. He would have been about eight years older than Villa.

[2] Villa had been at war since the 1910 Revolution in which Francisco Madero ousted long-time dictator Porfirio Diaz.

BEN WILLIAMS: PEACE OFFICER

Deputy U. S. Marshal Ben Williams (in white shirt) is seated beside Marshal Creighton Foraker. W. C. Kennedy is seated at far right. Photo was taken at Raton in July 1894.
(Photo Courtesy Walter Haussaman, Albuquerque New Mexico.)

Ben Williams is not a name frequently mentioned in the annals of the old west, and yet he served at various times as deputy U. S. Marshal, Doña Ana County Deputy Sheriff to Pat Garrett, Las Cruces town constable and chief special agent for the Santa Fe Railroad.[1] He played major roles in several significant episodes of his time, and he engaged in several life-threatening confrontations.

Williams was born in France in 1861.[2] He is believed to have arrived in the United States in 1873. Not much is known of his early life, but by the late 1880s he was working as a bill collector for the Singer Sewing Machine Company in and around Las Cruces. This occupation was described as "challenging work" at the time.

By 1890 he was self-employed as a detective in El Paso. He was hired to secure the release of one Dr. William Bolton from jail in Juarez, Mexico where he was being held on a murder charge. This was not possible by legal means, or bribery, so Williams contrived a plan involving subterfuge to accomplish his goal. Dr. Bolton was able to walk out of the jail unmolested, wearing the uniform of a soldier in the U. S. Army. A group of irate Mexicans offered a large reward for Williams, dead or alive. He is believed to have never returned to Mexico.

In 1894 he was hired to work as a stock detective for the Southeastern New Mexico Stock Growers Association, for which organization Albert Jennings Fountain served as chief prosecutor. The job afforded Williams an opportunity to observe the growing cattle herd of Oliver Lee, a loyalist to Fountain's arch political enemy, Albert Bacon Fall. Through Fountain's good offices, Williams was appointed Las Cruces town constable, and through the same procedure, Fall had Lee appointed a deputy sheriff. Lee then went after Williams, with a vengeance.

During the early summer of 1895, Lee arrested Williams for carrying firearms.[3] Williams made bond and was released from custody. On August 16, Lee arrested Williams again, on the same charge. Historian A. M. Gibson tells what happened next:

> "Out on bail again, Williams, on the night of September 14, was walking along Main Street [in Las Cruces]. As he fronted Desseur's Building three men stepped from the shadows—Albert Fall and Joe Morgan he recognized immediately; the poor light prevented him from identifying the third party. Morgan put his pistol in Williams face and fired. The constable moved at Morgan's motion; the bullet whined past his temple, but the point-blank blast gave him a bad powder burn. Williams staggered back, threw his left arm over his face, drew with his right, and fired twice at Morgan, one bullet hitting his arm. Fall's shot passed through the crown of Williams' hat. As he returned Fall's shot, Morgan fired again, the bullet entering Williams' left arm at the elbow and passing out the shoulder. The shot spun the constable around. He fired twice at Morgan, hitting him again, then as he turned and ran for cover across the street, two additional shots were fired at him by the third party still hiding in the shadows."

Fall said later that he and Morgan—Fall's brother-in-law—shot at Williams simply because they didn't like him; that there was no political significance in the matter. It was Williams, however, who was indicted for the shooting affray, though nothing ever came of it. Williams was named chief deputy to Sheriff Numa Reymond the following year.

Through a set of political convolutions, Pat Garrett was named chief deputy the same year—Sheriff Reymond left town for an extended European vacation—and Ben

Williams continued as Garrett's right-hand-man. Garrett was elected in his own right in 1898 and Williams was once again chief deputy. In this capacity, Williams faced his next formidable challenge.

Garrett's primary law enforcement goal was to solve the mystery of the disappearance of Col. Fountain and his son, Henry, which had occurred in February 1896. The investigation led to suspects Oliver Lee, Jim Gililland and Bill McNew. Warrants were issued and McNew was soon arrested. Lee and Gililland managed to avoid arrest by staying away from Las Cruces and visiting various ranches in Tularosa Basin. In July 1898, two of Garrett's deputies, Clint Llewellyn and José Espalin, discovered that Lee and Gililland were visiting the Cox Ranch on the east slope of the Organ Mountains. They also learned that the wanted men would soon be riding east, to Lee's Wildey Well Ranch.[4]

Garrett assembled a posse made up of himself, Llewellyn and Espalin, Ben Williams and Kent Kearney. All were described as experienced gun-hands, except for Kearney who was a former schoolteacher. The posse trailed the outlaws to the Wildey Well ranch. The particulars vary widely regarding what happened next. Garrett's version held that the officers learned from people inside the house that Lee and Gililland were hiding on the roof of the adobe structure. The sheriff ordered Llewellyn to guard the people inside the house while he positioned Williams under a water tank. Garrett, Kearney and Espalin would ascend a ladder to the roof. Kearney went first and peered over the parapet to discover the posse's quarry. Garrett claimed that he demanded surrender at that point. The response was gunfire from the roof, and Kearney was severely wounded in the shoulder and groin and fell to the ground. All the remaining deputies returned fire but Lee and Gililland had the positional advantage. Espalin sought cover along a wall and had no opportunity to continue firing. Williams returned fire, aiming at rifle flashes, but the wanted men shot holes in the tank he used for concealment. He was obliged to remain in place and be soaked with water.

This episode was probably Garrett's most humiliating setback. He was forced to retreat from the ranch empty handed, and Kent Kearney died in the unsuccessful effort.[5]

Williams continued to serve with Sheriff Garrett until 1901 when he took a position as Special Agent with the Atchison, Topeka & Santa Fe Railroad. He remained with the Santa Fe for many years, and rose to the rank of Chief Special Agent. He was involved in a number of incidents that involved gunplay and his son credited him with running the KKK out of El Paso. He was described as a quiet, well-mannered, well-dressed man who did not look the part of gunfighter. He is reported to have been married "about" eight times, and to have fathered two children, a son and daughter. He was also said to have been "…still looking at girls up until 1934."

Upon his retirement, he opened a detective agency in El Paso. He died there in 1935 of cancer. He'd invested all his money in bank stock, and the Great Depression had wiped him out. He died penniless.

———————

[1] One list of "gunslingers" in far west Texas and southern New Mexico in the 1890s lists Williams along with such notables as Bat Masterson, John Wesley Hardin, John Selman and Pat Garrett.

[2] His own son believed him to have been born in Ireland, but his birth certificate shows place of birth as France.

[3] Some sources indicate that it was perfectly legal for Williams to be armed. Other say it was technically illegal.

[4] Also spelled *Wildy*.

[5] Lee and Gilliland were arrested later, tried and acquitted of killing Henry Fountain.

BOOTLEGGER SHOOTS ROSWELL MARSHAL: ROY WOOFTER DEAD

Roy Woofter, Roswell City Marshal
(Photo Courtesy of Roswell Police Department)

The city of Roswell in southeastern New Mexico enacted a prohibition ordinance in 1910 that made illegal the sale of beer and liquor within the community. While the law was supported by a sizable number of citizens, especially among the churchgoers, it was strongly opposed by others, and several bootleggers continued to sell booze.

City Marshal Roy Woofter was earnest in enforcing the law. His investigation led him to suspect that Jim Lynch was selling beer from his boarding house at the corner of First Street and Richardson Avenue. Lynch apparently knew that Marshal Woofter was aware of his illegal activities. One mid-week evening in late May 1911, Lynch was heard to say, "I'll shoot that star full of holes if I catch him peeping around my house."

Upon a complaint made by Marshal Woofter, a warrant was issued for a search of Lynch's house. On May 26, 1911, around 5:00 in the afternoon, Marshal Woofter along with Roswell city policemen—and brothers—Ed and Henry Carmichael arrived to execute the search. They found Lynch in an alley behind the Smoke House, near his residence, with two other men, Fred Higgins and Red Preston. Lynch objected to the search at a time when his wife was out of town. Woofter assured him that the search *would* be conducted. Lynch, along with Higgins and Preston accompanied the officers to the Lynch house. Lynch told the officers they had nothing to fear from him and he opened his coat to show them he was not armed.

The group of six entered by the front door. They found nothing in the first room they entered and before Woofter could enter the second room, Lynch went through the door, slammed it in the marshal's face and locked it. Woofter knocked on the door and kicked it several times but Lynch would not open up or respond. One of the Carmichael brothers went out the front door and around the house toward the back door while Woofter went around the house, along the porch, in the opposite direction. Witnesses said the marshal's hands were at his sides and he had not drawn his gun.

As he passed a window, a voice called out: "Keep off my back porch!" A shot fired from inside hit the marshal in the belly.

Woofter clutched his stomach and faltered but did not fall. He managed to stagger to where Henry Carmichael stood. "Lynch has shot me. Save me. Let Lynch go."

The Carmichael brothers along with Higgins and Preston managed to get the marshal to the house next door. They summoned an ambulance and Woofter was taken to St. Mary's Hospital where he was attended by four surgeons. The .45 caliber rifle bullet, a U. S. A. ball weighing 405 grains, had done great damage. One doctor reported that the exit wound was large enough that three fingers could be inserted into it. In spite of the doctor's best efforts, the officer died the next morning about 5:00 o'clock. Before he died, however, he made a long and specific statement in which he identified the voice of the man who shot him as belonging to Jim Lynch.

Chaves County sheriff's deputies Jim Johnson and Clarence Young arrived at the scene to find Lynch in his house, behind a locked door, holding the Winchester rifle in his hands. They ordered Lynch out of the house, and he told them to come in. Deputies responded that the door was locked. Lynch told them use a knife to unhook the screen door. They declined. At last, Lynch opened the door and handed one of the deputies his rifle. He was arrested and taken to jail.

After Lynch was removed from the scene, the Carmichael brothers and a fireman completed the search of the house. They found a barrel of beer and an icebox containing a large amount of bottled of beer.

On a change of venue, Lynch was tried at Carlsbad in mid October 1911. The defendant's family engaged the services of high-priced Texas legal talent to make the case that Lynch acted only in defense of his home. He claimed that he believed the officers had no right to be there. Lynch also claimed that he fired only when Woofter reached for his gun. The jury didn't believe any of it and took only one hour to convict Lynch of murder in the first degree.

Roy Woofter had resided in Roswell for about five years at the time of his death. A native of West Virginia, he'd previously served as a peace officer at Albia in southeastern Iowa. He'd moved to Roswell for his health and joined the Police

Department in July 1909, and became city marshal in October of the same year. He married Margaret Forsyth three years before his death. They had no children. His remains were returned to Iowa for burial.

A Roswell newspaper reported that Reverend P. T. Ramsey said of Marshal Woofter that he "submerged every private interest, the comforts of home and his own personal safety to act against the criminal element. Fearless in his duty he had gone forth and because of that duty he now lay cold in death."

———————

UNCLE DICK WOOTTON: HIS LIFE AND TIMES

Uncle Dick Wootton was one of the more engaging characters in the history of New Mexico and one of the most often overlooked. He was a contemporary of the Bents—Charles, William and George—Cerán St. Vrain and Kit Carson.

"I got acquainted with Kit Carson the first time in the fall of 1837, I think it was in October. I was in his company a great deal at different times up to the time of his death," Wootton said in 1883.

Richens Lacy Wootton[1] was born in Mecklenburg County, in south-central Virginia in 1816. He received a "business education" as a young man and worked on tobacco plantations in Virginia and cotton plantations in Mississippi. None of that appealed to him as much as the prospects of adventure—and profit—in the Rocky Mountain West. He made his way to Independence, Missouri, and from there to Bent's Fort near the present day La Junta, Colorado, arriving in 1836. His adventures began almost at once.

He set out on a trapping venture with a dozen or so others. They traveled west to California and then back, taking a year and half to make the trek. Then he spent some time working as a hunter for the Bents at a time when the plains were so thick with buffalo that herds of thousands stretched as far as the eye could see.

In the years leading up to the American occupation of New Mexico in 1846, he was, he said, "engaged in taking goods to New Mexico. I might really say, smuggling them in." This gave him the background to go into business after 1848. While he was absent from Taos at the time of the 1847 rebellion, he did participate in the volunteer force which quelled uprising. He is reported to have killed a single rebel, probably an Indian, with a tomahawk. He became the sutler for the First Dragoons at Taos for a time.

Word reached Uncle Dick that sheep sold in California for about ten times what they could be purchased for in New Mexico. He had no experience in herding woolies, but the opportunity was too good to pass up. In early 1852, Wootton purchased 9,000 sheep for $5,000 and with a contingent of 22 men—14 herders and eight guards—he set out from Taos headed west for Sacramento, California, 1600 miles away.[2]

In addition to the natural barriers he faced, his troop had to contend with Indians, too. Wootton had become acquainted with Utes of southern Utah on his earlier sojourn, and knew they demanded tribute from those who trespassed on their land, and he was prepared to pay. Through a series of ill-advised actions and misunderstandings, the Ute chief, Uncotash, came to believe that Wootton intended to cheat him. Indians disarmed and surrounded the guards and Uncotash accused the sheep man of trying to deceive him.

"I tried to pacify and explain to the old heathen, but he kept railing at me until I got mad," Wootton said later.

With that, Wootton began scuffling with the chief. One report says he grabbed Uncotash around the waist and wrestled him to the ground then sat on his chest— Wootton is said to have weighed 240 pounds—with a knife at the Indian's throat. The chief recognized the error in his own ways, and surrendered. Wootton paid the tribute with some bonus supplies thrown in to assure no further trouble with the Utes.

"I had never been so badly scared in my life. Just at that time I think an old-fashioned Mexican dollar would have bought my entire outfit."

He endured other tribulations but managed to deliver his flock to California in the spring of 1853 with the loss of only about 100 head, an amazing accomplishment. He sold them en masse for $50,000. One report indicates that with all expenses paid, Wootton cleared about $14,000. Many others, including Kit Carson, trailed herds of sheep to California in the early 1850s, and made huge profits.

Wootton also engaged in Indian trading and freight hauling for a few years, and then moved north to Cherry Creek, Colorado[3] in the Winter of 1858. As fate would have it, supply trains from the east had been held up by bad weather, so Wootton's wagon load of trade goods, including two barrels of Taos Lightening,[4] were welcomed to the community. It being Christmas Eve, Wootton could well afford to give away the whiskey, and he did. Some historians trace this event as the origin of the sobriquet "Uncle Dick," bestowed in gratitude for the party.

By the middle 1860s, Uncle Dick occupied land in the Ratón Pass on the New Mexico-Colorado border. He blasted and scraped out a rough wagon road about 27 miles long and installed a chain gate in front of his house. He began collecting tolls from those who used the road at a rate of $1.50 per wagon and five or ten cents per head for livestock. He even charged famed cattleman Oliver Loving ten cents a head to drive his herd through the pass on his road. Observers at the time claimed that Uncle Dick hauled whiskey kegs full of silver coins to the bank in Ratón.

His toll road was even legitimized in 1867 when Lucien B. Maxwell, owner of the vast Miranda-Beaubien land grant,[5] deeded Wootton some 2500 acres of land. In return, Wootton granted Maxwell free use of his turnpike for life.

A brief digression here. Uncle Dick is said to have collected his tolls with a club if it became necessary, and there was only one exception: Indians were allowed to pass free of charge. And yet, Wootton was one of few old-time mountain men to come out in support of Colonel John Chivington who conducted the Sand Creek Massacre in which about 150 Indians, mostly women and children, were slaughtered in 1864. An enigma to be sure.

In 1878, Uncle Dick gave up the rights to his toll road to the Atchison, Topeka & Santa Fe Rail Road in exchange for $25 worth of groceries per month for life (some sources say the amount was $50), and a lifetime pass on the railroad. He died near Trinidad, Colorado in 1893.

Certainly, within the context of his times, Wootton was a wealthy man by the time of his death, but no mention is made of what became of his fortune. Nor is mention made of his personal life. Historians note that he was married four times, but nothing is reported about his wives, except that when he went to Cherry Creek in 1858, his wife accompanied him, and she was an Indian.

---

[1] Some historians indicate that his name was Richard. The most definitive, however, all agree on Richens. His last name is also sometimes spelled Wooton.

[2] Prospectors and miners in California would have much preferred beef to mutton, but sheep were much easier to move, and they could eat, and survive, on sparse grass that would not support cattle.

[3] Denver would grow up around the confluence of Cherry Creek and the South Platte River.

[4] One observer said this about Taos Lightening: "Its whiskey [that] ain't worth three skips of a louse."

[5] This became known as the Maxwell Grant.

ALBUQUERQUE'S MARSHAL YARBERRY KILLS TWO MEN: SENTENCED TO HANG

Milt Yarberry happened to be handy when a group of businessmen decided Albuquerque's new town—which sprang up with the arrival of the railroad in 1880—needed a peace officer. Yarberry, about 34 years old, tall, skinny, stoop-shouldered and illiterate, was named town marshal in spite of a work history that included stints as cattle thief and killer in the company of Mysterious Dave Mather and Dave Rudabaugh, both renowned criminals. His reputation as a gunhand seems to have been the deciding factor.

It's generally believed that *Yarberry* was an alias and no one seems to know for sure what his real name was. One source says he called himself John Armstrong when he rustled cattle with Mather and Rudabaugh in Sharp County, Arkansas. Another says he used the name Johnson when he shot and killed a man in a Texarkana, Texas, saloon brawl. Legend holds that Milt told his friend, Elwood Maden, his real name just before he died but Maden carried the secret to his own grave. Some believe that the Albuquerque Yarberry borrowed the name from Milton Yarberry who was a respected Colorado lawman.

At different times, Milt owned saloons, billiard parlors and dance halls in Colorado and New Mexico, all ventures at which he failed.

As Albuquerque's town marshal, he was a high-handed bully.

A young grass widow named Sadie Preston soon attracted Milt's attention. Sadie also attracted the attention of a young railway messenger and rake named Harry Brown. Brown had his own reputation as gunhand. He claimed to have single-handedly prevented the robbery of an AT&SF train by Dave Rudabaugh, and others, near Kinsley, Kansas in January 1878. Brown didn't refute a report that he'd killed two of the robbers, but in fact he didn't kill either one. None of the outlaws were killed at the scene of the robbery, and the one who died was killed during the pursuit, and Brown didn't participate in that.

In Albuquerque, Brown had a reputation for heavy drinking and trouble-making.

On Sunday afternoon, March 27, 1881, Harry and Sadie went for a ride in a hired hack. They dropped by a restaurant on Railroad Avenue (now Central Avenue) to get a bite to eat. Sadie was inside when Milt approached Harry outside, on the street. One source says Yarberry called Brown out. Whatever the circumstances, they exchanged unpleasant words. One witness reported that he heard Brown say, "I wouldn't be afraid of you if you were marshal of the United States."

The hack driver looked around in time to see Milt pump a bullet or two into Harry's chest. Brown fell and Milt shot him a couple more times as he lay on the ground. Harry Brown was 24 years old at the time of his death.

Milt immediately surrendered himself to Sheriff Perfecto Armijo. He was indicted for murder and brought to trial where he argued that the shooting was a matter of self-defense. Milt claimed Harry was reaching for a gun at the time he fired. But no gun was found on Brown's person. Milt claimed that Sadie Preston took the gun. He also argued that Brown had threatened to kill him on sight, and Brown had a reputation as a dangerous man.

Acquitted of all charges, Milt went back to work patrolling the streets of Albuquerque. But he couldn't stay out of trouble.

Yarberry and gambler Frank Boyd spent the better part of Saturday afternoon, June 18, 1881, drinking in Madsen's Hotel bar in Albuquerque's new town. That's what they were doing when they heard a shot fired. The report came from a restaurant down the street. Milt, in his official capacity, walked over to see to the commotion. Boyd tagged along.

"Who's firing?" the marshal demanded of restaurant patrons.

"There goes the man," a bystander said and pointed to Charles Campbell who was crossing the street.

What happened next is unclear. One report says Milt simply pulled his gun and shot at Campbell until the man fell, and then shot him some more.

Another story goes that Yarberry shouted, "Stop! I want you," or perhaps, "Hold up your hands!" after which Yarberry and Boyd both opened fire. They emptied their guns—ten or twelve shots—and Campbell, hit three times, fell dead.

"I've downed the son-of-a-bitch," Milt said to Boyd and he danced a little jig around the body.

No gun was found on or around Campbell's body and no evidence showed him to be the man who fired the shot in the restaurant in the first place. Campbell would have been an unlikely suspect in any event; an inoffensive man who kept to himself, he was a carpenter for the Atlantic & Pacific Railroad. He'd been in Albuquerque less than a month at the time of his death.

Milt turned himself into Sheriff Armijo and again argued self-defense. His plea fell on largely deaf ears. Milt cooled his heels in the Santa Fe jail—Sheriff Armijo saved him from a lynch party in Albuquerque—while a Grand Jury in Bernalillo County indicted him for murder in the fall of 1881.

Boyd left Albuquerque shortly after the Campbell shooting and headed west. His horse caved in somewhere near Grants Camp (now Grants) and he stole a fresh mount from a couple of Navajo Indians. He may have killed one of them, but history is not clear on the point. Boyd was soon overtaken by a larger band of armed Navajos who shot him full of holes and recovered their horse. They left the gambler's body where it fell.

Yarberry's trial in May 1882 lasted three days before the jury deliberated briefly and convicted the former marshal as charged, with first-degree murder. He was sentenced to hang three weeks hence but a series of appeals prevented that.

In September, Milt and three others, including Billy Wilson, one of William Bonney's (Billy the Kid) cohorts, escaped from the Santa Fe jail. Milt's luck had all turned bad. Santa Fe Police Chief Francisco "Frank" Chavez recaptured him three days later, cold and hungry and only a few miles from town, and took him back to jail.

All appeals finally failed and February 9, 1883, was set as the date of execution. In the meantime, Milt wiled away his time by playing the fiddle. He impressed a newspaperman with his aplomb by playing a fast version of *Old Zip Coon*. But Milt didn't have the intestinal fortitude he appeared to have. He simply stayed drunk most of the time as he watched the date of his death approach. Santa Fe County Sheriff Romulo Martínez allowed him a daily bottle of whiskey.

On the appointed day, Milt was moved from Santa Fe to Albuquerque by train, escorted by 16 Santa Fe militiamen, Santa Fe County Sheriff Martinez and Colfax County Sheriff Mace Bowman (reputed to be a fast man with a gun). From New Albuquerque to Old Town, a troop of Albuquerque militiamen did the escort duties with a great deal of pomp and ceremony.

The atmosphere in town that day was carnival-like, and Milt, as the center of attention, was downcast, but not reticent.

When asked by a reporter how he felt, Milt replied, "I feel tolerable, under the circumstances."

He was housed in the small adobe jail that was surrounded by an eight-foot fence near what is now La Hacienda Restaurant and Cantina in Old Town. Citizens who wanted to watch Milt come to the end of his trail occupied the roofs of houses in the neighborhood. Some paid as much as a dollar for the privilege.

Authorities fed Milt his final meal: cranberry pie, ale and a pint of whiskey. He said his confession to a priest from San Felipe de Neri Church and gave away what few possessions he owned. Elwood Maden brought the condemned man a new suit of clothes. Milt then told Maden his real name and the "true" story of his life, which Maden never repeated. At 2:40 p.m., Milt was taken into the jail yard.

Instead of mounting a scaffold for the hanging, Milt stood flat-footed on the ground. The noose end of a rope was placed around the condemned man's neck and the other end was affixed to a lever-like beam that was part of an elaborate device designed to yank the man upwards instead of dropping him through a trap door. The device had been constructed based on plans that had appeared in a recent issue of *Scientific American* magazine.

With rope in place, Milt offered up his final words:

"You are going to hang [me] not for the murder of Campbell, but for the killing of Brown." This really doesn't do Milt's final words justice. The complete speech lasted for more than 16 minutes and continued as the hood was placed over the condemned man's head. Milt paused and a tight rope prevented further utterance.

A rope cut with an ax allowed a 400-pound counterweight to drop snapping Milt upwards and breaking his neck. A newspaper reporter present at the execution wrote, "...the noise made in breaking the neck was quite loud. Death resulted almost instantaneously."

One newspaper reported that Milt was **"JERKED TO JESUS."**

Milt's body was carried to the Santa Barbara Cemetery with the rope still in place around his neck. A tombstone placed on the grave has long since disappeared, but it was an appropriate monument. Yarberry's name was misspelled as Yarbery.

Milt Yarberry is the only New Mexico lawman ever executed.

REFLECTIONS ON THE DEATH OF COLE YOUNG, TRAIN ROBBER

The train robbery began at about 7:20 p.m. on October 2, 1896. Seven robbers commandeered A. & P. train number 2 near the Rio Puerco about 35 miles southwest of Albuquerque.

It was not a smooth operation from the beginning, and one of the outlaws felt called upon to take a few shots at the brakeman and the conductor to gain control of the train. He killed neither, but shot a finger off the brakeman's hand and shattered the man's lantern. The shots got the attention of H. W. "Will", a deputy U. S. Marshal who was aboard one of the passenger cars. Loomis had been pursuing one of the robbers and had information that the train would likely be robbed.

Armed with a big bore double-barreled shotgun, the deputy marshal stepped down from the train. He noted a group of men standing near the train's engine, with one man standing apart from the rest. He selected that man as his target and fired. The man staggered and fell to his knees, but regained his feet and disappeared into the darkness. The deputy's second shot hit nothing. The robbers returned the fire—one report says about 30 shots were fired—but they didn't hit anything either. Loomis ducked for cover as a bullet zinged past his ear.

The outlaws, among them Will "Black Jack" Christian, acted as if they would go ahead with the robbery in spite of the interruption. They attempted to uncouple the express car from the rest of the train, but they couldn't get it done. Then they discussed using dynamite they'd hidden nearby to blow open the express car door. They were foiled in that plan when several armed trainmen protected the car. Eventually, they abducted the train's fireman and took him some distance from the scene where they robbed him of his personal possessions, including his tobacco, then let him go.

As they rode away, one of the outlaws called out for his fallen comrade.

"I can't come. I am done for," was the reply from the dark.

The robbers rode on. So much for loyalty among thieves. All they got for their trouble was what they were able to steal from the fireman and the attention of every lawman in two territories.

The train pulled out for Isleta Junction while Loomis remained behind to search for the body of the man he'd shot. He soon found it, bloody and face down. The outlaw held a six-gun in his left hand. It contained three spent cartridges.

The dead outlaw was one Cole Young, also known as Cole Estes and several other aliases. Sources describe him as smallish in stature, five feet six, or so, and weighing 145 pounds. He was 25 years old at the time of his death. He had $1.45 in his pocket and a receipt showing that he'd bought his hat in Wilcox, Arizona. An autopsy revealed that five buckshot pellets had hit him: four in the chest and one in the face. He'd bled to death.

Thus ended the career of an outlaw who may have been named Cole Young. No one but the undertaker attended his funeral at Fairview Cemetery in Albuquerque, and his grave marker disappeared years ago.

From a modern perspective, Young is only interesting because no one seems quite sure who he really was. One highly respected source identifies him as Code Young, with Cole Estes as an alias. Another flatly says that his name was Cole Young. After his death, a man from Deming, New Mexico, identified him as Cole Estes and suggested that he changed his name to Young after he left Deming a few months before he was killed, subsequent to a robbery indictment. On the other hand, two railroad workers who had known him in Trinidad, Colorado, several years *before* his death officially identified him as Cole Young. Another source says that he may have been wanted by the law in Texas, and his name was not Young *or* Estes, but may have been Bob or Tom Harris.[1]

Will "Black Jack" Christian was killed in a gunfight with lawmen about six months later, in April 1897, near Clifton, Arizona, and there was some question about his identity, too. Only one of the remaining Rio Puerco train bandits was officially identified: George Musgrave, alias Jesse Miller, Jesse Williams and Jeff Davis. It seems safe to assume that Will Christian's brother Bob was present, too, but then Bob may not have actually been Will's brother, but rather an Oklahoma killer named Tom Anderson.

What all of this suggests is that some of what is written about the Old West is based on conflicting reports and speculation. One source says that Cole Young rode with Tom "Black Jack" Ketchum, and that is most probably wrong. Another says that he was killed while hiding on the tender of a train after a failed bank robbery at Nogales, Arizona, nearly a week after he was actually killed in New Mexico. The bottom line seems to be that aside from what few documents there are, and aside from newspaper accounts (and remember that news writers then had the same problems with identification that history writers have today), one is free to pick and choose what he wants to believe about many of the characters of the Old West.

There is one other thing about the demise of Cole Young that merits comment. Marshal Will Loomis was in a passenger car. He only heard shots. He did not see who fired them and he did not know for sure why they had been fired. He only assumed that something was wrong; that a train robbery was taking place. He armed himself, stepped down from the train, picked a target and fired. It was no more than coincidence that, in the dark, he shot an outlaw, and the one he'd been hunting for weeks. What if it had been someone else? What if it had been one of the train's crewmen?

Modern peace officers would not likely fire under similar circumstances; without confirming the events taking place; without knowing the identity of the target; without issuing a warning; or without being fired upon first.

---

[1] Albuquerque history writer Don Cline believes that the name *Code* was incorrect from the beginning. Cline has never found any reference to Code Young or Estes. He

believes some earlier researcher misunderstood, or misstated, the name, and subsequent writers compounded the error.

NEWSPAPER/PERIODOCAL SOURCES

Alamogordo News,
> February 15 & 22, March 1 & 8, 1923.
> July 20, 1933.
Albuquerque Journal, (and *Morning Journal)*
> March 11, 1884.
> Nov. 23 & 27, 1886.
> August 29, 1904.
> July 3, 1909
> January 28, 29, 30 & 31, 1911
> November 20, 1911, April 25, 26, 1913
> January 7, 8, 9, 10, 12, 16 & 23; April 29;
> May 1 & 3; October 14, 26 & 27; and December 30, 1912.
> February 2, 1916.
> February 21, 22, 24, 25 & 26, 1916.
> February 14 & 15, and April 6, 1923.
> December 23, 1930; January 17, 1934.
> May 3, 1932.
> July 15 & 17, 1933
> April 14 & 15, 1952.
> December 18, 1979. Andy Gregg, "Impact Magazine."
> May 31, 1988.
> July 20, 1981 & July 10, 1994.
> September 9, 1990, "Savior Sought for 'Sin City'," by Fritz Thompson.
> December 14, 2003 "Fort Union Guarded New Mexico Frontier for 40 Years"
>> by James Abarr.
Albuquerque Tribune,
> Nov. 20, 1961, Howard Bryan, "Off the Beaten Path."
> February 27, 1995.
Artesia *Advocate*
> July 20 & 27, 1933
> August 3, 1933.
Associated Press,
> April 25, 1913.
Cibola County *Beacon*
> July 18, 2003 "They went west to Seboyeta," by Abe Peña.

Clayton Citizen,
>   July 2 & 9, 1909.
Deming Graphic,
>   March 16, 1904, February 25 & September 1, 1916.
>   May 5, 1932.
Deming Headlight,
>   November 24, 1911.
>   February 25, & September 8, 1916; March 9 & 23;
>   April 6 & 13, 1917.
Doña County Sheriff's Department *Employee Newsletter*
>   Undated. Lt. West Gilbreath, "Just a Little Bit of History."
El Cronicon (Publication of the Sandoval County, NM, Historical Society
>   Martha Liebert. "Hagan," Vol. 14, No. 3, Sept. 2003.
El Paso Times,
>   May 3, 1932.
Gallup Independent,
>   April 4, 5, 15 & 17, 1935.
Golden Era (Lincoln)
>   February 5, 1885, October 1, 1885.
Las Vegas *Optic,*
>   July 20, 1881
Mesilla News,
>   January 5 to 16, 1884.
Daily New Mexican,
>   July 16 & 17, 1885.
Lubbock *Morning Avalanche,*
>   April 19, 1932
National Association & Center for Outlaw and Lawman History,
>   University of Wyoming, Laramie, Vol XV, No. 2, April-June, 1991.
>   Chuck Hornung, "The Mystery Death of Federal Prohibition Officer Ray
>   Sutton."
New Mexico Historical Review,
>   July 1956, P. J. Rasch, "The Horrell War."
>   January 1960, William J. Parish. "The German Jew and the Commercial
>   Revolution in Territorial New Mexico, 1850-1900." .
>   April 1991, William E. Tydeman. "A New Deal for Tourists: Route 66
>   And the Promotion of New Mexico."
>   October 1991, Kevin J. Fernlund. "Senator Holm O. Bursum and the
>   Mexican Ring, 1921-1924."
>   April 1996, Michael Welsh, "Often Out of Sight, Rarely Out of Mind: Race
>   and Ethnicity at the University of New Mexico."
>   July 1996, Jan Bender Shetler, "Of Boundary Shifters and Disappearing
>   Tribes: Reverberation between East Africa and the American
>   Southwest."
>   October, 1996, Sandra K. Mathews-Lamb. "Designing and Mischievous
>   Individuals: The Cruzate Grants and the Office of the Surveyor
>   General."

Off Duty Magazine.
  September/October 1990. Robert A. Weaver, Jr. "Over the Hump."
Old West Magazine
  Summer, 1985. "Cole Young, Train Robber." By Donald Cline
Password (Publication of the El Paso County, Texas, Historical Society).
  Spring, 1982, "Ben Williams, Lawman," by R. A. Suhler.
Pecos Valley Argus,
  Friday, February 19, 1897.
Peñasco Valley *News and Hope Press*
  July 21, 1933.
Prime Time,
  August 2003, "Ghosts of Lake Valley Tell a Tale" by Marc Simmons.
Quarterly of the National Association for Outlaw and Lawman History,
  "The Shooting of the Old West" by Dennis McCowan.
Raton Guard,
  June 30 & July 7, 1882.
Ratón Range,
  January 31, February 8 & 14, 1989. Mike Pappas, "Officer Vanishes in
  Prohibition Drama."
The Roadrunner (Publication of the New Mexico State Police Association)
  Summer, 1992.
Roswell Daily Record
  February 15, 1901.
  May 27, 29, 30, 31; June 19 & 26;
      October, 13, 14, 16 & 19, 1911.
  August 3, 4, & 7; September 1; October 10 & 17, 1931.
  July 22, 1990.
  June 2, 2000; "Will Rainbolt..." by Elvis E. Fleming.
  September 24, 1995. "Woofter only Roswell lawman killed in performance of
      duty," by Sgt. John Halvorson, Roswell Police Department
Santa Fe New Mexican,
  July 12, 17, 18, 19, 20, 21 & 25; August 16, 1899
Silver City *Daily Press,*
  February 22, 1937.
Silver City *Enterprise*,
  March 19, 1886; January 21, September 30, & December 3, 1887; June 8 &
  July 6, 1888.
  May 19, 1893.
Silver City *Independent*,
  August 30, September 6 & 9, 1904.
Spirit Magazine,
  Fall/Winter, 1993/94. Marc Simmons. "Kit Carson's Homeland, The Man
  and the Legend."
True West,
  April 1991, "They Called Him Mister Kemp" by Bill O'Neal.

January 1992, "When New Mexico Invaded Colorado" by Fred M. Johnson.

Wild West,

April 1994, "Siege Warfare in the Southwest," by Michael Antonucci.

December 1994, "Gunfighters & Lawmen," by Jon Guttman.

December 2001, "Some Prominent New Mexicans May Have Been Accessories to the Murder of Pat Garrett," by Pete Ross.

October 2003. "Red Pipkin: Outlaw from the Black River Country," by Karen Holliday Tanner & John Tanner

December 2003, "Westerners," by Louis Kraft

December 2003, "The Real Villains of Sand Creek," by Gregory F. Michno

BIBLIOGRAPHY

Don E. Alberts. *The Battle of Glorieta, Union Victory in the West* (College Station: Texas A & M University Press, 1998).
_____. *Rebels on the Rio Grande: The Civil War Journal of A. B. Peticolas* (Albuquerque: The Merit Press, 1993).
Bob Alexander. *Dangerous Dan Tucker, New Mexico's Deadly Lawman* (Silver City: High-Lonesome Books 2001).
_____. *Fearless Dave Allison: Border Lawman* (Silver City: High Lonesome Books, 2003).
_____. *Lawmen, Outlaws, and S.O.Bs* (Silver City: High Lonesome Books, 2004).
_____. *Sacrificed Sheriff: John H. Behan* (Silver City: High Lonesome Books, 2002).
Larry D. Ball. *Desert Lawmen, The High Sheriffs of New Mexico and Arizona 1846–1912*, (Albuquerque: University of New Mexico Press, 1992).
_____. *The United States Marshals of New Mexico & Arizona Territories 1846-1912* (Albuquerque: The University of New Mexico Press, 1978).
Edward S. Barnard, Editor. *Story of the Great American West* (Reader's Digest Association, Inc., 1977).
Charles & Mary Beard. *A Basic History of the United States*. (New York: Doubleday, Doran & Co. 1944).
Warren A. Beck. *New Mexico: A History of Four Centuries*. (Norman: University of Oklahoma Press, 1962).
Warren A. Beck & Ynez D. Haase. *Historical Atlas of New Mexico*. (Norman: The University of Oklahoma Press, 1969).
Martha Fall Bethune. *Race With The Wind, The Personal Life of Albert B. Fall* (A Novio Book, 1989).
Dee Brown. *The American West*. (New York: Touchstone Books, 1994).
_____. *Fighting Indians of the West*. (New York: Ballantine Books, 1974).
Howard Bryan. *Incredible Elfego Baca* (Santa Fe: Clear Light Publishers, 1993).
_____. *Robbers, Rouges and Ruffians, True Tales of the Wild West*. (Santa Fe: Clear Light Publishers, 1991).
_____. *Wildest of the Wild West*. (Santa Fe: Clear Light Publishers, 1988).
Don Bullis, *New Mexico's Finest: Peace Officers Killed in the Line of Duty, 1847-1999* (Santa Fe: New Mexico Department of Public Safety, 2000).
_____. *The Old West Trivia Book* (Baldwin Park: Gem Guides Book Co., 1993).

Walter S. Campbell. *Kit Carson: The Happy Warrior of the Old West* (Boston: Houghton Mifflin Company, 1928).

John C. Ceremony. *Life Among the Apaches* (Santa Fe: The Rio Grande Press, 1968).

Thomas E. Chávez. *An Illustrated History of New Mexico* (Albuquerque: University of New Mexico Press, 1992).

_____. *Spain and the Independence of the United States* (Albuquerque: University of New Mexico Press, 2002).

Neil M. Clark, ed. *Campfires and Cattle Trails, Recollections of the Early West in the Letters of J. H. Harshman* (Caldwell, Idaho: The Caxton Printers, 1970).

Click, Mrs. N. H. (Cora). *Us Nesters in The Land of Enchantment*, (Privately Printed, 1980).

Donald Cline. *Alias Billy the Kid.* (Santa Fe: Sunstone Press, 1986).

Kyle S. Crichton. *Law and Order, Ltd, the Rousing Life of Elfego Baca* (Santa Fe: New Mexican Publishing Corporation).

James A. Crutchfield, *Tragedy at Taos, The Revolt of 1847* (Plano, Texas: The Republic of Texas Press, 1995).

Robert K. DeArment. *George Scarborough, The Life and Death of a Lawman on the Closing Frontier* (Norman: The University of Oklahoma Press, 1992).

M. Morgan Estergreen. *Kit Carson: a Portrait in Courage* (Norman, The University of Oklahoma Press, 1962).

Erna Fergusson. *Murder & Mystery in New Mexico,* (Boulder: Lightning Tree Press, 1948).

_____. *New Mexico, A Pageant of Three Peoples.* (New York: Alfred A. Knopf, 1964).

Floyd S. Fierman. *Guts and Ruts, The Jewish Pioneer on the Trail in the American Southwest* (KTAV Publishing, 1985).

Elvis E. Fleming. *Captain Joseph C. Lea: From Confederate Guerrilla To New Mexico Patriarch* (Las Cruces: Yucca Tree Press [In cooperation with the Historical Society for Southeast New Mexico], 2002).

_____. *J. B. "Billy" Mathews, Biography of a Lincoln County Deputy.* (Las Cruces: Yucca Tree Press, 1999).

Francis & Roberta Fugate. *Roadside History of New Mexico* (Missoula: Mountain Press Publishing, 1989).

Maurice Fulton, *History of the Lincoln County War* (Tucson: University of Arizona Press, 1968).

Nasario García. *Tata: A Voice from the Rio Puerco* (Albuquerque: The University of New Mexico Press [in cooperation with the Historical Society of New Mexico], 1994).

Patrick F. Garrett. *The Authentic Life of Billy the Kid.* (Norman: University of Oklahoma Press, 1965).

Shannon Garst. *William Bent and His Adobe Empire* (New York: Julian Messner, Inc., 1957).

Noel B. Gerson. *Kit Carson: Folk Hero and Man* (Garden City: Doubleday & Company, 1964).

A. M. Gibson. *The Life and Death of Colonel Albert Jennings Fountain* (Norman: University of Oklahoma Press, 1965).

West Gilbreath. *Death on the Gallows, The Story of Legal Hangings in New Mexico1847-1923* (Silver City: High Lonesome Books, 2002).

Thelma S. Guild & Harvey L. Carter. *Kit Carson: A Pattern for Heroes* (Lincoln London: The University of Nebraska Press, 1984).

George P. Hammond and Edgar Goad. *The Adventure of Don Francisco Vasquez de Coronado* (Albuquerque: University of New Mexico Press).

Dee Harkey. *Mean as Hell*, (Albuquerque: University of New Mexico Press, 1948).

Fred Harrison. *Hell Holes and Hangings*. (Clarendon, Texas: Clarendon Press, 1968)

H. B. Henning, ed.. *George Curry, 1861-1947, An Autobiography* (Albuquerque: University of New Mexico Press, 1958).

Peter Hertzog. *Little Known Facts About Billy the Kid*. (Santa Fe: Press of the Territorian, 1964).

_____. *Outlaws of New Mexico* (Santa Fe: Sunstone Press, 1984.)

Tony Hillerman. *The Great Taos Bank Robbery and Other Indian Country Affairs*. "Othello in Union County." (Albuquerque: University of New Mexico Press, 1973.)

George Hilliard. *Adios Hachita, Stories of a New Mexico Town* (Silver City: High-Lonesome Books, 1998.)

Conrad Hilton. *Be My Guest* (Englewood Cliffs: Prentice-Hall, 1957).

Paul Horgan. *The Centuries of Santa Fe*. (Santa Fe: William Gannon, 1976).

_____. *Great River*. (Austin: Texas Monthly Press, 1984).

Chuck Hornug. *The Thin Gray Line*. (Fort Worth: Western Heritage Press, 1971)

David Hsi and Janda Panitz, Eds. *From Sun Daggers to Space Exploration*. "Archaeology and Anthropology in New Mexico: The First Century" by Linda S. Cordell and David Stuart (Albuquerque: New Mexico Journal of Science, 1986).

Frances Ingmire. *Texas Rangers, Frontier Battalion, Minute Men, Commanding Officers, 1847-1900* (St. Louis: Ingmire Publications,1982).

Myra Ellen Jenkins and Albert H. Schroeder. *A brief History of New Mexico* (Albuquerque: University of New Mexico Press, 1974).

Michael Jenkinson. *Ghost Towns of New Mexico, Playthings of The Wind* (Albuquerque: University of New Mexico Press, 1967).

William Weber Johnson. *Heroic Mexico: The Narrative History of a Twentieth Century Revolution* (New York: Harcourt Brace Jovanovich, 1968).

Robert Julyan, *The Place Names of New Mexico* (University of New Mexico Press, 1996).

William Loren Katz. *The Black West*. (Garden City: Anchor Press/Doubleday, 1973).

William A. Keleher. *The Fabulous Frontier* (Albuquerque: University of New Mexico Press, 1962).

_____. *The Maxwell Land Grant*. (Albuquerque: University of New Mexico Press, 1942).

_____. *Turmoil in New Mexico, 1846-1868* (Albuquerque: University of New Mexico Press, 1952).

_____. *Violence in Lincoln County* (Albuquerque: University of New Mexico Press, 1957.)

Charles Kelly. *The Outlaw Trail, A History of Butch Cassidy and His Wild Bunch* (New York: Bonanza Books, 1959).

Bruce King. *Cowboy In The Roundhouse*. (Santa Fe: The Sunstone Press, 1998).

Lily Klasner (Eve Ball, ed.), *My Girlhood Among Outlaws* (Tucson: The University of Arizona Press, 1972).

Howard R. Lamar. *The Far Southwest, 1846-1912, A Territorial History* (Albuquerque: University of New Mexico Press, 2000).

Carole Larson. *Forgotten Frontier* (Albuquerque: University of New Mexico Press, 1993).

William H. Leckie. *The Buffalo Soldiers: A Narrative of the Negro Cavalry in the West* (Norman: University of Oklahoma Press, 1967)

Seymour B. Liebman. *A Guide to Jewish Reverences in the Mexican Colonial Era, 1521-1821* (Philadelphia: University of Pennsylvania Press).

Ralph Looney. *Haunted Highways*. (Hastings House Publishers).

Jacqueline Maketa. *From Martyrs To Murderers, The Old Southwest's Saints, Sinners & Scalawags*. (Las Cruces: Yucca Tree Press, 1993).

Leon Claire Metz. *The Encyclopedia of Lawmen, Outlaws and Gunfighters* (New York: Checkmark Books, 2003).

_____. *Pat Garrett, The Story of a Western Lawman* (Norman & London: The University of Oklahoma Press, 1974).

_____. *The Shooters* (El Paso, Mangan Books, 1976).

Denis McLoughlin. *Wild and Woolly, An Encyclopedia of the Old West* (New York, Barnes & Noble, 1995).

Robert Mullin. *A Chronology of The Lincoln County War*. (New Mexico Historical Review, 1957-58).

David F. Myrick. New Mexico's Railroads (Colorado Railroad Museum).

Milton C. Nahm. *Las Vegas and Uncle Joe: The New Mexico I Remember*. (Norman: University of Oklahoma Press, 1964).

Jay Robert Nash. *Encyclopedia of Western Lawmen & Outlaws* (New York: DaCapo Press, 1994).

Bill O'Neal. *Encyclopedia of Western Gunfighters* (Norman & London, University of Oklahoma Press, 1979).

Miguel Antonio Otero. *My Life on The Frontier, 1864-1882* (Albuquerque: University of New Mexico Press, 1987).

_____. *My Nine Years As Governor of the Territory of New Mexico,1897-1906* (Albuquerque: University of New Mexico Press, 1940).

Gordon Owen. *Las Cruces, New Mexico 1849-1999: Multicultural Crossroads*. (Las Cruces: Red Sky Publishing, 1999).

_____. *The Two Alberts: Fountain and Fall* (Yucca Tree Press, 1996).

Chuck Parsons. *Clay Allison, Portrait of a Shootist* (Seagraves, Texas: Pioneer Book Publishers, 1983).

Richard Patterson. *Historical Atlas of the Outlaw West*. (Boulder: Johnson Books, 1985).

T. M. Pearce, ed. *New Mexico Place Names, A Geographical Dictionary* (Albuquerque: University of New Mexico Press, 1965).

Abe Pena. *Memories of Cibola: Stories from New Mexico Villages* (Albuquerque: University of New Mexico Press, 1997).

Ted Raynor. *The Gold Lettered Egg & Other New Mexico Tales* (privately printed, 1962).

Ruben Salaz Marquez. *New Mexico: A Brief Multi-History* (Albuquerque: Cosmic House, 1999).

Adolph Saenz, *Politics of A Prison Riot* (Corrales: Rhombus Publishing, 1986).

Carl Schenck, Editor. *Indians of the Southwest*. (Capricorn Books, 1973).

James E. & Barbara Sherman, *Ghost Towns and Mining Camps of New Mexico* (University of Oklahoma Press, 1975).

Marc Simmons. *Albuquerque, A Narrative History* (Albuquerque: University of New Mexico Press, 1982).

_____. *Kit Carson & His Three Wives: A Family History* (Albuquerque: The University of New Mexico Press, 2003).

_____. *New Mexico, An Interpretive History* (Albuquerque: University of New Mexico Press, 1977).

_____. *Spanish Government in New Mexico* (Albuquerque: University of New Mexico Press, 1968).

_____. *Spanish Pathways: Reading in the History of Hispanic New Mexico* (Albuquerque: University of New Mexico Press, 2001).

_____. *Ranchers, Ramblers, and Renegades, True Tales of Territorial New Mexico*. (Santa Fe: Ancient City Press, 1984).

_____. *When Six-Guns Ruled: Outlaw Tales of Southwest* (Santa Fe: Ancient City Press 1990).

C. L. Sonnichsen. *I'll Die Before I'll Run, the Story of the Great Feuds of Texas* (Lincoln & London: University of Nebraska Press, 1951).

John Stoutenburgh, Jr. Dictionary of the American Indian (New York: Wing Books, 1969).

John Upton Terrell. *Apache Chronicle, The Story of The People*. (Apollo Edition, 1974.)

Dan T. Thrapp. *Encyclopedia of Frontier Biography* (Lincoln & London: University of Nebraska Press, 1988).

Robert J. Torrez and David Harrell. *New Mexico Blue Book, 1995-1996*. "History of the Land of Enchantment." (Santa Fe: New Mexico Secretary of State).

Robert M. Utley. *Frontier Regulars: The United States Army and the Indian, 1866-1891*. (Lincoln: University of Nebraska Press, 19730.

_____. *High Noon in Lincoln, Violence on the Western Frontier* (Albuquerque: University of New Mexico Press, 1987).

David Wallechinsky and Amy Irving Wallace. *The People's Almanac*. (New York: Doubleday & Co., 1975).

Walter Prescott Webb, *The Texas Rangers, A Century of Frontier Defense* (Austin: University of Texas Press, 1935).

Peter & Mary Ann White, Eds. *Along the Rio Grande, Cowboy Jack Thorp's New Mexico.* (Santa Fe: Ancient City Press, 1988).
John P. Wilson, *Merchants Guns & Money, The Story of Lincoln County and Its Wars* (Santa Fe: Museum of New Mexico Press, 1987).

OTHER PUBLICATIONS/SOURCES

Alamogordo Public Library: Howard Brooks, oral history tapes, September 1975 & Murray E. Morgan (1906-1988), Report on the Rutherford affair prepared in 1976.
Albuquerque Police Department.
Rufus J. Dunnahoo, Funeral Record
Elvis E. Fleming. "Chaves County Deputy Sheriff Rufus J. Dunnahoo, 1879-1931: Killed in the Line of Duty," June 2, 1998.
"Fort Union." A brochure prepared by the National Park Service.
New Mexico Blue Book (Published by the Office of the Secretary of State)
New Mexico State Police Yearbook, Anniversary 1935-1995.
The WPA Guide to 1930s New Mexico. University of Arizona Press, 1940.
The Old West, Time-Life Books, Alexandria, Virginia, 1980.
"This is Grants." Booklet published by the Grants, New Mexico, Community Development Committee in 1969.

CORRESPONDENCE & INTERVIEWS

Michael Archibeque, President, Sandoval County Historical Society
Mrs. Rosie Armijo, extensive correspondence, spring 2004.
Patrick Baca of Sandia Pueblo, conversations over many years.
Phil Bibo of Grants, New Mexico. Conversations, 1967-2003.
Don F. & Doris M. Bullis of Bowling Green, Ohio, both of whom had personal knowledge of Clyde and Carrie Tingley and Tingley Farms. Numerous conversations.
Virginia Chavez, Bernalillo, New Mexico.
Yolanda Cline, Fort Sumner, New Mexico, correspondence, August 21, 1990.
Jack Coussons, Captain, Luna County Sheriff's Department, correspondence, May 22, 1991.
Randy Dunson. "The Abo Pass Gang." Unknown publisher.
Marjorie Ferguson. "The Acculturation of Sandia Pueblo." Master of Arts Thesis, UNM, 1931.
Elvis Fleming, Historian, City of Roswell, correspondence, December 9, 1999.
Sam Gomez, Cpl., Gallup Police Dept., May 1989.
The Grazier family of Rio Rancho, New Mexico.
George Griego, Bernalillo, New Mexico.
Terry Humble, Silver City, New Mexico.
Lee Johnson, Sheriff, Union County, NM, October 22, 1999.
William Kuehl, Retired New Mexico Peace Officer.
Martha Liebert, Sandoval County Historical Society, September 2003.
Cindy Martinez, Lincoln County Heritage Trust, correspondence, September 11, 1995.
Lorella Montoya Salazar, Bernalillo, New Mexico.
Ruben Montoya, Bernalillo, New Mexico.
Edward Piasano of Sandia Pueblo, conversations over many years.
Thomas J. Ryan, Chief (Ret.), Silver City (New Mexico) Police Dept., correspondence, October 2 & 23, 1991.
Coleen Salazar of the Lincoln County Heritage Trust.
Socorro County Historical Society
Socorro County Chamber of Commerce.
Lalo Torres, Former Mayor of Bernalillo, New Mexico.
Robert J. Torrez, New Mexico State Historian (Ret.). "Executions in Territorial New Mexico," 1989 (Unpublished).
Martha Plotner Williams, Correspondence, July 8, 1982.

INDEX

ABOUT THE AUTHOR

Don Bullis graduated from Eastern New Mexico University at Portales in 1970 with a degree in American History and Literature. In the years since, he as served in a number of positions, most notably as a small-town newspaper editor/columnist, and peace officer. He retired in 2002 after serving as a New Mexico deputy sheriff, town marshal, organized crime commissioner, and criminal intelligence operational supervisor.

His earlier books include *The Old West Trivia Book* published in 1993, *New Mexico's Finest: Peace Officers Killed in the Line of Duty, 1847-99* published in 2000, and *Bloodville*, published in 2002.

Bullis is Sheriff of the Albuquerque Corral of Westerners International, a docent at Corrales' Casa San Ysidro and Albuquerque's Old Town, an active member of the Western Writers of America, SouthWest Writers, The Western History Association and the Sandoval County Historical Society.

He lives in Rio Rancho with his wife, Gloria.

Books from Science & Humanities Press

HOW TO TRAVEL—A Guidebook for Persons with a Disability – Fred Rosen (1997) ISBN 1-888725-05-2, 5½ X 8¼, 120 pp, $9.95 18-point large print edition (1998) ISBN 1-888725-17-6 7X8, 120 pp, $19.95

HOW TO TRAVEL in Canada—A Guidebook for A Visitor with a Disability – Fred Rosen (2000) ISBN 1-888725-26-5, 5½X8¼, 180 pp, $14.95 MacroPrintBooks™ edition (2001) ISBN 1-888725-30-3 7X8, 16 pt, 200 pp, $19.95

AVOIDING Attendants from HELL: A Practical Guide to Finding, Hiring & Keeping Personal Care Attendants 2nd Edn—June Price, (2002), accessible plastic spiral bind, ISBN 1-888725-72-9 8¼X10½, 125 pp, $16.95, School/library edition (2002) ISBN 1-888725-60-5, 8¼X6½, 200 pp, $18.95

If Blindness Comes – K. Jernigan, Ed. (1996) Strategies for living with visual impairment. 18-point Large type Edition with accessible plastic spiral bind, 8¼X10½, 110 pp, $7 (not eligible for quantity discounts— distributed at cost with permission of the National Federation of the Blind)

The Bridge Never Crossed—A Survivor's Search for Meaning. Captain George A. Burk (1999) The inspiring story of George Burk, lone survivor of a military plane crash, who overcame extensive burn injuries to earn a presidential award and become a highly successful motivational speaker. ISBN 1-888725-16-8, 5½X8¼, 170 pp, illustrated. $16.95 MacroPrintBooks™ Edition (1999) ISBN 1-888725-28-1 $24.95

Value Centered Leadership—A Survivor's Strategy for Personal and Professional Growth—Captain George A. Burk (2003) Principles of Leadership & Total Quality Management applied to all aspects of living. ISBN 1-888725-59-1, 5½X8¼, 120 pp, $16.95

Paul the Peddler or The Fortunes of a Young Street Merchant—Horatio Alger, jr A Classic reprinted in accessible large type, (1998 MacroPrintBooks™ reprint in 24-point type) ISBN 1-888725-02-8, 8¼X10½, 276 pp, $16.95

The Wisdom of Father Brown—G.K. Chesterton (2000) A Classic collection of detective stories reprinted in accessible 22-point type ISBN 1-888725-27-3 8¼X10½, 276 pp, $18.95

24-point Gospel—The Big News for Today – The Gospel according to Matthew, Mark, Luke & John (KJV) in 24-point type is about 1/3 inch high. Now, people with visual disabilities like macular degeneration can still use this important reference. "Giant print" books are usually 18 pt. or less ISBN 1-888725-11-7, 8¼X10½, 512 pp, $24.95

Buttered Side Down - Short Stories by Edna Ferber (BeachHouse Books reprint 2000) A classic collection of stories by the beloved author of Showboat, Giant, and Cimarron. ISBN 1-888725-43-5, 5½X8¼, 190 pp, $12.95 MacroPrintBooks™ Edition (2000) ISBN 1-888725-40-0 7X8¼,16 pt, 240 pp $18.95

The Four Million: The Gift of the Magi & other favorites. Life in New York City around 1900—O. Henry. MacroPrintBooks™ reprint (2001) ISBN 1-888725-41-9 7X8¼, 16 pt, 270 pp $18.95; ISBN 1-888725-03-6, 8¼X10½, 22 pt, 300pp, $22.95

Bar-20: Hopalong Cassidy's Rustler Roundup— Clarence Mulford (reprint 2000). Classical Western Tale. Not the TV version. ISBN 1-888725-34-6 5½X8¼, 223 pp, $12.95 MacroPrintBooks™ edition ISBN 1-888725-42-7, 8¼X6½, 16 pt, 385pp, $18.95

Nursing Home – Ira Eaton, PhD, (1997) You will be moved and disturbed by this novel. ISBN 1-888725-01-X, 5½X8¼, 300 pp, $12.95 MacroPrintBooks™ edition (1999) ISBN 1-888725-23-0,8¼X10½, 16 pt, 330 pp, $18.95

Perfect Love-A Novel by Mary Harvatich (2000) Love born in an orphanage endures ISBN 1-888725-29-X 5½X8¼, 200 pp, $12.95 MacroPrintBooks™ edition (2000) ISBN 1-888725-15-X, 8¼X10½, 16 pt, 200 pp, $18.95

The Essential Simply Speaking Gold – Susan Fulton, (1998) How to use IBM's popular speech recognition package for dictation rather than keyboarding. Dozens of screen shots and illustrations. ISBN 1-888725-08-7 8¼ X8, 124 pp, $18.95

Begin Dictation Using ViaVoice Gold -2nd Edition– Susan Fulton, (1999), Covers ViaVoice 98 and other versions of IBM's popular continuous speech recognition package for dictation rather than keyboarding. Over a hundred screen shots and illustrations. ISBN 1-888725-22-2, 8¼X8, 260 pp, $28.95

Ropes and Saddles—Andy Polson (2001) Cowboy (and other) poems by Andy Polson. Reminiscences of the Wyoming poet. ISBN 1-888725-39-7, 5½ X 8¼, 100 pp, $9.95

Tales from the Woods of Wisdom - (book I) - Richard Tichenor (2000) In a spirit someplace between The Wizard of Oz and The Celestine Prophecy, this is more than a childrens' fable of life in the deep woods. ISBN 1-888725-37-0, 5½X8¼, 185 pp, $16.95 MacroPrintBooks™ edition (2001) ISBN 1-888725-50-8 6X8¼, 16 pt, 270 pp $24.95

Me and My Shadows—Shadow Puppet Fun for Kids of All Ages - Elizabeth Adams, Revised Edition by Dr. Bud Banis (2000) A thoroughly illustrated guide to the art of shadow puppet entertainment using tools that are always at hand wherever you go. A perfect gift for children and adults. ISBN 1-888725-44-3, 7X8¼, 67 pp, 12.95 MacroPrintBooks™ edition (2002) ISBN 1-888725-78-8 8½X11 lay-flat spiral, 18 pt, 67 pp, $16.95

MamaSquad! (2001) Hilarious novel by Clarence Wall about what happens when a group of women from a retirement home get tangled up in Army Special Forces. ISBN 1-888725-13-3 5½ X8¼, 200 pp, $14.95 MacroPrintBooks™ edition (2001) ISBN 1-888725-14-1 8¼X6½ 16 pt, 300 pp, $24.95

Virginia Mayo—The Best Years of My Life (2002) Autobiography of film star Virginia Mayo as told to LC Van Savage. From her early days in Vaudeville and the Muny in St Louis to the dozens of hit motion pictures, with dozens of photographs. ISBN 1-888725-53-2, 5½ X 8¼, 200 pp, $16.95

The Job—Eric Whitfield (2001) A story of self-discovery in the context of the death of a grandfather.. A book to read and share in times of change and Grieving. ISBN 1-888725-68-0, 5½ X 8¼, 100 pp, $12.95 MacroPrintBooks™ edition (2001) ISBN 1-888725-69-9, 8¼X6½, 18 pt, 150 pp, $18.95

Plague Legends: from the Miasmas of Hippocrates to the Microbes of Pasteur-Socrates Litsios D.Sc. (2001) Medical progress from early history through the 19th Century in understanding origins and spread of contagious disease. A thorough but readable and enlightening history of medicine. Illustrated, Bibliography, Index ISBN 1-888725-33-8, 6¼X8¼, 250pp, $24.95

Sexually Transmitted Diseases—Symptoms, Diagnosis, Treatment, Prevention-2nd Edition – NIAID Staff, Assembled and Edited by R.J.Banis, PhD, (2005) Teacher friendly --free to copy for education. Illustrated with more than 50 photographs of lesions, ISBN 1-888725-58-3, 8¼X6½, 200 pp, $18.95

The Stress Myth -Serge Doublet, PhD (2000) A thorough examination of the concept that 'stress' is the source of unexplained afflictions. Debunking mysticism, psychologist Serge Doublet reviews the history of other concepts such as 'demons', 'humors', 'hysteria' and 'neurasthenia' that had been placed in this role in the past, and provides an alternative approach for more success in coping with life's challenges. ISBN 1-888725-36-2, 5½X8¼, 280 pp, $24.95

Behind the Desk Workout – Joan Guccione, OTR/C, CHT (1997) ISBN 1-888725-00-1, Reduce risk of injury by exercising regularly at your desk. Over 200 photos and illustrations. (lay-flat spiral) 8¼X10½, 120 pp, $34.95 Paperback edition, (2000) ISBN 1-888725-25-7 $24.95

Copyright Issues for Librarians, Teachers & Authors–R.J. Banis, PhD, (Ed). 2nd Edn (2001) Protecting your rights, respecting others'. Information condensed from the Library of Congress, copyright registration forms. ISBN 1-888725-62-1, 5¼X8¼, 60 pp, booklet. $4.95 postpaid

Rhythm of the Sea --Shari Cohen (2001). Delightful collection of heartwarming stories of life relationships set in the context of oceans and lakes. Shari Cohen is a popular author of womens' magazine articles and contributor to the Chicken Soup for the Soul series. ISBN 1-888725-55-9, 8X6.5 150 pp, $14.95 MacroPrintBooks™ edition (2001) ISBN 1-888725-63-X, 8¼X6½, 16 pt, 250 pp, $24.95

Bloodville -- Don Bullis (2002) Fictional adaptation of the Budville, NM murders by New Mexico crime historian, Don Bullis. 5½ X 8¼, 350 pp ISBN: 1-888725-75-3 $14.95 **MacroPrintBooks**™ edition (2003) 16 pt. 8¼X11 460pp ISBN: 1-888725-76-1 $24.95

Once in a Green Room: A Novel—Keri Baker (2001). After being raped and having an abortion while in college, a young woman struggles to deal with her feelings and is ultimately helped by the insights she gains from her special education students. Contact information for help groups throughout the United States. Part of proceeds contributed to RAINN. ISBN 1-888725-38-9, 5½X8¼, 160 pp, $14.95 MacroPrintBooks™ edn (2001) ISBN 1-888725-61-3, 8¼X6½, 16pt, 200 pp, $24.95

To Norma Jeane With Love, Jimmie -Jim as told to LC Van Savage (2001) ISBN 1-888725-51-6 The sensitive and touching story of Jim Dougherty's teenage bride who later became Marilyn Monroe. Dozens of photographs. "The Marilyn book of the year!" As seen on TV. 5½X8¼, 200 pp, $16.95 MacroPrintBooks™ edition ISBN 1-888725-52-4, 8¼X6½, 16 pt, 290pp, $24.95

Riverdale Chronicles--Charles F. Rechlin (2003). Life, living and character studies in the setting of the Riverdale Golf Club by Charles F. Rechlin 5½ X 8¼, 100 pp ISBN: 1-888725-84-2 $14.95 **MacroPrintBooks**™ edition (2003) 16 pt. 8¼X6½, 16 pt, 350 pp ISBN: 1-888725-85-0 $24.95

The Cut--John Evans (2003). Football, Mystery and Mayhem in a highschool setting by John Evans ISBN: 1-888725-82-6 5½ X 8¼, 100 pp $14.95 **MacroPrintBooks**™ edition (2003) 16 pt. ISBN: 1-888725-83-4 $24.95

Inaugural Addresses: Presidents of the United States from George Washington to 2008 -2nd Edition– Robert J. Banis, PhD, CMA, Ed. (2001) Extensively illustrated, includes election statistics, Vice- presidents, principal opponents, Index. coupons for update supplements for the next two elections. ISBN 1-888725-56-7, 6¼X8¼, 350pp, $18.95

Eudora Light™ v 3.0 Manual (Qualcomm 1996) ISBN 1-888725-20-6½, extensively illustrated. 135 pp, 5½ X 8¼, $9.95

50 Things You Didn't Learn in School–But Should Have: Little known facts that still affect our world today (2004) by John Naese, . ISBN 1-888725-49-4, 5½X8¼, 200 pp, illustrated. $16.95

Republican or Democrat? (2004) Moses Sanchez, who describes himself as "a Black Hispanic" thinks for himself, questions the stereotypes, examines the facts and makes his own decision. Early Editions Books ISBN 1-888725-32-X 5½X8¼, 176pp pp, $14.95

republicanordemocrat.us and democratorrepublican.us

The Way It Was-- Nostalgic Tales of Hotrods and Romance Chuck Klein (2003) Series of hotrod stories by author of Circa 1957 in collaboration with noted illustrator Bill Lutz BeachHouse Books edition 5½ X 8¼, 200 pp ISBN: 1-888725-86-9 $14.95 MacroPrintBooks™ edition (2003) 16 pt. 8¼X6½, 350pp ISBN: 1-888725-87-7 $24.95

The Way It Was

Nostalgic Tales of HotRods and Romance

Chuck Klein

"...a delightful mix of anecdote, observation, and social history. A book so masterfully written, you can almost smell new upholstery on the street rod. This is definitely the best read..."

Paul Taylor, Publisher. Route 66 Magazine

"...a classic recipe for hours of delightful entertainment.... If this is your first time reading Chuck Klein, it's just like eating chocolate. Once you have the first bite, you know you'll be coming back for more. "

Carl Cartisano, Cruisin' Style Magazine

a new American classic, conjuring up images of good, clean fun for the "hot-rodders" of yesterday and today....a fun, fast read that appeals to the kid in all of us." --

Aaron Lasky, Hot Rod DeLuxe, CK DeLuxe, & Kingpin Magazines

"Your book is great. You have captured the feel and texture of the 'fifties in each story. It's a wonderful read ...which accurately portrays and preserves the magic of the era".

Dusty Rhodes, WSAI Radio, Cincinnati

"As varied as the vehicles --a 1960 Corvette, a '57 Chevy, a 1937 Ford pick-up truck-- and the people who drive them--eager teenagers cruisin' for dates, a sailor on furlough, a young woman who understands a "two-eighty-three engine, bored sixty thousandths over"-- these well crafted tales are a veritable potpourri of American road lore." "Bet you can't read just one!"

Michael Lund, Author of the Growing Up on Route 66 Series

Route 66 books by Michael Lund

Growing Up on Route 66 —Michael Lund (2000) ISBN 1-888725-31-1 Novel evoking fond memories of what it was like to grow up alongside "America's Highway" in 20th Century Missouri. (Trade paperback) 5½ X8¼, 260 pp, $14.95 **MacroPrintBooks™** edition (2001) ISBN 1-888725-45-1 8¼X6½, 16 pt, 330 pp, $24.95

Route 66 Kids —Michael Lund (2002) ISBN 1-888725-70-2 Sequel to *Growing Up on Route 66*, continuing memories of what it was like to grow up alongside "America's Highway" in 20th Century Missouri. (Trade paperback) 5½ X8¼, 270 pp, $14.95 **MacroPrintBooks™** edition (2002) ISBN 1-888725-71-0 8¼X6½, 16 pt, 350 pp, $24.95

A Left-hander on Route 66--Michael Lund (2003) ISBN 1-888725-88-5. Twenty years after the fact, left-hander Hugh Noone appeals a wrongful conviction that detoured him from "America's Main Street" and put him in jail. But revealing the details of the past and effecting a resolution of his case mean a dramatic rearrangement of his world, including troubled relationships with three women: Linda Roy, Patty Simpson, and Karen Murphy. (Trade paperback) 5½ X8¼, 270 pp, $14.95 **MacroPrintBooks™** edition (2002) ISBN 1-888725-89-3 8¼X6½, 16 pt, 350 pp, $24.95

Miss Route 66--Michael Lund (2004) ISBN: 1-888725-96-6. In this novel, Susan Bell tells the story of her candidacy in Fairfield, Missouri's annual beauty contest. Now married and with teenage children in St. Louis, she recounts her youthful adventure in this small town along "America's Highway." At the same time, she plans a return to Fairfield in order to right injustices she feels were done to some young contestants in the Miss Route 66 Pageant. Throughout this journey she wonders what, if anything, was feminine in the "Mother Road" of the 1950s. (Trade paperback) 5½ X8¼, 270 pp, $14.95. **MacroPrintBooks™** edition (2002) ISBN 1-888725-97-4 8¼X6½, 16 pt, 350 pp, $24.95.

AudioBook on CD-- Miss Route 66 ISBN: 1-888725-12-5 by Michael Lund unabridged 5 CD's --7 Hours running time. $24.95

Route 66 Spring-- Michael Lund (2004) ISBN: 1-888725-98-2. The lives of four young Missourians are changed when a bottle comes to the surface of one of the state's many natural springs. Inside is a letter written by a girl a dozen years after the end of the Civil War. Lucy Rivers Johns ' epistle contains a sad story of family failure and a powerful plea for help. This message from the last century crystallizes the individual frustrations of Janet Masters, Freddy Sills, Louis Clark, and Roberta Green, another group of Route 66 kids. Their response to the past charts a bold path into the future, a path inspired by the Mother Road itself. (Trade paperback) 5½ X8¼, 270 pp, $14.95. **MacroPrintBooks™** edition (2002) ISBN 1-888725-99-0. 8¼X6½, 16 pt, 350 pp, $24.95.

Route 66 to Vietnam Michael Lund (2004) ISBN 1-59630-000-0 This novel takes characters from earlier works in the Route 66 Novel Series farther west than Los Angeles, official destination of the famous highway, Route 66. Mark Landon and Billy Rhodes find the values they grew up on challenged by America's role in Southeast Asia. But elements of their upbringing represented by the Mother Road also sustain them in ways they could never have anticipated. . (Trade paperback) 5½ X8¼, 270 pp, $14.95. **MacroPrintBooks**™ edition (2004) ISBN 1-59630-001-9. 8¼X6½, 16 pt, 350 pp, $24.95.

Our books are guaranteed:

If a book has a defect, or doesn't hold up under normal use, or if you are unhappy in any way with one of our books, we are interested to know about it and will replace it and credit reasonable return shipping costs. Products with publisher defects (i.e., books with missing pages, etc.) may be returned at any time without authorization. However, we request that you describe the problem, to help us to continuously improve.

Journey to a Closed City with the International Executive Service Corps

describes the adventures of a retired executive volunteering with the senior citizens' equivalent of the Peace Corp as he applies his professional skills in a former Iron Curtain city emerging into the dawn of a new economy.

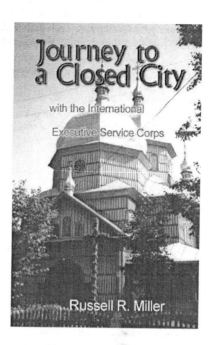

Before this adventure, Russ Miller spent 20 years traveling to over 100 countries as Sr.Vice President of International Development.

Since retiring, he has served as an advisor with the World Bank, United Nations Development Program, and the Vienna-based United Nations Industrial Development Organization, as well as the International Executive Service Corps.

This book is essential reading for anyone approaching retirement who is interested in opportunities to exercise skills to "do good" during expense-paid travel to intriguing locations.

Journey to A Closed City should also appeal to armchair travelers eager to explore far-off corners of the world in our rapidly-evolving global community.

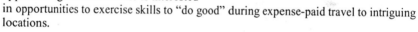

Journey to a Closed City with the International Executive Service Corps—Russell R. Miller (2004) ISBN 1-888725-94-X, Describes the adventures of a retired executive volunteering with the senior citizens' equivalent of the Peace Corp as he applies his professional skills in a former Iron Curtain city emerging into the dawn of a new economy.This book is essential reading for anyone approaching retirement who is interested in opportunities to exercise skills to "do good" during expense-paid travel to intriguing locations. Journey to A Closed City should also appeal to armchair travelers eager to explore far-off corners of the world in our rapidly-evolving global community. paperback, 5½X8¼,270pp,$16.95 **MacroPrintBooks**™ edition (2004) ISBN 1-888725-94-8, 8¼X6½, 18 pt, 150 pp, $24.95

Books by Don Bullis

Bloodville Regular size print edition. Fictional adaptation of the Budville, NM murders by New Mexico crime historian, Don Bullis. (2002) $14.95 5½X8¼, 200 pp, $14.95 MacroPrintBooks™ edition ISBN 1-888725-76-1, 16 pt, $24.95

Bullseye (2005) ISBN 1-888725-80-X, 5½ X 8¼, 200 pp, $14.95 MacroPrintBooks™ edition ISBN 1-888725-81-8, 16 pt, $24.95

Ellos Pasaron por Aqui — 99 New Mexicans and a Few Other Folks (2005) ISBN 1-888725-92-3, 6½ X 8¼, 350 pp, $16.95 MacroPrintBooks™ edition ISBN 1-888725-93-1, 350pp 8¼ X 11, 16 pt, $24.95

Order form			
Item	Each	Quantity	Amount
Missouri (only) sales tax 6.075%			
Priority Shipping			$4.00
	Total		

𝕾cience & 𝕳umanities 𝕻ress
PO Box 7151
Chesterfield, MO 63006-7151
(636) 394-4950
sciencehumanitiespress.com